Investigations in Cognitive Grammar

I0901859

Investigations in Cognitive Grammar

by

Ronald W. Langacker

Mouton de Gruyter
Berlin · New York

Mouton de Gruyter (formerly Mouton, The Hague)
is a Division of Walter de Gruyter GmbH & Co. KG, Berlin.

⊗ Printed on acid-free paper which falls within the guidelines
of the ANSI to ensure permanence and durability.

The Library of Congress has cataloged the first edition as follows:

Langacker, Ronald W.
Investigations in cognitive grammar / by Ronald W. Langacker.
p. cm. – (Cognitive linguistics research ; 42)
Includes bibliographical references and index.
ISBN 978-3-11-021434-5 (hardcover : alk. paper) – ISBN 978-3-11-021435-2 (pbk. : alk. paper)
1. Cognitive grammar. I. Title.
P165.L365 2009
415–dc22
2009003853

Bibliographic information published by the Deutsche Nationalbibliothek

The Deutsche Nationalbibliothek lists this publication in the Deutsche Nationalbibliografie; detailed bibliographic data are available in the Internet at http://dnb.d-nb.de.

ISBN 978-3-11-021435-2

Cover design: Martin Zech, Bremen.
Cover photo: Speed/www.photocase.com
Typesetting: OLD-Media OHG, Neckarsteinach.
Printed in Germany.

To David and Sharon

Preface

In its general outline, Cognitive Grammar (CG) has been in existence for roughly three decades. Over this span of time it has not changed in any fundamental way. It has of course been subject to refinement and elaboration. Still, its continued evolution has mostly been a matter of working out the specifics of its application to varied linguistic phenomena. In a symbolic account of grammar, the key problem is to characterize the semantic structures it incorporates and serves to express. Progress in CG has therefore come about primarily through detailed conceptual analysis in numerous domains, requiring no substantial modification of the basic descriptive framework.

Reports of this progress are scattered in many venues often not readily accessible. The need to make them easily available was accommodated by two previous volumes in this series (Langacker 1990a, 1999a) and has now resulted in a third. The present volume brings together a dozen innovative papers reflecting recent work. Although they were first written independently, and pertain to diverse topics, they have been revised and integrated to form a coherent whole. And while they deal with important grammatical problems in considerable depth and analytical detail, the presentation builds from fundamentals and introduces the background needed for comprehension.

One source of the volume's coherence is that a number of overlapping topics are examined in multiple chapters viewing them from different perspectives and in relation to one another. Among the topics covered in this fashion are grammatical constructions (their general nature, their metonymic basis, their role in grammaticization), nominal grounding (quantifiers, possessives, impersonal *it*), clausal grounding (its relation to nominal grounding, an epistemic account of tense, a systemic view of the English auxiliary), the "control cycle" (an abstract cognitive model with many linguistic manifestations), finite clauses (their internal structure and external grammar), and complex sentences (complementation, subordination, coordination). Though necessarily selective, the book thus provides a reasonably comprehensive survey of current research in CG and gives some indication of its future directions.

Contents

Chapter 6 Enunciating the parallelism of nominal and clausal grounding

Chapter 7 The English present: Temporal coincidence vs. epistemic immediacy

Chapter 11 Subordination in Cognitive Grammar

Chapter 12 The conceptual basis of coordination

Publication Sources

Chapter 1. Constructions in Cognitive Grammar
2003 *English Linguistics* 20, 41–83.

Chapter 2. Metonymy in grammar
2004 *Journal of Foreign Languages* 6, 2–24.

Chapter 3. A constructional approach to grammaticization
To appear *Linguistics*. Special issue. Guest editors: Suzanne Kemmer and Martin Hilpert

Chapter 4. Possession, location, and existence
2004 In Augusto Soares da Silva, Amadeu Torres, and Miguel Gonçalves (eds.), *Linguagem, Cultura e Cognição: Estudos de Linguística Cognitiva*, vol. 1, 85–120. Coimbra: Livraria Almedina.

Chapter 5. On the subject of impersonals
To appear In Mario Brdar, Milena Zic Fuchs, and Stefan Th. Gries (eds.), *Converging and Diverging Trends in Cognitive Linguistics.* Amsterdam/Philadelphia: John Benjamins.

Chapter 6. Enunciating the parallelism of nominal and clausal grounding
2008 In Jean-Rémi Lapaire, Guillaume Desagulier, and Jean-Baptiste Guignard (eds.), *Du Fait Grammatical au Fait Cognitif [From Gram to Mind: Grammar as Cognition]*, 17–65. Pessac: Presses Universitaires de Bordeaux.

Chapter 7. The English present: Temporal coincidence vs. epistemic immediacy
To appear In Frank Brisard (ed.), *Cognitive Linguistic Approaches to Tense and Aspect.* Amsterdam/Philadelphia: John Benjamins.

Chapter 8. A functional account of the English auxiliary
Original paper.

Chapter 9. Aspects of the grammar of finite clauses
2004 In Michel Achard and Suzanne Kemmer (eds.), *Language, Culture and Mind*, 535–577. Stanford: CSLI Publications.

Chapter 10. Finite complements in English
2008 *Journal of Foreign Languages* 10, 2–35.

Chapter 11. Subordination in Cognitive Grammar
2008 In Barbara Lewandowska-Tomaszczyk (ed.), *Asymmetric Events*, 137–149. Amsterdam/Philadelphia: John Benjamins.

Chapter 12. The conceptual basis of coordination
To appear In Seana Coulson (ed.), *Language in Action*. Stanford: CSLI Publications.

The papers are published with permission. They appear in their original form except for some emendations made to avoid excessive redundancy. Also, bibliographical entries, section numberings, and other typographical elements have been adjusted to the Mouton style, temporary and incomplete references have been updated, and cross-references to the original volumes have been deleted.

Chapter 1
Constructions in Cognitive Grammar

1. Architecture

More than one linguistic theorist has voiced the opinion that cognitive linguists, including myself, fail to recognize the existence of grammar. That is simply false. The question is not whether grammar exists – for it does – but rather, what is it like? Cognitive Grammar (CG) diverges from standard assumptions in two fundamental respects: (i) its claim that grammar is symbolic in nature; and (ii) its focus on constructions (rather than "rules") as the primary objects of description (Langacker 1987a, 1990a, 1991, 1999a).

The first claim denies the autonomy of syntax. Crucially, though, we need to distinguish between two definitions of autonomy that have often been confused. By the first definition, syntax (and more generally, grammar) is autonomous unless it is fully predictable in terms of meaning and other independent factors. Let us call this **weak autonomy**. It implies that grammar does not just "fall out" or emerge automatically from other phenomena. Rather, it has to be specifically learned by children and explicitly described by linguists. Observe that weak autonomy says nothing about the nature of grammatical structure, bearing only on its non-predictability. The second definition says that grammar is autonomous by virtue of being distinct from both lexicon and semantics, constituting a separate level of representation whose description requires a special set of irreducible grammatical primitives. Let us call this **strong autonomy**.

All cognitive linguists accept weak autonomy. Grammar exists and has to be described as such. Only its nature and proper characterization are at issue. The basic claims of CG presuppose weak autonomy but constitute a radical alternative to strong autonomy. For one thing, CG holds that lexicon, morphology, and syntax form a continuum, divided only arbitrarily into discrete components. Moreover, it claims that lexicon and grammar are fully describable as **assemblies of symbolic structures**, where a symbolic structure is simply the pairing between a semantic structure and a phonological structure (its semantic and phonological **poles**). This has several consequences. First, grammar is not distinct from semantics, but rather incorporates semantics as one of its two poles. Second, grammatical description does not rely on special, irreducible grammatical primitives, but only on symbolic structures, each reducible to a form-meaning pairing. Third, every construct validly posited in grammatical description has a semantic pole and is therefore meaningful (though the meanings are often quite schematic).

Like Construction Grammar, CG takes constructions, rather than "rules", to be the primary objects of grammatical description (Fillmore 1988; Fillmore, Kay, and O'Connor 1988; Goldberg 1995; Croft 2001; cf. Langacker 2005c). Grammar comprises regularities of varying degrees of generality – patterns that speakers internalize and that linguists need to discover and describe. What are these patterns like, and how can we best describe them? Three kinds of devices have commonly been employed in linguistic description: rules, filters, and schemas. These imply different kinds of relationships between specific expressions (e.g. sentences) and the patterns they manifest.

By **rules**, I mean constructive rules analogous to the phrase structure rules and transformations of classic generative syntax. What is important here is the notion that rules and expressions are quite different in nature and related only indirectly. It is only required that, through their cumulative application, some set of rules serve collectively to "construct" a given expression. Rules do not necessarily resemble the expressions they help derive. **Filters** are negative statements indicating that a particular configuration of elements is not permitted. By definition, filters are distinct from the expressions they help describe. **Schemas** bear the closest relation to expressions. They are templates for expressions, representing the abstracted commonality of sets of expressions parallel in certain respects. Schemas are thus are directly analogous to the expressions they characterize apart from their level of specificity.

In CG, grammatical patterns are represented by means of schemas. A **construction** is defined as either an expression (of any size), or else a schema abstracted from expressions to capture their commonality (at any level of specificity). Expressions and the patterns they instantiate are thus the same in their basic nature, differing only in degree of specificity. Both specific expressions and abstracted schemas are capable of being entrenched psychologically and conventionalized in a speech community, in which case they constitute established **linguistic units**. Specific expressions with the status of units are traditionally recognized as lexical items. More schematic units correspond to what is traditionally regarded as grammar. The difference, though, is a matter of degree, and in CG these form a continuum. Every construction – whether lexical or grammatical – is characterized as an assembly of symbolic structures.

CG is highly restrictive owing to the **content requirement**. The elements permitted in a linguistic description are limited to: (i) semantic, phonological, and symbolic structures that actually occur as (parts of) expressions; (ii) schematizations of permitted structures; and (iii) categorizing relationships between permitted structures. Thus the only elements ascribable to a linguistic system are those which are either part of the primary data (namely, occurring expressions), hence directly apprehended, or else emerge from the primary data by means of the basic psychological phenomena of schematization and categorization. Ruled out by the content requirement are such elements as filters, purely syntactic primitives (with neither semantic nor phonological content), and derivations from underlying structures.

Let us then consider what the content requirement does permit. Permitted first, as shown in Figure 1.1, are semantic structures (abbreviated S) and phonological structures (P). These can be of any size and any degree of internal complexity. A symbolic structure (Σ) consists in the linkage of a semantic and a phonological structure (its two poles). Symbolic structures combine with one another (in ways to be discussed) to form assemblies of symbolic structures, which can also be of any size and any degree of internal complexity. When these assemblies are specific (rather than schematic), they constitute expressions (E), such as words, phrases, clauses, etc.[1]

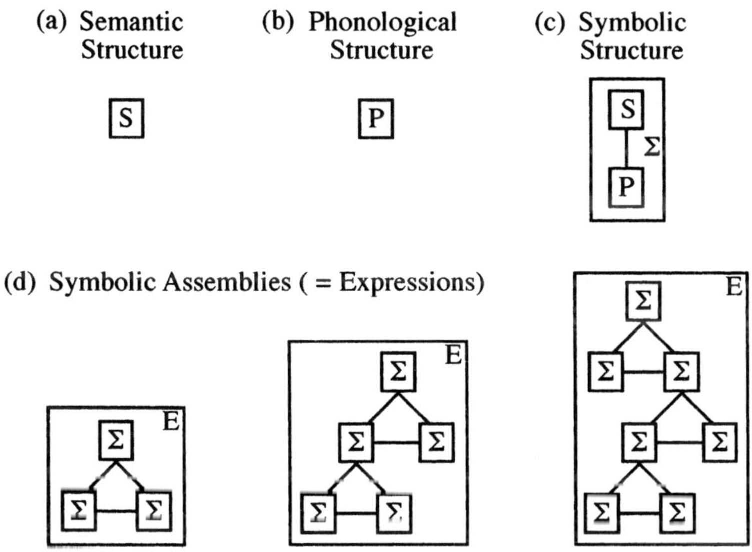

Figure 1.1

1 When those expressions are entrenched and conventionalized, they are recognized as lexical items.

Permitted next, as shown in Figure 1.2, are schemas (Sch). Each represents the abstracted commonality observable in sets of occurring expressions, or in schemas previously extracted. Schematization can be carried to whatever level of abstraction the data supports.

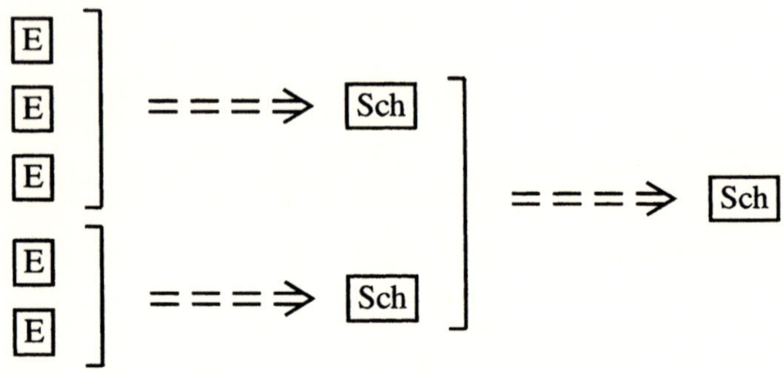

Figure 1.2

Also permitted are relationships of categorization, of which there are two basic sorts, described in Figure 1.3. One sort is the relation between a schema and more specific structures in which the schema is immanent (i.e. observable without distortion). These more specific structures thus elaborate (or instantiate) the schema. For this I use a solid arrow. A dashed arrow represents extension, implying some conflict between the categorizing structure and the one it categorizes. In this case the categorizing structure can be regarded as a prototype (at least in local terms).

Figure 1.3

A linguistic system thus comprises vast networks of structures linked by categorizing relationships, as sketched in Figure 1.4(a). Included in such networks are specific expressions with the status of conventional units, as well as schemas representing various levels of abstraction (or schematicity). Of course, a particular expression – whether fixed or novel – is categorized simultaneously by many schemas, each corresponding to a particular facet of its structure. Collectively, the set of schemas which categorize it constitutes its structural description (i.e. its interpretation with respect to the linguistic system), as shown in Figure 1.4(b). The expression is well-formed (or "grammatical") to the extent that these categorizations involve elaboration rather than extension.

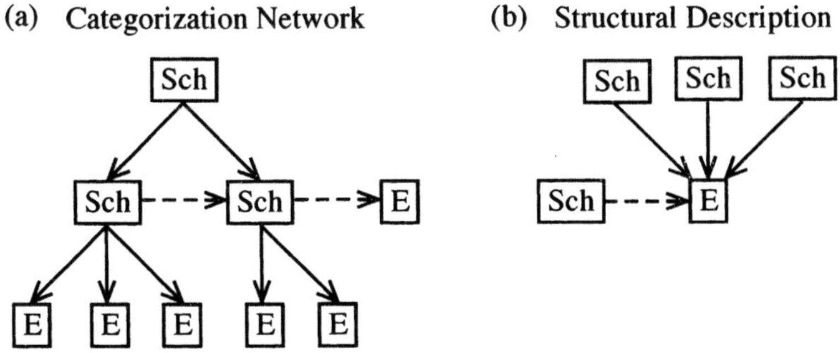

Figure 1.4

In this framework, grammatical patterns are captured by **constructional schemas**, i.e. schematic symbolic assemblies (Langacker 1987a: ch. 10, 1988a, 2000). A constructional schema describes, in schematic terms, how simpler expressions combine to form a more complex expression. It can therefore function as a template guiding the formation of new expressions, and also serves to categorize the relevant facets of such expressions, as shown in Figure 1.5.

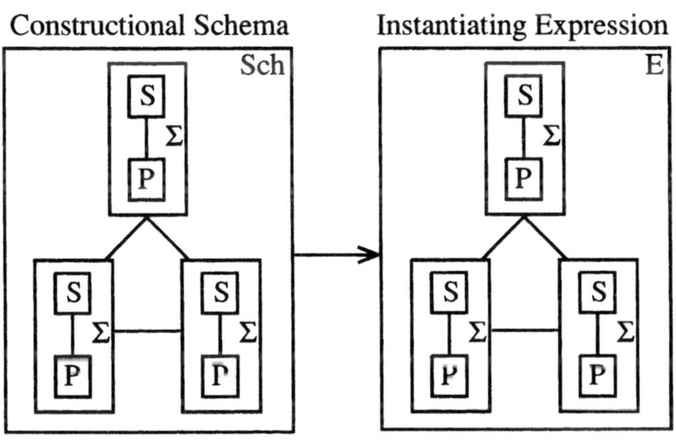

Figure 1.5

Why does grammar exist? There would be no need for grammatical patterns if a minimal symbolic structure (i.e. a morpheme) were available to symbolize every notion we might have occasion to express. That of course is not feasible because conceptualization is so flexible and open-ended. Grammar allows the formation of symbolically complex expressions capable of evoking novel conceptions of any degree of complexity. It does so by means of constructional schemas. Each such schema is a pattern for combining simpler symbolic structures to form more complex ones. As such, it specifies how their component elements are semantically integrated, and how they are phonologically integrated to symbolize their semantic integration. Consequently, patterns of semantic composition can be identified as the semantic poles of constructional schemas. Semantic composition is not distinct from grammar, but constitutes the semantic pole of grammar (just as lexical meanings are not distinct from lexical items, but constitute their semantic poles). These patterns of semantic composition do not completely determine the meanings of complex expressions (Langacker 2003b). Here, though, I will concentrate on grammatical constructions and the compositional aspects of linguistic meaning captured by constructional schemas.

2. Basic semantic notions

To describe in detail the CG view of grammatical constructions, I must first introduce some basic notions pertaining to semantic structure. In cognitive semantics, meaning is identified with conceptualization, in the broadest sense. Pivotal to linguistic semantics is our ability to **construe** the same situation in alternate ways (Langacker 1993a). Among the dimensions of construal are the level of specificity at which a situation is characterized, the perspective adopted for "viewing" it, and the degree of prominence conferred on the elements within it.

By **specificity** (or conversely, **schematicity**) I mean the level of precision and detail at which a situation is characterized (how coarse-grained or fine-grained). This can be exemplified by an expression hierarchy like that in (1). Under appropriate circumstances, the same entity might be designated by any of these expressions.

(1) *thing* → *object* → *vehicle* → *truck* → *pick-up truck* → *battered old pick-up truck*

Perspective is multifaceted. Two of its facets are vantage point, illustrated by the contrast in (2), and direction of mental scanning, exemplified in (3). Sentence (2)a construes the situation as being seen from a vantage point in the attic, (2)b from a vantage point down below. The sentences in (3) describe precisely the same situation. They contrast semantically by inducing us to mentally scan through the scene in opposite directions in building up to its full conception.

(2) a. *Come on up into the attic!*
b. *Go on up into the attic!*

(3) a. *From home plate to the pitcher's mound, the grass has all been worn away.*
b. *From the pitcher's mound to home plate, the grass has all been worn away.*

There are many kinds of prominence that need to be distinguished. Only two concern us directly, namely **profiling** and **trajector/landmark** organization. Each is strongly motivated in purely semantic terms, and subsequently proves essential for describing grammar (cf. Langacker 1993b, 1999c).

Every expression evokes some conception – simple or complex – as the basis for its meaning. Within its conceptual **base**, an expression singles out a particular substructure as a kind of focus of attention. This substructure, called the **profile**, is the one the expression designates (its conceptual referent). For example, as sketched in Figure 1.6(a), the word *arc* evokes as its base the conception of a circle, within which it profiles any segment.[2] The base for *roof* is the conception of a house, within which it profiles the upper part that covers it. Two expressions can have exactly the same base yet differ in meaning because of the alternate profiles they impose on it. For instance, *husband* and *wife* both evoke as their base the conception of a male (M) and a female (F) linked in a relationship of marriage (represented by double lines). The semantic contrast between them is not a matter of conceptual content, but rather one of prominence, the choice of profile.

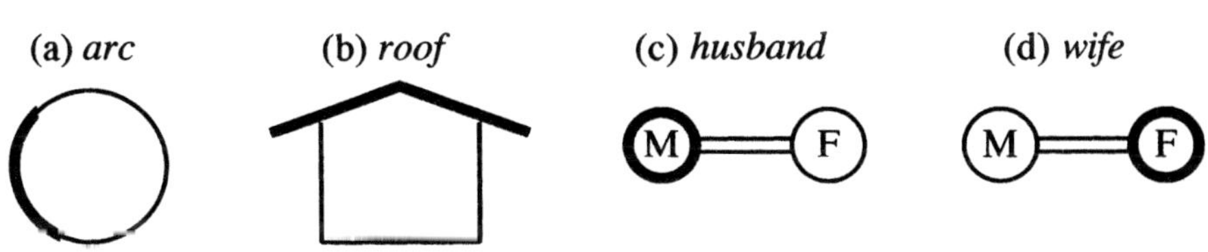

Figure 1.6

Crucially, an expression can profile either a **thing** or a **relationship**. Both notions are defined quite abstractly (Langacker 1987b). Here I can merely note

2 Observe that heavy lines indicate profiling.

that things are not limited to objects or physical entities, and a relationship does not necessarily involve multiple participants. The expressions in Figure 1.6 profile things. Some examples of profiled relationships are given in Figure 1.7. As abbreviatory notations, I often employ circles or ellipses to represent things, and various kinds of lines or arrows for relationships. Note further that, because the conception of a relationship presupposes and incorporates the conception of its core participants, those participants are part of the profiled relation and are thus depicted with heavy lines.

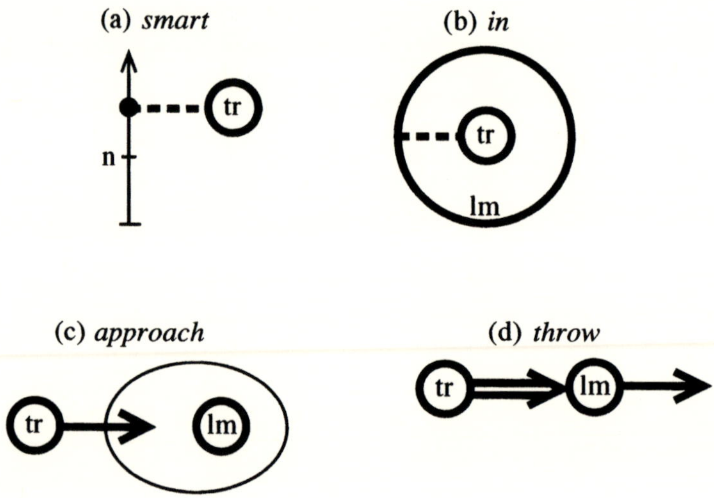

Figure 1.7

The adjective *smart* exemplifies a one-participant relation. The profiled relationship consists of this participant (shown as a circle, since a person is a kind of thing) being situated beyond the norm (n) on a scale of intelligence. Prototypically, the preposition *in* profiles a two-participant relationship of spatial inclusion (but cf. Vandeloise 1991, ch: 13). The verb *approach* profiles an event in which one participant moves (single arrow) toward the other without reaching it, but does arrive in its neighborhood (given as an ellipse). In the case of *throw*, one participant exerts force (double arrow) on the other, causing it to move rapidly along an extended trajectory.

With expressions that profile relationships, a second kind of prominence comes into play. It consists in the degree of prominence conferred on the participants in the profiled relation. There is generally a **primary focal participant**, called the **trajector** (tr). This is the participant the expression is concerned with locating or characterizing. Often there is also a **secondary focal**

participant, called a **landmark** (lm). Metaphorically, we can think in terms of primary and secondary spotlights, which can be directed at different elements within the scene onstage. Trajector and landmark can also be characterized as primary and secondary figures within the profiled relationship (Langacker 1999c, 2001a).

Relational expressions that evoke essentially the same content for their base can nonetheless differ in meaning by virtue of their profiles and/or their trajector/landmark alignment. A well-known example is the contrast between *like* and *please*. For both, we can posit a conceptual base involving two participants, with the roles of stimulus and experiencer, which interact as shown in Figure 1.8. The stimulus somehow impinges on the experiencer, who perceives or apprehends it and has a positive (+) affective reaction. The verb *like* describes the experiencer's role in this interaction, so the experiencer functions as trajector, whereas *please* focuses the stimulus. Focusing one or the other participant naturally serves to highlight those aspects of the overall relationship it is responsible for. Consequently, the profile of *like* saliently includes the experiencer's apprehension of the stimulus, while that of *please* centers on the latter's stimulation of the former.

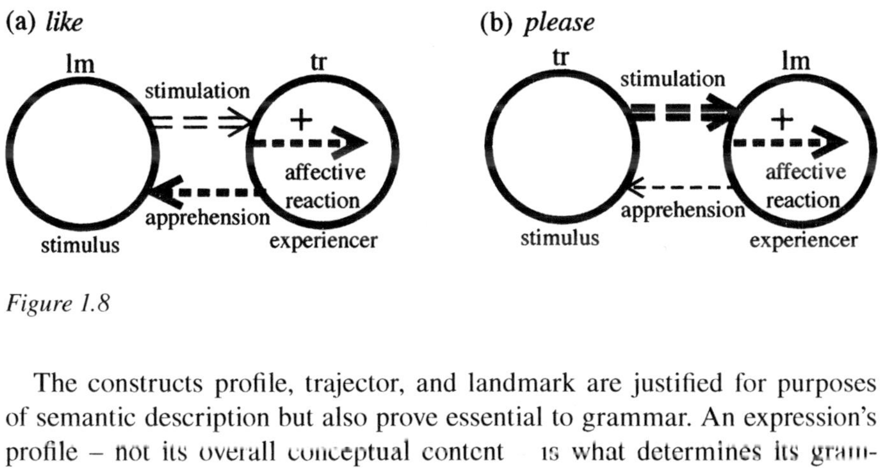

Figure 1.8

The constructs profile, trajector, and landmark are justified for purposes of semantic description but also prove essential to grammar. An expression's profile – not its overall conceptual content – is what determines its grammatical category. For instance, a noun profiles a thing, as in Figure 1.6. Such classes as verbs, adjectives, adverbs, and prepositions profile various sorts of relationships. A verb designates a **process**, defined as a relationship followed in its evolution through time. The other classes mentioned profile relationships that are **non-processual** (or **atemporal**) – though time may well be involved, the profiled relationship is viewed holistically (rather than being scanned sequentially through time). They are distinguished by the nature of their focal participants. An adjective (e.g. *smart*) has a thing as trajector, but no focused landmark. An adverb is comparable except that its trajector is a relationship rather than a thing. By contrast, a preposition (e.g. *in*) does have a thing as focused landmark, while its trajector can either be a thing or a relationship.

Trajector/landmark organization provides the conceptual basis for the grammatical notions subject and object. A subject can be characterized as a nominal expression that specifies the trajector of a profiled relationship, and an object as one that specifies the landmark of a profiled relationship. Hence the subject of *like*, for example, designates the experiencer, and that of *please* the stimulus. Conversely for their objects.

3. Prototypical constructions

A construction is simply an assembly of symbolic structures. The CG characterization is basically the same whether a construction is specific or schematic, whether it is fixed or novel, and whether it is morphological or syntactic.

In a typical construction, two **component** symbolic structures are integrated to form a **composite** symbolic structure. They are integrated at both the semantic and the phonological poles, their phonological integration serving to symbolize their semantic integration. At either pole, integration is effected by correspondences (marked by dotted lines) that equate particular elements within the two component structures. To form the composite structure, corresponding elements are superimposed, their specifications being merged (or "unified"). As a consequence, component elements that correspond each correspond to the merged composite element derived by their superimposition.

Consider the phrase *smart woman*, sketched in Figure 1.9. The two component structures, *smart* and *woman*, are shown at the bottom. The composite expression *smart woman* is shown at the top. At the semantic pole, the adjective *smart* profiles a relationship that situates its trajector on a scale of intelligence. The noun *woman* profiles a thing. To simplify the representation, its many semantic specifications are simply abbreviated as W. The semantic integration of *smart* and *woman* hinges on a correspondence between the adjective's trajector and the noun's profile. By superimposing these elements and merging their specifications, we obtain the composite semantic structure, in which a thing characterized as a woman is located on a scale of intelligence. The composite expression profiles the woman (a kind of thing), so the overall expression is classed as a noun.

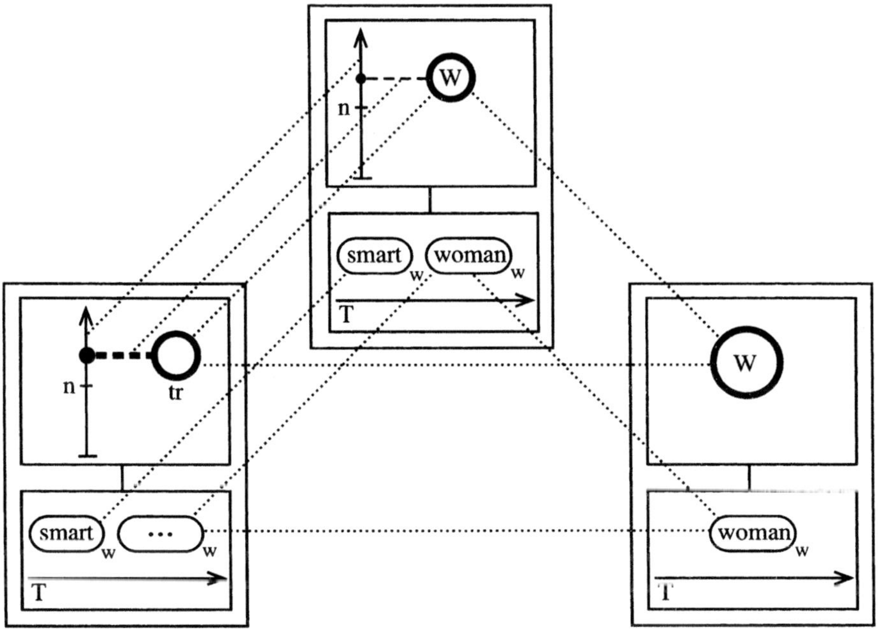

Figure 1.9

This semantic association of *smart* and *woman* is symbolized by the integration of these words at the phonological pole.[3] That is, the fact that *smart* qualifies *woman* semantically is symbolized by the fact that these words occur together in the speech stream in a particular linear (i.e. temporal) order. The speech stream is represented diagrammatically by the arrow labeled T (for processing time). The horizontal correspondence line equates *woman* with the word that directly follows *smart* in the speech stream. Phonologically, then, the composite expression derived by superimposing corresponding elements is *smart woman*.

The dynamic language employed above – saying that the component structures are "integrated" to form the composite structure by "superimposing" and "merging" corresponding elements – should not be taken too seriously. It is not being claimed that, in terms of actual processing, the component structures exist first, and the composite structure only subsequently. Nor is the composite structure seen as being constructed out of the component structures, which supply all its content. The composite structure is viewed as an entity in its own right, which may have properties not derived from either component.

3 Words are indicated by ellipses subscripted with lower-case 'w'.

More neutrally, then, I say that a construction is an assembly of symbolic structures linked by correspondences and categorizing relationships. Figure 1.9 illustrates how they are linked by horizontal and vertical correspondences. I will now describe how they are also linked by categorizing relationships. Though I will concentrate on the semantic pole, all the constructions discussed must be understood as being bipolar.

It is typical for one component structure to contain a salient schematic element which the other component structure serves to elaborate. This schematic element, corresponding to the profile of the other component, is called an **elaboration site** (or **e-site**) and is marked here by shading. In Figure 1.10, the semantic pole of *smart woman*, the elaboration site is the trajector of *smart*. The trajector is quite salient, the primary focus within the profiled relationship. Within the adjective itself it is also quite schematic; elaboration by *woman* serves to make it more specific.

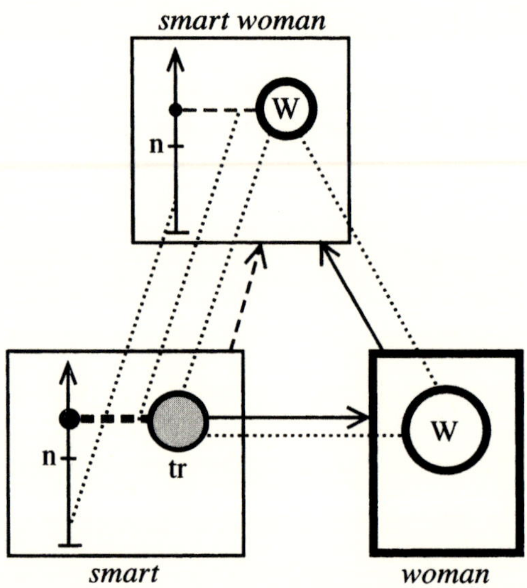

Figure 1.10

The vertical arrows in Figure 1.10 indicate that the two component structures (taken as wholes) categorize the composite structure (taken as a whole). In what sense is their relationship one of categorization? Within a construction, the composite structure has special status: it stands in the foreground as the structure primarily employed for higher-level purposes. The component structures tend not to be invoked for their own sake, but rather as stepping stones allowing one to arrive at the composite structure. I take this asymmetry as being a special case of the asymmetry inherent in the relation between a categorizing structure and the target of categorization. Moreover, the composite structure is an entity in its own right, often with special properties not strictly derivable from the meanings of component elements considered individually. In other words, the composite structure is not literally constructed out of the components – the stepping stones are not building blocks. Rather, the components serve merely to evoke and motivate certain facets of the composite conception. As a general matter, the relation between them is more akin to categorization than strict composition.

In Figure 1.10, the categorizing relationship between the component structure *woman* and the composite structure *smart woman* is one of elaboration (solid arrow). This is because the two are fully consistent in their specifications and *smart woman* offers a finer-grained characterization of the profiled entity. On the other hand, the relation between *smart* and *smart woman* is given with a dashed arrow, indicating extension rather than elaboration. Considered as wholes, *smart* and *smart woman* are inconsistent in their specifications, particularly in regard to profiling: *smart* profiles a non-processual relationship, whereas *smart woman* profiles a thing. Thus, while *smart* contributes to the composite conception (or motivates a certain aspect of it), it is not precisely schematic with respect to it.

This is quite typical. In a construction, it is normally the case that the profile of one component structure, but not of the other, corresponds to the composite structure profile. The component structure whose profile is thus inherited at the composite structure level is called the **profile determinant**. Diagrammatically, the profile determinant is enclosed in a heavy-line box. In Figure 1.10, *woman* functions as profile determinant because *smart woman* designates the woman, not the relationship of being intelligent.

The phrase *smart woman* represents a specific symbolic assembly, i.e. an expression. This expression instantiates a constructional schema describing a general syntactic pattern for combining adjectives with nouns. Diagrammed in Figure 1.11 is the semantic pole of this schema, representing the abstracted commonality of countless adjective + noun sequences. The component structure on the left is the schematic representation of an adjective: it profiles a non-processual relationship of unspecified nature, except that its trajector is a thing, with no focused landmark. The component structure on the right is the schematic representation of a noun, which profiles a thing. The adjectival trajector functions as elaboration site and corresponds to the nominal profile. The noun is the profile determinant, so the composite structure profiles a thing which, as an unprofiled part of its conceptual base, participates in the relationship coded by the adjective. At the phonological pole, the schema specifies that the adjective directly precedes the noun in the speech stream.

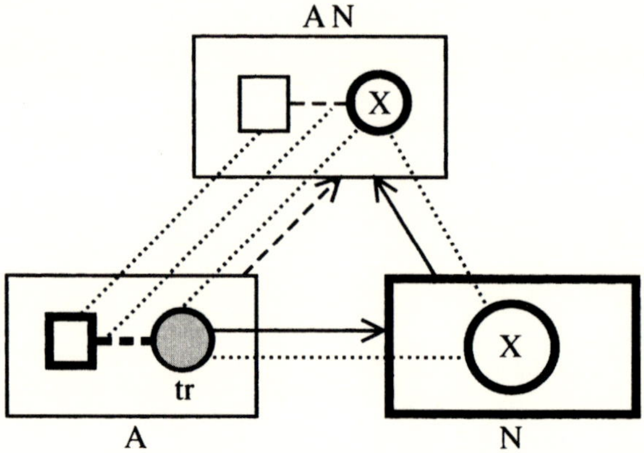

Figure 1.11

Constructional schemas provide the patterns a language makes available for the production of complex expressions. These schemas are themselves symbolic assemblies, hence meaningful, although their meanings are generally quite abstract. Their skeletal meanings are immanent in (i.e. they "lie within") those of instantiating expressions, which elaborate them ("flesh them out") in their own individual ways.

A constructional schema's semantic pole constitutes a **constructional meaning**, the schema's contribution to the overall meaning of composite expressions. With more abstract schemas, like Figure 1.11, constructional meaning is limited to specifying the grammatical category of symbolic elements, as well as organizational properties: how these elements relate to one another in terms of correspondences, categorization, and profile determinance. For instance, the specification that *smart woman* designates the woman (rather than the property of being intelligent) is a function of the entire construction, not of the component lexical items. It is likewise an aspect of constructional meaning that the profiled woman is the trajector of *smart* (the person whose intelligence is specified), rather than having some other role.

Whether specific or schematic, symbolic assemblies can in principle be of any size. When there are more than two component structures, it is usual for an assembly to exhibit multiple levels of organization, such that a composite structure at one level functions in turn as component structure with respect to another, "higher" level. The result is a kind of constituency. However, the constituency hierarchies posited in CG are not comparable to the syntactic "tree structures" of generative grammar, which are generally conceived as purely formal objects with no intrinsic conceptual or phonological content. On the contrary, CG constituency hierarchies consist solely of symbolic structures, each comprising a semantic and a phonological pole. Grammatical constituency is simply the order in which simpler symbolic structures are progressively integrated to form more complex ones.

Consider the nominal expression *smart woman with a PhD*, sketched in Figure 1.12 (ignoring the article). It consists of several canonical constructions: *smart woman*, already examined; a prepositional phrase, where *with* takes a nominal object; and the higher-level construction where the composite expressions *smart woman* and *with a PhD* combine as component structures to form the overall expression.

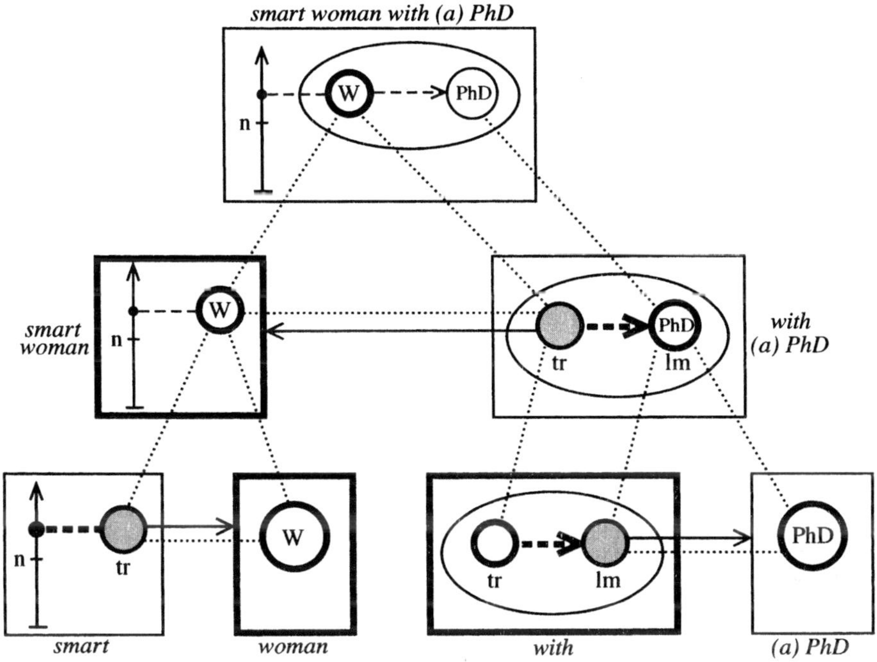

Figure 1.12

The representation of *with* is meant to indicate that it profiles a non-processual, essentially possessive relationship such that the trajector anchors an experiential **dominion** (Langacker 1993c) in which the landmark can be found. The schematic landmark functions as e-site, corresponding to the profile of the nominal component *a PhD*. Since the composite structure *with a PhD* profiles the possessive relationship (not the academic degree), *with* is the profile determinant at this level. At the higher level, the schematic trajector of the prepositional phrase corresponds to the profile of *smart woman*, which elaborates it and imposes its own profile on the higher level composite structure. Hence the overall expression, *smart woman with a PhD*, designates the woman.

Some basic grammatical notions are straightforwardly characterized in terms of symbolic assemblies as described thus far. As the term is most commonly understood, for example, a **head** can be defined as the profile determinant at a given level of organization (cf. Zwicky 1985; Hudson 1987). It is the component structure whose profile is inherited at the composite structure level, thereby determining the grammatical category of the composite expression. *Woman* is thus the head in the nominal expression *smart woman*, and *with* in the prepositional phrase *with a PhD*. Granted the constituency shown in Figure 1.12, the head at the higher level of organization, for the expression as a whole, is *smart woman* (and by extension, *woman* – as the head within the head).

We can go on to characterize the notions **complement** and **modifier** in terms of whether a component structure elaborates or is elaborated by the head. More specifically, a complement is a component structure which **elaborates** a salient substructure of the head. In Figure 1.12, the nominal expression *a PhD* is thus a complement of *with*, since it elaborates a salient substructure of *with*, namely its landmark (a focal participant). Conversely, a modifier is a component structure a salient substructure of which is **elaborated by** the head. Hence *smart* modifies *woman* in Figure 1.12, since the head – *woman* – elaborates its trajector. In the same way, *with a PhD* modifies *smart woman* at the higher level.

I should emphasize that these definitions refer exclusively to conceptual factors – profiling, profile determinance, correspondence, elaboration – observable at the semantic pole of symbolic assemblies. Despite their utility for describing grammar, these constructs are ultimately semantic in nature, not autonomous grammatical primitives.

4. Non-prototypical constructions

The constructions examined so far are reasonably considered canonical, or prototypical. They have a number of typical properties: (i) there are two component structures; (ii) one component profiles a thing, the other a relationship; (iii) the nominal profile corresponds to a focal participant of the relationship (its trajector or landmark); (iv) that participant is schematic, being elaborated by the nominal component; (v) the composite structure inherits its profile from one of the two component structures.

Grammatical constructions are nonetheless highly varied and deviate from the prototype in myriad ways (Langacker 1988b, 1999b, 2005a). Ultimately, it is only required that a construction comprise an assembly of symbolic structures linked by correspondences. Even this must be qualified if we make the terminological decision to regard single morphemes as constructions, so that all of lexicon and grammar can be described as residing in constructions. With this approach, a morpheme constitutes a **degenerate** construction, a symbolic assembly consisting of just one symbolic element. Hence there is no distinction between component and composite structures, nor any correspondences.

Also deviating from the prototype are constructions with more than two component structures. The previous example, *smart woman with a PhD*, might be analyzed in this fashion. On this account, diagrammed in Figure 1.13, *smart* and *with a PhD* modify *woman* at the same level of constituency, in a tripartite construction.[4] It will be observed that, despite the difference in constituency, the overall composite structures in Figures 1.12 and 1.13 are identical, and the necessary semantic and grammatical relationships are expressed in both (e.g. *woman* is the head, modified by *smart* and *with a PhD*).

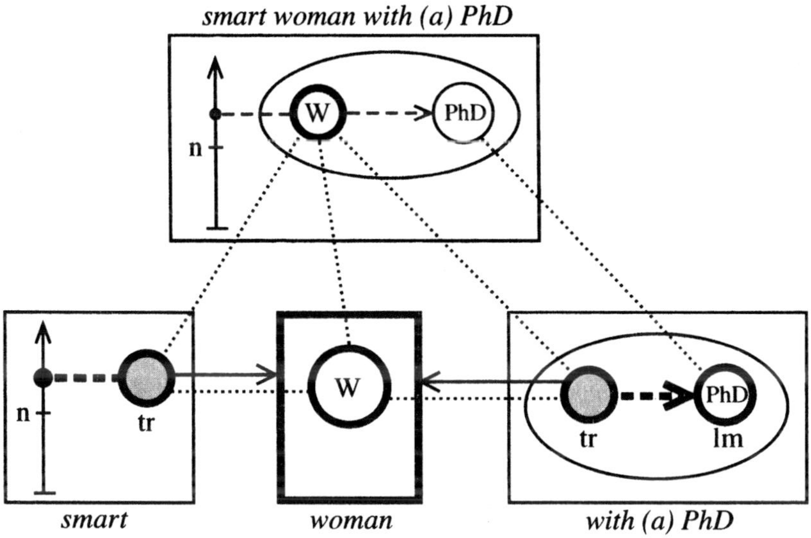

Figure 1.13

Which constituency is correct, the one in Figure 1.12 or the one in Figure 1.13? Actually, I suspect both of them are. In CG, essential grammatical relationships are conceptual in nature and captured by correspondences, not in terms of constituent structure. The same relationships can be captured with alternate constituencies, with the empirical consequence that constituent structure is often flexible, variable, and even indeterminate (Langacker 1995a, 1997a). In the case at hand, evidence for two alternate constituencies is pro-

4 I omit the internal structure of the prepositional phrase.

vided by the intonational possibilities in (4), where a slash ('/') indicates a slight pause. It is further corroborated by the ability of *one* to refer anaphorically to either *smart woman* or just *woman*, as seen in (5).

(4) a. *smart woman / with a PhD*
b. *smart / woman / with a PhD*

(5) a. *They're looking for a* ***smart woman*** *with a PhD, not* ***one*** *with just a masters.*
b. *A smart* ***woman*** *with a PhD is happier than a brilliant* ***one*** *with just a masters.*

More generally, a number of adjectival modifiers can be strung together with no indication of any particular constituency hierarchy, especially when pronounced with pauses between them and with equal degrees of stress: *big / ugly / vicious / dog*. In this case I see no reason not to posit a multipartite construction, as seen in Figure 1.14. Each adjective ascribes a property to the modified noun, so the trajector of each corresponds to its profile.[5]

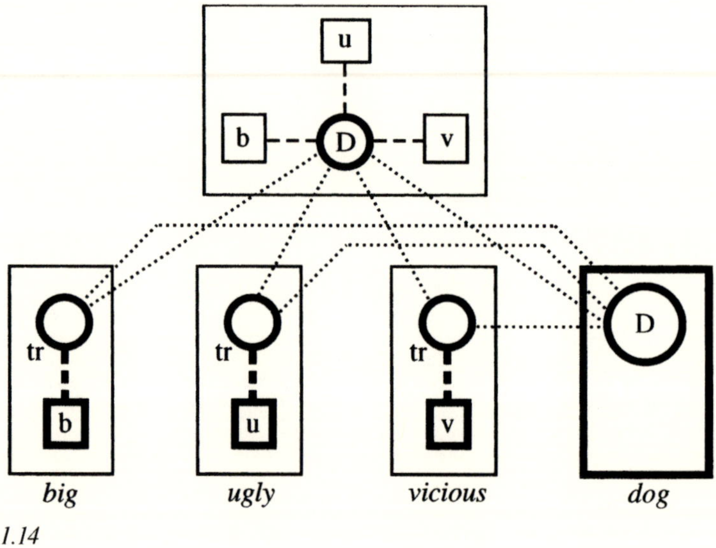

Figure 1.14

Many constructions depart from the prototype because they lack a head, or profile determinant, defined as a **single** component structure whose profile corresponds to the composite structure profile. Here we can distinguish three subcases. A unique profile determinant may be absent (i) because the compo-

5 Here I simplify by not indicating elaboration or e-sites.

nent structure profiles correspond to one another, so they all correspond to the composite structure profile; (ii) because the composite structure profile represents a conflation of the component structure profiles and is not equivalent to any one of them individually; or (iii) because the composite structure profile is distinct from that of any component.

The first case is exemplified by **appositional** constructions, where two nominal expressions each describe the same nominal referent, in different ways. The nominal components range in size from simple nouns to full noun phrases:

(6) a. *pussy cat; sailor boy*
  b. *my friend Henry Kissinger; the famous French novelist Marcel Proust*
  c. *the {fact / claim / idea / notion / myth} that syntax is autonomous*

Abstractly, such expressions have the organization sketched in Figure 1.15. Each component structure profiles a thing, these things correspond, and both correspond to the composite structure profile.

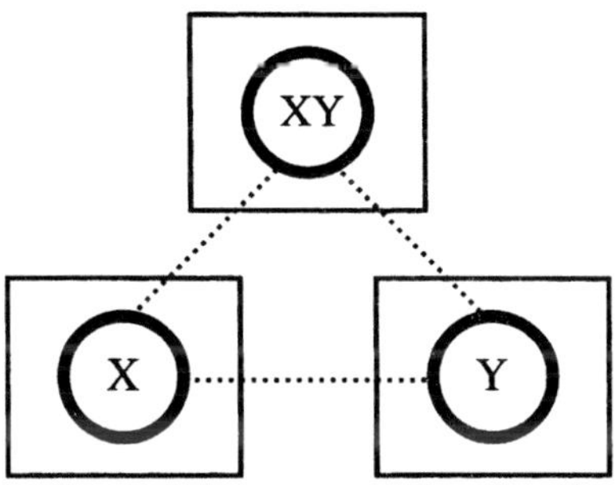

Figure 1.15

In cases like (6), we could make either of two terminological decisions: to say that both component structures are heads, or that neither is (since neither functions **uniquely** as profile determinant). I tend to follow the latter practice, essentially arbitrarily. I make the same terminological choice in the situation where the composite structure profile conflates the profiles of its components, none of which is thus equivalent to it taken individually. A favorite example is the "nested locative" construction:

(7) *The hammer is in the garage, on the workbench, behind the electric saw.*

Any number of locatives can be strung together in this manner, with no apparent grouping into constituents. Each successive locative specifies the trajector's location with greater precision (confines it to a smaller area). For our purposes, the important point is that the composite locative expression – *in the garage, on the workbench, behind the electric saw* – simultaneously locates the trajector with respect to three different landmarks. No one of these locative relationships stands out as the single location described by the overall expression. Rather, as shown in Figure 1.16, all three specifications are simultaneously valid and equally focused. The profiled relationship is complex, for it evidently conflates the simple relationships expressed by the individual component structures.

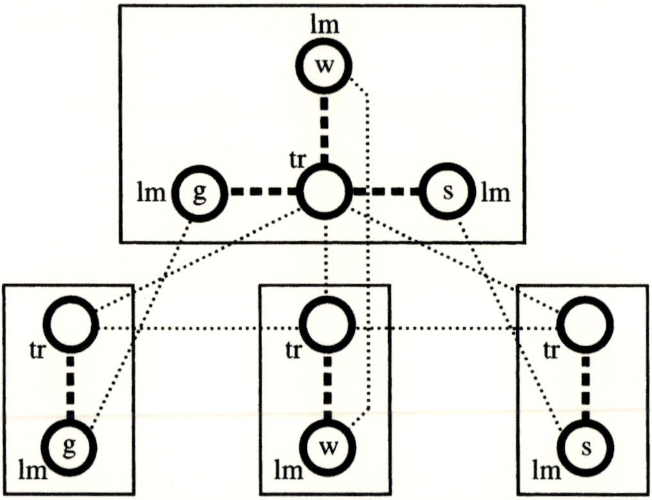

Figure 1.16

In the third type of construction lacking a head (traditionally called **exocentric**) the composite structure profile is distinct from that of both component structures. An example is *pickpocket.* In the verbal expression *pick someone's pocket*, the verb *pick* has the conceptual value sketched at the lower left in Figure 1.17: the trajector exerts a force (double arrow), thereby inducing some object to move (single arrow). This object moves from its original location, which is focused as the landmark, into the trajector's dominion (sphere of control). The noun *pocket* designates a location, shown as a rectangle, which functions as a kind of container. The circle within it represents the contents of the container, while the larger circle represents the article of clothing of which it is a part. In the compound *pickpocket*, correspondences identify the contents of the pocket with the object that moves, and the pocket itself with the landmark of *pick* (the location emptied of its contents). However, the composite structure does not inherit the profile of either *pick* (the action) or *pocket* (the location). Instead it profiles the actor, corresponding to *pick*'s trajector. Thus neither element of the compound functions as profile determinant.

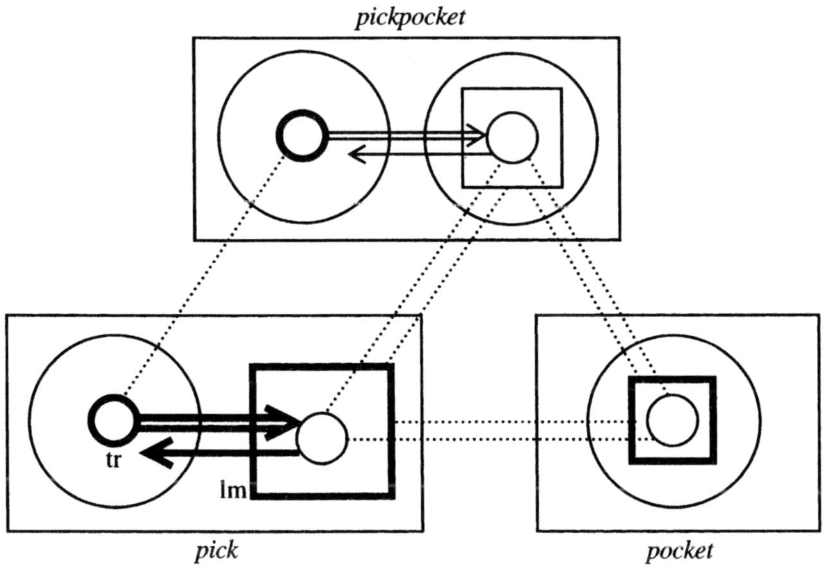

Figure 1.17

Pickpocket is idiosyncratic, in that the second element of an English compound normally functions as profile determinant (cf. Tuggy 2003). This can be contrasted with cases where an aspect of constructional meaning, while not inherited from either component, is nonetheless regular in the sense that it is specified by a productive constructional schema. Consider equative sentences in those languages where referential identity is marked simply by juxtaposing two nominal expressions. In Luiseño (a Native American language), a sentence like (8) predicates identity despite the absence of any verb or morphological element expressing this meaning.

(8) *Wunaal ya'ash no-kaytu.* (that man my-enemy) 'That man is my enemy.'

This is not an idiosyncratic expression but a regular construction, where equative sentences are productively formed using any appropriate combination of nominal expressions (NML). The constructional schema specifies that both component structures profile things, whereas the composite structure profiles a relationship of identity between them (given as a double line). As shown in Figure 1.18, the relationship profiled by the clause emerges at the level of the overall construction rather than coming from either component, but does so in accordance with a productive pattern. A particular expression like (8) is thus quite regular in formation, despite the absence of a head.

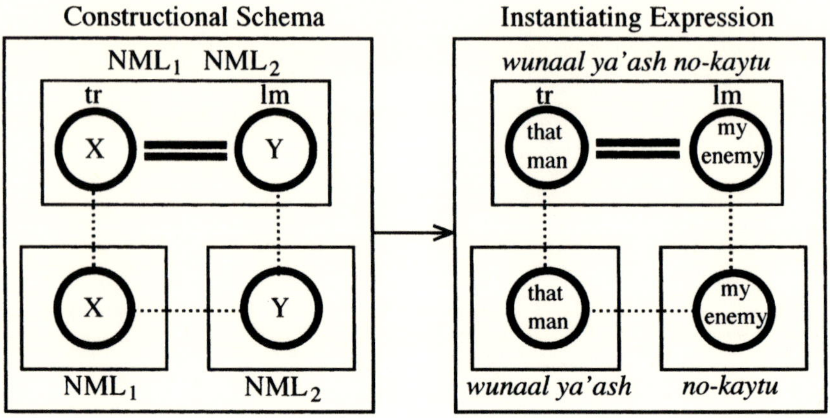

Figure 1.18

Equational and appositional constructions are non-prototypical in that both component structures profile things. Grammatical combination does not require a predicate-argument relationship, such that a nominal component specifies a relational participant. Moreover, an elaboration site does not have to be a thing, but may itself be a relationship. This is the case with adverbs, e.g. *fast*, whose trajector is a process situated on a scale of rapidity. In Figure 1.19, a box represents the schematic process functioning as the adverb's trajector. It will be seen that a phrase like *move fast* is analogous to *smart woman*.

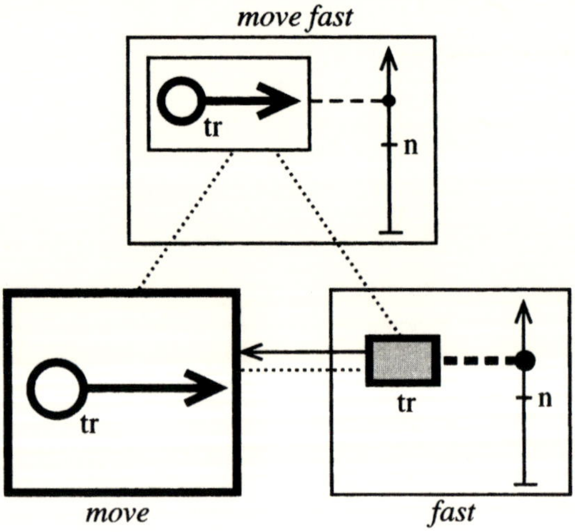

Figure 1.19

Nor is it required that an elaboration site be a focal participant. An e-site, defined as a substructure corresponding to the profile of the other component, need not even be particularly salient within the elaborated structure. An example is the compound *woman smart*, which is made-up but perfectly natural and well-formed. I interpret it as meaning 'smart in regard to women'. We know that people often exhibit intelligence with respect to certain topics but not others. The notation in Figure 1.20 is meant to indicate that the property of being smart holds only in a particular domain of knowledge (represented as an ellipse), namely the one centered on a particular topic (given as a circle). This topic functions as e-site, being elaborated by *woman*. Though pivotal to the expression's interpretation, this e-site is not a focal participant of *smart*, nor is it highly salient.

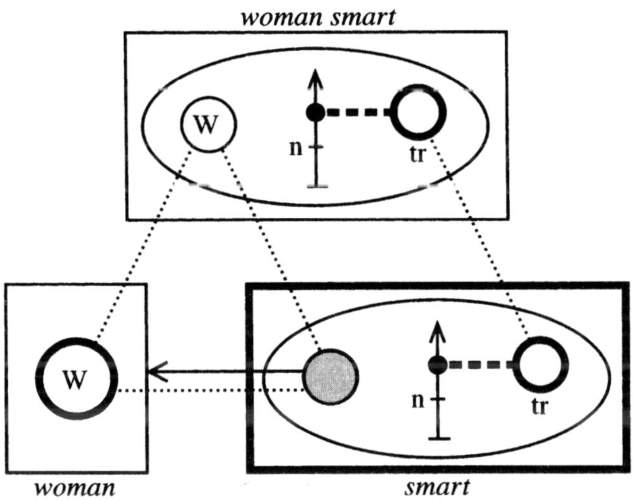

Figure 1.20

Observe that the phrase *smart woman* and the compound *woman smart* have the same component structures but very different composite meanings. They differ in their constructional meanings, contributed by the constructional schemas they instantiate. *Smart woman* instantiates the schema for the adjectival modification of nouns, sketched in Figure 1.11. On the other hand, *woman smart* instantiates a semantically more flexible schema for compounds, where in general the second element functions as profile determinant. Thus, whereas *smart woman* profiles the woman, the compound *woman smart* profiles the relationship.

Of course, it is not even necessary that there be an e-site at all. Two component structures are capable of combining grammatically even in cases where neither contains a substructure corresponding to the other's profile. Consider the composite expression *go away angry* (e.g. *Don't go away angry!*). The meaning of *go away* makes no intrinsic reference to the mental state of its trajector, nor does *angry* evoke an action which this mental state accompanies.

Their integration is sketched in Figure 1.21. The arrow labeled 't' stands for time. As a complex verb, *go away* profiles a process, where development through time is salient as a matter of definition. The solid bar along the time arrow represents the span of time through which the event is followed in its temporal evolution. Being an adjective, *angry* merely profiles the situation of its trajector exhibiting a certain property. Continuation through time is not essential to its characterization – if a person is angry during a certain span of time, that person is angry at any single instant during that time span. It is however part of our understanding of *angry* that this emotion occurs in bounded episodes, enduring for some time on each occasion. A bar along the time arrow represents the duration of one such episode.

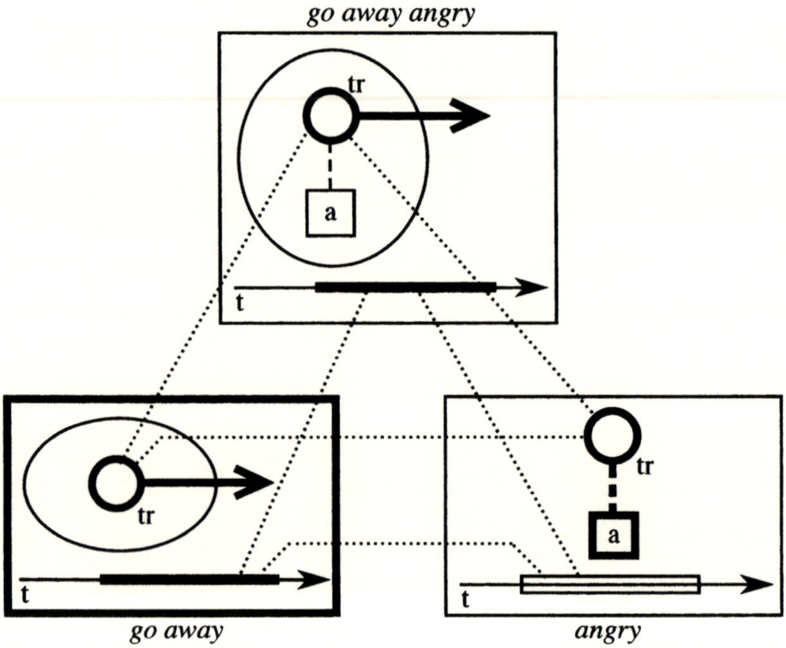

Figure 1.21

Although neither component structure elaborates a salient substructure of the other, they are integrated by virtue of two correspondences. First, their trajectors correspond – the person who goes away is the one who is angry. Second, the span of time through which the departure occurs is equated with the time span constituting one episode of anger; the expression cannot mean that the trajector goes away at one time and is angry at another, only that the two are temporally coincident.

Because neither component structure elaborates a salient e-site within the other, we cannot describe *angry* as either a complement or a modifier of *go away*. In cases like this the non-head component (*angry*) is generally called an **adjunct**. I should note that in CG the status of elements as complements, modifiers, or adjuncts is a matter of degree, reflecting the relative salience of particular notions within the global meanings of component structures. It is neither expected nor required that a particular term be obviously or uniquely applicable. That is, notions like complement, modifier, and adjunct are not unanalyzable grammatical primitives, but rather convenient labels for typical sorts of configurations that emerge with various degrees of distinctness in grammatical constructions.

An e-site sometimes exhausts the content of a component structure, rather than being limited to a proper substructure of it. This is commonly the case with derivational elements, which I generally analyze as being schematic for the category they derive. Consider the nominalizing suffix *-er*, as in *swimmer*, *complainer*, *teacher*, *philanderer*, etc. Prototypically, it forms a noun designating some kind of actor. As shown in Figure 1.22, it can then be characterized as evoking for its base the schematic conception of an active process, which I have indicated by means of an arrow with ellipses (...). Within this base, it profiles the actor, a thing. The schematic process, representing the entire conceptual content of the suffix, functions as e-site in this construction, being elaborated by a specific verb, in this case *throw*. Since *-er* is the profile determinant, the composite expression designates the actor in the specific process of throwing, and since it profiles a thing, *thrower* is a noun.

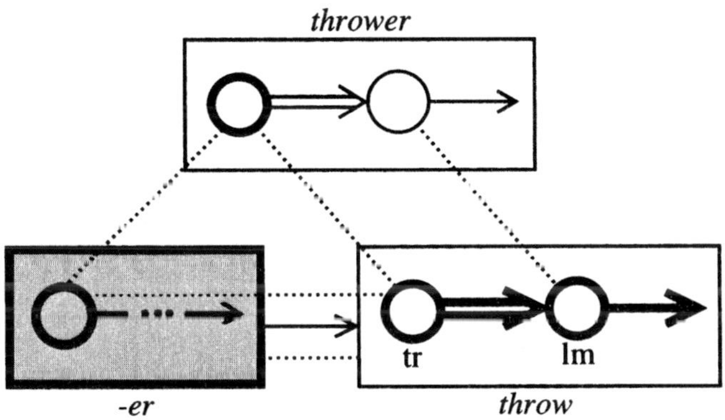

Figure 1.22

When established as lexical items, symbolically complex expressions vary in their degree of **analyzability**, defined as the extent to which speakers recognize the semantic contributions of component elements. Novel expressions are fully analyzable, since the speaker has to construct them from component elements on the basis of their meanings. Established expressions may be less analyzable. They come as prepackaged assemblies, whose composite forms and meanings are well-known and well-rehearsed, so it is not essential that the component structures be mentally accessed individually. In fixed and frequently occurring expressions, there is thus an overall tendency for component elements to be activated only to a lesser degree, and perhaps not on every occasion of their use.

The result is that familiar expressions can often be ranked in terms of their degree of analyzability, e.g. *flinger* > *complainer* > *computer* > *propeller* > *drawer.* A novel expression like *flinger* 'something that flings' is fully analyzable. The lexical item *complainer* is highly analyzable (it is always understood as 'one who complains'), but the others listed are progressively less so. In using the term *computer,* we do not always specifically think of it as 'something that computes', and a *propeller* is seldom thought of as 'something that propels'. At the extreme endpoint of the scale, a form like *drawer* may be fully unanalyzable, in which case it constitutes a single morpheme.

Degree of analyzability is an important dimension of linguistic organization which has largely been neglected. It is unproblematic in CG, where constructions are viewed as assemblies of symbolic structures. Since the composite structure is a distinct entity, existing in its own right, in established expressions it can perfectly well be activated independently of the component structures. The contrast between a fully analyzable expression like the novel *flinger* 'something that flings' and a partially analyzable form like *computer* is represented in Figure 1.23. Words in capital letters are used here to abbreviate the semantic structures, and lower-case letters for phonological structures. Dashed-line boxes enclose structures that are activated only partially or only sporadically.

On this view, the analyzability of a composite expression into component morphemes is a matter of degree – a form like *propeller* is neither completely monomorphemic nor completely bimorphemic. Moreover, once degree of analyzability is recognized and accommodated, other well-known problems of classic morphemic analysis disappear (Langacker 1995a).

First, as seen in Figure 1.24(a), it is quite possible for just one symbolic component to be recognized within a more complex expression. For instance, the *day* of *Monday, Tuesday, Wednesday,* etc. is certainly recognized by contemporary speakers, but the residue (*Mon, Tues, Wednes,* etc.) is not. We can simply characterize these expressions as **defective constructions** having a composite structure but only one (partially recognized) component structure.

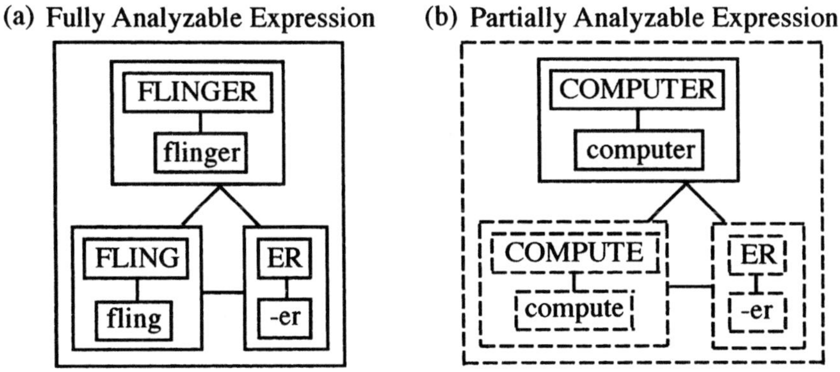

Figure 1.23

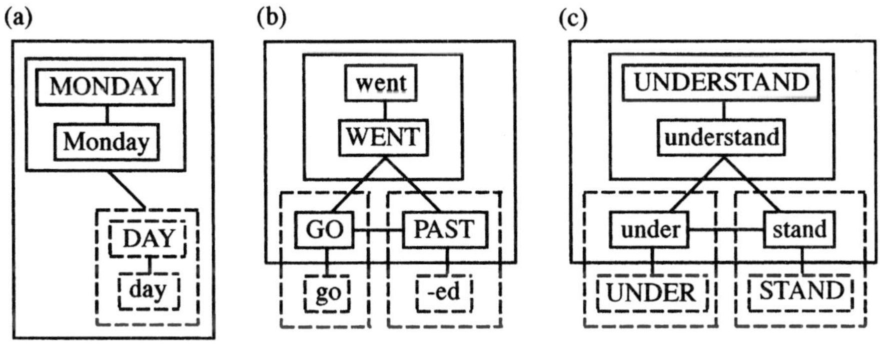

Figure 1.24

Beyond this, we can readily handle cases of **phonological suppletion** and **semantic opacity**. A case of suppletion is *went*, the past tense of *go*. Semantically the components GO and PAST are clearly evident, but phonologically there is just a single, essentially unanalyzable form. As shown in Figure 1.24(b), the symbolic unit *went* can be characterized as comprising a full, bipolar composite structure, while being defective in regard to component structures, which have a semantic pole but not a phonological pole.

Conversely, as shown in Figure 1.24(c), it is possible for a construction to be defective by including only the phonological poles of the component structures. An example is *understand*, which is clearly analyzable into the morphological elements *under* and *stand*, but which speakers find semantically opaque, making no connection to the meanings of the preposition and the verb. In the case of both *went* and *understand* the only symbolic link is at the composite structure level. However, these constructions still conform to the content requirement.

5. Grammatical dependencies

In CG, grammatical dependencies are non-configurational. They reside in semantic relationships, primarily correspondences between conceptual substructures, not in any particular constituency configuration. Two basic kinds of grammatical dependencies are subject and object relationships. Both subjects and objects are complements: nominal expressions which respectively elaborate the trajector and the landmark of a profiled relationship.

Let us take the expression *Jennifer likes that boy.* It is normally ascribed the constituency shown in Figure 1.25, where the verb and object form a constituent excluding the subject. This corresponds to the normal intonational grouping, where a slight pause is possible between *Jennifer* and *likes that boy*: *Jennifer / likes that boy.* However, in deliberate speech it is possible to divide the sentence into three intonational units: *Jennifer / likes / that boy.* This suggests a tripartite structure, and while I do not claim that intonation always correlates with constituency, it is at least one factor that bears on it. As a secondary pattern, I presume that English allows the constituency shown in Figure 1.26. The configurational difference between Figures 1.25 and 1.26 has no effect on grammatical dependencies. In both structures, by tracing horizontal and vertical correspondence lines we find that *Jennifer* functions as the subject of *like*, and *that boy* as its object.

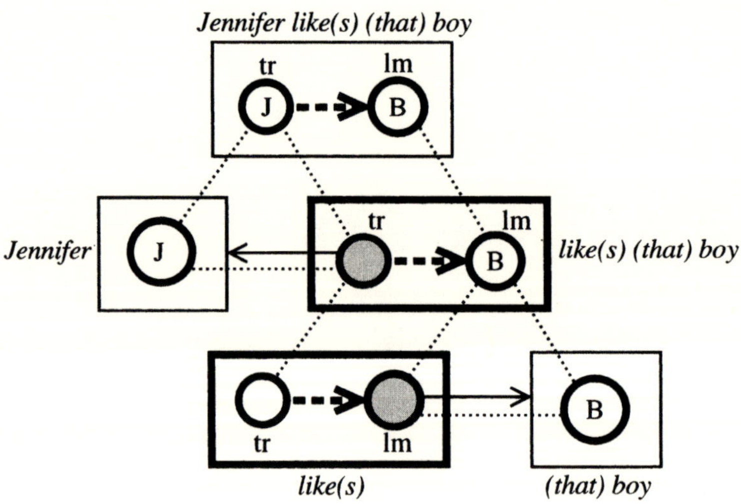

Figure 1.25

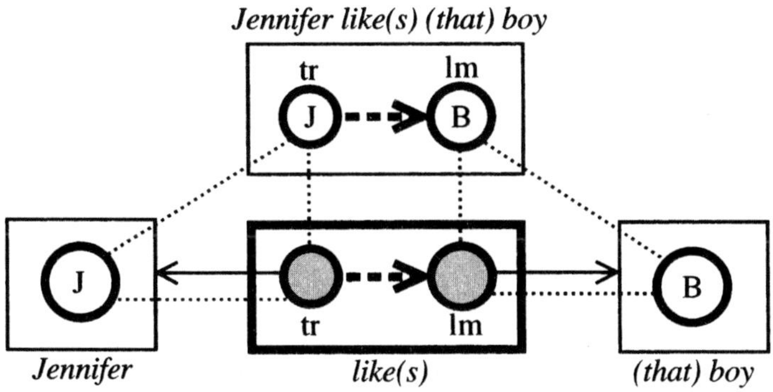

Figure 1.26

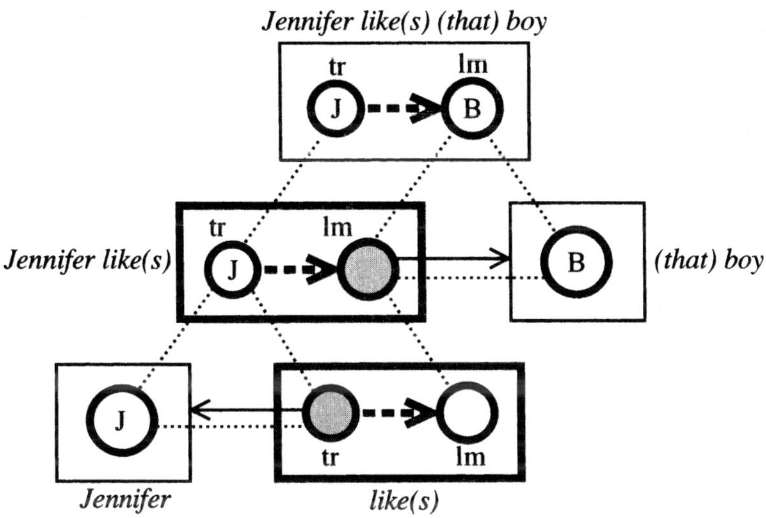

Figure 1.27

What about the other possibility, where subject and verb form a constituent, as shown in Figure 1.27? This too gives rise to the same composite structure and the same grammatical relations: *Jennifer* as subject, *that boy* as object. Though a pause after *like* is not very natural (*?Jennifer likes / that boy*), there are various more elaborate constructions where positing a subject + verb constituent does seem necessary. Among these are a clause-internal topic construction, as in (9)a, coordinate structures like (9)b,[6] and object relative clauses, as in (9)c–d. To

6 See Chapter 12 for a different perspective on coordinate expressions of this sort.

accommodate such expressions, I would simply posit a constructional schema allowing subject and verb to combine directly. This schema may be limited to larger contexts, represented by more complex constructional schemas, in which the verb's landmark is elaborated at a higher level of grammatical organization. In (9)a, for instance, the landmark of *likes* is specified in a higher-level construction by a nominal functioning simultaneously as object and clausal topic.

(9) a. *That boy Jennifer likes (this one she doesn't).*
b. *Jennifer likes, and Sharon really admires, the boy who lives next door.*
c. *The boy that Jennifer likes finally called.*
d. *The boy finally called that Jennifer likes.*

This approach to grammatical dependencies easily accommodates various phenomena that were handled in classic transformational grammar by means of derivations from underlying structures. An example is "relative clause extraposition". Because sentences like (9)c–d are effectively equivalent semantically, and modification was thought to require grammatical co-constituency, a deep structure analogous to (9)c was posited for both expressions. Sentences like (9)d were then derived by an optional transformation serving to extrapose the relative.

The CG account is sketched in Figures 1.28–29, ignoring everything not essential to the point at hand. In 1.28, the relative clause combines with the head noun in a canonical modifying construction. I have not shown the internal structure of the relative, which is a subject + verb constituent, equivalent to the lower portion of Figure 1.27. At the composite structure level, it profiles the process of liking, with a specified trajector (Jennifer) and a schematic landmark. It modifies the head noun, *boy*, by virtue of a correspondence between its landmark and the nominal profile. This correspondence identifies *boy* as the semantic object of *like*. At the higher level of organization, the subject nominal *the boy that Jennifer likes* elaborates the trajector of *call* (whose processual profile is simply represented as a solid arrow).

The alternative expression in (9)d, with an extraposed relative, is diagrammed in Figure 1.29. Here *the boy* and *finally called* are integrated in the usual fashion to form a clause at the lower level of constituency. The relative, *that Jennifer likes*, combines with this clause as a whole in the higher-level construction. However, while the two clauses combine as wholes, their integration hinges specifically on a correspondence between the landmark of the relative and the main clause trajector. Owing to this correspondence, the relative functions to describe the boy, which is identified as the semantic object of *like*. This is not a canonical modifying construction, since the head – which is the full main clause, *the boy finally called* – does not per se elaborate the landmark of the relative. The semantic effect of modification is nonetheless achieved.

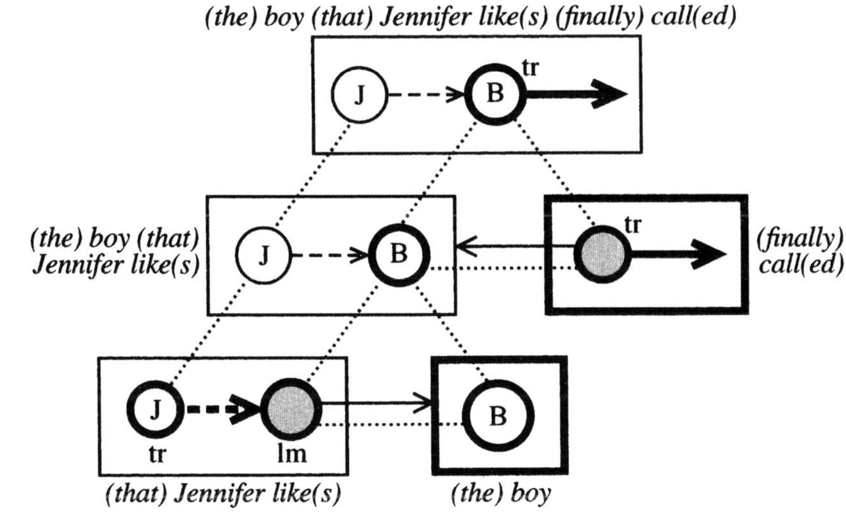

Figure 1.28

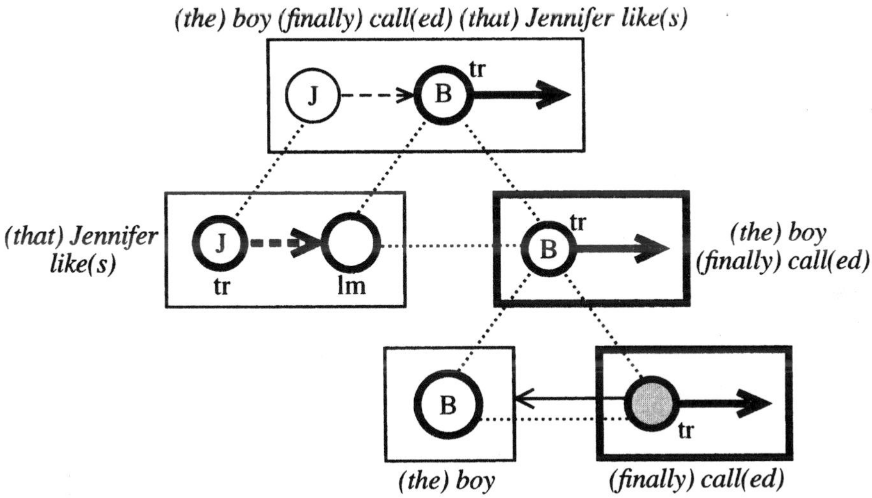

Figure 1.29

Relative clause extraposition does not come for free – speakers have to learn the construction (and the various restrictions on it), and linguists have to describe it by positing the appropriate constructional schemas. Still, this alternative grammatical option does not require any special theoretical apparatus (like deep structures and transformations). It is straightforwardly accommodated with the same theoretical devices employed for the basic pattern.

In Figures 1.28–29, correspondences identify the boy as being both the trajector of *call* and the landmark of *like.* Accordingly, in the composite semantic structure this same individual is simultaneously depicted as participating in both relationships. It is usual and unproblematic for the same conceptual element to have multiple roles, each pertaining to a particular relationship coded at a particular level of organization. In (10), for example, *a rock* functions simultaneously as the landmark (object) of *throw* and as the trajector (subject) of *into the pond.*

(10) *She threw a rock into the pond.*

Their integration is sketched in Figure 1.30. At the first level of constituency, *a rock* elaborates the landmark of *throw* in a normal direct object construction. *Throw* implies that the landmark, due to the force exerted by the trajector, moves rapidly along an extended spatial path. *Throw* itself of course evokes this path only schematically. Still, the conception of the landmark successively occupying all the spatial positions defining a path is an inherent aspect of *throw*'s meaning, and in the higher-level construction it functions as an elaboration site. Shown as a rectangle in Figure 1.30, this substructure of *throw a rock* is elaborated by the path prepositional phrase *into the pond*, which describes the path in more specific detail. Through horizontal and vertical correspondences, the rock is thus identified as both the landmark of *throw* and the trajector of *into the pond.*

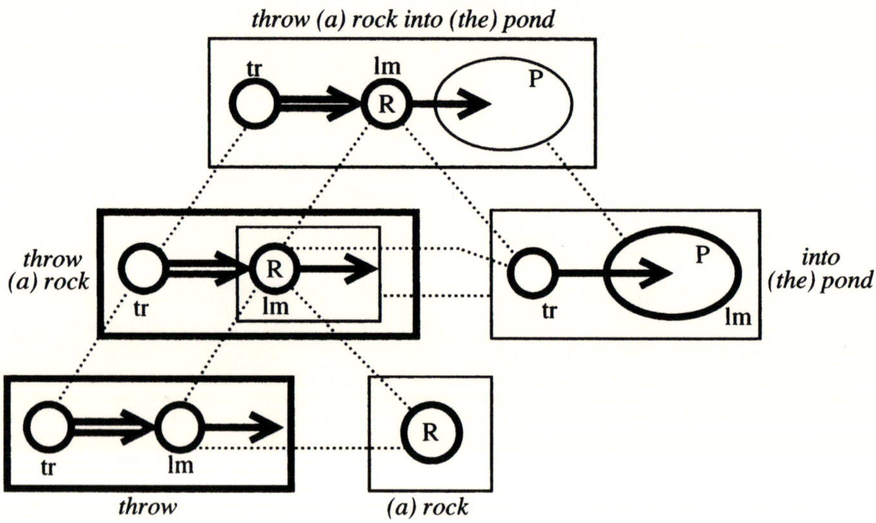

Figure 1.30

A final, more elaborate example is the following Luiseño sentence (cf. Langacker 1973):

(11) *Noo poy ngee-vichu-ni-q.* 'I made him want to leave.'
I him leave-want-make-TNS

Syntactically, it consists of a morphologically complex verb together with a subject and an object pronoun. Semantically, we need to show that the speaker is the "logical subject" of 'make' (i.e. the one who does the making), while the object 'him' has multiple roles: as the semantic object of 'make' (the target of the agent's force), and as the semantic subject of both 'want' and 'leave'.

In Figure 1.31, I show how the verb stem *ngeevichuni* 'make want to leave' is progressively assembled. The component elements are *ngee* 'leave', *-vichu* 'want', and *-ni* 'make'. The root *ngee* profiles the trajector's motion away from some original location. The suffix *-vichu* 'want' designates the trajector's desire (dashed arrow) for the occurrence of some process, which functions as a kind of landmark (a **relational** landmark rather than a nominal one). Since *-vichu* is only used for cases where the process desired is one carried out by its trajector, a correspondence internal to its semantic pole identifies the trajector of *-vichu* with the actor of the landmark process. Finally, *-ni* profiles an act of causation (double arrow), where the force is directed at a target (a nominal landmark) by way of inducing some occurrence (a relational landmark). The nominal landmark is simultaneously the target of force and the trajector of the schematic process induced.

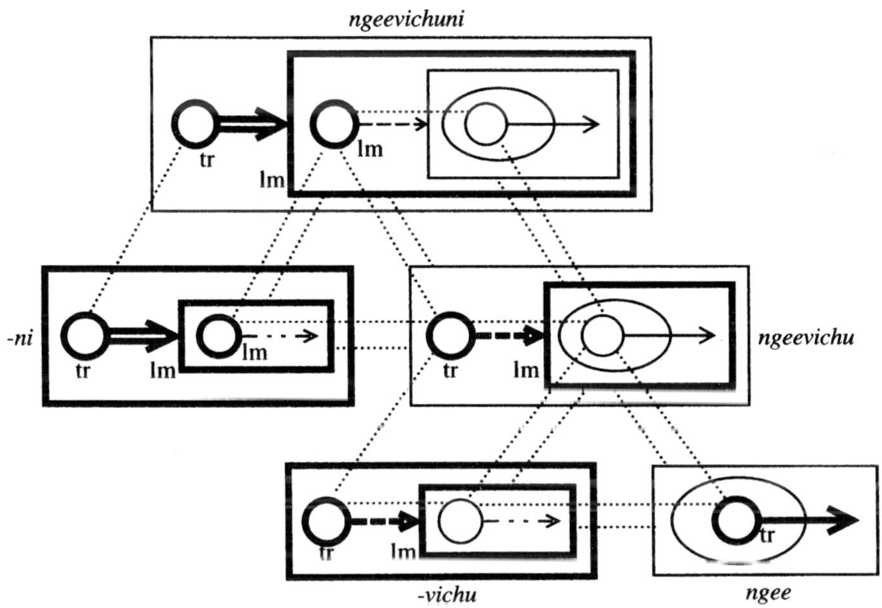

Figure 1.31

The verb stem is straightforwardly assembled by constructions representing two successive levels of morphological organization. At the lower level, *ngee* 'leave' specifies the schematic process functioning as the landmark of *-vichu* 'want', i.e. the desired event. The composite expression *ngeevichu* thus profiles the process of the trajector desiring an event consisting of the trajector leaving. At the higher level of organization, *ngeevichu* specifies the caused occurrence schematically evoked by *-ni* 'make'. The nominal landmark of *-ni* is thus identified with the trajector of *ngeevichu*, i.e. with the person who has the desire and the one who does the leaving. At higher levels of organization (not shown), the subject pronoun *noo* 'I' elaborates the trajector, and the object pronoun *poy* 'him' specifies the landmark. The speaker is thus identified as the causer, and 'him' as the target of force, the wanter, and the leaver.

6. Constituency

The foregoing examples suggest how CG handles the complexities of grammatical structure without positing syntactic tree structures. To the extent that it is valid, the information captured in such tree structures is also captured in the CG account based on symbolic assemblies. Three kinds of information are represented in classic generative phrase trees: constituency, linear order, and category membership (via node labels). It is not denied that these kinds of information need to be provided, only that their expression requires a separate, autonomous formal device.

Given that basic grammatical categories have conceptual characterizations, and that an expression's category is determined by the nature of its profile, category information is inherent in each symbolic structure in an assembly, as an aspect of its semantic structure. In Figure 1.30, for example, *throw* is a verb because it profiles a process, *rock* is a noun because it profiles a thing, and *into* a preposition because it profiles a non-processual relationship with a thing as landmark. Higher-level categories are also susceptible to semantic or symbolic characterization. A full noun phrase – what I call a **nominal** – profiles a thing which is **grounded**, i.e. a grammaticized indication is given of its relation to the speech situation. The composite expressions *a rock* and *the pond* are thus identified as nominals by virtue of being grounded by the indefinite and definite articles. Similarly, a prepositional phrase can be characterized as a symbolic assembly in which a nominal elaborates the preposition's landmark. *Into the pond* is thus a prepositional phrase (though I have not shown the full assembly in Figure 1.30).

Linear order is actually temporal order in the speech stream. As such, this aspect of symbolic assemblies is specified at the phonological pole of each symbolic structure. In Figure 1.9, for instance, the composite phonological structure of *smart woman* indicates that the word symbolizing the adjective directly precedes the word symbolizing the noun (T = processing time). Importantly, this dimension of phonological structure, exploited for grammatical (symbolizing) purposes, is given as part of the internal structure of each symbolic element. It is not essential that linear order be represented in these diagrams by relative position on the page of the component symbolic structures.

Finally, constituency is a matter of a composite structure in one construction functioning in turn as component structure in another – the order in which simpler symbolic structures are successively integrated to form progressively more elaborate symbolic structures. It is just a matter of hierarchy, a general feature of cognitive organization, even motor routines.

A crucial point is that grammatical constituency pertains to the external arrangement of symbolic structures, taking these as wholes (i.e. as **bipolar** entities). This external hierarchical arrangement need not coincide with any hierarchical structure evident internally at the semantic or phonological pole of symbolic elements. That is, grammatical constituency need not parallel any purely conceptual hierarchy manifested in the semantic pole of component or composite symbolic structures, nor any purely phonological hierarchy manifested in their phonological poles. Internally, at each pole, any hierarchical arrangement is determined locally, by factors that are intrinsically conceptual or intrinsically phonological (hence **unipolar** – see Langacker 1987a: § 2.3.1.2).

For example, in casual pronunciation the definite article cliticizes to the following word, with which it forms a single intonational unit. A nominal such as *the smart woman* therefore shows the intrinsically phonological organization indicated in (12)a. Semantically, however, the article does not pertain to the adjective, but to the entire nominal expression. For semantic and grammatical purposes, we want to say that it combines with the remainder of the nominal as the last step in assembling it, implying the constituency in (12)b.

(12) a. (*th'smart*) (*woman*) [unipolar (purely phonological) constituency]
b. (*the*) (*smart woman*) [bipolar (grammatical) constituency]

This apparent discrepancy is unproblematic given the distinction between **grammatical hierarchy** – pertaining to the external arrangement of symbolic structures as bipolar entities – and the **phonological hierarchy** internal to each symbolic structure at its phonological pole, viewed as a purely phonological (unipolar) entity. Unipolar phonological structure involves the grouping of segments into syllables, syllables into words, words into phonological phrases, etc. The phonological elements directly relevant to grammar are those defined in bipolar terms, i.e. through their participation in symbolic relationships. We should not expect that these will always coincide with natural phonological units (e.g. morpheme boundaries do not necessarily coincide with syllable boundaries), nor that the two will mirror one another in their hierarchical arrangements.

Diagrammed in Figure 1.32 is the phonological pole of *th'smart woman*, for the normal pronunciation (12)a. In terms of grammatical constituency, where phonological elements are delimited by their participation in symbolic relationships, the constituency is the expected one, represented in (12)b. At the lower level of organization, *smart* and *woman* combine to form *smart woman*, and then, at the higher level of organization, the definite article combines with this to form the full nominal. In casual speech, the definite article cliticizes to the following word. I represent its clitic status by showing the consonant *th* as combining with a word to form a higher-level word. Of course, internally to the definite article the word it combines with is specified only schematically. In the construction, this word is put in correspondence with the **first** word of the other component structure, in this case *smart*. The composite phonological structure is thus as given in (12)a.

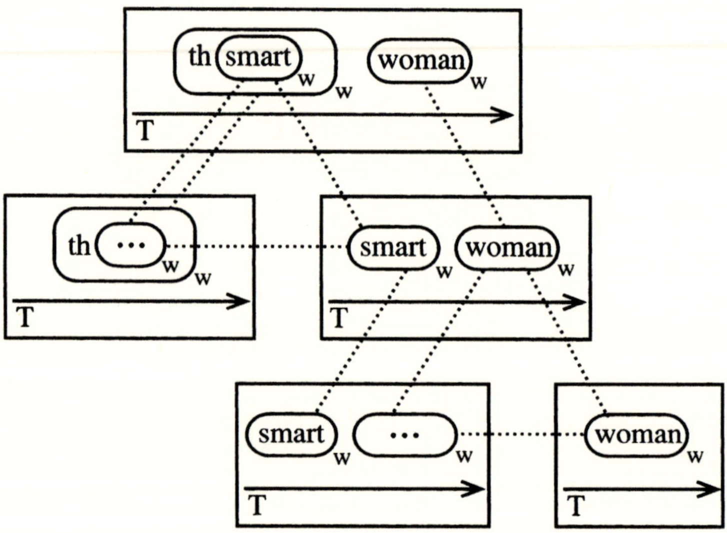

Figure 1.32

The expression's semantic pole is sketched in Figure 1.33. Grammatically, i.e. in terms of the external relationships between semantic structures, *woman* and *smart* combine at the lower level of constituency, with *smart woman* then combining with *the* at the higher level. Internally, the semantic structures of *smart*, *woman*, and *smart woman* are just as shown in previous diagrams. As for the article, the contextual definiteness it conveys is represented by dashed arrows indicating that the speaker (S) and hearer (H) are able to direct their attention to the same focused entity, characterized schematically as a thing. In the higher-level construction, this thing functions as an e-site. It corresponds to the profile of *smart woman*, which elaborates it.

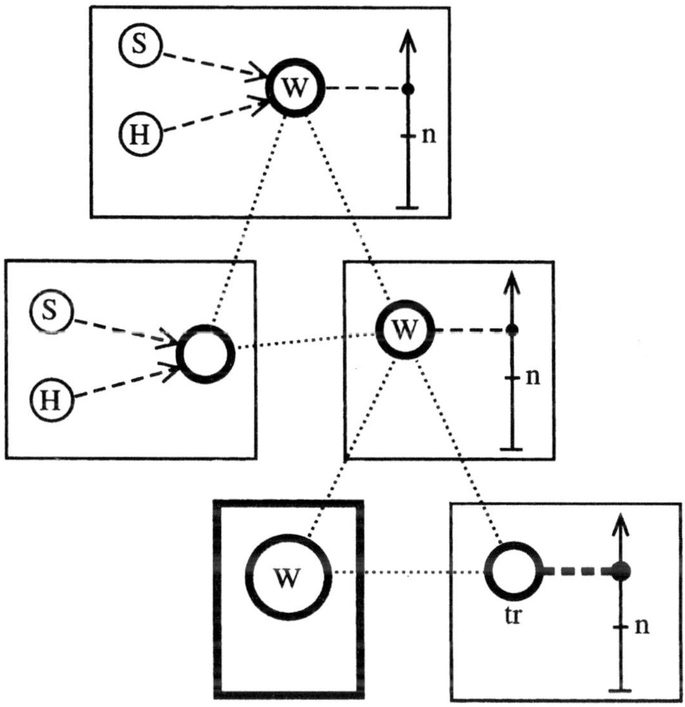

Figure 1.33

How can the definite article pertain to the noun *woman* in particular when it combines grammatically with the composite expression *smart woman*? The answer is that *smart woman*, despite its grammatical complexity, **profiles** the woman at the composite structure level. That is, the woman is the conceptual referent of the composite expression, just as it is for *woman* individually. Since profiling determines grammatical category, the composite expression *smart woman* is itself a complex noun. The definite article can thus combine with it by virtue of a correspondence between their profiles, just as it can with a simple noun. In short, the grammatical constituency, where *smart* and *woman* are on a par, is not isomorphic to the internal conceptual organization at the composite structure's semantic pole, where only the woman stands in profile.

Grammatical constituency is straightforwardly accommodated in CG as a particular form symbolic assemblies can assume. In this section and the previous one, however, I have tried to show that it is less central, and its role more limited, than is commonly assumed. When it is properly distinguished from purely conceptual and purely phonological organization, and when the pivotal role of correspondences is recognized, grammatical constituency can be seen as non-essential and often variable. It is not fundamental, but emerges as a special case from other, more basic phenomena (Langacker 1995a, 1997a).

7. Conclusion

The question is often posed whether grammar is predictable from semantics and other independent factors. From a negative answer to that question, it is generally concluded that grammar constitutes an autonomous formal system. I suggest, however, that this conclusion is unwarranted, if only because the reasoning fails to distinguish between strong and weak autonomy. The non-predictability of grammar, i.e. weak autonomy, does not itself determine what kinds of units are needed to describe it. In particular, it does not establish the claim of strong autonomy: that grammar is distinct from both lexicon and semantics, constituting a separate level of representation whose description requires a special set of irreducible grammatical primitives. I have outlined an alternative view which accommodates weak autonomy while denying strong autonomy. In CG, grammar and lexicon form a continuum fully describable as assemblies of symbolic structures (form-meaning pairings). On this account, it makes no sense to ask whether grammar is predictable from meaning, since grammar **incorporates** meaning, as one of its two poles. The question is analogous to asking whether the phonological shape of a lexical item can be predicted from its semantic value. While the answer is clearly negative, it does not establish the independence of lexicon from semantics. A dictionary listing only lexical forms, without their meanings, would not be very interesting.

A more reasonable question to pose is why grammar should exist in the first place. I can best conclude by quoting a previous answer (Langacker 1999b: 55):

> Grammar would not exist if lexical units were available to symbolize every conception we wanted to express. But they are not. Lexical units form a limited set, while the conceptions we want to encode linguistically are open-ended and indefinitely varied. To overcome this, we resort to complex expressions consisting of multiple

lexical elements. Each lexical component evokes some facet of the overall conception, one singled out precisely by virtue of being susceptible to individual symbolization. Collectively, these individually symbolized conceptual "chunks" give enough information about the composite conception intended by the speaker that the addressee, in context, is able to reconstruct some approximation to it. However, this reconstruction requires some indication of how the conceptual chunks are supposed to fit together. The role of grammar is to provide this information.

Chapter 2
Metonymy in grammar

Grammar consists in assemblies of symbolic structures linked by correspondences. In Chapter 1, I made the simplifying assumption that the corresponding elements can always be precisely specified. The present chapter argues that this basic picture needs qualification. Correspondences are indeed crucial for semantics and grammar, but owing to the conceptual complexity of linguistic meanings, there are limits to the precision of their specification. While the specific connections shown in diagrams are valid and essential as first approximations, in a coarse-grained view, they prove more flexible and variable when viewed at a higher resolution.

1. Indeterminacy

An assumption usually made in syntactic theory and description is that particular elements combine with one another in very specific and determinate ways. Syntactically, for example, the sentence *Alice likes Bill* involves a specific structural configuration, with the elements *Alice*, *likes*, and *Bill* inserted in particular slots. Semantically, the predicate LIKE has two arguments, which ALICE and BILL instantiate in accordance with their syntactic roles.

(1) a. $[\ [\text{Alice}]_{NP}\ [\ [\text{likes}]_{V}\ [\text{Bill}]_{NP}\ ]_{VP}\ ]_{S}$
    b. LIKE(x,y)   x = ALICE   y = BILL

This supposed property, that it is possible to give a definite and precise specification of the elements connected to one another and how they are connected, will be referred to as **determinacy**. The doctrine of determinacy belongs to a broader conception of language, mind, and meaning, which holds that language is a separate mental "module", that syntax is autonomous, and that semantics is well-delimited and fully compositional. This broader conception is not however well-founded. Over the last few decades, research in cognitive linguistics has demonstrated that grammar is not autonomous from semantics, that semantics is neither well-delimited nor fully compositional, and that language draws on more general cognitive systems and mental capacities from which it cannot be neatly separated. The issue of determinacy must therefore be re-examined from this newer perspective.

I suggest that the usual situation is not one of determinacy, but rather **indeterminacy** (Langacker 1998a). Precise, determinate connections between specific elements represent a special and perhaps unusual case. It is more common for there to be some vagueness or indeterminacy in regard to either the elements participating in grammatical relationships or the specific nature of their connection. Otherwise stated, grammar is basically **metonymic**, in that the information explicitly coded linguistically does not itself establish the precise connections apprehended by the speaker and hearer in using an expression. Explicit indications evoke conceptions which merely provide mental access to elements with the potential to be connected in specific ways – the details have to be established from other considerations. Metaphorically speaking, explicit linguistic coding gets us into the right neighborhood, but from there we have to find the right address by other means. Perhaps the crude diagrams in Figure 2.1 capture the spirit of this proposal. If diagram (a) reflects the archetypal conception of classic syntactic theory, diagram (b) is more reflective of linguistic and cognitive reality.

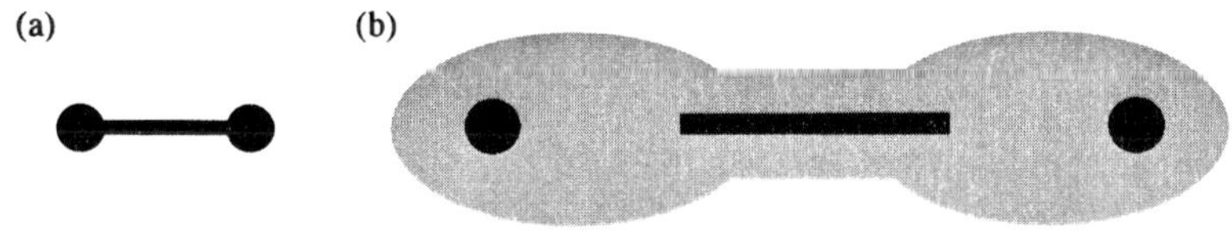

Figure 2.1

2. Active zones

I am claiming that grammar is basically metonymic in nature. In contrast to the standard view that particular elements combine in very specific and determinate ways, I am suggesting that the canonical situation is actually one of indeterminacy. This is not apparent from the diagrams in Chapter 1, which show specific connections between specific elements, in the form of correspondences (dotted lines). It is not that those diagrams are wrong; working out the correspondences – determining which particular substructures correspond to one another between the components of a symbolic assembly – is critical for describing it explicitly. The point, rather, is that constructions can also be viewed in finer grained conceptual detail, where a range of variation may be observed.

Let me first say that indeterminacy in grammar is not an excuse for vague or imprecise description. If a construction is indeterminate in some respect, as a matter of principle we still have to describe the construction, including its indeterminacy, and we still want our characterization to be explicit and precise, even in regard to the nature and extent of the indeterminacy. We must not confuse indeterminacy at the level of the **phenomenon** with indeterminacy at the level of its **description**.

In standard approaches to syntax and semantics, indeterminacy fails to become apparent because there is no real attempt to deal with conceptual structure. Assumptions made in truth-conditional semantics specifically exclude from its scope of concern the very factors that are most responsible for indeterminacy – factors like construal, imaginative phenomena, and encyclopedic semantics. Formulas like (1)b say nothing about the actual conceptualizations they represent. There is no attempt, for instance, to spell out the internal conceptual structure of a predicate; however complex this may be, it is simply represented by means of an atomic, unanalyzable symbol (e.g. LIKE). And obviously, syntactic structures like (1)a are not intended, and not able, to capture the specific details of the conceptualizations evoked by the expressions described.

Indeterminacy starts to become apparent as soon as one adopts a conceptualist semantics and a symbolic view of grammar that incorporates semantics as one of its poles. Instead of merely saying that elements combine with other, as unanalyzed wholes, it becomes necessary to say precisely **how** they combine, in terms of their conceptual integration. Here too, matters look determinate under certain conditions that are quite common given practical constraints: for selected examples; in preliminary analyses that do not go into very much conceptual detail; and in describing general patterns, where the whole point is to abstract away from the specifics of individual expressions. For instance, if we consider prepositional phrases in general, we can posit a constructional schema based on a correspondence between two specific elements, namely the landmark of the preposition and the profile of its nominal object. It is only when we look more closely at the conceptual import of specific expressions that the extent of grammatical indeterminacy begins to reveal itself.

I first became aware of this, over two decades ago, through cases involving a **discrepancy** between **profile** and **active zone** (Langacker 1984). Let us confine our attention to cases where a nominal expression, which profiles a thing, combines with a relational expression with respect to which it functions as subject or object. This is a matter of the nominal profile corresponding to the trajector or the landmark of the profiled relationship. Yet in many cases the thing profiled by the nominal is not precisely the same as the one that actually participates in that relationship. There is a discrepancy between the profile of the nominal and its active zone. An entity's active zone, with respect to a profiled relationship, is defined as that facet of it which most directly and crucially participates in that relationship.

Consider sentence (2):

(2) *The cigarette in her mouth was unlit.*

The subject nominal, *the cigarette in her mouth*, is syntactically analogous to Figure 1.12, *smart woman with a PhD.* The head noun *cigarette* specifies the trajector of *in*, and the nominal *her mouth* specifies its landmark. Thus, if *in* has the spatial meaning shown in Figure 2.2(a), the expected import of (2) is that the entire cigarette was inside the cavity identified as her mouth. It would then be very fortunate that the cigarette was not lit. But of course, that is not the way we understand the sentence. We do not take it as meaning that the cigarette, as an undifferentiated whole, was inside the mouth, as an undifferentiated whole. Instead we interpret it as meaning that a particular portion of the cigarette (one end) was contained in a particular portion of the mouth (a segment of the lips). Those portions constitute the **active zones** of the cigarette and of the mouth with respect to the *in* relationship. There is in each case a **discrepancy** between the active zone and the nominal profile. One end of a cigarette is not what we take to be the referent (profile) of *cigarette*. Nor is part of the lips what we identify as the referent of *mouth*. The entities we explicitly mention with the subject and object nominals are not the ones most directly and crucially involved in the profiled relationship.

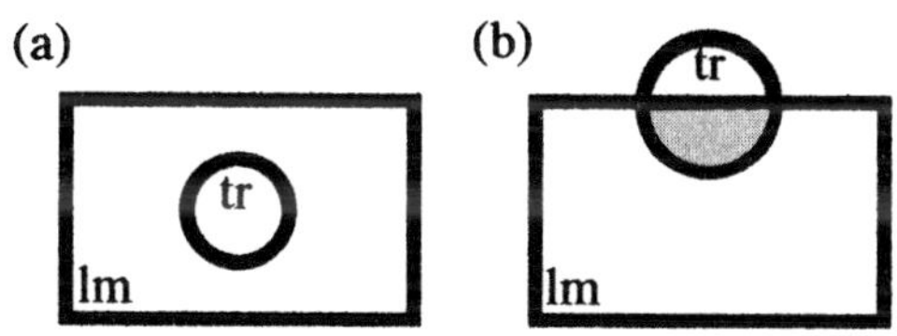

Figure 2.2

This situation – **profile/active-zone discrepancy** – is not at all unusual. In fact, it is quite common, even typical. Sticking with *in*, for the moment, the examples in (3) are all quite normal (cf. Vandeloise 1991: ch. 13). They respectively correspond to the diagrams in Figure 2.2. The expressions in (3)a exemplify full spatial inclusion: the entire trajector is inside the landmark, and no one portion of the landmark stands out as the only one directly involved. In other words, the entities profiled by the subject and object nominals participate as wholes in the profiled relationship. In (3)b, on the other hand, only a portion of the trajector is spatially included in the landmark (and in some cases only part of the landmark is involved). This portion of the trajector, indicated by shading, constitutes its active zone with respect to the *in* relation.

(3) a. *the cake in the oven; the letter in the envelope; the air in the balloon; the dresser in the bedroom; the food in my stomach*

b. *the swan in the water; the axe in your hand; the arrow in the target; the sword in the scabbard; the cork in the bottle*

Such discrepancies are typical for subjects and objects.[1] The verbs in (4)a, for example, designate processes involving different facets of a person, yet the subject nominal refers to this person as an undifferentiated whole. A verb like *hit* is quite vague as to which portions of the trajector and the landmark participate directly. Any part of the landmark might be affected. We can overcome this indeterminacy by adding a prepositional phrase to specify the active zone, as in (4)b. Of course, this does not completely resolve the indeterminacy. If she hit me in the arm, was it the left arm or the right? Where on the arm did she make contact? We can never be totally precise, and usually we do not even try. With respect to the trajector of *hit*, the active zone is typically the fist, but that is only the default. Here as well the options can be spelled out using a prepositional phrase, as in (4)c. Note that the active zone need not even be a subpart of the subject. It might be a stick which the subject is holding, or even a projectile which she throws, like a baseball. In (4)d, what is actually perceived – a sound or a cloud of dust – is merely associated with the entity profiled by the object nominal, not a subpart of it. As for the subject, only the speaker's perceptual apparatus is directly involved in the profiled relationship.

(4) a. *The boy {blinked / waved / coughed / meditated / yawned / stretched / smiled / urinated}.*

b. *She hit me (in the {arm / stomach / mouth / back / leg / knee / neck}).*

c. *She hit me (with {her left hand / her elbow / the top of her head / a stick / a baseball}).*

d. *I can {hear a piano / see the elephants in the distance* [only a cloud of dust is visible]*}.*

The only requirement is that the active zone be **associated** with the nominal referent in some evident fashion. Being identical to the profiled entity and being a subpart of it are special cases of association. We easily manage the imprecision and indeterminacy inherent in profile/active-zone discrepancy. In fact, we do not even notice it. The reason is that we are able to make sense of discrepant expressions by exploiting general knowledge. For example, every expression in (3) evokes a basic scenario, a familiar aspect of everyday life in

1 For examples involving adjective + noun combinations, see Sweetser 1999.

our culture. This encyclopedic cultural knowledge – not any narrow, dictionary-type definitions of the component lexical items – gives us what we need to properly understand the expressions. We know that the whole cake goes in an oven, but that only part of a swan is below the surface of the water. Of course, this default knowledge can always be overridden in special contexts. If we see a swan diving to the bottom of a pond, *the swan in the water* would be interpreted along the lines of Figure 2.2(a), not 2.2(b).

But why does profile/active-zone discrepancy occur in the first place? It is actually both natural and often necessary from the cognitive standpoint. In many cases complete precision and accuracy in describing a relational participant is simply not possible. Discrepant expressions are natural because they profile, and thus make linguistically prominent, entities that have greater cognitive salience. Usually, for example, a whole is more salient than its parts.

Thus many expressions exhibit meanings comparable to the structure shown in Figure 2.3. The profiled relationship does not itself directly connect the entities put in profile as trajector or landmark. Rather, the directly connected enties (the shaded active zones) are either part of the profiled participant or merely associated with it. This entire configuration has the potential to be entrenched and conventional. The verb *hear*, for instance, has an established meaning analogous to the structure shown – it is quite usual to say things like *I hear a piano.*

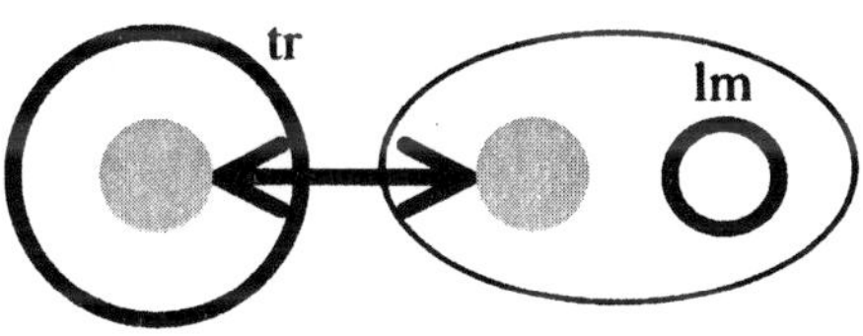

Figure 2.3

3. Reference point constructions

In cases of profile/active-zone discrepancy, a nominal expression focuses attention on a thing, its profile, which the grammatical construction connects with the trajector or the landmark of a profiled relationship. Usually, though, the specific nature of that connection is indeterminate. The nominal profile evokes an array of associated entities, and all we know for sure is that one of those entities can supposedly be identified as a direct participant in the relationship.

But which one? This is often apparent from the content of the relational component. In (5), the verbs *review* and *weigh* respectively direct our attention to the textual and physical aspects of the book; evoking these as active zones makes the sentence coherent. Quite commonly, however, the relational element fails to resolve the indeterminacy. For instance, the sentence *I like the book* could equally well pertain to its content or its physical appearance. In such examples we rely on context and general knowledge. Thus in (3), it is only through standard cultural scenarios that we can determine the specific configuration most likely intended.

(5) *I have to review this book, which weighs 5 pounds.*

Profile/active-zone discrepancy exploits our **reference point** ability (Langacker 1993c). This is our capacity for invoking one conceived entity as a reference point (R) in order to establish mental contact with another, i.e. to **mentally access** one conceived entity **through** another. The entity accessed in this way is called the **target** (T) in the reference point relationship. The set of entities accessible through a given reference point (the set of potential targets) are collectively referred to as its **dominion** (D). The basic elements of a reference point relationship are sketched in Figure 2.4(a). Dashed arrows indicate the path of mental access.

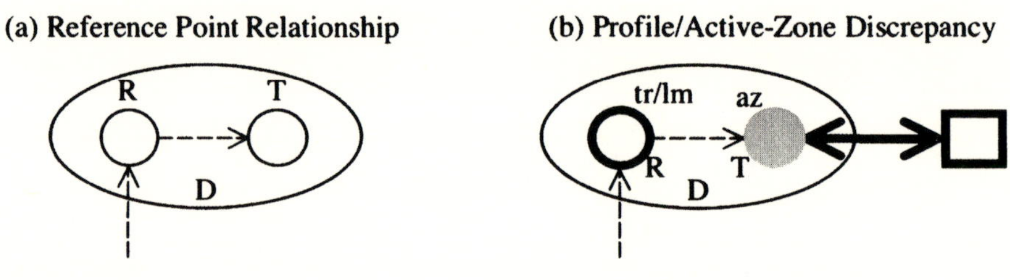

Figure 2.4

Figure 2.4(b) shows profile/active-zone discrepancy as a particular application of our reference point ability. Functioning as reference point is the profile of a subject or object nominal, which the construction puts in focus as trajector or landmark of a profiled relationship. By directing attention to the nominal profile we activate or make accessible an array of associated entities, which constitute the reference point's dominion. The task is then to find a target which can serve as its active zone for participating in the profiled relationship. The active zone is usually left implicit, since it is not sought for its own sake, but only as a way of connecting the nominal referent with the profiled relationship.

In other cases, the kind of indeterminacy inherent in profile/active-zone discrepancy represents a construction's basic motivation and central conceptual import. Often these constructions do not even have an explicit relational component. They are simply concerned with invoking a nominal profile in order to direct attention to another, associated entity. This target is sought for its own sake, not just as active zone for a profiled relationship. In these reference point constructions, the target is therefore made explicit, often being focused as profile, as shown in Figure 2.5.

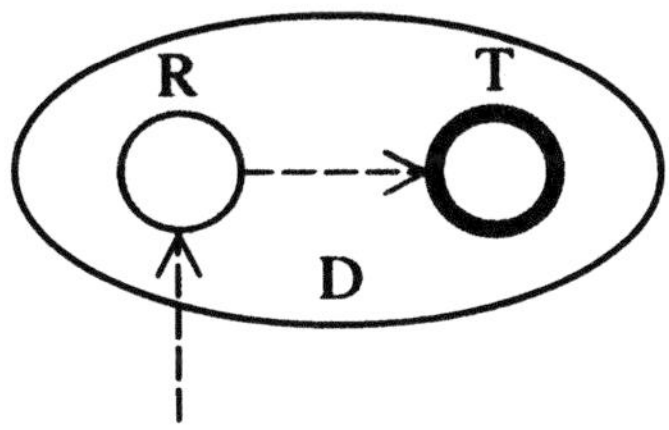

Figure 2.5

I have argued, for example, that **possessive** constructions have the reference point relationship as their schematic semantic value (Langacker 1993c, 1995b; Chapter 4). While particular kinds of relationships are prototypical – notably ownership, kinship, and part-whole relations – expressions like (6) indicate that possessive constructions are extremely varied in the specific kinds of relationships they are used for. What they all have in common is merely the abstract commonality of the possessor functioning as conceptual reference point providing mental access to the entity possessed.

(6) *the mayor's cellphone, Joe's mother, my foot, the baby's diaper, their office, his problems, your candidate, my bus, the student's qualifications, our displeasure, her migraine, the dog's fleas, the bank's current interest rate, Oswald's assassination [of Kennedy], Kennedy's assassination [by Oswald]*

The possessive morpheme *'s* evokes the configuration in Figure 2.5 as its schematic meaning (Taylor 1996). When the reference point and the target are specified by the possessor nominal and the possessed noun, the full expression has the same organization and the same profiling, except that at this level the reference point is identified as a particular individual and the target as a specific instance of the type evoked by the noun, an instance identified by virtue of being located in the reference point's dominion. Even here there is anything but complete determinacy in regard to their relationship or, as a consequence, in regard to the target's identification. Does *my foot* refer to the left foot or the right foot? Or is it even part of my own body? If I am an artist, it might be the foot that I am currently drawing. If I am a surgeon, it might be the foot that I am responsible for operating on (as opposed to the one my partner is going to operate on). *My bus* could be the bus I am scheduled to take, but it could also be the bus I drive, the one I designed, the one I am betting on to win the cross-country bus race, and so on indefinitely. Despite certain conventionally established defaults, the construction leaves open the precise nature of the connection between possessor and possessed. Minimally, it merely indicates that one is mentally accessible in relation to the other.

Another manifestation of reference point relationships are **topic** constructions, as in (7). They consist of a nominal, which functions as topic, followed by a clause which expresses a proposition somehow pertaining to the topic. When the topic and the clause are separated by an intonation break, there are two successive "windows of attention" (Chafe 1994: ch. 5; Langacker 2001b), each with its own profile: the nominal profiles a thing, and the clause a process.

(7) a. ***Your uncle, he*** *really should get married.*
b. ***That color,*** *I just don't like* ***it****.*
c. ***The lottery,*** *I never have any luck.*

To say that the clause "pertains to" the topic means that the proposition it expresses fits somewhere in the body of knowledge evoked by the topic nominal. Thus we can characterize the nominal profile as a reference point, the associated body of knowledge as the dominion accessible through it, and the proposition as a target, i.e. as one element in the reference point's dominion. This is shown in Figure 2.6. If the proposition is "about" the topic, the nominal referent must somehow figure in the proposition expressed by the target clause. It has some role in this proposition, usually indicated in English by means of a coreferential pronoun, like *he* in (7)a and *it* in (7)b. In diagram (a), a small circle represents the nominal referent in its role in the clausal proposition (coreference is shown as a dotted correspondence line).

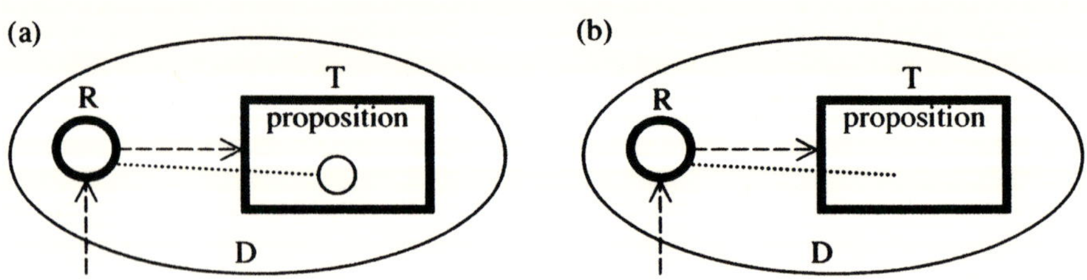

Figure 2.6

In many languages, the topic construction does not include a resumptive pronoun. Occasionally this happens in English, e.g. (7)c. There is then no way to be sure what role the topic plays in the proposition, only that it has **some** role, possibly quite peripheral. This is shown in Figure 2.6(b). Such expressions are indeterminate in regard to how the topic and the clause are connected, and where the proposition fits in the topic's dominion. There is often a default, supplied by context or general knowledge. Thus (7)c would normally mean that I never have any luck at winning the lottery. But given appropriate circumstances, it might instead mean that I never have any luck in getting the winner of the lottery to marry me, or in running it successfully.

Closely related to topic constructions are the **double subject** constructions found in many languages. The examples in (8) are from Japanese:

(8) a. *Taroo-ga fuku-ga itsumo hade-da.* 'Taro always has gaudy clothes.'
Taro-s clothes-s always gaudy-be

b. *Rokugatsu-ga ame-ga yoku furu.* 'June always has a lot of rain.'
June-s rain-s often fall

c. *Kono koosokudooro-ga ookuno torakku-ga tooru.*
this freeway-s many truck-s pass
'This freeway has many trucks pass on it.'

Like topic constructions, these sentences consist of a nominal followed by a clause. They differ from a standard topic construction in that the entire expression constitutes a single, higher-level clause, which incorporates the lower-level clause as one component. What happens in a double subject construction is that the two elements of a topic construction – nominal and clause – are incorporated as trajector and landmark of a profiled relationship that is not explicitly indicated by any verb. As shown in Figure 2.7, this relationship is nothing other than the reference point relation responsible for the trajector's topic status with respect to the lower-level clause.[2] Most relevant here is the absence of any explicit indication of the role played by the subject/topic nominal in the target proposition, expressed by the lower-level clause. The precise connection between topic and proposition has to be supplied on the basis of context or general knowledge.

---

2 Evidence for this analysis (justified more fully in Kumashiro and Langacker 2003) includes the absence of an intonation break after the first nominal, suggesting that the entire expression indeed constitutes a single clause, as well as the fact that the first nominal can take the subject marker *-ga*.

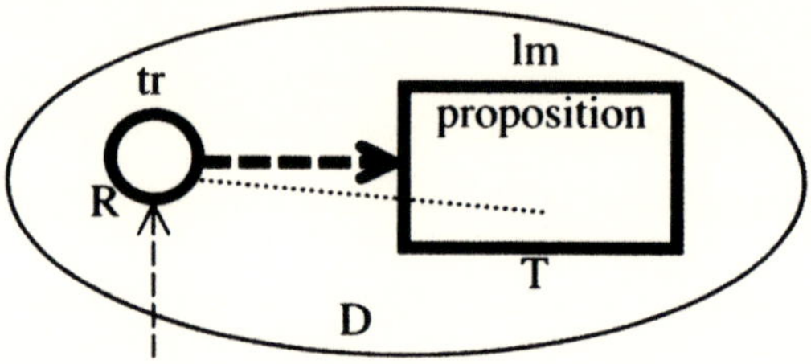

Figure 2.7

4. Complex things and relationships

Many expressions pertain to collections of entities, or to single, higher-order entities clearly recognized as consisting of individual elements. These complex entities are a major source of indeterminacy. Plural nouns are an obvious example. When a plural specifies the trajector or the landmark of a relational expression, there is usually some indeterminacy as to how the profiled relationship engages the complex entity.

In some cases, a default interpretation follows from a predicate's meaning. For instance, the adjectives in (9) induce the respective interpretations in Figure 2.8. *Intelligent* ascribes to its trajector a property that is usually characteristic of individuals. Barring special circumstances, (9)a implies that each woman individually displays a certain property (represented as a box), that of intelligence. Thus the profiled adjectival relationship comprises multiple **atomic** relationships, each projecting to a single woman. On the other hand, the property of being *numerous* can only be ascribed to a set of entities viewed collectively, as a single but complex whole. So (9)b implies only one atomic relationship.

(9) a. *Those women are intelligent.*
b. *The problems with that idea are numerous.*

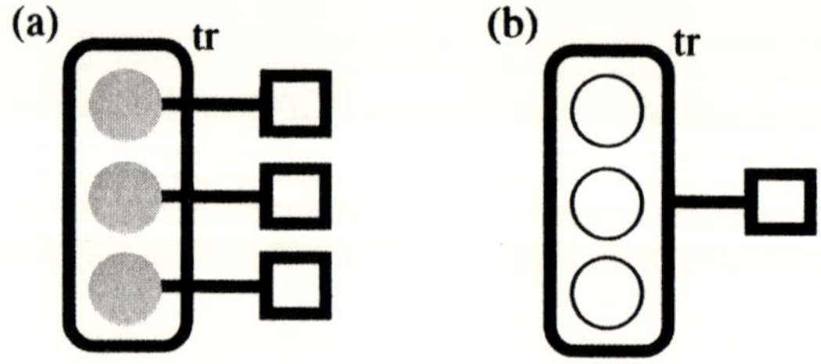

Figure 2.8

Yet many predicates fail to impose a default interpretation. One of these is *heavy*, as in (10), which can easily be interpreted along the lines of either 2.8(a) or 2.8(b). That is, the property of being heavy can plausibly be ascribed to each box individually, or to all the boxes taken collectively.

(10) *These boxes are heavy.*

With multiple plural participants, the indeterminacy is often much greater. For instance, sentence (11) has an open-ended set of significantly different interpretations, a few of which are diagrammed in Figure 2.9.

(11) *The two men lifted the two boxes.*

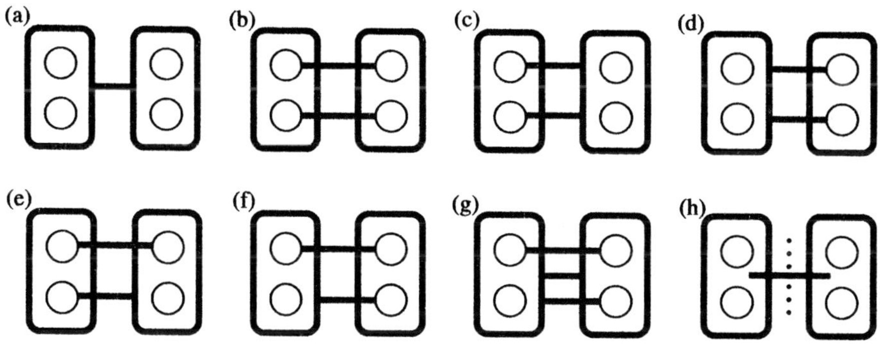

Figure 2.9

One interpretation, represented in diagram (a), is that the two men, acting together, lifted the two boxes together. Hence there is only one atomic event of lifting, in which both the men and the boxes participate collectively. Alternatively, each man may have lifted a single box, implying two atomic events, as shown in (b). Another possibility, shown in (c), is that each man individually lifted the two boxes together. Or conversely, the men may have collectively lifted each box individually, as in (d). It is also conceivable that one man lifted one box, while the other lifted both boxes, as in (e). Or conversely once more, one box was lifted by a single man and the other by both men, as in (f). Yet another option, shown in (g), adds to (f) a further atomic event in which the men jointly lift the boxes together. Other possibilities are easily imagined. In sum, all we know for sure is that lifting was done and that two men and two boxes were somehow involved as agents and patients. We do not know how many atomic events there might have been, nor how any such event projects to the individuals subsumed by the subject and object nominals. I have tried to indicate this indeterminacy in diagram (h).

English verbs and adjectives give no morphological indication of whether they profile a single, atomic relationship or a complex relationship consisting of multiple atomic ones. The singular/plural contrast induced by so-called "verb agreement" does not itself indicate the number of atomic relationships, as we see in (9), where the plural form *are* occurs with both configurations. Nor does the verb mechanically agree with the subject. Rather, the verb inflection makes an independent semantic contribution (Reid 1991; Barlow 1992), emphasizing either the trajector's unitary nature or its internal multiplicity. This specification encourages a corresponding construal of the profiled relationship as being either simple or complex, but does not strictly determine that choice.

Exemplified in (12) are three kinds of nominal expressions displaying this ambivalence. The collective noun *faculty* lends itself to either of two construals: as a deliberative body capable of joint decisions; or as a set of individuals who make individual decisions. While in either case the subject in (12)a profiles a collective entity consisting of all faculty members, the choice of singular *has* vs. plural *have* indicates which aspect of its decision-making capacity engages the profiled process of acceptance. The contrast in (12)b hinges on whether drinking and smoking are seen as two distinct vices, each of which fails individually to improve one's health, or whether they are construed as two facets of a single unhealthy behavioral complex. And in (12)c, the flying is attributable to either the individual geese or the flock as a whole. Obviously, a flock can fly only by virtue of its individual members doing so, but we can opt to highlight either the individual or the collective aspect of the motion.

(12) a. ***The faculty*** *{has / have} accepted the new curriculum.*
b. ***Drinking and smoking*** *{does / do} not improve your health.*
c. ***A flock of geese*** *{was / were} flying overhead.*

By emphasizing the trajector's unitary or multiplex nature, the verb inflection in (12) gives an indication of how the subject links up with the profiled clausal relationship. The subject nominal does not itself impose a choice, for with either construal its has the same form and the same grammatical structure (i.e. there is no difference in component elements, correspondences, or constituency). It is therefore indeterminate how the nominal referent engages the profiled relationship when there happens not to be any verb inflection to indicate it:

(13) a. *The new curriculum has been accepted by* ***the faculty****.*
b. ***Drinking and smoking*** *will not improve your health.*
c. *We saw* ***a flock of geese*** *flying overhead.*

With respect to (12)c, a flock and the geese constituting it are coextensive and referentially identical. Yet *flock* is a count noun, and *geese* a plural mass noun. What about the subject nominal as a whole? Objectively, it has the same profile with either the unitary or the multiplex construal – in either case it refers to the same set of objects. Conceptually, however, a unitary entity like a *flock*, a *stack*, or a *week* is just as real to us – just as much a single, bounded object – as is a *goose*, a *plate*, or a *day*. We can thus say that *a flock of geese* has two alternate profiles. It can either designate the flock, construed as a single, discretely bounded entity, or else the mass coextensive with (and delimited by) that entity. These two options are respectively shown in Figure 2.10(a) and (b), using circles for intrinsically bounded entities and an ellipse for a mass (where bounding is extrinsic). The small circles represent geese, the large one a flock. The ellipse represents a mass consisting of geese. The construction tells us that this mass is limited in extent – specifically, it is coextensive with the flock (the double line indicates their coincidence).

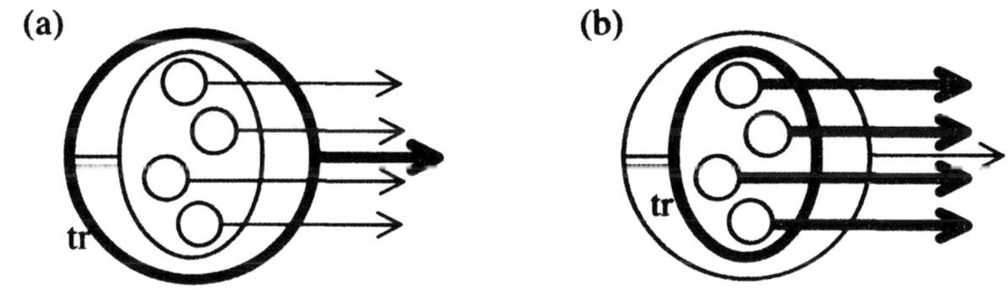

Figure 2.10

Hence the nominal profile can fall on either of two **conceived** entities that are **objectively** coincident. Depending on whether it is construed as designating the referent's unitary or multiplex aspect, it is compatible with either a uniplex or a multiplex interpretation of *fly*, as shown in the diagram by arrows. But since *fly* itself is morphologically the same under either interpretation, the choice between 2.10(a) and (b) is indeterminate unless verb inflection should happen to indicate how its trajector is construed.

I want to emphasize that, in CG terms, this is not a matter of how the nominal is put together syntactically. Under either interpretation, the phrase *flock of geese* consists of the same elements, connected by the same correspondences, and with the same constituency.[3] The difference is solely a matter of which aspect of the referent is singled out for profiling at the composite structure level. The variation is not a problem in CG, for there is no requirement that the composite structure inherit its profile from any particular structural position. The alternate interpretations can be seen as an instance of metonymy in a fairly narrow sense of the term (shift in profile).

3 This is discussed more fully in Chapter 3. (See also Langacker 1992a, 1997a.)

If a flock of geese is multifaceted, a barrel of oil is even more so. First, *a barrel of oil* exhibits a contrast analogous to that observed for *a flock of geese*, whereby it designates either the container or its contents. But *barrel* also functions as a unit of measurement, in which case there need be no physical container at all. There are thus a number of possibilities as to the referent and how it engages a profiled relationship, and particular examples may be indeterminate in either respect.

Certain points will emerge more clearly if we shift to the plural. Consider, then, the various ways of interpreting the phrase *three barrels of oil.* We can start with cases where the primary focus is on the plural mass consisting of physical containers. Here there are two basic possibilities with respect to how the profiled mass engages a relationship: the barrels can participate in the relationship either collectively or individually. In (14)a, the predicate *stacked* imposes a collective construal, while in (14)b *sit* suggests an individual construal, as respectively shown in diagrams (a) and (b) of Figure 2.11. But in other examples the connection is indeterminate. One can *see* three barrels of oil individually or collectively, and one can *load* them in either fashion (e.g. by rolling them individually or by lifting them together with a crane).

(14) a. *Three barrels of oil were stacked in the basement.*
b. *Three barrels of oil were sitting in the basement.*
c. *I saw three barrels of oil on the truck.*
d. *They loaded three barrels of oil onto the truck.*

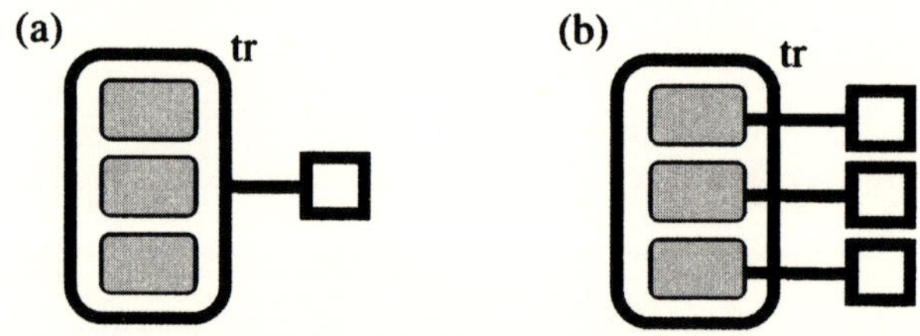

Figure 2.11

In other uses, focus shifts to the oil contained in the barrels, which can still be construed as physical entities actually holding the substance. An example is (15), where only the oil itself participates in the burning, as sketched in Figure 2.12. Note, however, that in the subordinate clause we can construe the relative pronoun *which* as referring to either the oil or to the barrels per se. This shows how easily we can shift back and forth between two construals of the same situation coded by the same expression with the same grammatical structure. Even when *which* refers anaphorically to *three barrels of oil*, where the substance is in focus, it can itself be taken as indicating the containers. Participation in different relationships evokes different facets of this complex entity.

(15) *To heat our house last winter we burned the three barrels of oil which had been sitting in the basement for several years.*

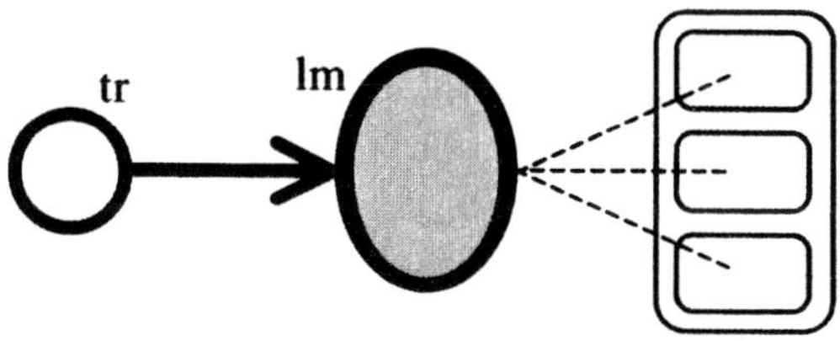

Figure 2.12

Figures 2.11 and 2.12 characterize the alternate ways of construing *three barrels of oil* in terms of a difference in profiling: [*three* ***barrels*** [*of oil*]] vs. [*three barrels* [*of* ***oil***]]. This contrast is orthogonal to another one, namely whether *barrel* is taken as designating a physical container or a unit of measurement. In the latter sense, metonymically related to the first, it profiles the volume defined by a barrel's interior. As such, it is typically conceived in relation to a scale for measuring quantity in terms of this volumetric unit. While the notion of a physical container is still evoked to some degree, no actual container need be involved. Physical containers figure in the conception of the scale only as **virtual** entities in terms of their **potential** for holding a given quantity.

In (16), *three barrels of oil* does not refer directly to either oil or physical barrels. While these are certainly part of the background conception, what the expression actually designates is a volumetric quantity. Thus, as shown in Figure 2.13, these expressions invoke a scale for measuring volume, where the basic unit of measurement is the volume defined by a barrel. Since this is true in both (16)a and (16)b, which are otherwise identical, what could be responsible for the contrast between the plural verb *are* in (16)a and the singular *is* in (16)b? The difference, indicated in the diagrams, is whether the profiled quantity is primarily conceived as a **set** of volumetric units or as a **point** on the scale they serve to calibrate. The latter construal emerges as the association with physical barrels recedes further into the background.

(16) a. *Three barrels of oil* ***are*** *equivalent to 126 gallons.*
b. *Three barrels of oil* ***is*** *equivalent to 126 gallons.*

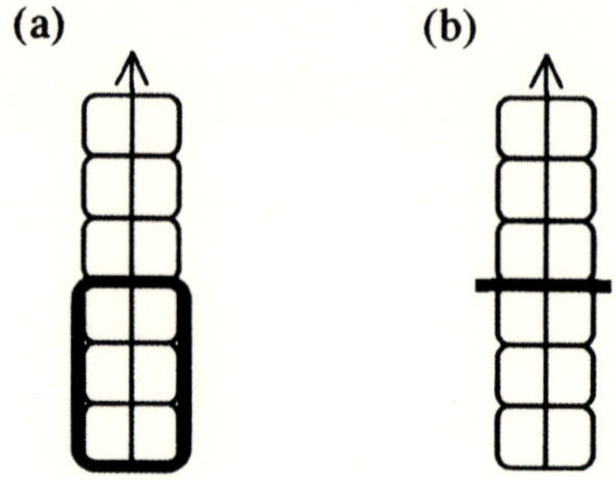

Figure 2.13

This metonymic shift from set of units to location on a scale represents a general pattern, observed with many other kinds of units and scales, exemplified in (17). They vary as to whether the set interpretation is still accessible.

(17) a. *Eleven days in Cairo {was / were} more than we had planned on.*
b. *For this recipe two cups of flour {is / are} enough.*
c. *Thirty degrees {is / *are} a big difference in temperature.*
d. *Fourteen dollars {was / *were} a lot to pay for that.*

Finally, we see from the anaphoric pronouns in (18) that *three barrels of oil* can also be construed as either singular or plural in cases where it designates the oil and where the barrels once again are units of measurement (*pipe in* rules out their interpretation as physical containers). The constrast, sketched in Figure 2.14, is a matter of whether the oil is conceived as the union of three barrel-sized portions or simply as an undifferentiated mass corresponding to three units on the scale of measurement.

(18) a. *We piped in* ***three barrels of oil****, but* ***they*** *ran out, so we had to pipe in another.*
b. *We piped in* ***three barrels of oil*** *and burned* ***it*** *over the winter.*

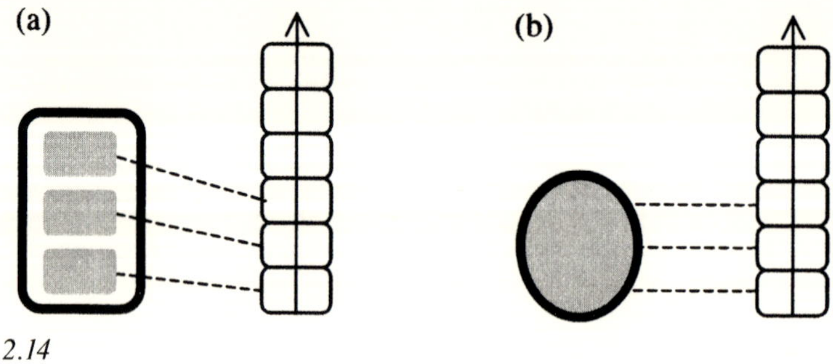

Figure 2.14

These subtly different ways of interpreting *three barrels of oil* have very real grammatical consequences. They determine such factors as singular vs. plural verb inflection, selection of co-referring pronoun, and which predicates the expression can combine with. It would be quite implausible (and certainly gratuitous) to suppose that each interpretation is uniquely associated with a distinct grammatical structure. I suspect that *three barrels of oil* is put together grammatically in the same way for all the interpretations considered, the sole differences residing in the choice of composite structure profile. Commonly, though, there is nothing that forces a single, unique construal. In view of these multiple options, metonymically related to one another, the specific nature of the nominal's grammatical connection with other elements is often indeterminate. The nominal evokes a complex conceptualization with a number of profiling options. In effect, its occurrence in a particular grammatical construction merely tells us to hook it up in any way that makes sense.

5. Other phenomena

Indeterminacy can be observed in many other grammatical phenomena. Let me mention just a few by way of conclusion.

There is often indeterminacy in regard to how an adverbial expression hooks up with a clause in which it has a modifying function. A case in point is the trajector of *on* in (19). What specifically is it that is conceived as being *on* the door? It can hardly be the entire event – the door's surface is not the global setting for my pounding. Nor is it me, at least not all of me, for only my fist makes contact with the door. Intuitively, I am inclined to identify the trajector of *on* as being the blow or the force transmitted. In any case the point of connection is vague or indeterminate. Descriptively, I would probably take the verb *pound* as being the trajector of *on the door*, without specifying any particular active zone for its participation in the *on* relationship. The point of connection is **sublexical**, an aspect of the scene not individually singled out for explicit mention.

(19) *I pounded on the door.*

Various sorts of indeterminacy figure in anaphora, e.g. the connection between a personal pronoun and its antecedent. This is another kind of reference point relationship (van Hoek 1995, 1997). The antecedent nominal establishes its referent as a reference point whose dominion is some portion of the ongoing discourse. Within this stretch of discourse, it provides the basis for determining the reference of a pronoun, which is thus a target in the sense that the intended referent is mentally accessible via the antecedent. This relationship is usually independent of any particular structural configuration. The antecedent can lie at some distance from the pronoun, in a wide variety of structural positions with respect to it. At the most schematic level, we merely know that a pronoun's reference can be ascertained because it occurs in the dominion of a nominal serving as reference point for its interpretation.

There is further indeterminacy when a pronoun lacks an explicit nominal antecedent. In some cases the intended referent is not mentioned explicitly, but is evident from the discourse context (Hankamer and Sag 1976). Alternatively, the referent may be accessible metonymically, as in (20), from Japanese (Yamanashi 2003; Langacker 1996). The pronoun *sore* refers to the food in the bowl, but only the bowl is mentioned directly. Of course, many languages carry indeterminacy one step further by not even using a pronoun in certain circumstances. A vacant argument slot can be just as effective as a pronoun in prompting the search for a referent. And despite the indeterminacy, we usually manage to find the intended referent in the discourse or the context of speech. The referent is commonly the speaker or the hearer, since these are always accessible in the discourse context to serve as point of connection. In (20), the main clause trajector is left implicit but is understood by default as being the speaker.

(20) ***Donburi**-ga detekita node, suguni* ***sore**-o tabeta.*
bowl-s served since instantly it-o ate
'As soon as the bowl was served, I ate it [the food].'

Yet another kind of indeterminacy in pronominal reference is actual vagueness as to the intended referent (Gensler 1977; Chapter 5). Especially with the pronoun *it*, there are times when even the speaker – though clearly referring to something – would not be able to say just what. Suppose, for example, that a teenage girl is denied permission to go to the movies with her boyfriend. One can imagine her protesting to her parents by saying *It's just not fair!*. What does the pronoun *it* refer to in this context? The decision? The fact that permission was denied? The prospect of staying home on Friday night? The general circumstances? The misery of being a teenager? The plight of not being in control of her life? All of these? Some combination of them? In all likelihood the speaker has no single, precisely delimited referent in mind. This vagueness of reference is not however the same as absence of reference.

A final example concerns the internal structure of nominal expressions. In (21), there is indeterminacy as to how the definite article *the* and the quantifier *four* connect with the remainder of the nominal, which singles out a **type** of thing as the entity being identified or quantified.

(21) a. *The [**hard-working [Japanese]**] have achieved prosperity.*
b. *She has four [**brilliant [students]**].*

The definite article indicates that a single instance of the specified type is uniquely identifiable in the current discourse context. But what is that type? In (21)a it can either be *Japanese* or *hard-working Japanese*. In the former case, the set of Japanese as an undifferentiated whole offers itself as the obvious unique instance of this plural type. The adjective *hard-working* does not itself contribute to characterizing the type in question. It does however contribute in the second interpretation, where only those Japanese who are hard-working are said to have achieved prosperity. Depending on whether or not the adjective contributes to characterizing the specified type, it is sometimes described as being used either "restrictively" or "non-restrictively" (by analogy to relative clauses). In the CG account, this is simply a matter of which type specification potentially available within the nominal is put in correspondence with the type invoked by the article.

Likewise, *four* evokes a plural type and indicates the size of a set constituting one instance of it. In (21)b the type in question can either be just *students* (in which case she only has four, all of whom are brilliant) or else *brilliant students* (in which case she probably has additional students of lesser caliber). This is not a structural difference in the sense of there being different constituency or constituents representing different categories. It is simply a matter of how the component elements are connected by correspondences, in this case at the type level. But despite its non-structural nature, the contrast is still in the realm of grammar. In the CG perspective, grammar is nothing more than assemblies of symbolic structures linked by correspondences. Neither the indeterminacy of many connections nor the conceptual nature of the elements connected offers any basis for claiming that the phenomena at issue are semantic rather than grammatical or pragmatic rather than semantic.

These examples could be multiplied indefinitely. The indeterminacy they manifest is not in any way atypical, even in "core" areas of grammar. They demand a revision in what traditionally has been the default conception of grammatical structure, as well as a theoretical perspective in which they are seen as natural rather than problematic. A perspective of this kind is available in CG, set in the broader context of cognitive linguistics.

Chapter 3
A constructional approach to grammaticization

If grammaticization is characterized as the evolution of grammatical elements from lexical sources, it is with the understanding that the locus of change is an encompassing construction. For instance, the source of future *gonna* is not the verb *go* by itself, but the entire *be going to* construction, involving the progressive and an infinitival purpose clause. Ideally, a complete account of grammaticization must therefore include a description of the construction at various evolutionary stages, from source to end result.

From a cognitive-functional perspective, one should not expect to find a specific number of distinct historical stages occurring in a strictly determined sequence. Nor should one expect the situation at a given stage to be simple and clear-cut. Both meanings and constructions are complex and multifaceted. Certain aspects of their characterization, and the changes affecting them, are matters of degree. And at any one time, a language exhibits competing analyses as well as variants representing multiple diachronic stages (Heine 1992). Dealing with these complexities, either synchronically or diachronically, requires a constructional, usage based framework (Barlow and Kemmer 2000; Langacker 2000).

Still, it all starts with the description of particular constructions, characterized in CG as assemblies of symbolic structures, i.e. form-meaning pairings (Chapter 1). To describe a construction fully, one has to specify: (i) the meaning of each component element; (ii) how these meanings are integrated to form composite conceptions at different levels of organization; and (iii) how the construction relates to others (its position in intersecting networks of constructions and constructional variants). I will illustrate these factors and their interaction by examining the quantifying expression *a lot of* (Langacker To appear b).

1. The source construction

Superficially, expressions of the form *a lot of X* are parallel to nominals like *a woman from Brazil*, consisting of a determiner, a head noun, and a modifying prepositional phrase. Presumably the source structure instantiated some variant of this construction. The example is analyzed in Figure 3.1, on the assumption (which is not essential) that the article and noun form a constituent. The article is a **grounding** element, i.e. it specifies the discourse status of the nominal referent vis-à-vis the **ground** (G), comprising the speech event and its participants (Langacker 2004c). Heavy lines indicate that *woman* and *Brazil* profile (i.e. designate) things, while *from* profiles a relationship whose trajector (tr) and landmark (lm) – its primary and secondary focal participants – are also things. Dotted lines represent the correspondences which specify how component elements are integrated to form composite conceptions at successively higher levels of organization.

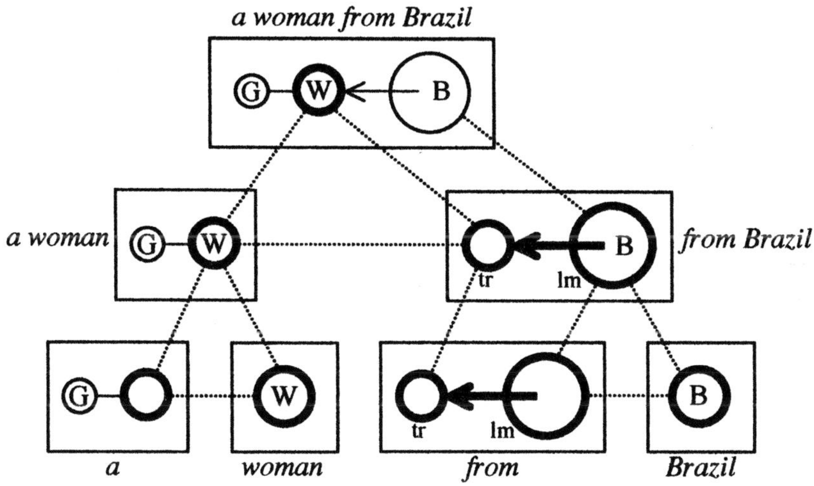

Figure 3.1

If Figure 3.1 approximates the source construction, in terms of grammatical organization, the end result of grammaticization is likely to be a simple quantifying construction, analogous to the one with *many* and *much*. At least in certain contexts, *a lot of* appears to be winning the competition with *many*, as seen in (1)a, and has largely supplanted *much*, as in (1)b.

(1) a. *We ate {a lot of / ?many} cookies.*
b. *We drank {a lot of / ??much} milk.*

The basic construction with *many* or *much* is sketched in Figure 3.2(a). I will use an ellipse (as opposed to a circle) to represent a mass, be it plural (as with *cookies*) or non plural (as with *milk*). The quantifier profiles a mass characterized only as surpassing the norm (n) on a scale of magnitude. The construction simply identifies that mass with the one profiled by the noun, so the composite expression designates a quantified mass of the type it specifies (given as X). Structure (a) instantiates the constructional schema in (b), which is the same except that it abstracts away from the specification of any particular quantity.

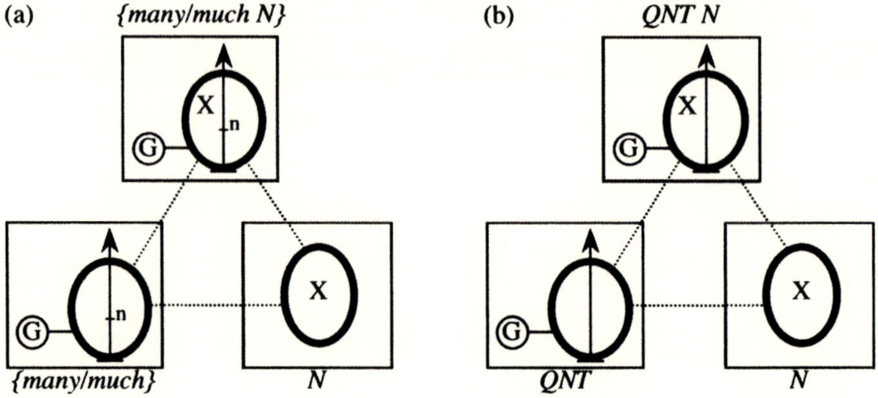

Figure 3.2

I have shown the quantifier as a grounding element, a point which requires elaboration. In and of themselves, *many* and *much* are not grounding elements, but **absolute quantifiers** (Langacker 1991: § 2.3.2) which profile relationships (cf. *Our problems are many*; *The many problems we face*). Most typically, however, such quantifiers occur in nominals grounded by zero, the unmarked option for indefinite mass nouns. The quantifier depicted in Figure 3.2 represents the conflation of the quantifying and zero grounding functions; this should probably be regarded as a derived value of such quantifiers. Their status as nominal grounding elements is most evident in expressions that lack a lexical head (e.g. *Many were broken*).

If *a lot of X* starts out with a structure analogous to Figure 3.1, and winds up with one like Figure 3.2, where *a lot of* is reduced to a monomorphemic quantifier, what are the stages connecting them? What happens to the article and preposition, which are not preserved as separate elements? Where are we now in this overall development? For the reasons cited above, I would not posit a specific sequence of stages that are well-defined and discretely different. It need not be the case, for instance, that changes affecting the article and the preposition occur in any particular order. Nor does the situation at any one stage necessarily reduce to a single, consistent analysis. I suspect that in alotta uses *a lot of* is not too far removed from being analyzed as a monomorphemic quantifier, as in Figure 3.2. But at the same time (right now, that is) various phenomena indicate a coexisting analysis closer to the one in Figure 3.1. In other words, there still exists an analysis with the constituency in Figure 3.1, where *a*, *lot*, and *of* retain their identities as article, noun, and preposition.

(2) a. [[a lot] [of X]] b. [alotta X]
ART N P NML QNT N

So if (2)a is developing into (2)b, this process has not yet run its course. Evidence for the persistence of (2)a includes the existence of the variants in (3). The sequence *a lot* – not *alotta* – occurs in anaphoric and adverbial uses. We find the reinforced variant *a whole lot*, just as with nouns like *pile*, *flock*, *bunch*, etc. Suggesting the continued status of *a lot* as a singular count noun with an indefinite article is the expected plural *lots*. Beyond this, there may still be some connection with expressions like those in (3)d, where *lot* retains the original meaning 'group/collection'.

(3) a. *We ate a lot.* (**We ate alotta.*)
b. *a whole lot of X* (*a whole {pile / flock / bunch} of X)*
c. *lots of X* (*{tons / scads / oodles} of X; a ton ~ tons)*
d. *They're a sorry lot. We should get rid of the lot of them.*

Thus *a lot of* belongs to a family of expressions all of which support the analysis in (2)a. One could argue, of course, that the connections among them are rather tenuous, hardly sufficient to prevent its reanalysis as (2)b. And indeed, I do not doubt that (2)b is emerging. Nonetheless, additional evidence based on grammatical behavior all points to (2)a as the primary analysis, or at least one that is still accessible. One difference between (2)a and (2)b is that X is a full nominal (i.e. a noun phrase) in the former, but simply a noun in the latter. The distinction is not always evident with indefinites, due to the option of zero grounding. X can however be definite, as in (4), which argues for (2)a:

(4) a. *a lot of them* (**many them)*
b. *a lot of that cherry-flavored whisky* (**much that cherry-flavored whisky)*

Expressions like (5) also require this analysis:

(5) *They have a lot – maybe even a whole collection – of impressionist paintings.*

Further supporting (2)a is the possibility of preposing the prepositional phrase, as in (6)a:

(6) a. (i) *Of that I have a lot.* (ii) *That's something of which I have a lot.*
b. (i) *That I have a lot of.* (ii) *That's something I have a lot of.*
c. (i) *That song I know the words to.* (ii) *That's a song I know the words to.*

To be sure, *of* can also be left behind, as in (6)b. But that merely illustrates the phenomenon known as "preposition stranding", as in (6)c.

2. Component meanings

How, then, are expressions like (2)a put together? The first task is to specify the meanings of *lot* and *of*.[1] The sense of *lot* that concerns us is the one manifested in expressions that instantiate the general pattern in (7), i.e. expressions of the form *a N of X*, where N is the noun in question and X describes a mass (plural or non-plural). This represents a special case of the pattern in Figure 3.1, distinguished by several properties: (i) the preposition is *of*; (ii) X is a mass term; and (iii) the referents of N and X are **coextensive**. Their coextension can be of different sorts. With nouns like *box* and *barrel*, N is a container and X the content which fills it. Nouns like *pile* and *stack* designate a bounded entity characterized by its spatial configuration, X being the constitutive mass which assumes that configuration. Nouns like *flock* and *collection* are similar, except that they are non-specific about spatial configuration, placing more emphasis on the collective function of the constitutive entities. And nouns like *ton*, *yard*, and *gallon* are units of measurement, used to assess the extension of X along some scale.

(7) ***a N of X:*** *a box of nails; a barrel of oil; a pile of dirt; a stack of plates; a flock of sheep; a collection of paintings; a ton of coal; a yard of fabric; a gallon of milk*

These types of noun differ in the extent to which N exists independently of X. I roughly describe them in (8), without pretending that the list is exhaustive or that the types are sharply distinct or non-overlapping (e.g. *flock* is intermediate between configurational and group nouns). A container is a distinct physical object that exists independently of its content. Configurations and groups may be physical, but they are not distinct from their constitutive entities – they are coextensive with them in the strongest sense. A unit of measure per se is non-physical, consisting in extension along a scale; it is physically manifested only as an aspect of what it measures.

(8) a. **Container** (*box*, *barrel*): physical object; distinct from content; has a shape; has a containing function.
b. **Configuration** (*pile*, *stack*): physical; not distinct from constitutive entities; has a shape; has no specific function.
c. **Group** (*flock*, *collection*): not necessarily physical; not distinct from constitutive entities; has no specific shape; has a particular function.
d. **Measure** (*ton*, *yard*, *gallon*): non-physical (scalar); physically manifested only as an aspect of constitutive entities; has no shape (only extension along a scale); has a measurement function.

---

1 The meaning of *a* will be considered later.

In Figure 3.3 I offer diagrammatic representations for these types of nouns. I am using a circle to indicate a bounded entity (corresponding to count nouns) and an ellipse for a mass (not inherently construed as bounded). A container noun profiles a bounded object distinct from a mass that fills it. I make no diagrammatic distinction between a configuration and a group, which are alike in that the bounded entity they profile is indistinguishable from the mass which constitutes it; I use two lines (like an equal sign) to represent this strong co-extensiveness. Finally, a measure noun designates a bounded entity consisting only of some extension along a scale, corresponding to one facet of what is measured (such as weight, area, or volume).

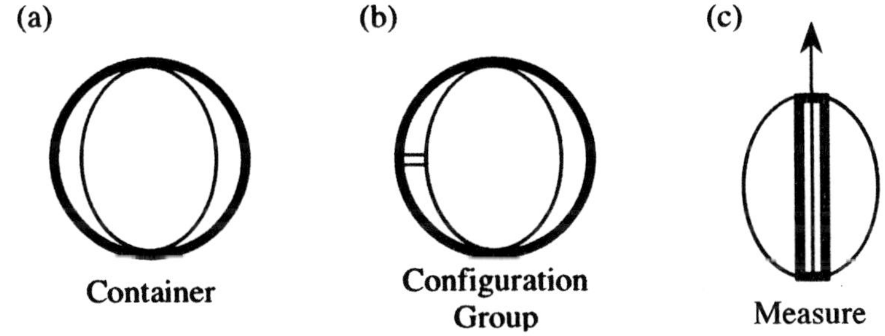

Figure 3.3

As noted in Chapter 2, a particular expression of the form *a N of X* may have multiple specific interpretations, and a particular N may have multiple conventionally established senses. We see in (9), for instance, that the composite expression *a barrel of oil* can designate either the container, its content, a mass equivalent in volume to its content, or a unit of measurement pure and simple. As for *barrel* itself, its established meanings include at least the container sense and the unit of measurement sense.

(9) a. *They rolled **a barrel of oil** down the ramp.* [container]
b. *We burned **a barrel of oil** that had been sitting in the basement.* [content]
c. ***A barrel of oil** leaked from the storage tank.* [measured mass]
d. ***A barrel of oil** is 42 gallons.* [unit of measurement]

Container, configuration, and group nouns can all develop into measure nouns, as observed in (10). The original meaning can be retained, and may even still be primary, as in the case of *cup*. Container nouns seem especially prone to this development, probably because containers usually have a fairly specific size. The configuration noun *bunch* figures in the quantifying expression *a bunch of X*, which rivals *a lot of X* for its prevalence and degree of grammaticization. As for *lot*, the group noun sense still exists, if only marginally.

(10) a. (i) *The **cup** broke.* (ii) *This recipe calls for a **cup** of blueberries.*
b. (i) *He bought a large **bunch** of grapes.* (ii) *He owns a **bunch** of hotels.*
c. *The auction started well. Every item in the first **lot** attracted a **lot** of bidders.*

The development of a measure sense is sketched in Figure 3.4. At the initial stage, the noun profiles a container, configuration, or group per se; while it may have a typical size, this is not a central semantic specification. But since it designates a bounded entity, it serves a **unitizing** function with respect to a mass by delimiting the portion that is coextensive with it. This gives it the potential to serve a **quantifying** function, where the size of an instance is measured in terms of the units thus defined. Employing the noun in this fashion heightens the salience of its size specification. Moreover, through the kind of phrasal metonymy exemplified in (9)b–c, it might be used for a unit of mass whose association with the container, configuration, or group is merely recalled or imagined. This interpretation is sketched in diagram (b). The measure sense results from a shift in profile (metonymy) whereby the noun specifically designates the unit of measurement (extension along a scale), association with a container, configuration, or group receding into the background. Eventually this association may disappear altogether.

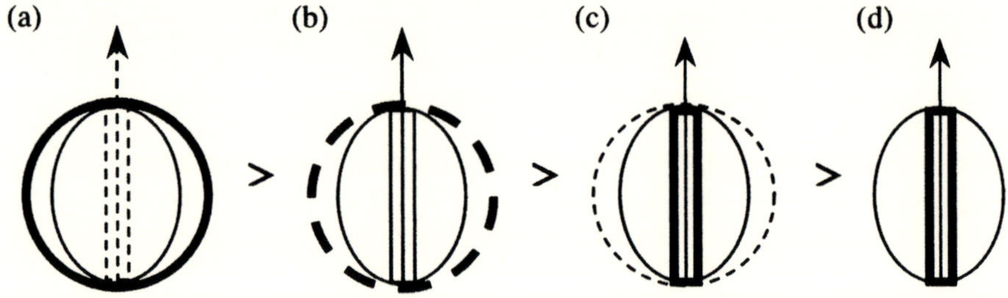

Figure 3.4

The *lot* that appears in *a lot of X* at least approximates this final stage. In contrast to *barrel*, *flock*, and even *bunch*, it does not at all evoke the conception of a bounded entity coextensive with the quantified mass. It is not entirely clear why *lot* has evolved to indicate a large quantity rather than a small one. Presumably this reflects an original emphasis on the constitutive entities being exhaustive of the group defined for a certain purpose. Be that as it may, I will take diagram (d) as representing the sense of *lot* in *a lot of X*. As a pure measure expression, it lends itself to adverbial uses, where it does not quantify a mass but rather the intensity or frequency of a process: *I like it a lot*; *She complains a lot* (cf. *He hit it a ton*).

The uses and senses of the preposition *of* are too complex to examine here in any detail. As a schematic characterization, I have suggested (Langacker 1992a) that *of* profiles an **intrinsic relationship** between its trajector and landmark. For describing *a lot of X* and related expressions, we can focus on two particular kinds of intrinsic relationship: that in which the trajector is a **restricted subpart** of the landmark, as exemplified in (11)a, and that in which the trajector and landmark are **coextensive**, as in (11)b.

(11) a. **Restricted subpart:** *the back of my hand; the center of the room; most of the elephants; a portion of the rice; the first chapter of his thesis; the roof of that house; two of those packages; a bite of this pizza; the surface of the moon; the floor of the closet*

b. **Coextension:** *a line of posts; a bar of soap; a can of soup; a mound of dirty clothes; a grove of orange trees; a herd of cattle; an array of sensors; a house of straw; the state of California; the mystery of his disappearance; that idiot of a president*

Though seemingly at odds with one another, these two senses are related to one another in various ways, the first being their common status as types of intrinsic relationship. For each sense, a plausible path of evolution can be suggested starting with the original meaning 'from'. That, however, is well beyond the scope of this analysis. A further connection is that coextension represents the limiting case of a restricted subpart: the case that emerges when the degree of the trajector's restrictiveness vis-à-vis the landmark falls to zero (cf. Langacker 1982). Finally, I note that many uses are ambivalent between the two senses, both being observable in the overall situation. Consider *a slice of cake*. The overall expression may be interpreted as profiling the bounded entity *slice* (N), as shown in Figure 3.5(c). But what about *cake* (X)? Does it refer to the larger mass from which the slice is taken, as in 3.5(a)? Or just to the portion which constitutes the slice, as in 3.5(b)? It may be possible to force a particular interpretation, e.g. by using an overtly grounded nominal object which clearly designates a larger whole: *a slice of that cake which you baked last night*. But often the matter is indeterminate.

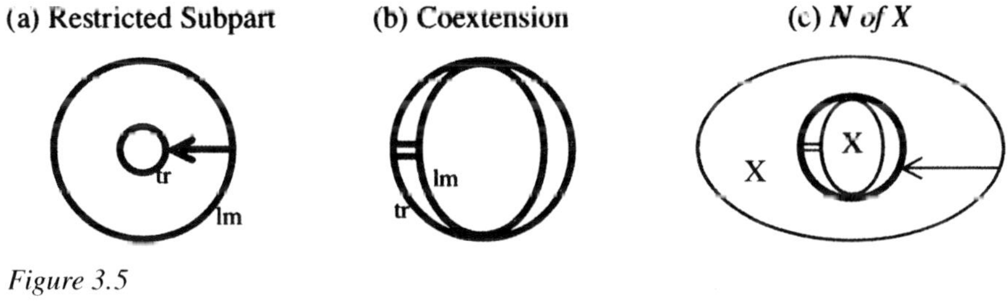

Figure 3.5

3. Integration

Having considered the meanings of the component elements, we can now describe their integration to form composite conceptions at different levels of organization. For sake of comparison, we can usefully start with expressions that have not grammaticized to the same extent as *a lot of X*. Consider the phrase *a flock of those sheep*, which might occur in the context of (12). The context makes it clear that the referent of *flock* (N) is only a portion of the mass designated by the prepositional object *those sheep* (X). The expression then has the structure sketched in Figure 3.6.

(12) *The sheep you imported from New Zealand are getting to be a problem.* ***A flock of those sheep*** *is messing up my lawn.*

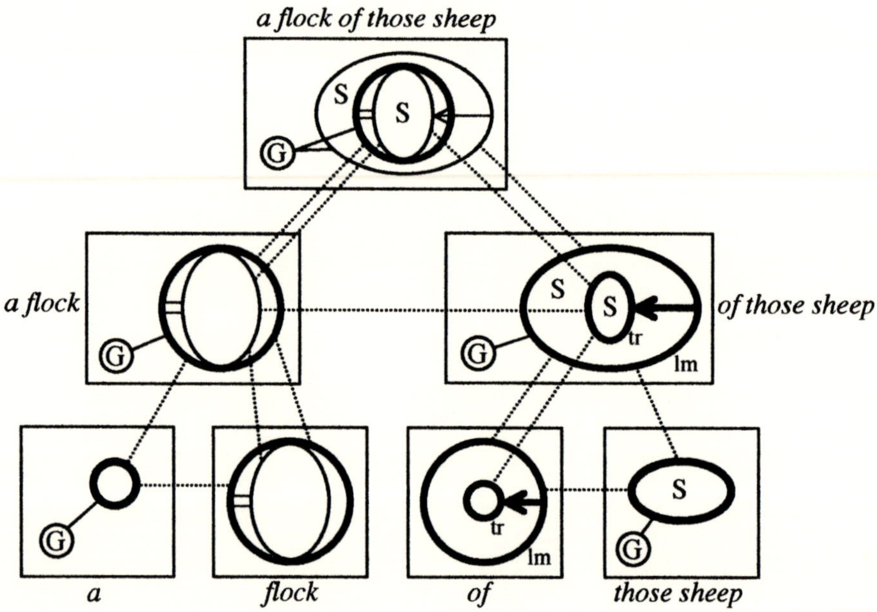

Figure 3.6

The noun *flock*, grounded by the indefinite article, profiles a bounded entity which is coextensive (in the strong sense) with a plural mass. *Of* profiles the relationship which a proper subpart bears to a whole. Its landmark is elaborated by the nominal *those sheep* (grounded by the demonstrative) to form a prepositional phrase, which therefore designates the relationship that a restricted mass of sheep bears to a more inclusive mass. At the higher level of organization, the schematic mass delimited by *flock* is put in correspondence with the trajector of the prepositional phrase (the usual configuration in a modifying construction). Hence the composite structure profiles a flock consisting of sheep drawn from a larger mass of sheep.[2]

Since a group and its constitutive entities are strongly coextensive, it is hardly surprising that expressions like *a flock of those sheep* are sometimes interpreted as referring not to the group per se but rather to the plural mass it comprises. Indicating this metonymic shift is the plural verb in (13), in contrast to the singular verb in (12). When interpreted in this manner, the expression has the structure shown in Figure 3.7.[3] It is just the same as Figure 3.6 except for the composite structure profile. Note that this constructional variant is **exocentric**, as the composite structure profile is not the same as that of either component structure. While the two analyses are very similar, the difference between them is grammatically significant – depending on the choice of profile, the composite expression is either a count noun (hence the verb *is*) or a plural mass noun (hence the verb *are*). Expressions like *a flock of those sheep* are thus susceptible to alternative analyses which compete with one another. It is not always evident which analysis is intended, or whether the speaker is even making the distinction. In the absence of verb agreement (e.g. *A flock of those sheep would mess up my lawn*) the matter may simply be indeterminate.

(13) *A flock of those sheep* **are** *messing up my lawn.*

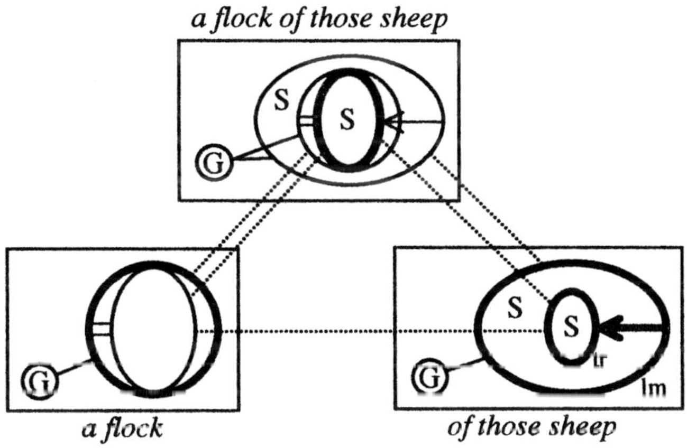

Figure 3.7

2 I have not shown the internal structure of *those sheep*, nor am I making any notational distinction among the various kinds of nominal grounding.

3 Only the highest level of organization is indicated.

There is also competition between alternative analyses along another dimension. To force the restricted subpart interpretation, I had to construct the context in (12) and use a demonstrative to ground the prepositional object. It is far more typical in expressions of this sort for the prepositional object to be a simple noun, e.g. *a flock of sheep*. Of course, due to the option of zero grounding a plural or non-plural mass noun may itself constitute a full, grounded nominal, hence able to function as a subject or object. The instance it designates can be of any size relative to the maximal extension of the type. The profiled instance may be contextually delimited (as in *I saw sheep on the lawn*), or it may be unrestricted, in which case the profiled instance is equivalent to the maximal extension (e.g. *I hate sheep*).

So in the expression *a flock of sheep*, it is still possible to analyze *sheep* as a full, grounded nominal. Here too it might be interpreted as designating a larger mass (perhaps the maximal extension of the type) from which the flock is drawn. If so, *a flock of sheep* has the analyses in Figures 3.6 and 3.7, differing from them only in how the prepositional object is grounded. But since a zero-grounded mass can be of any size, we have another option (just as with *a slice of cake*): instead of designating a more inclusive mass, *sheep* can also be interpreted as designating the very instance of the type which constitutes the flock. In this case *of* is understood as indicating coextension (rather than a restricted subpart relation), as in (11)b and Figure 3.5(b). There may be no direct way to detect the difference. Indeed, in a previous description (Langacker To appear b) I adopted the analysis in Figures 3.6 and 3.7 precisely in order to accommodate examples with a definite determiner, like *a flock of those sheep*. But there is no real reason to suppose that *a flock of sheep* and *a flock of those sheep* have to be parallel in all respects. Given the prevalence of competing analyses and coexisting variants, it seems quite reasonable to suppose that the interpretive possibilities afforded by zero grounding allow the emergence of an alternative analysis in which the component elements are integrated in a different fashion. It is a tighter integration, in accordance with a general tendency for grammaticization to correlate with a higher degree of conceptual overlap (Langacker 1992b, 2003c).

Since the meaning of *flock* involves coextension, which dovetails with a central sense of *of*, interpreting *of* in this manner is natural if not inevitable. Expressions like *a flock of those sheep*, which specifically invoke a larger mass, seem rather marginal and require more contextual support. I take them as representing a constructional variant that is now secondary but still available when need arises. For expressions like *a flock of sheep*, with zero grounding, the interpretation based on coextension is now (I presume) the default. With this analysis as well we have the option of profiling either the flock or the sheep which constitute it, as reflected in the choice of *is* vs. *are* in (14).

(14) *A flock of sheep {is / are} grazing on my lawn.*

In Figure 3.8, I show this default analysis under the second option, where *a flock of sheep* designates the sheep.[4] The indefinite nominal *sheep* profiles a plural mass which might be of any size. It specifies the landmark of the preposition *of*, which profiles a relationship of coextension. At the higher level of organization, that relationship is identified with the one inherent in the meaning of *flock*: its trajector corresponds to the flock per se, its landmark to the mass which constitutes it. At the composite structure level, therefore, these two relationships of coextension collapse into one: they are two encodings of the same relationship.[5] In this way the referent of *sheep* is delimited and bounded by *flock*.

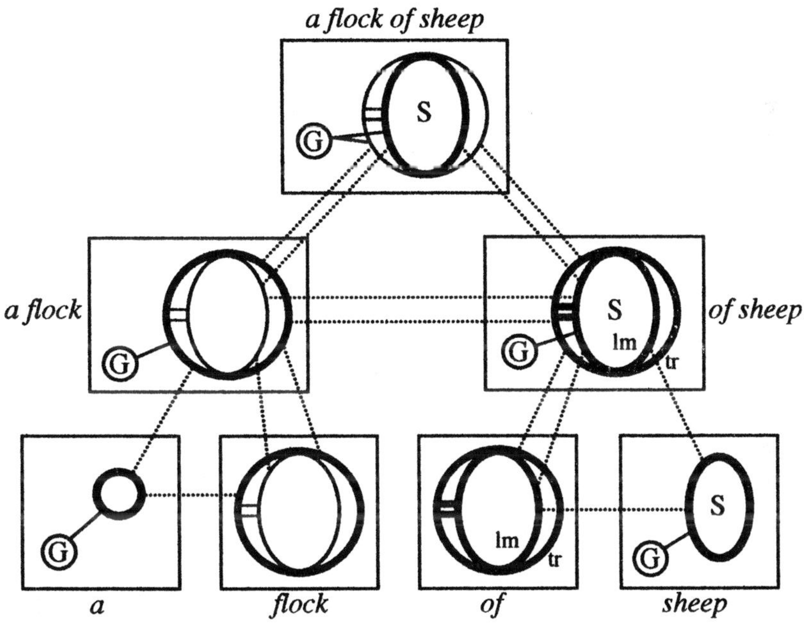

Figure 3.8

Tighter integration – reflected in multiple correspondences and a greater degree of conceptual overlap – is characteristic of more highly grammaticized expressions. The type of overlap in Figure 3.8 represents a step in the evolution

4 The first option would be the same apart from the composite structure profile, as in Figures 3.6 and 3.7.

5 One could say that they are themselves coextensive.

of *a lot of* in the direction of being a monomorphemic quantifier. But we are not there yet. If the end result will be something like (2)b, the structure in (2)a is still alive and well. Indeed, *a lot of X* still allows the restricted subpart interpretation, where X is a full, grounded nominal that designates a larger mass from which the quantified mass is drawn. Thus (15)a is analogous to (13). In contrast to *flock*, however, *a lot of X* requires a plural verb when X is a plural noun: we cannot say **A lot of sheep is on my lawn.*

(15) a. *A lot of those sheep are scrawny.*
b. *A flock of (those) sheep {is / are} on my lawn.*
c. *A lot of (those) sheep {*is / are} on my lawn.*
d. *An admirer of sheep {is / *are} on my lawn.*

Evidently, the overall expression *a lot of X* can only designate the quantified mass, not the bounded unit of measurement profiled by *lot* individually.[6] That is, the construction is necessarily exocentric, as shown for *flock* in Figures 3.7 and 3.8. We can relate this to the fact that *lot* has largely lost its group noun sense, so – in contrast to *flock* – the mass is the only tangible entity available to function as the nominal referent (see Figure 3.4(d)). In expressions of the form *a N of X*, therefore, the metonymic shift observed in Figures 3.7 and 3.8 is obligatory in the case of *lot*, optional for nouns like *flock*, and impossible for a noun like *admirer*, which is not based on coextension.

Expressions like *a lot of sheep* can thus have a structure analogous to either Figure 3.7 or Figure 3.8, depending on whether *of* profiles a restricted subpart relationship or one of coextension. With zero grounding of *sheep*, the former is the less likely alternative, though presumably still available. The mass with respect to which *lot* functions as a unit of measurement is then identified with a mass of sheep viewed as a restricted subpart of a larger mass (most likely the maximal extension, i.e. the set of all sheep). The restricted mass it quantifies is profiled by the expression as a whole, at the composite structure level, even though it is not profiled by either component structure.

Figure 3.9 represents the more likely analysis (analogous to Figure 3.8), where *of* profiles a relationship of coextension. In combination with *a lot*, this coextension is identified with the inherent relation between a unit of measurement and the mass it quantifies. Once again, the quantified mass is profiled at the composite structure level. Here, though, the profiled mass is not specifically portrayed as being drawn from a larger one. There is a tighter conceptual in-

6 It profiles this unit in expressions comparable to (9)d or to the following, where measurement per se is at issue: *A lot is more than a little.*

tegration, in that the intrinsic relationship evoked by *of* collapses with the one inherent in the meaning of *lot*.

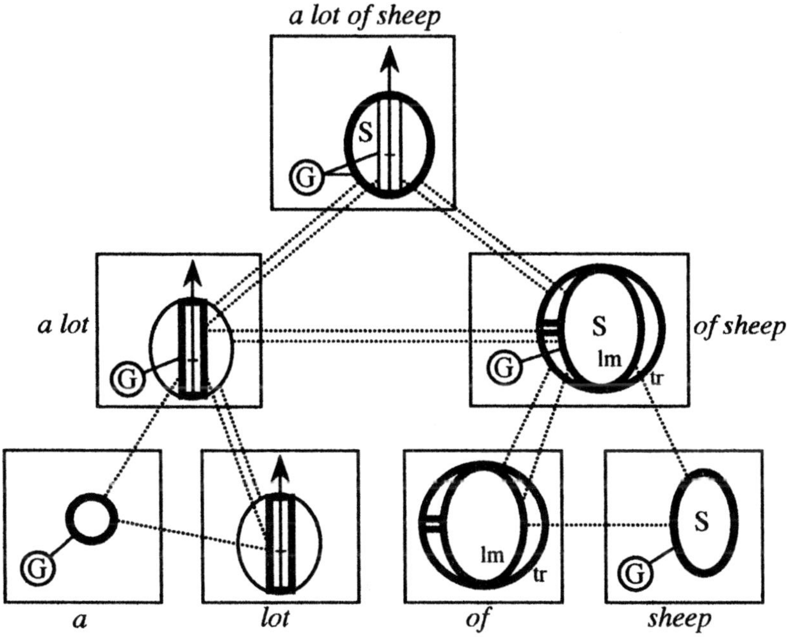

Figure 3.9

The structure in Figure 3.9 corresponds to (2)a, where *a lot* and the *of*-phrase are the major constituents, and the prepositional object is a nominal (not just an ungrounded noun). Earlier I provided a variety of evidence that this analysis is still available, if not the primary one. It represents a construal made possible by zero grounding of the prepositional object, since overt grounding – as in (15)a – induces the conception of a mass other than the one quantifed by *lot*. The structure in Figure 3.9, which does not invoke a larger mass, is presumably in the process of grammaticizing into a simple quantifying construction along the lines of (2)b. It is not unlikely that an essentially monomorphemic variant of *alotta* has already emerged for certain speakers. If so, it probably coexists with the analysis in Figure 3.9, where the constitutive elements are still recognizable to some extent. It is of course a basic tenet of CG that the **analyzability** of complex fixed expressions is a matter of degree (Langacker 2000). *A lot of* has a long way to go before it reaches the point of zero analyzability and reanalysis as a strictly monomorphemic expression.

4. The indefinite article

Supposing that this development eventually runs its course, let us consider what must happen along the way. The structures in Figure 3.9 and (2)b differ in three basic respects. First, the article *a* and the preposition *of* lose their status as separate morphemes, either disappearing phonetically or being incorporated in the monomorphemic *alotta*. Concomitantly, there is a realignment of constituency, so that *a*, *lot*, and *of* – so long as there is still any vestige of analyzability – form a group that combines as a whole with the following nominal element. Finally, this element is reanalyzed as a noun rather than a full, independently grounded nominal. I am not prepared to specify the temporal sequencing of these developments, or the extent to which one presupposes or induces another. I will discuss them in the order listed, with no claim that it is necessarily chronological. More important than chronology, I suspect, is the independent existence of nominals of the form QNT+N, as in Figure 3.2. This construction offers a model for an alternative analysis, whether it facilitates the changes or merely provides a way to assimilate the resulting structure in the grammatical system.

In expressions like *a woman from Brazil*, the indefinite article functions as grounding element for the nominal as a whole. It singles out an instance of the type specified by the head noun, *woman*, and indicates that it was not previously accessible in the discourse as the unique instance of this type. Clearly, though, the function of *a* in *a lot of X* must be rather different. It combines directly with *lot*, but due to the metonymic shift, *lot* is not the head noun: the entity it profiles is not profiled by the nominal as a whole. Indeed, with the structure in Figure 3.9 there is no head noun so defined (this is what makes the construction exocentric). The indefinite article does still function here as a grounding element, but only locally, for the nominal *a lot*, rather than globally, for *a lot of sheep* overall.

Even in local terms, *a* does not have quite the same semantic value as in other uses. The reason is that *lot*, as a measure noun, does not specify a type with multiple instances which have to be distinguished or identified. The entity it designates is abstract – a vaguely delimited degree of extension along a scale – and as such is unique: there is only one *lot*, not a bunch of different *lots* that have to be distinguished from one another. In this respect *lot* is comparable to a number, like *seven*, which is also unique and abstract. In terms of uniqueness, *lot* is further comparable to a proper name, e.g. *George Lakoff*, which also specifies a type with just one instance (Langacker 2004c). When the indefinite article combines with *lot*, therefore, its referential function is much attenuated. While *lot* has an abstract referent (just as a number does), its uniqueness renders vacuous the function of singling out a particular instance of its type.

Why, then, is *lot* not grounded by zero (as in the case of *seven* or *George Lakoff*), or by the definite article (the usual marker of contextual uniqueness)? Obviously, the choice of article is due to historical conservatism: we say *a lot* (rather than *the lot* or just *lot*) because it constitutes a fixed expression whose form was established at a stage when the meaning of *lot* was such that the indefinite article had its normal value. The fact that this is no longer the case creates the potential for the indefinite article to lose its status as a separate symbolic element. On the one hand, it might be reanalyzed as part of a monomorphemic quantifier: *alotta*. Alternatively, it might disappear altogether. Being phonologically minimal and having no essential semantic function, it would seem quite susceptible to phonetic erosion.

But this has not yet happened. Not only is the indefinite article still a separate element (cf. *a whole lot of X*), but it still has a discernible meaning consistent with a vestigial grounding function. We can see its meaningfulness by observing that *a lot of X* has a particular place in paradigms of quantifying expressions. As I noted at the outset, *a lot of* (as well as *lots of*) is competing with *many* and *much*. By now it is well established as a central member of the English quantifier system. Among the core members listed in (16)a–b, the older ones combine directly with a noun, whereas the newcomers – *lot*, *lots*, and *bunch* – require the preposition *of*. More to the point, the indefinite article that accompanies *lot* and *bunch* also appears in the core members *a few* and *a little*. Also related are the less grammaticized expressions in (16)c–d, where *a* still alternates with *one* and other numerals (*a dozen X*, *one dozen X*, *two dozen X*).[7]

(16) a. *many X, much X, few X, little X, a few X, a little X, several X, three X*
b. *a lot of X, lots of X, a bunch of X*
c. *a dozen X, a hundred X, a thousand X*
d. *a cup of X, a barrel of X, a yard of X, a ton of X, a case of X*

So even within the core inventory, the indefinite article figures in several English quantifiers: *a lot of, a bunch of, a few, a little*. Moreover, the paradigmatic relationship among *few*, *little*, *a few*, and *a little* clearly demonstrates the article's segmentability and meaningfulness in these expressions. All four quantifiers specify a value lower than the norm. They differ along two axes. *Few* and *a few* are used with plural masses (*few cookies*, *a few cookies*), *little* and *a little* with non-plural masses (*little milk*, *a little milk*). Along the second axis, *few* and *little* are negative expressions, governing negative polarity items

7 I consider only **absolute** quantifiers, not the **relative** quantifiers (*all*, *most*, *some*, *no*, *every*, *each*, *any*), since *a lot of* most closely resembles the former. (See Langacker 1991: § 2.3.3.)

such as *any*, whereas *a few* and *a little* are positive despite the limited quantity they indicate:

(17) a. ***Few*** *politicians have* ***any*** *principles.*
b. ***Little*** *political rhetoric has* ***any*** *substance.*
c. **A* ***few*** *politicians have* ***any*** *principles.*
d. **A* ***little*** *political rhetoric has* ***any*** *substance.*
e. **A* ***bunch of*** *politicians have* ***any*** *principles.*
f. **A* ***lot of*** *political rhetoric has* ***any*** *substance.*

Observe that *a lot of* and *a bunch of* behave analogously to *a few* and *a little* in this respect.

I have proposed (Langacker To appear b) that these quantifiers have the conceptual import sketched in Figure 3.10, where dashed arrows represent a path of mental scanning. *Many* and *much* (also *lots*) specify a quantity that departs from the norm in a positive direction, while *few* and *little* are based on scanning in a negative direction. In terms of quantity, *a few* and *a little* are comparable to *few* and *little* – the quantity specified lies toward the lower end of the scale. They are however positive expressions by virtue of how the specified quantity is mentally accessed: instead of scanning downward from the norm, they are based on upward scanning from the scalar origin. I propose that *a lot* and *a bunch* are comparable, except that the upward scanning goes beyond the norm. On this account, the expressions in (c) and (d) share a component of meaning: they all specify a quantity through upward scanning from the scalar origin, i.e. as a **positive increment** starting from the baseline of zero. This notion of a positive increment is what I take to be the semantic contribution of the indefinite article in these expressions. Though abstract, it is quite consistent with the article's basic value, where it occurs with count nouns (which profile bounded entities) and designates a single instance of the specified type.

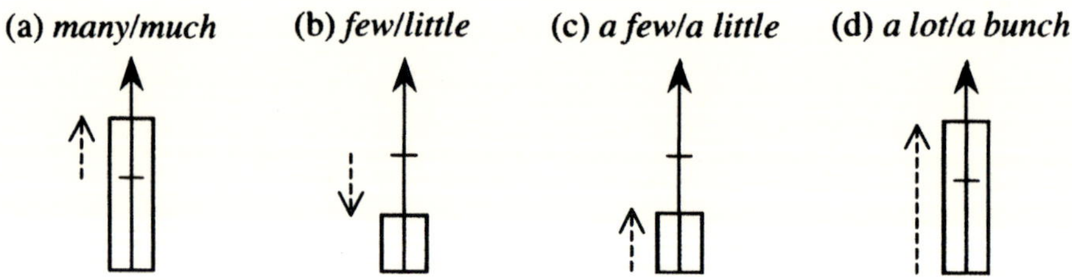

Figure 3.10

The *a* that appears in *a lot* is therefore meaningful, and *a lot* is subtly distinct in meaning from *many* and *much*, despite their being equivalent in the quantities they indicate. Essentially the difference is one of analyzability, with *a* and *lot* construing the quantity in terms of incrementation by a single measurement unit. But with fixed expressions, analyzability – the extent to which component conceptions are activated along with the composite conception – is a matter of degree that tends to decline with continued frequent use. When it falls to zero, the resulting, unanalyzable expression will not necessarily retain the semantic nuances contributed by the component elements. Most likely, then, a monomorphemic *alotta* will wind up with the meaning of *many* and *much*, as sketched in diagram (a).[8]

5. Restructuring

In sum, semantic developments affecting *lot* and the construction as a whole result in the indefinite article's attenuation and susceptibility to loss, whether through incorporation in a monomorphemic quantifier or total disappearance. The preposition *of* is likewise susceptible to loss in either fashion, also due to semantic developments in the construction as a whole. When it profiles a restricted subpart relationship, *of* makes a substantial semantic contribution by introducing an element not evoked by *lot*: a larger entity (its landmark) from which the quantified mass is drawn. But in Figure 3.9, where *of* profiles a relationship of coextension, it fails to contribute anything not already implicit in *lot* itself. As a measurement noun, *lot* itself includes the notion of coextension inherent in the relation between a measurement unit and the mass it quantifies. Semantically, therefore, *of* is fully subsumed in the meaning of *lot*: its trajector is identified with the measurement unit, its landmark with the quantified mass, and the profiled relationship of coextension with the intrinsic coextension of a measurement unit and what it measures. Because the entity specified by the prepositional object figures schematically in the meaning of *lot*, the preposition is not essential – the quantified mass could perfectly well be specified by a noun (like *sheep*) that directly combines with *lot* and elaborates its schematic reference to this mass. There is thus the potential for a monomorphemic quantifier to emerge (*alotta*) and combine with the quantified noun, just as in Figure 3.2.

Even while *a* and *of* are still segmentable and meaningful, expressions of the form *a lot of X* are capable of being assimilated to the global construction in Figure 3.2(b). That is, we can envisage a stage intermediate between (2)a and (2)b. At this stage the sequence *a lot of* is still internally analyzable, as in (2)a

8 It will however be slightly more schematic by virtue of neutralizing the distinction between a plural and a non-plural mass.

or Figure 3.9, but forms a constituent which, as a composite whole, functions as the quantifier in Figure 3.2(b). This analysis is shown in Figure 3.11. Possibly it coexists and competes with (2)a/Figure 3.9 at the present time. While I cannot be sure that a structure precisely like Figure 3.11 exists at any stage, it at least provides a tangible basis for discussing the transition from (2)a to (2)b, where *alotta* functions as a monomorphemic quantifier.

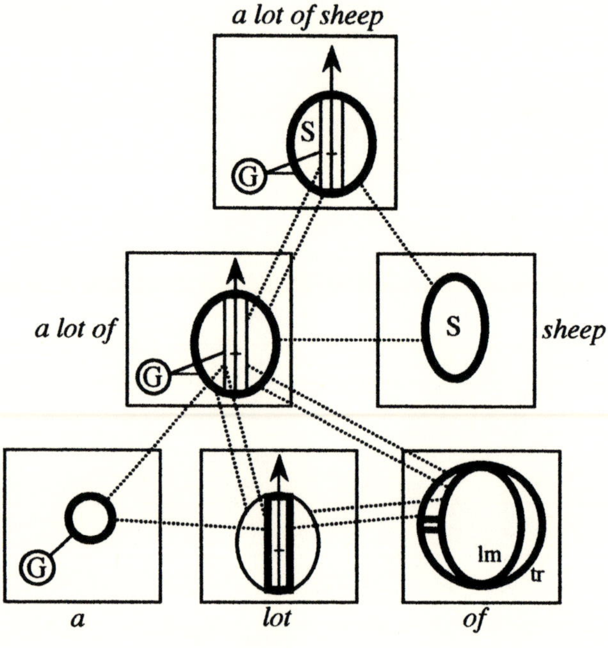

Figure 3.11

The differences between Figures 3.9 and 3.11 can all be ascribed to the expression being interpreted as instantiating the constructional schema in Figure 3.2(b). Most evident is the change in constituency, which brings the expression into line with the bipartite structure QNT+N. From the standpoint of CG, where constituency is seen as non-essential and often variable (Langacker 1997a), this is not a momentous adjustment. Less visible but grammatically more significant is the reinterpretation of *sheep* as a noun, rather than a full nominal (or "noun phrase"). This is possible due to the zero grounding option for English indefinites: there is no distinction in form between *sheep* as a plural noun, which merely specifies a type of mass, and *sheep* as a nominal designating an instance of that type (indefinite and unrestricted in terms of size). Being a simple noun, *sheep* then functions as lexical head in the overall expression, being grounded by the quantifier in accordance with the pattern in Figure 3.2(b). The complex form *a lot of* fills the quantifier role.

A lot of serves this function by virtue of its composite structure assuming the value of QNT in Figure 3.2(b). The value shown represents the conflation of an absolute quantifier's basic meaning with the import of zero grounding, resulting in a derived grounding quantifier.[9] As a grounding element, QNT profiles the grounded entity, namely the quantified mass. And in accordance with its zero grounding component, the grounding relationship (the discourse status of the mass) is that of indefiniteness. But while zero grounding does not itself impose any restriction in regard to size, the grounding quantifier inherits the size specification of the quantifier. *A lot of* thus profiles a mass whose magnitude is specified by *lot*.

From a structure like Figure 3.11, the transition to (2)b is straightforward: it is basically just a matter of the composite expression *a lot of* losing its analyzability, whereby – *ipso facto* – it constitutes a monomorphemic quantifier. I have already noted that *a* and *of*, though meaningful, are semantically dispensable in the context of the overall construction. The preposition is wholly subsumed in the meaning of *lot*, so nothing is lost if it disappears or is no longer recognized as a separate element. As for *a*, which grounds *lot* (not the nominal as a whole), it has no real referential function, but merely indicates that the specified quantity is construed as a positive increment from the baseline of zero. This is not the only way to conceptualize a larger-than-normal mass: an alternative construal, exemplified by *many* and *much*, is based instead on upward scanning from the norm (Figure 3.10).[10] Should *a* and *lot* lose their separate identities, therefore, the former construal will fade away and the latter will naturally emerge.

Given the basic tendency for fixed expressions to gradually lose their analyzability, we can expect *a lot of* to eventually coalesce into a simple, monomorphemic quantifier, as shown in Figure 3.12. It will then be equivalent to *many* and *much* (Figure 3.2(a)), except for neutralizing the distinction between a plural and a non-plural mass. It may well be that *a lot of X* already has the structure in Figure 3.12, for some speakers or even for all speakers some of the

9 By contrast, with **relative quantifiers** (*all*, *most*, *every*, etc.) the grounding function is intrinsic (Langacker 1991: § 2.3.2). The reanalysis of absolute quantifiers as grounding elements is outside the scope of this discussion.

10 Both meanings invoke the same essential content, including the notion of a scale, a baseline of zero, and a norm. The difference in construal is a matter of relative prominence: whether the baseline or the norm is foregrounded within the overall conception.

time. I have argued, however, that the structure in Figure 3.9 is still accessible, if not primary. The coexistence of multiple stages in the grammaticization process is, of course, to be expected (Heine 1992).

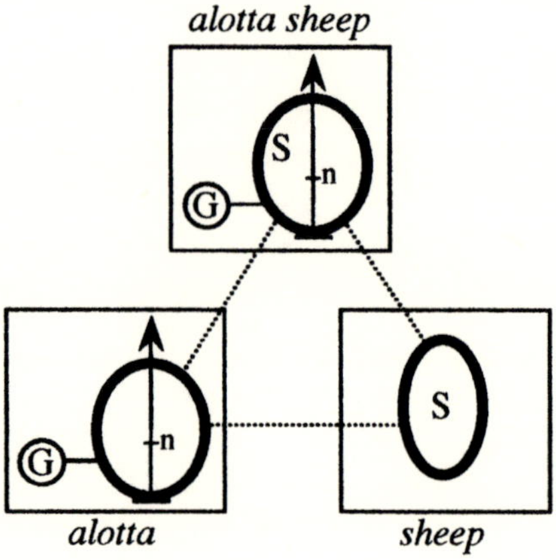

Figure 3.12

The picture I have sketched is complex but hopefully realistic. If we take seriously the view that grammaticization affects constructions, rather than isolated elements, a full description has to deal with these constructions in all their semantic and grammatical specificity. I have tried to illustrate, for one specific case, what such an account might look like. In particular, I have tried to indicate how the various factors involved – the meanings of component elements, their conceptual integration, and relations to other constructions – interact with one another. Describing these factors and their interaction, in a reasonable amount of explicit detail, is a key to both synchronic and diachronic analysis.

Chapter 4
Possession, location, and existence

Possessive constructions raise numerous issues of semantic and grammatical description. Among the questions to be addressed here are the following: (i) What is the semantic value of possessive elements and possessive constructions? (ii) How does nominal possession serve a grounding function? (iii) What is the relationship between nominal and clausal possession? (iv) What is the relationship between the different kinds of clausal possessive constructions? (v) How do clausal possessive predicates grammaticize from their lexical sources? (vi) What is the relationship among possession, location, and existence?

1. What is "possession"?

Semantically, the traditional label **possessive** is anything but self-explanatory. The term itself does not adequately define or delimit the phenomenon, since possessive constructions apply to a much wider range of circumstances than does either the verb *possess* or the noun *possession* in their non-technical uses. A notion like 'ownership', even interpreted rather loosely, comes nowhere near exhausting the range of cases covered by a nominal possessive (*X's Y*) or a clausal possessive (*X has a Y*). This has led some analysts to propose that linguistic possession implies nothing more than the existence of some association or relationship between possessor and possessed. For instance: "… *A has B* expresses that there is some state relation between 'A' and 'B' and … leaves a more precise specification of this relation to the context" (Bendix 1966: 120).

As seen in (1)a, the variety of examples does suggest a description having this level of generality. However, the mere notion that there exists an association or relationship between possessor and possessed is not quite sufficient, as it fails to account for the asymmetry in possessive expressions. While there are exceptions (e.g. *the doctor's patient* vs. *the patient's doctor*), in general the possessor and possessed cannot be reversed, as observed in (1)b.

(1) a. *the doctor's wallet; Sam's cousin; my elbow; the supervisor's desk; your rook; the baby's pacifier; his complaints; Ellen's favorite singer; our train; her athletic ability; his mother's illness; the cat's fleas; their exasperation; the students' average age; Booth's assassination [of Lincoln]; Lincoln's assassination [by Booth]*

b. **the wallet's doctor; *the athletic ability's she; *the fleas' cat; *the average age's students; *the assassination's Lincoln*

My own proposal for a semantic characterization starts from a general claim of CG: that certain fundamental and universal grammatical notions – among them noun, verb, subject, object, and possessive – can be characterized semantically at both the **prototype** level and the **schema** level. The prototype is based on an experientially grounded **conceptual archetype**. The schematic characterization (claimed to be valid for all instances) invokes a basic **cognitive ability** which is **immanent** in the archetype (i.e. "lies within it"). First manifested in the archetype, this cognitive ability is later extended to other cases.

It seems fairly evident that ownership, kinship, and whole/part relationships are prototypical for possessive constructions, with ownership arguably being more central than the others (Taylor 1996). These are the kinds of notions that I identify as conceptual archetypes – fundamental aspects of everyday experience which are cognitively basic and apprehended as gestalts despite their analytical complexity. The term *possession* reflects the archetype of ownership. What about a schematic description? For this level I have proposed a characterization in terms of what I call the **reference point** ability (Chapter 2: § 3).

Diagrammed in Figure 4.1, the reference point ability is our capacity to invoke one conceived entity as a means of establishing mental contact with another, i.e. mentally accessing one entity **via** another. The conceptualizer (C) first directs attention to the entity serving as **reference point** (R). Attending to R evokes a set of associated entities, collectively called its **dominion** (D), one of which is the **target** (T). A reference point relationship is thus a matter of sequenced mental access, where directing attention to R makes it possible to then direct attention to T.

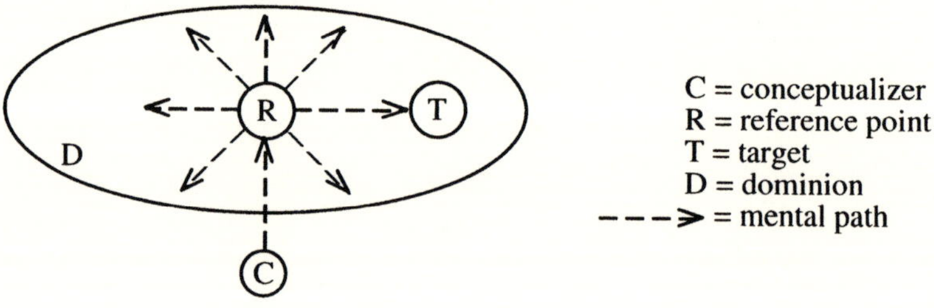

Figure 4.1

Since the reference point ability is independent of any particular conceptual content, it is sufficiently abstract and flexible to accommodate the full range of possessive expressions. At the same time, it is inherently asymmetrical, thus accounting for the typical irreversibility of possessive relationships. It therefore seems reasonable as a schematic characterization of possessives.

Reference point accounts have also been given of topic constructions, the subject and object relations, and pronominal anaphora (van Hoek 1995, 1997). Evidence for the reference point analysis is therefore provided by the many grammatical phenomena observable cross-linguistically in which the notions possessor, subject, topic, and pronominal antecedent display a special affinity to one another (Langacker 2001a; Kumashiro and Langacker 2003). To take just one example, I characterize trajector and landmark – expressed as grammatical subject and object – as reference points evoked by way of mentally accessing a profiled relationship. This directly accounts for the cross-linguistically prevalent use of possessive locutions to express the trajector and landmark of a nominalized verb (e.g. *Booth's assassination*, *Lincoln's assassination*). A nominalized verb profiles an abstract thing (produced by conceptual reification), so the relation which the trajector or landmark bears to it is then a reference point relationship between two things, which is just what possession is claimed to be.

Further supporting the reference point account is the fact that the possessive archetypes – ownership, kinship, and whole/part relations – are all clear examples of reference point organization. This is perfectly evident in the case of kinship expressions, for a person is not an *uncle*, a *sister*, or a *grandfather* intrinsically, but only in relation to a particular **reference individual**. In a phrase like *Sherridan's grandfather*, it is only with reference to Sherridan that the person designated qualifies as a grandfather. Likewise, a part is apprehended and characterized as such only in relation to the whole. A *mane*, for example, only qualifies as such by virtue of its place on a lion or a horse. Viewed in isolation from the lion, a *lion's mane* is just a mass of hair.

What about ownership? Typically a given person owns a considerable number of possessions, each of which he controls and can access when desired. Thus, mentally accessing a particular person affords a way of mentally accessing a substantial array of associated objects – those which this person controls. The opposite is not true; typically a given object is connected to just one person in this fashion. In terms of cognitive efficiency, therefore, it is easier to identify possessions in relation to their owner than conversely. People also have far greater cognitive salience to us than do typical possessions. We know and recognize far more people as individuals than we do wallets, beds, or bank accounts. We think of the world as being populated by people, each of whom has an assortment of possessions, rather than thinking of the world as being populated by wallets, beds, bank accounts, etc., each of which has a person attached. These factors point to a clear asymmetry in which owners are natural reference points, their possessions being targets.

It is important to understand how the possessive schema is immanent in the possessive archetypes. In prototypical instances of possession, the possessor (R) actively controls the possessed (T) in some manner – physically, socially, or experientially. The flip side of R controlling T is that R has an exclusive privilege of access to T. In the case of ownership (e.g. *my pen*), R manipulates T, determines where T is kept, and can use T whenever desired. This control also has social and experiential components. Others acknowledge these privileges. Moreover, R knows where T is and determines whether others can use it. Similarly, a kinship relation entails an array of culturally expected modes of social interaction. One interacts with a parent, a child, or a grandchild in a way that others are not allowed or expected to. This privileged social access is basically exclusive: there are few if any other people for whom *my sister* is a sister. Likewise, a part usually belongs to just one highest-level whole. I am the only one who can use *my stomach* for digestion. I also have the exclusive privilege of experiencing it (e.g. when it hurts) and controlling its location (when I move, it goes along with me).

This active control by R is part of the situation evoked and alluded to by possessive expressions. In my terminology, it is **onstage** and **objectively construed**, i.e. it functions as an **object** of conception. It is represented in Figure 4.2 by a solid arrow. With respect to this onstage relationship, the dominion (D) can be interpreted as the set of targets over which R exercises control, the region within R's purview. Also seen in Figure 4.2 are dashed arrows representing the path of mental access on the part of C, the conceptualizer (primarily the speaker). C's activity is not part of the situation described. Rather, it is **offstage** and **subjectively construed**, i.e. it inheres in the **subject** of conception – an aspect of the conceptualizing process that is not itself conceived. This subjectively construed relationship, whereby C invokes R as a reference point to mentally access T, is posited for all possessives, constituting their schematic characterization. By contrast, the objectively construed relationship of R controlling T is prototypical but does not extend to all instances.

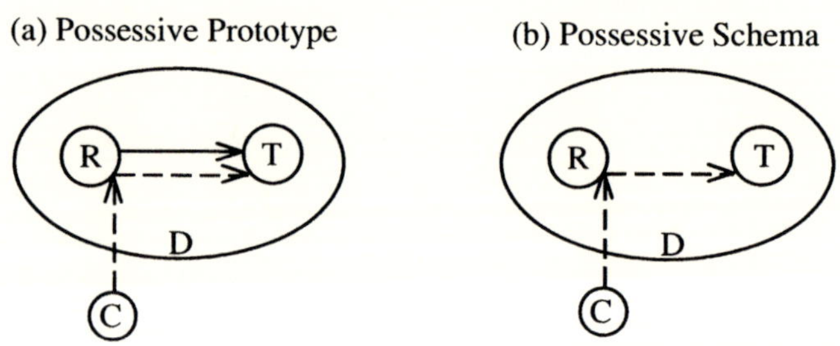

⟶ = access/control by R (physical, social, experiential)

- - - -> = mental access by C

Figure 4.2

The two paths of access – objective control by R, mental access by C – are closely related. R's objective relationship to T provides the basis for the subjective relationship of C using R to mentally access T. It is precisely by virtue of C apprehending R's control of T that C traces a mental path from R to T. Moreover, C's subjective mental path is immanent in (lies within) C's conception of the objective relationship: sequenced mental access – first conceptualizing R, then T – is an inherent aspect of conceptualizing R controlling T.

While prototypical, an objectively construed relationship of the possessor controlling the possessed becomes more tenuous with more peripheral exemplars and is often absent altogether. In cases like (2), it is hard to discern any real sense in which R objectively controls or has privileged access to T. Here the possessor's role in the onstage situation is essentially a passive one. R does however function as a reference point, providing a mental point of access invoked by the conceptualizer to identify a particular target.[1] This is the schematic import of possessives, inherent in all instances.

(2) *his age; the dog's enormous size; the applicant's nationality; the table's rough surface; my critics; the door's hinges; their situation; Kennedy's assassination; our very existence; the car's present location; her complexion; the year's most tragic event; the moon's average surface temperature*

The relation between the possessive prototype and the possessive schema qualifies as an instance of **subjectification**, in my sense of the term (Langacker 1990b, 1998b, 1999e) as opposed to Traugott's (e.g. 1989). As I define it, subjectification occurs when an objectively construed relationship fades away, leaving behind a subjectively construed relationship that was immanent in it (inherent in its conception). We can see this process as either a developmental change, assuming that a child masters prototypical possessives earlier than examples like (2), or else a diachronic one pertaining to the grammaticization of possessive elements and constructions. Of course, the prototype does not disappear as the more schematic value emerges. Both are necessary in a full description of possessive phenomena.

2. Possessive grounding

Nominal possessives, as in ***Sally's*** *friend* or ***my*** *new car*, generally function as determiners. In CG terminology, they are **grounding** elements, analogous to

1 In the final example, for instance, one knows that the average surface temperature in question is that of the moon, not the sun.

articles and demonstratives. Grounding is a grammaticized means of specifying the epistemic status of a thing or process with respect to the **ground**, i.e. the speech event and its participants. Characteristic of a full nominal (i.e. noun phrase) or a finite clause, grounding is the means by which the speaker and hearer coordinate their mental reference to things and events in a discourse (Langacker 1991, 2002a, 2004c; Brisard (ed.) 2002).

In the CG analysis, a lexical noun or verb merely specifies a **type** of thing or process. A nominal or a finite clause designates a **grounded instance** of a thing or process type. Let me briefly discuss these notions, focusing just on nominal expressions. The difference between a type and an instance, I suggest, is that an instance is specifically thought of as occupying a particular **location**, in contrast to other instances. In the case of things, it is most commonly space that functions as the **domain of instantiation** (Langacker 1991: § 2.2). In the case of processes, it is always time.

If (at a given moment) two things of the same type occupy exactly the same location, they are (in our naive conception) the same instance. If they are different instances, they occupy different locations. A type conception represents the abstracted commonality of its instances. It is schematic relative to its instances, and in particular abstracts away from the notion of being anchored to a particular location. The type conception is immanent in the various instance conceptions, which elaborate it at least by invoking this anchoring. These notions are depicted on the left in Figure 4.3, for a type 't', where dots represent distinguishing locations in the domain of instantiation (solid rectangle). On the right I give abbreviatory notations for instance conceptions.

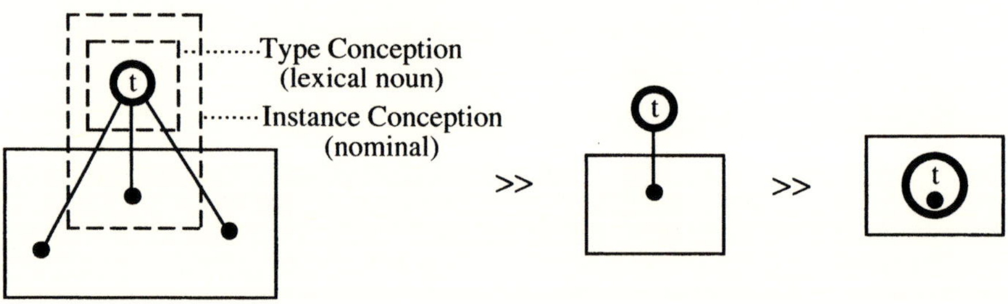

Figure 4.3

In saying that instances of a type are distinguished by their locations, it is not implied that the speaker or hearer actually knows what specific location an instance has at a given moment. The conception of a thing being anchored to a certain location is independent of the ability to **identify** the instance location in any objective way. In the absence of any specific identifying information, conceiving of an instance is a matter of declaring the existence of some such location, and perhaps of choosing a location arbitrarily in a spatialized representation invoked to conceptualize the situation being described in a discourse. An analogy can be drawn to the means of establishing discourse referents in American Sign Language, by pointing to arbitrary locations in sign space. I am positing an abstract conceptual analog of this pointing gesture as the basis for instance conceptions and nominal reference in spoken language.

Grounding can be thought of as either presupposing coordinated mental reference (as with a definite article) or else establishing it (e.g. with a demonstrative). In either case the result is that the speaker and hearer direct their attention to the same instance of the type in question. In Figure 4.4 coordinated mental reference is represented by the arrows leading from S and H to the profiled thing. Observe that grounding is sometimes effected by actual pointing (e.g. *this* [→] *one*). On the right is an abbreviatory notation for grounding.

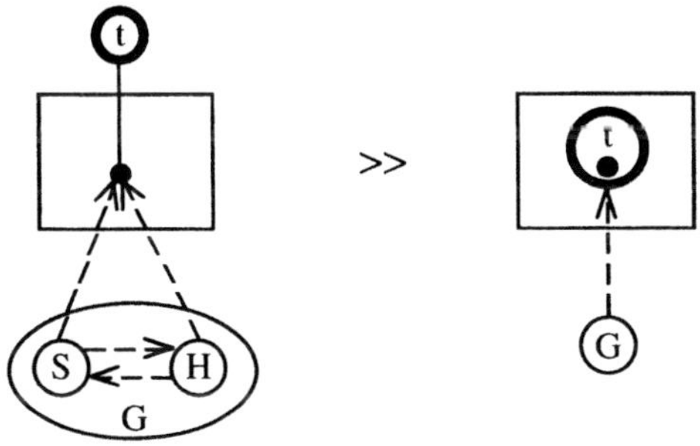

Figure 4.4

How, then, do possessives effect nominal grounding? To a significant extent our "cognitive map" of the entities that populate our world has the kind of organization abstractly represented in Figure 4.5. For a given type (t) there are many instances (t_i, t_j, t_k, etc.), which we generally do not know as individuals. There are as well certain kinds of entities – notably people – many of which we do know as individuals, so that we can identify them and refer to them in their own terms (e.g. with proper names). These can serve as **reference individuals** (R). They allow us to distinguish and identify other, less salient entities in relation to them. A particular reference individual controls a substantial number of other entities, having an exclusive privilege of access to them. On this basis we can partition our mental world into sets of entities each controlled by a single reference individual. This partitioning in turn provides a way of distinguishing and identifying instances of other types. A specific instance can be singled out and characterized as the one controlled by a particular reference individual.

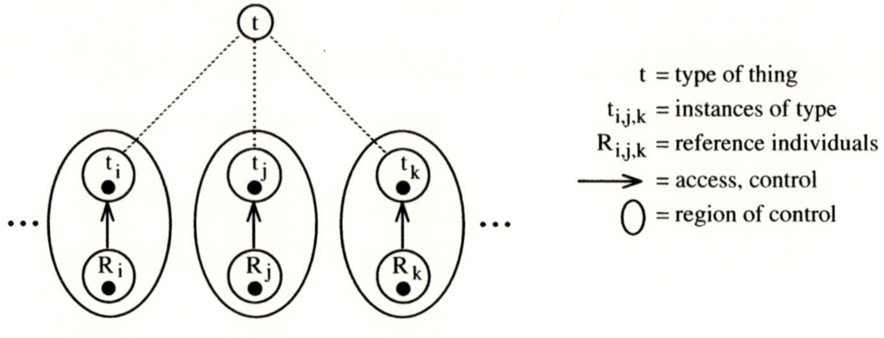

Figure 4.5

Thus, provided that the speaker and hearer direct their attention to the same reference individual, they can use it as a way to focus their joint attention on the same instance of some type, as shown in Figure 4.6.

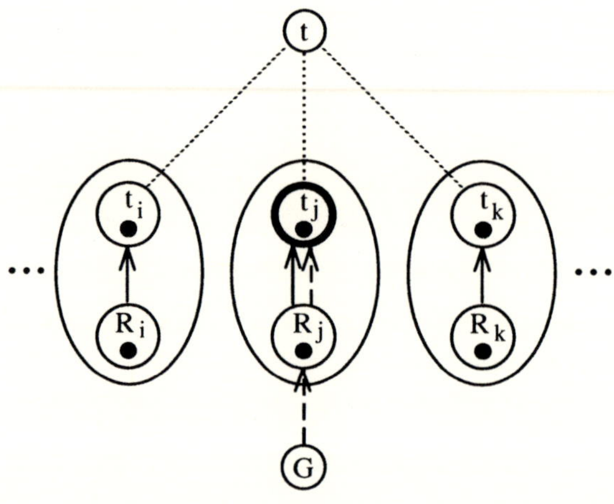

Figure 4.6

Once again, the grounded instance need not be objectively identifiable in any independent fashion – it is sufficient that it be singled out for discourse purposes. If you tell me that *Arthur's nephew* is getting married, I may have no way of knowing objectively who the nephew is; I could not recognize him on the street or in a police lineup. But for discourse purposes the nephew has been identified: it is the nephew located in Arthur's dominion (thus mentally accessible via the conception of Arthur).

3. Nominal and clausal possession

What is the relationship between a nominal possessive, such as *Jerry's house*, and a clausal possessive, e.g. *Jerry has a house*? The former profiles a thing, namely the entity possessed. The possessive relationship grounds the nominal by singling out a particular instance of the specified type (*house*). On the other hand, a possessive clause profiles the possessive relationship (*have*), i.e. it predicates possession rather than presupposing it. Here there are two basic alternatives, distinguished by whether the possessor functions as grammatical subject, or whether the entity possessed does. In CG terms, it is a matter of whether **primary focal prominence** – trajector status – is conferred on the reference point or on the target. These options are represented in Figure 4.7. For the time being we will concentrate on nominal possession and then on HAVE-type possessives, where R is chosen as subject.

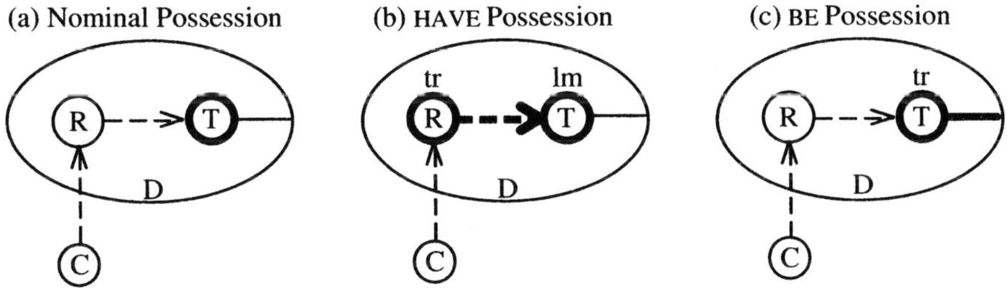

Figure 4.7

In these diagrams, I have added a solid line representing the relationship of T being located in D. This is not really distinct from the reference point relationship, just a particular facet of it. T being located in R's dominion, and T being accessible via R, can be thought of as two sides of the same coin (a matter of perspective). The essential point is that clausal possessives profile the possessive relationship rather than the entity possessed (T). The two kinds of possessive clauses differ as to which facet of the overall relationship they single out for profiling – that of R controlling T (minimally in the passive sense of providing mental access to T), or that of T being located in the region R controls (whether actively or passively).

There are two basic ways of indicating nominal possession. In many languages, it is marked by an explicit morphological element, such as English *'s*. Ignoring constituency (to keep the diagram simple), the English construction is represented in Figure 4.8. The possessive morpheme *'s* evokes a reference point relationship, where R and T are only schematic, and profiles T. In the construction, the profiles of the possessor nominal and the possessed noun correspond (dotted lines) to R and T, respectively.[2] At the composite structure level, therefore, the possessor is identified as Jerry, and the possessed as a house in Jerry's dominion. Although the noun *house* merely specifies a type, not an instance, the composite expression *Jerry's house* singles out a particular instance of this type precisely because of its location in this dominion. It is a grounded instance because a mental path is specified from G, through R (Jerry), to the house.

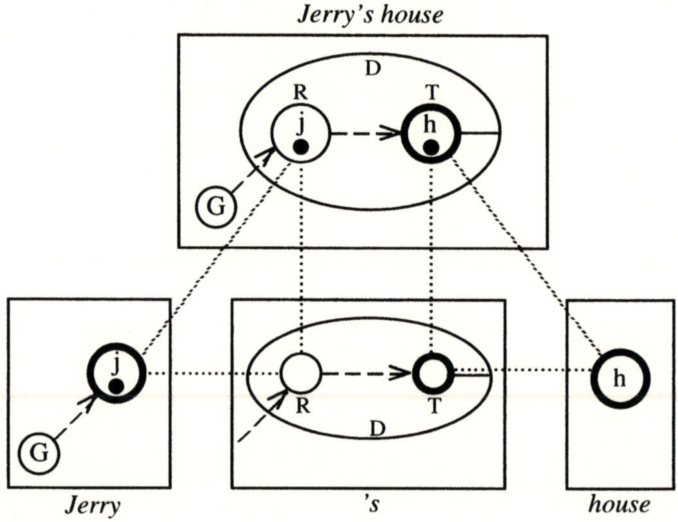

Figure 4.8

Many languages employ an alternative construction in which there is no overt possessive marker. Instead of *Jerry's house*, one would simply say the equivalent of *Jerry house*, indicating possession by means of simple juxtaposition of the possessor nominal and the possessed noun. An example from Tohono O'odham is given in (3).[3]

(3) *g huan kii* (ART Juan house) 'Juan's house' [Tohono O'odham]

This type of nominal possessive construction is diagrammed in Figure 4.9(a). The reference point relationship is not specifically contributed by either component element, but is rather a function of constructional meaning, emerging at

2 As a proper name, *Jerry* is internally grounded, representing what is presupposed to be the sole relevant instance of its type.

3 Tohono O'odham, Hopi, and Luiseño are Native American languages of the Uto-Aztecan family.

the composite structure level. The composite semantic structure is nonetheless the same as in Figure 4.8.

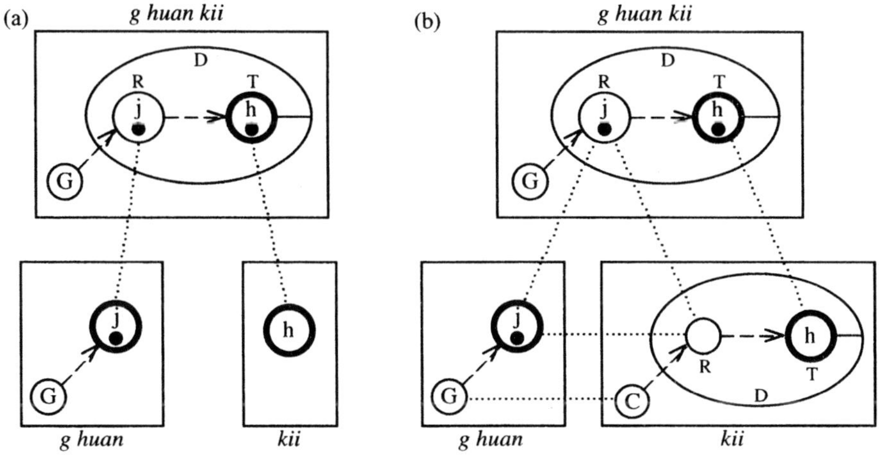

Figure 4.9

If we probe a little deeper into the lexical semantics of *kii* or *house*, we do find a reference point relationship corresponding to the one signaled by the overall construction. Central to the meaning of *house* is that a house has an owner (also an occupant, typically the same). When the diagram is elaborated to include this specification, it thus provides a correspondent for the nominal profile and introduces the reference point relationship evoked at the composite structure level, as shown in Figure 4.9(b). Of course, we could similarly elaborate the representation of *house* in Figure 4.8. In that case the reference point relationships invoked by *'s* and by *house* are put in correspondence to one another and merge in a single composite structure relationship.

4. HAVE possessives

Turning now to clausal possession with a HAVE-type predicate, I will first observe that many languages code the possessed with a simple noun rather than a full nominal. These are typical cases of noun incorporation, as in Hopi:

(4) *Pam kii-'yta.* (he house-have) 'He has a house.' [Hopi]

In this Hopi construction, *kii* 'house' combines morphologically with a schematic possessive verb to form a derived (and intransitive) verb stem. Since the object noun is ungrounded, the sentence does not actually refer to any specific house – it introduces the notion of a house only as a type specification. From the sentence we can however **infer** the existence of a house in the subject's dominion. This comes about through clausal grounding, in the absence of any indication that the profiled clausal relationship is anything other than real or actual.

The Hopi construction is sketched in Figure 4.10. The subject pronoun *pam* is internally grounded, the referent specified as being third person singular (3s). By contrast, *kii* 'house' simply makes a type specification; it does not itself single out an instance of the type. The verbal ending *-'yta* profiles a schematic reference point relationship. I have shown it as being grounded, though the grounding element is zero, corresponding to the unmarked case of a situation observed in current reality. A dot indicates that the profiled process is a particular instance of the process type ('have'), anchored in time (and thus distinct from other instances). This is the clausal analog of nominal grounding.

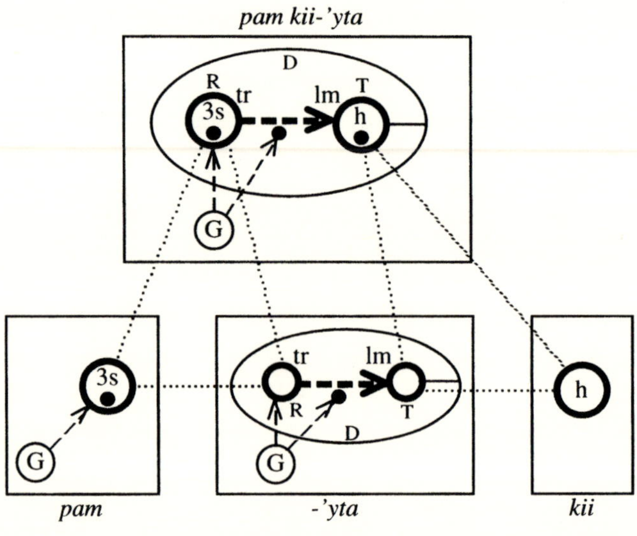

Figure 4.10

The pronoun *pam* is the subject because it specifies the trajector of the profiled relationship. *Kii* 'house' is the object in the sense that it specifies the landmark, but it is not a direct object, as the term is usually understood, for it is not a full, independent nominal distinct from the verb. Instead, it combines morphologically with the verbal ending to form a complex, grammatically intransitive stem with the approximate meaning 'have house', invoking the notion 'house' only as a type. However, if an actual person actually does participate in an instance of house-having, it follows as an inference that some actual house is involved. At the composite structure level, therefore, the landmark is represented (with a dot) as an instance of 'house', although its instantiation comes about inferentially (through the interaction of other factors) rather than being explicitly coded per se.[4]

Compare this sentence to its English translation, *He has a house.* In English the landmark is expressed by a full, independent nominal, which we can accept as being the clausal direct object (although *have* is quite low in transitivity). Being a full nominal, *a house* profiles a single grounded instance of the type *house.* This is shown in Figure 4.11, which is comparable to Figure 4.10 except for the indication of instantiation and grounding.

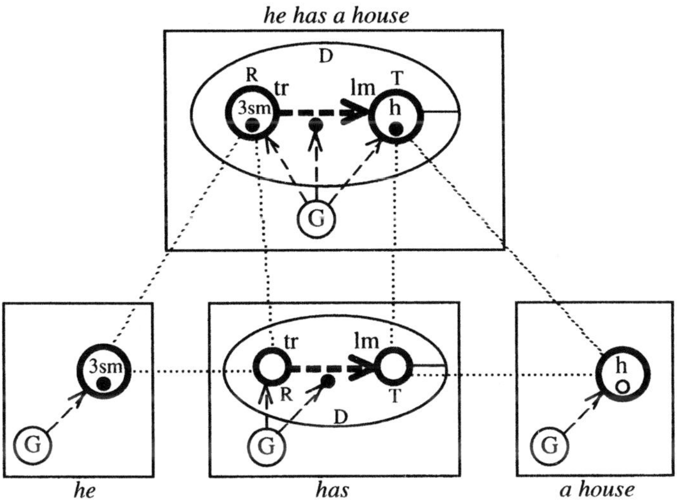

Figure 4.11

Observe, however, that for the nominal *a house* in Figure 4.11 I have used an empty dot instead of a filled dot. This reflects a subtle distinction that proves quite important for understanding clausal possession (and much else besides). The distinction I am making with a filled dot vs. an empty dot is the difference between an **actual** and a **virtual** instance of some type (Langacker 1999d). In surprisingly many cases, the entities we directly refer to linguistically are virtual (or fictive) in nature, even when we are talking about actual real-world situations. A virtual (or fictive) instance of a type is one that is "conjured up" (i.e. imagined) for some purpose, having no status outside the mental space constructed for that

4 It is not an important issue in CG whether this specification is considered semantic or pragmatic, for it is claimed that any strict line of demarcation is arbitrary.

purpose. In (5), for example, the nominal expressions shown in bold all designate virtual entities rather than actual individuals. The evocation of virtual entities is a constant, ubiquitous, and utterly normal aspect of linguistic expression.[5]

(5) a. *Evelyn hopes to invent* ***a perpetual motion machine.***
b. *Whenever we have* ***a party, a guest*** *breaks* ***a glass.***
c. *We don't have* ***a dog.***
d. *If you buy* ***a diamond ring,*** *you should insure* ***it.***
e. ***A kitten*** *is born with* ***blue eyes.***

The actual/virtual distinction pertains to the kind of mental space occupied by a nominal referent; it is not equivalent to the definite/indefinite opposition. The specific/non-specific contrast for indefinites, illustrated in (6), shows that an indefinite nominal can designate either an actual or a virtual instance of some type. In either case, it does establish a discourse referent that can be referred to anaphorically by a definite pronoun under the proper circumstances (Langacker 1996). As shown by Fauconnier (1985), a specific (i.e. actual) referent is construed as existing in actuality, not just in the mental space representing the subject's desire, whereas a non-specific (i.e. virtual) referent is construed as existing only in the desire space, not as corresponding to any actual individual. It is "conjured up" just to characterize that desire. Nonetheless, an instance of the type is established as a discourse referent.

(6) a. *He wants to marry* ***a Norwegian. She*** *is tall and blonde.* [specific/actual]
b. *He wants to marry* ***a Norwegian. She*** *has to be tall and blonde.* [non-specific/virtual]

Conversely, a definite nominal can designate a virtual entity. One example is a **role description**, as in (7). The referents of the highlighted nominals are not actual individuals, but virtual instances of their types (*engine, winner, president*) identified by their role within a **scenario** or **idealized cognitive model**. The role may come to be instantiated by an actual individual, or by different individuals at different times, but the role per se is just an imagined instance of the type, existing only in the mental space representing the scenario or model.

(7) a. *The most important consideration in buying a car is* ***the engine.***
b. ***The winner*** *will receive a very nice trophy.*

---

5 The term **non-referential** is sometimes used for virtual entities. The term is ill-advised, however, since virtual entities are readily established as discourse referents, referred to anaphorically by definite pronouns, e.g. *it* in (5)d.

c. *In this corporation,* ***the president*** *keeps getting younger.*

Let us now return to Figure 4.11, depicting the sentence *He has a house.* The unfilled dot indicates that the house referred to by the object nominal is a virtual instance of *house* rather than an actual one. This obviously requires clarification, since the sentence clearly does imply that a particular house – an actual instance of the type – is possessed. Indeed, the composite structure in Figure 4.11 does represent the house in question as an actual instance (with a filled dot). My suggestion, then, is that its actuality is inferred from other elements, not a property of the indefinite nominal per se. The inference is in some respects similar to the one in the Hopi example, though not quite the same, since in English the landmark is specified by a full nominal rather than a simple noun. Thus Hopi starts with just a type specification, and English with a grounded (albeit virtual) instance of that type. Despite the different starting points, the inference of an actual instance arises in much the same way.

What is the import of saying that the house referred to by the object nominal in Figure 4.11 is a virtual instance of the type? The motivation for this characterization is a general, though still very preliminary, claim concerning indefinite nominals. The claim is that indefinite nominals have a kind of **intrinsic virtuality** not shared by definites.[6] At the current stage in the discourse, a definite nominal – like *this shirt, the sofa, Bill Clinton,* or *my cat* – is generally taken as being sufficient to single out the intended referent **independently** of the clause containing it. Thus in (8)a the listener can supposedly identify the shirt from the object nominal alone, its participation in the clausal process providing supplementary information about it. For this reason a definite nominal can function as a topic, as in (8)b, an independently accessible conceptual reference point with respect to which the comment clause will then be interpreted.

(8) a. *I just bought* ***this shirt.***
b. ***This shirt,*** *I just bought it.*
c. *I just bought* ***a shirt.***
d. *****A shirt,*** *I just bought it.*

In and of itself, on the other hand, an indefinite nominal – e.g. *a shirt, some cat, any doctor* – merely directs the listener to conjure up (imagine) an instance of the type, **pending** the information provided by the clause that contains it. From (8)c the listener does indeed identify the intended discourse referent, but it is not independently known – the listener only identifies it after the fact, and only as the shirt the speaker just bought. Prior to its interpretation with respect

6 A similar idea has been proposed by Verhagen (1986: § 4.2).

to the content of the clause containing it, the shirt in question (at least from the hearer's standpoint) has no independently established referent. For this reason an indefinite is not felicitous as a topic, as seen in (8)d.

Intrinsically, then, an indefinite has a kind of **provisional** virtuality, if only for the listener.[7] A sentence like (8)c may however provide the information needed to overcome this provisional virtual status and establish the profiled instance as an actual one. Since the shirt participates in the buying, which itself is portrayed as actual, the shirt itself is inferred as being actual. The actuality of the indefinite nominal's referent is **derivative** of the actuality of the event profiled by the clause. Of course, the clausal process may itself be virtual, in which case the nominal referent remains virtual as well. The shirt in (9)a, for instance, is only a virtual one conjured up just to specify what did not happen (it makes no sense to ask *Which shirt is it that you didn't buy?*). By contrast, the independently established referent of the definite object in (9)b is interpreted as being actual despite the clausal negation.

(9) a. *I didn't buy* ***a shirt.***
    b. *I didn't buy* ***this shirt.***

The import of Figure 4.11 should now be clear. In *He has a house*, the house referred to has the kind of provisional virtuality just described, so far as the indefinite nominal itself is concerned. It is only its participation in the clausal relationship that identifies it and establishes its actuality. Since the having is portrayed as actual, the entity possessed must also represent an actual instance of its type, identified for discourse purposes simply as the one which *he has.*

These considerations make it possible to understand what is going on in an otherwise puzzling construction in Luiseño. Sentence (10) predicates possession of a basket. Observe, however, that the direct object incorporates a possessor prefix which expresses precisely the same possessive relationship that the clause asserts. How can that be? How can a nominal possessive be invoked to predicate the same possessive relationship that it itself presupposes?

(10) *Chaam=cha=po* *cham-tukmay-i 'ay-ma-an.* 'We will have a basket.'
     we=we=FUT our-basket-OBJ have-DUR-FUT [Luiseño]

My proposal is that the object nominal *cham-tukmay* 'our basket' is interpreted as a **role description**, analogous to the definites in (7). It is not construed as designating an actual basket, but only a virtual one, the one we might be expected to have given standard cultural models concerning people and their possessions.

7 Indeed, many indefinites – those grounded by *most*, *all*, *every*, *any*, *each*, and *no* – always designate virtual entities.

The possessive clause then establishes the basket as being actual, or as having whatever epistemic status is implied by the clausal content. In (10), since the profiled relation of having is projected as being actual in the future, the same will hold for the basket. The examples in (11) show that a nominal possessive – though it is definite and thus identifies its referent – does not preclude that its referent might be virtual rather than actual. As in (10), the nominal possessives are construed as role descriptions. The ears and the social skills referred to are those expected to exist given the idealized cognitive model of a kitten or a person. While actuality represents the default, the content of these sentences makes it clear that the nominal referents are only virtual, i.e. not manifested in actuality as expected.

(11) a. *The kitten was born deformed –* ***its ears*** *are missing.*
b. ***His social skills*** *are non-existent.*

In the case of (10) the basket is projected as being actual in the future. Essential elements of this sentence are diagrammed in Figure 4.12. Construed as a role description, the object nominal *cham-tukmay* 'our basket' profiles a virtual instance of 'basket' identified as the one expected to occur in the possessor's dominion. The clause profiles a possessive relationship and projects it as being actual in the future (tense is not indicated). Through the regular direct object construction, the verb's landmark corresponds to the nominal profile. Moreover, the possessive relationship invoked by the nominal is identified as (and thus collapses with) the one profiled by the verb – their reference points, targets, and dominions all correspond. In the composite expression, the basket in question is thus attributed the epistemic status implied by that of the clause in which it participates.

chaam(=cha=po) cham-tukmay(-i) 'ay(-ma-an)

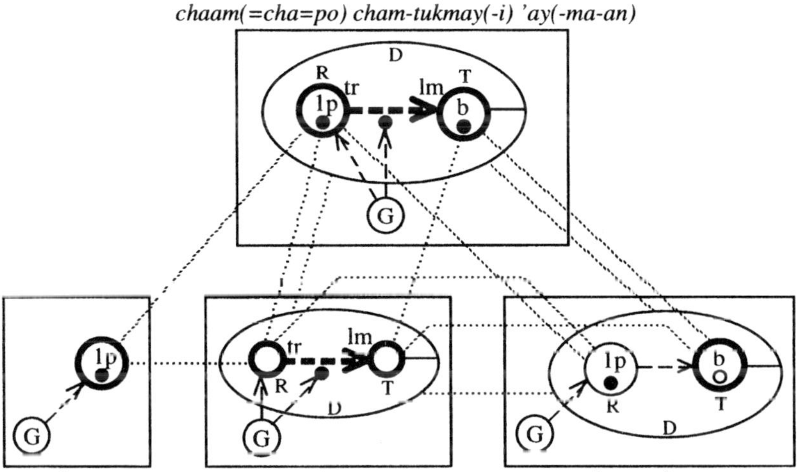

chaam *'ay* *cham-tukmay*

Figure 4.12

5. BE possessives

We have so far considered only HAVE-type possessive clauses. However, many languages express possession by means of clauses that are basically locative or existential in nature, often incorporating a predicate that can be roughly glossed as 'be' or 'exist'. In BE possessive constructions the target functions as clausal subject, the reference point being expressed in a locative phrase, as in (12)a, or as an indirect object, as in (12)b.

(12) a. *U menja kniga.* (at me [is] book) 'I have a book.' [Russian]
b. *Est Johanni liber.* 'John has a book.' [Latin]

Not only are locative/existential constructions commonly used for possession, but the converse also occurs, as in Mandarin:

(13) a. *Wǒ yǒu shū.* (I have book) 'I have a book.' [Mandarin]
b. *Zhūo-shàng yǒu shū.* 'The table has a book [on it].'/'There is a book on the table.'

The cross-linguistic prevalence of these associations has led some linguists to embrace the **localist hypothesis**, in which locative expressions are seen as basic, the source from which all the others derive. Lyons (1967: 390), who cited the data in (12)–(13), formulated the hypothesis as follows: "...In many, and perhaps in all, languages existential and possessive constructions derive (both synchronically and diachronically) from locatives." Similar proposals were made by Anderson (1971: ch. 7) in the context of his localist theory of case, and by Freeze (1992) from a generative perspective.

I will return to the localist hypothesis in the final section. The immediate task is to characterize BE possessive constructions. And in order to do that, we first need a characterization of locative and existential expressions.

Notions of location and existence are always relative to some **domain**, the default being space (and in particular, physical space in the "real world"). Though it is probably not sufficient, one way to think about their relationship is to treat an existential predication as a generalized, maximally schematic locative specification. Taking space as the domain, if I say that a unicorn is *here*, *there*, or *in the garden*, I restrict its location to a delimited spatial region, implying that if you search in that region you will find it. If I say instead that a unicorn *exists*, you will not know where to look for it. The existential predication implies that it can in principle be found, that if you were able to look everywhere you would find it somewhere, but does not itself do anything to narrow down the region of search. It is maximally schematic ("coarse-grained") in regard to the unicorn's location within the domain of existence. This way of viewing the distinction between location and existence is sketched in Figure 4.13.

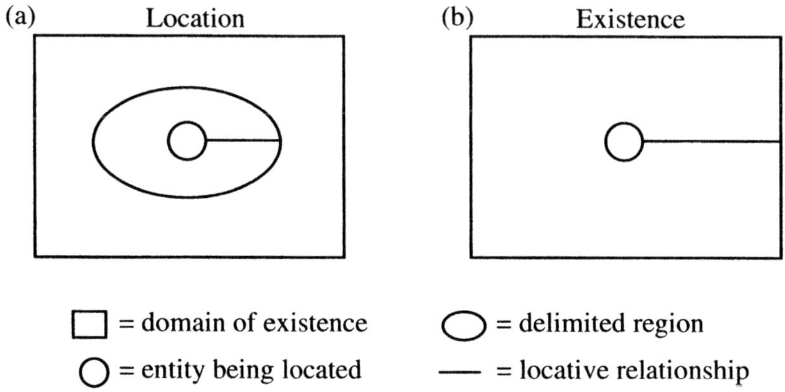

Figure 4.13

Typically a locative expression identifies the delimited region where an entity can be found by invoking a reference object. The reference object functions as a **spatial landmark**, with respect to which it specifies a **domain of search** (Hawkins 1984; Langacker 1993b, 2002b). For instance, the prepositions *above*, *beside*, and *in* have the organization shown in Figure 4.14. In each case the target of search (T) occupies a search domain (D) defined in relation to the reference object (R), *in* being the special case where the search domain and reference object are basically coextensive. The relationship profiled by a preposition or postposition is that of T occupying a location accessible via R. T is thus the trajector, and R the landmark. Diagram (d) is a schematic representation of locatives. It should not be read as implying that R is always inside D, but merely that R is invoked as a point of reference to "anchor" the domain of search.

In terms of its form, the Japanese construction in (14) is fairly typical of BE possessives. The verb *iru* predicates animate existence. The ending *-ni* has a variety of specific interpretations, often being glossed as 'to' or 'at'. It also marks indirect objects.

(14)	*Watashi-ni-wa*	*mago-ga*	*iru.* 'I have a grandchild.' [Japanese]
	I-to-TOP	grandchild-SUBJ	exist

Relevant aspects of this construction are diagrammed in Figure 4.15. The two primary constituents are the postpositional phrase *watashi-ni* 'to me' and *mago(-ga) iru* '(a) grandchild exists'. Each is constructed in the normal fashion:

watashi 'I' elaborates the landmark of *-ni* 'to' in a postpositional object construction; and *mago* elaborates the trajector of *iru* in the regular subject construction to form a minimal finite clause. As in previous examples, the actuality of the clausal subject is derivative of the profiled process ('exist') being actual.

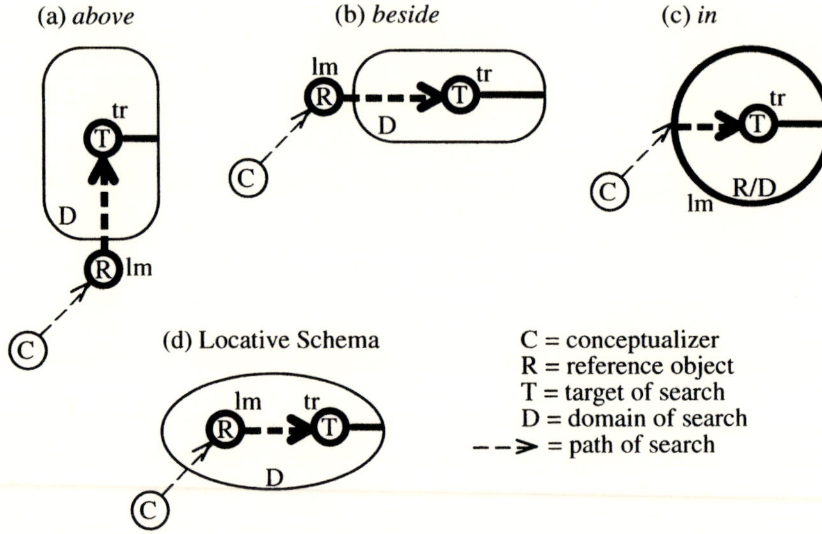

Figure 4.14

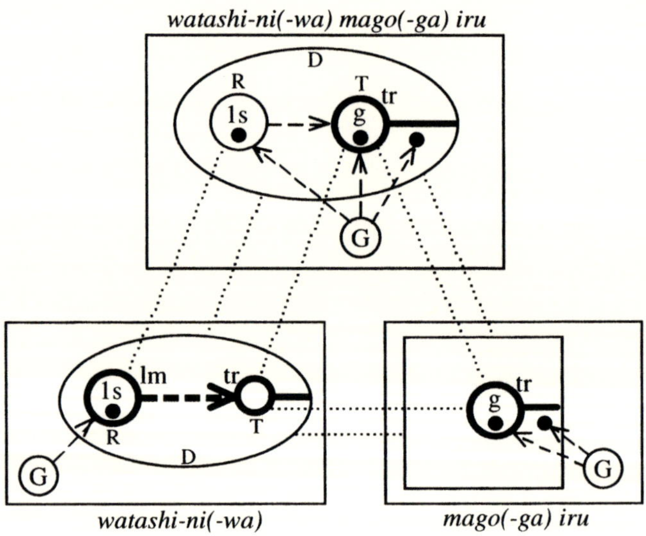

Figure 4.15

At the level of organization shown in the diagram, these two constituents are integrated to form the full sentence. Two correspondences are involved. First, their trajectors correspond: the thing which exists is equated with the entity located with respect to the speaker. Second, the domain of existence is identified with the domain of search in which the target can be found. In other words, the construction serves to localize the domain of existence, so the subject is said to exist specifically in the region anchored by the postpositional object (in this case the speaker). This region is not necessarily or even primarily a spatial one. As noted, *-ni* is the Japanese indirect object marker, and indirect object relationships are generally interpreted as being experiential in nature. Hence the central import of (14) is that a grandchild exists in the speaker's domain of experience. This amounts to possession, which also centers on experiential access.

The composite structure in Figure 4.15 instantiates the configuration for BE possession given earlier in Figure 4.7(c). There are various ways of structually implementing this general strategy of clausal possession. While Japanese *iru* is primarily existential, the corresponding predicates in Latin and Russian would generally be considered "copular", with a more general meaning and a wider range of uses.[8] I would be inclined to analyze such predicates as merely extending through time the relationship profiled by their complement, giving it the temporal extension necessary to function as a clausal head (cf. Langacker 1982, 1999e). The clausal construction is then quite comparable to Figure 4.15 except that the relationship profiled by BE is fully assimilated to the one profiled by the complement (hence the profiling and trajector/ landmark organization of the complement carry over to the composite structure level).

A more fundamentally different way of implementing the BE possessive strategy is found in Luiseño. As seen in (15), the possessor is not introduced through a locative complement to BE, but through a possessor prefix on the subject nominal. This construction resembles (10) in that a nominal possessive is invoked as part of a clausal construction serving to predicate precisely the same possessive relationship. Once again, the possessive nominal is evidently construed as a role description; internally to the subject nominal itself, the target is only a virtual instance of the type *peetum* 'younger brothers' or *qeesum* 'younger sisters', its status vis-à-vis actuality being determined by the clause containing it. Through lexical choices, the language makes it possible to indicate either the existence of this virtual entity (hence its actuality) or its non-existence.

---

8 Concomitant with this generalized semantic value is the omission of the Russian copula in the present tense.

(15) a. *Po-peet-um* *qal-wun.* 'He has younger brothers.'
his-younger:brother-PL be-PRES:PL [Luiseño]
b. *Po-qees-um=pum* *'oma-an.* 'He has no older sisters.'
his-older:sister-PL=they not:be-PRES:PL

Sentence (15)a is sketched in Figure 4.16, which should now be self-explanatory. Grammatically it is a normal subject construction, where the nominal profile corresponds to the verb's trajector. This existential clause has possessive function because the subject nominal incorporates a possessive relationship. As in Figure 4.15, the domain of existence is identified with the possessive dominion, so the existence is localized to this region. Thus, depending on whether the existence is portrayed as actual (by *qal* 'be') or non-actual (by *'oma* 'not be'), the entity possessed is specified – derivatively – as being actual or only virtual.

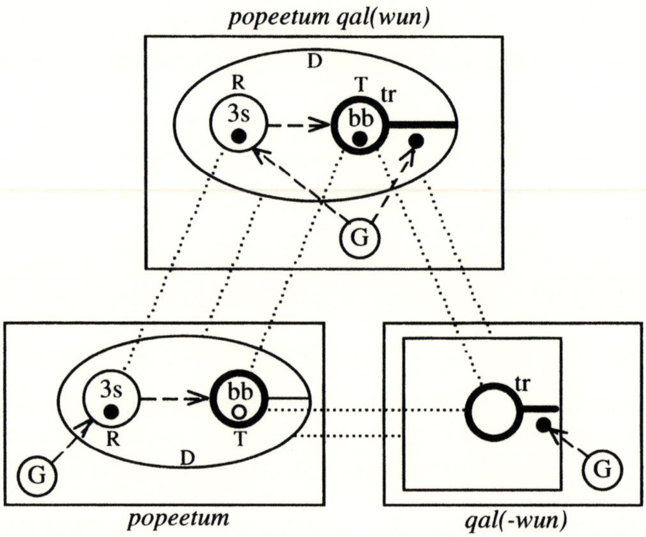

Figure 4.16

6. Diachronic perspective

The data and analysis I have presented corroborate the intimate connection, noted by Lyons and many others, between possessive and locative/existential expressions. Nevertheless, I believe that any strong formulation of the localist hypothesis (like the one quoted from Lyons) is empirically and theoretically untenable. It is theoretically untenable to the extent that it posits derivations from underlying structures in a synchronic description. Devices of this sort are proscribed in CG and increasingly disfavored in other theoretical traditions. Discussion of this general issue is beyond the scope of my presentation. Suffice it to say that, in a CG account, one is not permitted to treat a sentence like *He has a house* as the surface manifestation of an underlying structure like *At me is a house* or *To me a house exists*.

As a diachronic claim, the localist hypothesis conflicts with what has been learned about the historical origins of HAVE-type predicates. Verbs analogous to English *have* and Spanish *tener* (< Latin *tenēre* 'hold, keep, grasp') do not grammaticize from locatives, but from expressions designating physical occurrences in which the subject manipulates or otherwise acts on an object. The resulting constructions are "conceptually derived from a propositional structure that typically involves an agent, a patient, and some action or activity. In addition to 'take', a number of related action verbs can be employed, such as 'seize', 'grab', 'catch', and the like, but ... verbs like 'hold', 'carrry', 'get', 'find', 'obtain', 'acquire', or 'rule' can [also] be used" (Heine 1997: 91). While such verbs do imply that the subject controls (or comes to control) the object's location, the structures in question are basically agentive rather than locative.

For BE possessives a locative/existential source is however clearly indicated. The locative element in the source expression can have a range of original meanings, including 'at', 'from', 'to', and 'with' (Heine 1997: 5.2). As for the verbal element, I note that one possible source is a posture predicate: 'sit', 'stand', or 'lie'. For instance, the Luiseño stem *qal* in (15)a derives from the Proto Uto-Aztecan verb **katɨ* 'sit'.

If the affinity between possessive and locative/existential constructions does not reside in a common diachronic origin, nor in a common underlying structure, to what can we attribute it? The answer should already be apparent from the foregoing discussion and analyses: possessives and locatives share an abstract conceptual characterization based on the reference point ability. While they are grounded in different conceptual archetypes, reflected in their prototypical values, each archetype incorporates a reference point relationship – immanent within it – which may be all that remains as the constructions are extended to a wide range of non-prototypical uses. This abstract commonality is the link permitting locative constructions to be used for possession, and conversely.

With HAVE-type predicates, the basic evolutionary path starts with agentive verbs describing immediate physical control (e.g. 'hold', 'carry', 'get'). These represent specific actions. From there, the semantic change resulting in a prototypical possessive predicate involves **attenuation** in the degree of agentive control, with respect to several parameters (Langacker 1999e). First, a possessive predicate does not designate a specific action, but rather the potential to interact with the object when desired – saying that *I have an electric toothbrush* does not imply that I am using it right now, only that I have the privilege of doing so whenever I want. Possessive verbs are therefore imperfective (or stative) rather than perfective (active). Second, the possessor's control, when exercised, is not limited to physical interaction. It extends as well to abstract situations, with social and experiential factors being if anything more prevalent and important than physical ones, as seen in (16). Finally, there is attenuation in the extent to which the possessor is an active controller at all. In certain uses, like (16)e–f, the subject is only marginally an experiencer; it serves primarily as a spatial reference point indicating where the object can be found. At the extreme, e.g. (16)g, the possessor is completely passive, serving only a reference point function.

(16) a. *I have an electric toothbrush.*
b. *She has several dogs.*
c. *Jones has a very good job.*
d. *My brother has frequent headaches.*
e. *We have a lot of earthquakes in California.*
f. *Sherridan has brown eyes.*
g. *Their house has four bedrooms.*

The basic stages – source predicate, prototypical possessive, and generalized (schematic) possessive, are sketched in Figure 4.17. Observe that the relationship between diagrams (b) and (c) is essentially the same as the relationship, shown in Figure 4.2, between the possessive prototype and the possessive schema. The schematic characterization, where C traces a mental path via R to T, is immanent in the predicate and the construction at all stages. This subjectively construed path of mental access remains behind as all traces of active control by R fade from the picture.

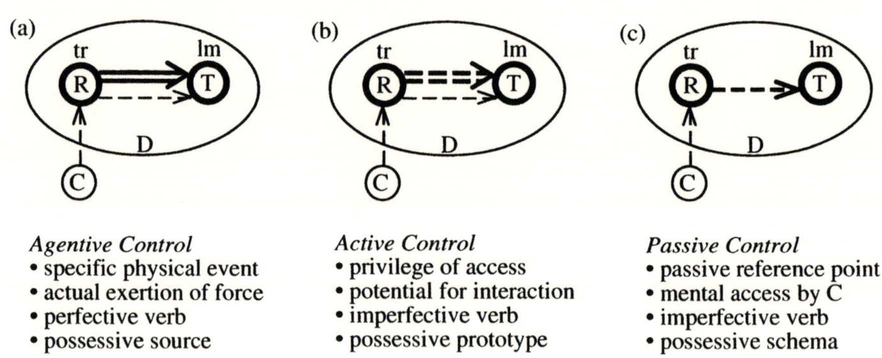

Figure 4.17

At the extreme, when all vestiges of active control have faded away, we are left with what amounts to a locative predication – R serves only as a reference point evoked by C in order to locate T. Spatially interpreted, R's dominion is then a locative domain of search. Of course, since the predicate was originally (and remains primarily) based on the notion of active control, R functions as trajector and T as landmark (in contrast to BE locatives, where T is the trajector). It can then be imagined that a language might adopt this sort of predicate as a basic means of expressing spatial location.

One such language is Mandarin, as exemplified in (13). The verb 'have' is regularly employed for locative/existential expressions with inanimate reference points, as in (13)b.[9] A relevant aspect of this construction is that the subject is construed as a **location** (rather than a **participant** – for the importance of this distinction, see Langacker 1993b; Shen 1996). The form *zhūo-shàng* consists of 'table' + 'top', so what the nominal actually profiles is the top (a location) rather than the object as a whole. When a location functions as reference point for a spatial search, it is a natural (if not an automatic) consequence that the functions of reference point and dominion (i.e. domain of search) collapse. The delimited region to which a location affords mental access, in order to find a target, is most readily identified as being that location itself.

Sentence (13)b is sketched in Figure 4.18. It is quite analogous to Figure 4.11, *He has a house*, except that R and D coincide. The location evoked as reference point is also the domain of search, where the target can be found.

We have already seen, in Figures 4.15 and 4.16, how BE-type predicates and locative/existential constructions can be appropriated for possessive use. The basic step is simply to equate the domain of existence with R's dominion. Of course, a full account must also consider semantic developments affecting the locative element and the locative/existential predicate. Here I can offer just a few comments of a programmatic nature.

How does a locative element, e.g. an adposition meaning 'at' or 'to', come to indicate a possessive relationship? Essentially this is the inverse of the development sketched in Figures 4.2 and 4.17, in which the notion of active control on the part of R attenuates to the point where R is left with only the passive role of spatial reference point. The inverse development, where a locative comes to be used for general possession, is a matter of R's passive role being strengthened. Instead of merely serving as a spatial reference point allowing C to mentally access T, R becomes an active controller with physical, social, and/or experien-

9 English does something comparable, e.g. *The table has a book on it*, but it is not the general locative pattern and has special semantic and grammatical properties, including the obligatory incorporation of a prepositional phrase.

tial access to T. The dominion is no longer interpreted in purely spatial terms – if anything, experiential factors predominate.

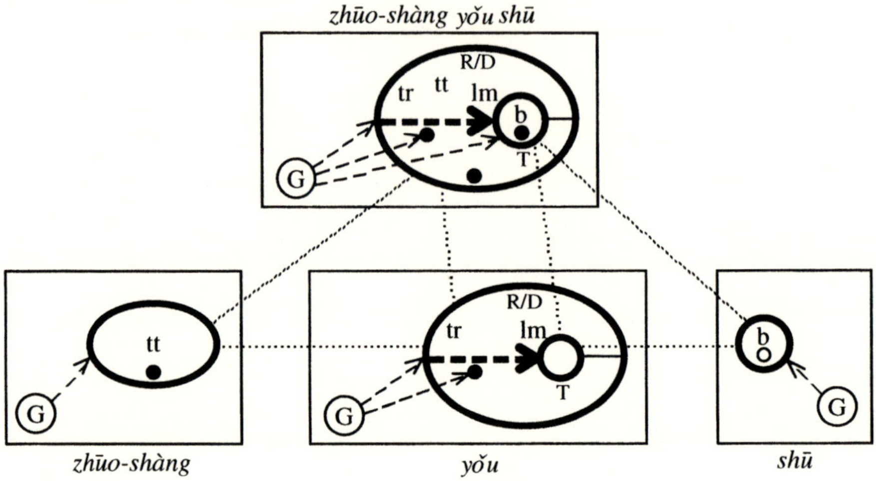

Figure 4.18

Does this inverse direction conflict with the idea that semantic developments in grammaticization tend to be unidirectional? Not really, since the attenuation of R's role pertains to the grammaticization of an agentive verb, while this strengthening of R's role pertains to the grammaticization of a spatial preposition. They represent different kinds of grammaticization, with distinct starting points and endpoints. Traugott (1988) has suggested that the initial stage of grammaticization involves strengthening, or semantic enrichment, even if weakening or attenuation predominates in later stages. Accordingly, the strengthening of R's role is not unexpected as part of a spatial preposition being extended to possessive use. We can interpret this as an instance of either metaphor or metonymy (the two are not inconsistent). In terms of the former, location in a spatial region anchored by a landmark constitutes the source domain, projected metaphorically onto the target domain of something being within a possessor's sphere of control. The metonymic interpretation hinges on the correlation between spatial proximity and the possibility of access or control: it is generally by virtue of something being close to us spatially that we are able to use it or experience it. Shifting to a primarily possessive value is then a matter of the strengthening of pragmatic inference.

I have already indicated that one source of a BE-type predicate is a posture predicate: 'sit', 'stand', or 'lie'. For instance, Spanish *estar* derives from Latin *stāre* 'stand' (Langacker 1999e), and Luiseño *qal* from Proto Uto-Aztecan

kati* 'sit'. Here I would only add that this development does involve semantic weakening. In particular, it represents subjectification, as defined in CG: an **objectively construed relationship fades away, leaving behind a **subjectively** construed relationship that was **immanent** in it (inherent in its conception). A verb like SIT or STAND profiles an imperfective process with two relational components: the notion of the trajector exhibiting a certain posture and spatial orientation; and the notion of the trajector remaining in a single spatial location. "Bleaching out" of the posture specification leaves behind the notion of being in a certain place. Further attenuation, in the form of abstracting away from the idea of a particular spatial location (and even physical space), results in an existential predicate.

I hope to have shown in reasonably precise detail how a HAVE possessive construction can be extended to locative/existential use, and conversely, how a locative/existential BE construction can assume possessive function. In view of this extensive overlap between possessives and locatives, both of which instantiate the abstract notion of a reference point relationship, one more type of diachronic development can be anticipated: **reanalysis**, whereby a HAVE construction is reinterpreted as a BE construction, or the opposite. While I suspect that this is in fact a frequent occurrence, I have not done any serious investigation along these lines.

One apparent case has however come to light. It concerns the Japanese construction illustrated previously, where possession is expressed by predicating existence within the possessor's dominion. In terms of its form, (14) is a classic example of a BE possessive construction employing a locative/existential predicate. In particular, observe that – as expected in a BE construction – the target is marked as subject (by *ga*). There is evidence, however, that this possessive construction based on *iru* 'exist' is in the process of being reanalyzed. Specifically, Kumashiro (2000: § 4.4.2) has shown that subject properties are split: while T functions as subject at the predicate level (in terms of subject honorification marked on the verb), R functions as subject at the clause level (in terms of being a controller for reflexives). Should this development run its course, R would eventually take over as subject in all respects. In effect, the construction would be reanalyzed as a HAVE possessive, with *iru* then meaning 'have'.

In terms of its CG description, this change is fairly minimal. The basic development is summarized in Figure 4.19. Since HAVE and BE possessives involve all the same conceptual elements, it is simply a matter of shifting the profile from the relationship of T being located with respect to R, to the associated relationship of R controlling (providing mental access to) T. This implies (and perhaps is even instigated by) a shift in primary focal prominence from T to R. R is then the trajector, coded as grammatical subject, leaving T as landmark. A shift in profile is simply metonymy, an utterly ubiquitous linguistic phenomenon.[10]

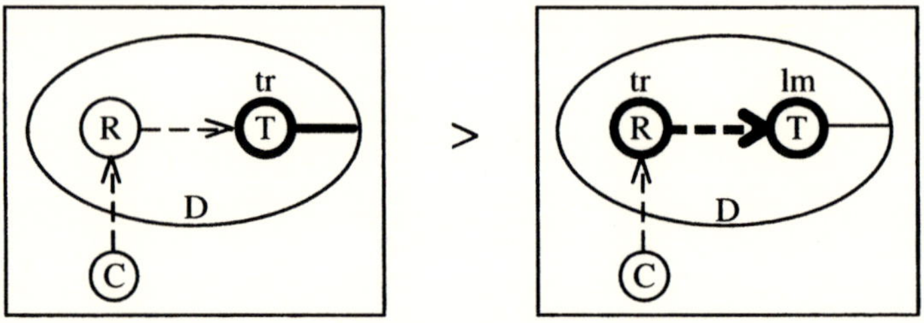

Figure 4.19

Obviously, I cannot claim to have analyzed any of the constructions or phenomena discussed here in all their rich detail. I believe, however, that the broad outlines of a comprehensive account are starting to emerge. At the very least, it should be evident that a revealing analysis of these phenomena requires the simultaneous consideration of many factors: synchronic, diachronic, and crosslinguistic; lexical, grammatical, and semantic. All of these must figure in a comprehensive description and are necessary for a thorough understanding of any part of this complex picture.

10 For parallel cases, see Langacker 1999a: ch. 12.

Chapter 5
On the subject of impersonals

1. The problem

The problem is *it*. By "it", I mean the *it* illustrated by the sentences in (1). This hapless formative is treated by the reigning theoretical orthodoxy as a second-class linguistic citizen. It suffers the indignity of being described by a whole series of derogatory words, such as "expletive", "pleonastic", "epenthetic", and even "dummy", which clearly imply its lack of reality, virtue, or intelligence. It (i.e. *it*) does not deserve this abuse. To have a more neutral term that does not discriminate or prejudge its character, I will refer to it as the **impersonal** *it*.

(1) a. ***It** is obvious that my novel will never be published.*
b. ***It**'s hard to wash a cat.*
c. ***It** seems that the fire started in the attic.*
d. ***It**'s embarrassing when you can't remember someone's name.*
e. ***It**'s in April that we go to Japan.*
f. ***It** is very peaceful without the children around.*
g. ***It** rained last night.*

We need not dwell on generative accounts, where – in accordance with the doctrine of autonomous syntax – *it* is treated as a purely formal object to be inserted and discarded at will. It is, though, worth recalling the classic transformational analysis based on the "extraposition" of a subject complement clause. On this account, *it* is either inserted as subject when the complement clause is extraposed, or alternatively, is base-generated along with the complement and is deleted when the latter remains in place (Rosenbaum 1967). At best this analysis covers only part of the data. Observe that *it* alternates with a subject complement clause only for the first two examples in (1), as seen in (2):

(2) a. *That my novel will never be published is obvious.*
b. *To wash a cat is hard.*
c. **That the fire started in the attic seems.*
d. **When you can't remember someone's name is embarrassing.*
e. **That we go to Japan is in April.*
f. **Without the children around is very peaceful.*
g. **Last night rained.*

Especially problematic is the notion occasionally entertained that *it* is a cataphoric pronoun with the extraposed clause as its antecedent. If so, their relationship directly violates the most robust restrictions otherwise imposed on where pronouns and antecedents can occur relative to one another (Langacker 1969; Reinhart 1983; van Hoek 1995, 1997). One idea that does make sense is the distinction between so-called "pro drop" languages (e.g. Spanish), which allow omission of a pronominal subject, and languages where an overt subject is required. English *it* provides the needed subject when nothing else is available. Likewise for its counterpart in other languages (e.g. French *il*, German *es*, Dutch *er*).

(3) a. ***It** seems that **she** is very intelligent.*
b. ***Il** semble qu'**elle** est très intelligente.* [French]
c. *Parece que es muy inteligente.* [Spanish ("pro drop")]

I accept the notion that English finite clauses require an overt subject (with various qualifications that do not concern us), and that impersonal *it* provides one when needed. Still, the mere fact that it serves this grammatical function does not entail the formalist view that *it* is just an empty syntactic shell uninhabited by any semantic spirit. The central claim of CG is that lexicon and grammar form a continuum fully describable as assemblies of symbolic structures, each of which pairs a semantic structure and a symbolizing phonological structure (Langacker 1987a, 1990a, 1991, 1999a). From this perspective, the very first question one should ask is: What does *it* mean? This is not by way of avoiding grammar, but is rather the first and crucial step in the investigation of impersonal constructions. If we want to understand their grammatical structure, we must first understand their semantic import. What, then, is the conceptual structure of impersonal expressions? To paraphrase Bill Clinton, that depends on what the meaning of *it* is.

Cognitive and functional linguists have made various proposals concerning its meaning. *It* (or its congener in other languages) has variously been described as designating a **mental space** (Lakoff 1987: 542; Smith 2000), an **abstract setting** (Langacker 1993b), the **immediate scope** (Achard 1998: § 7.2), and what I call a **field** (Langacker 2002c). Kirsner (1979: 81) ascribes to Dutch *er* the meaning of "low situational deixis", often interpreted as "general presence or availability", or "mere sceneness" – i.e. an entity is "on the scene", but "the identity of that scene is immaterial". As an abstract meaning shared by all uses of *it*, Bolinger (1977: 84–85) describes it as "a 'definite' nominal with almost the greatest possible generality of meaning, limited only in the sense that it is 'neuter' ... It embraces weather, time, circumstance, whatever is obvious by the nature of reality or the implications of context".

Obviously, a definitive semantic description has not yet been established. The conceptual characterizations cited are, however, all in the same ballpark. They are kindred in spirit, and if there is any inconsistency among them, it is of a very subtle nature. The notions alluded to, and how they relate to one another, do of course stand in need of clarification. Though hardly desirable, the current confusion is certainly understandable. Coming up with clear, explicit, and convincing descriptions of abstract concepts is not at all an easy task. Even harder, perhaps, is the characterization of maximally general notions. Yet the difficulty of pinning down its meaning precisely does not constitute a valid argument that *it* is meaningless. Nor does its generality. In the words of Bolinger (1977: 85), "our mistake has been to confuse generality of meaning with lack of meaning".

The semantic characterization of *it* and the constructions it appears in cannot be dealt with in isolation. Their analysis demands a broad perspective, where they are seen against the background of related phenomena, from which they emerge as special cases. I am going to pursue three broad avenues of approach to the problem, each providing clues about some aspect of it. I will then try to fit these pieces together into a coherent overall account. The first avenue will be a comparison with related constructions. Here I suggest that impersonal constructions – themselves quite varied – fall within a considerably broader range of constructions allowing focal prominence to be conferred on different aspects of a complex scene. In the second avenue of approach, *it* will be compared to other pronouns – both impersonal pronouns and personal pronouns in their "impersonal" uses. The third avenue will be to examine a basic cognitive model referred to as the **control cycle**. This model proves essential for explicating the conceptual organization of impersonal expressions.

2. Alternations in focal prominence

2.1. Basic grammatical notions

As it must, given its central claim, CG offers conceptual characterizations of basic grammatical constructs. A key notion for this purpose is that of profiling, one kind of prominence: within the overall conception it evokes as its base, an expression profiles some substructure, i.e. puts it in focus as the entity it designates (refers to). An expression's grammatical category is determined by the nature of its profile (Langacker 1987a: chs. 5–7, 1987b). A noun profiles a thing (abstractly defined), as does a nominal. A verb profiles a process, as does a finite clause. A process is characterized as a relationship apprehended by tracking its development through time. Adjectives, adverbs, and prepositions profile various kinds of relationships that are non-processual.

An expression that profiles a relationship confers varying degrees of prominence on its participants. There is usually a primary focal participant, called the trajector (tr), and often a secondary focal participant, the landmark (lm). Trajector/landmark alignment provides the conceptual basis for the notions subject and object, as illustrated in Figure 5.1. The boxes represent major components of the composite expression *Floyd broke the glass.* The process designated by the verb is a complex event: the trajector causes (double arrow) the landmark to undergo an internal change (single arrow) whereby it becomes non-functional (nf). Through correspondences, the schematic relational participants are identified with the things profiled by the nominals *Floyd* and *(the) glass.* It is by virtue of elaborating the verb's trajector and landmark that the latter function as its subject and object (irrespective of constituency).

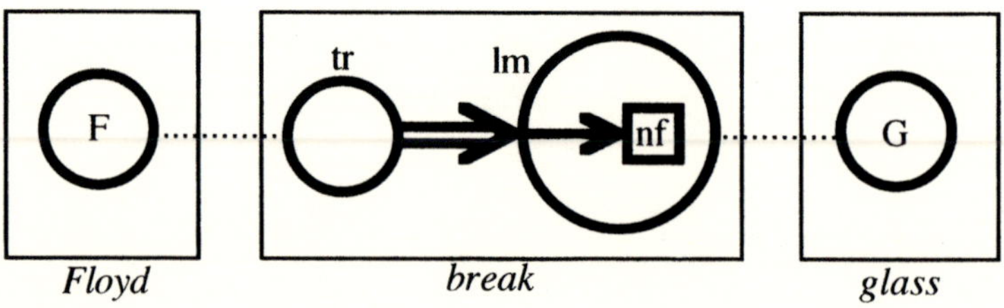

Figure 5.1

Crucially, the prominence of the profile, the trajector, and the landmark is not something inherent in the scene described. Rather, this prominence is imposed on elements of the scene by the linguistic structures employed in coding it, as an aspect of their meanings. The linguistic structures that concern us include the lexical meanings of verbs as well as various constructional schemas pertaining to clause structure (Langacker 1990a: ch. 9, 1991: part II, 1993d), e.g. the schemas, instantiated in Figure 5.1, describing the basic subject and object constructions. Intrinsic to every lexical and grammatical unit is a particular way of construing the conceptual content it evokes or applies to, and thus a particular way of viewing the situations coded by expressions that employ it. This has two important consequences. First, by using different expressions we can always portray a situation in alternate ways – the objective nature of a situation does not determine its linguistic coding or the specific meanings of the expressions describing it. Second, the elements made prominent linguistically need not be the most salient on non-linguistic grounds. There is of course a natural tendency for linguistic prominence to be conferred on elements with the greatest cognitive salience. Nonetheless, we have the linguistic means to focus whatever we like.

For example, the expressions in (4) could all be used to describe the same situation, highlighting different aspects of it through alternate choices of landmark (expressed by the first object nominal). The oft-noted contrast between (4)a and (4)b reflects the choice of conferring secondary focal prominence on either the topic of instruction or else the recipients of the knowledge. While these are certainly the most salient non-agentive elements in a teaching situation, we also have the option of focusing more peripheral elements, such as the kind of institution or the level of instruction. Instead of central participants in the profiled activity, these pertain to the circumstances in which it occurs.

(4) a. *Jack teaches* ***American history*** *to immigrant children.*
 b. *Jack teaches* ***immigrant children*** *American history.*
 c. *Jack teaches* ***elementary school.***
 d. *Jack teaches* ***fourth grade.***

Metaphorically, I think of trajector and landmark status as primary and secondary spotlights, which can be directed at different elements within a scene. Now a spotlight illuminates not only its target, but also the immediately surrounding area. Likewise, focusing some element as trajector or landmark serves as well to augment the salience of those facets of the overall situation it is directly involved in. Alternate assignments of focal prominence thus have the effect of adjusting the profiled relationship, either in terms of which facets of the situation are encompassed by the profile, or else in terms of their degree of prominence within it. Focused to the highest degree is the relational component corresponding to how the trajector interacts with the landmark. Focused to a secondary degree are the components corresponding to how the trajector and the landmark interact with the non-focal participant.

The well-known contrast between (4)a and (4)b emerges as a consequence. In (4)a there is greater emphasis on the theme moving (or becoming accessible) to the recipient. The ditransitive construction in (4)b places greater emphasis on the resultant situation in which the recipient apprehends or controls the theme. Examples (4)c–d take a different perspective on the overall situation by shifting secondary focal prominence to a circumstantial element that would ordinarily be left implicit. Hence the most prominent component relation is that of the teaching activity being situated with respect to the institution or its levels of instruction.

2.2. Actor defocusing

The contrasts in (4), resulting from alternate choices of landmark, are hardly insignificant. Yet linguists have generally paid more attention to those resulting from alternate choice of trajector, which have a more drastic impact on grammatical organization. Here the archetypal example is an active/passive alternation. The passive clause *the glass was broken* is partially diagrammed in Figure 5.2. The details of particular passive constructions are not our present concern. The important point is that trajector status is conferred on a participant which would otherwise – given the usual alignment imposed by the verb stem – be the landmark, expressed by a direct object. Instead, the nominal expressing this same participant functions as grammatical subject, precisely because it has trajector status.

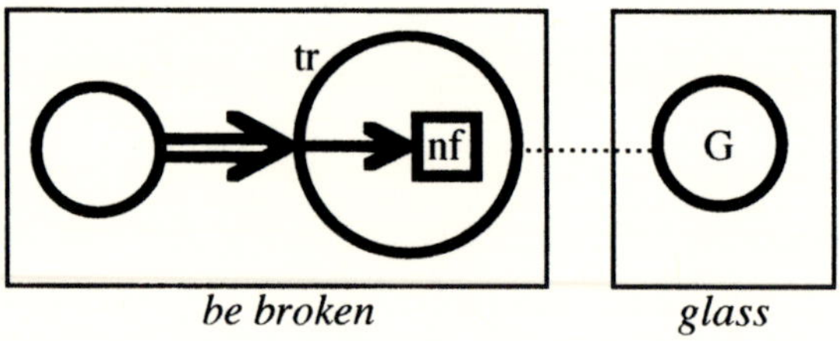

Figure 5.2

Specification of the agent is not an obligatory part of the passive construction. Indeed, its occurrence is relatively infrequent in ordinary conversation, and passives in many languages do not allow this option. This goes along with the claim, reflected in the diagram, that the passive agent does not have the status of a landmark: although it is (at least in English) a central participant in the profiled relationship, it is not a **focal** participant. This claim is in full accord with Shibatani's (1985) characterization of passives in terms of **agent defocusing**. A passive is used when there is motivation for leaving the actor implicit and unspecified, e.g. because it is unknown or because responsibility cannot be assigned to any single individual (van Oosten 1986). When there is discourse motivation both for focusing the patient and also for identifying the actor, the latter is specified periphrastically, by means of a *by*-phrase. Introduced as a prepositional object, the actor is not then a focal participant at the clausal level (Langacker 1990a: ch. 4, 1992a).

If it is not specified periphrastically, a passive agent is simultaneously defocused in two ways: the absence of focal prominence (trajector or landmark status); and also by remaining implicit and unspecified. By explicitly mentioning a participant and supplying a detailed characterization of it we necessarily direct attention to it, so leaving a participant implicit and unspecified renders it less prominent than it would otherwise be. These two complementary means of defocusing can work independently. In the case of a passive with a *by*-phrase, the lack of focal prominence works alone. Conversely, non-specification works alone in the kind of construction referred to as **impersonal** (or sometimes **impersonal passive**). An example from Hopi is given in (5). The sentence lacks an overt subject, and *taaqa* 'man' takes the usual object-marking suffix *-t*. This is not a passive (in any restrictive sense), because the verb's landmark does not assume the function of clausal trajector.

(5) *Taaqa-t niina-ya.* '[They] killed the man.' [Hopi]
man-OBJ kill-PL:SUBJ

The agents in Figure 5.2 and in (5) are left **unspecified**. What does this mean, precisely? It means that the notion of an agent is invoked, but that no indication is given of how that role is filled. For a given role, we can imagine a class of possible **candidates**, consisting of everyone (or everything) that could conceivably be selected to fill it. When the role is specified by a nominal expression, a correspondence is established between the role and the individual or set of individuals profiled by the nominal, as in Figure 5.3(a)-(b). When the role is left unspecified, there is no indication of what it corresponds to within the class of candidates. Invoking it implies that it is somehow filled, but no further information is provided.

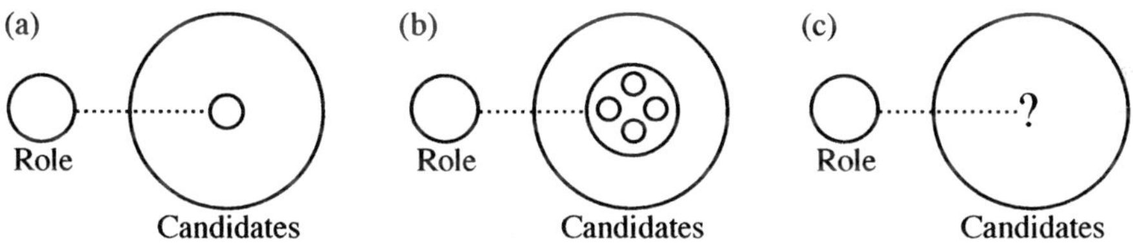

Figure 5.3

For an unspecified participant, various interpretations are possible. Conceivably a single individual is involved, but the speaker chooses not to identify it. This is ruled out in (5) by the verbal suffix indicating a plural subject. It could then be the case that an unknown group of individuals are involved, or perhaps most everybody in the class of candidates. A closely related possibility is that the statement is offered as a kind of generalization, being applicable – under appropriate circumstances – to any member of the candidate class. In this latter case I will speak of a **generalized** participant.

This notion is useful in describing a number of constructions involving a shift in focal prominence, so that a defocused role is readily interpreted in generalized fashion. A familiar case is the so-called "middle" construction. The verb *steer*, for instance, implies an agent and is basically transitive. In this construction, however, the spotlight of primary focal prominence falls on the theme, leaving the agent in the shadows. This construction tends to be used for general statements, like (6)a, which thus invokes a **generalized agent** – anyone driving the truck would experience the ease of steering it. Less typical but still possible is its use for specific events, as in (6)b, but even here the agent (presumably a particular individual) cannot be specified.[1]

(6) a. *This truck steers quite easily.*
b. *The truck steered quite easily (*by the workman).*

Consider next the lexically governed alternations in (7):

(7) a.	(i) *She tasted the soup.*	(ii) *The soup tastes salty.*
b.	(i) *She smelled the milk.*	(ii) *The milk smells sour.*
c.	(i) *She felt the cloth.*	(ii) *The cloth feels smooth.*
d.	(i) *She looked at the lawn.*	(ii) *The lawn looks healthy.*
e.	(i) *She listened to his voice.*	(ii) *His voice sounds pleasant.*

As transitives, the sensory predicates *taste*, *smell*, *feel*, *look at*, and *listen to* take as their subject a participant that combines the roles of actor and experiencer (the action serving to induce the experience). By contrast, their intransitive counterparts – *taste*, *smell*, *feel*, *look*, and *sound* – confer primary focal prominence on the **stimulus**, thus highlighting the quality it manifests to the senses. These predicates can be used for specific occurrences, and a particular experiencer can be specified periphrastically (e.g. *The soup tasted salty to her*). Still, these intransitives tend to be used for general statements, thus invoking a **generalized experiencer**. For instance, *The soup tastes salty* suggests that anybody tasting it would have the same sensation.

We begin to see a pattern here. Though English is an agent-oriented language (Ikegami 1985; Langacker 2004e, 2006a), it provides a range of alternative constructions in which trajector status is conferred on some element other than the most active participant, which would typically attract it. This participant – some kind of actor or experiencer – is further defocused by being left unspecified. Since no particular individual is singled out to fill this active role,

---

1 It can however be specified indirectly in its role as beneficiary, e.g. *The truck steered quite easily for me*. For discussion of the middle in functional terms, see van Oosten 1977; Langacker 1991: 334–335; Heyvaert 2003: ch. 6.

the construction lends itself to use in general statements, involving a generalized actor or experiencer. Besides the families of constructions exemplified in (6) and (7), this description applies to passives. For instance, *Bush cannot be trusted* invokes a generalized experiencer: anybody who might be tempted to trust him ought not do so.

2.3. Non-participant trajectors

The pattern is even wider. In the cases examined thus far, the alternative to an active trajector has been some other participant in the overall interaction. We have already seen, however, that focal prominence is sometimes conferred on more peripheral elements, which are not participants in any narrow sense, but are better described as pertaining to the circumstances of the interaction. Recall the landmarks in (4)c–d: *Jack teaches {elementary school / fourth grade}*. It also happens that primary focal prominence – trajector status – is conferred on non-participants.

One kind of entity that can function as trajector is a **location**. In (8), for example, the subject is not the actor with respect to the profiled activity, but merely the location where it occurs: it is the bees that swarm, the fires that blaze, the bells that ring, and the fleas that crawl. The role of the garden, the sky, the streets, and the cat is that of **host** to this activity, which pervades it, the actors being specified periphrastically by means of a *with*-phrase. A further property of this construction, established by Dowty (2000), is that the location is portrayed as the source of a sensory impression created by the ubiquitous activity – imagine, for instance, the visual and auditory impression of a garden filled with swarming and buzzing bees. This in turn implies an experiencer, for without an experiencer there is no visual or auditory sensation. The construction, however, leaves the experiencer unmentioned and unspecified. It is a **generalized experiencer**, the import being that anybody capable of observing the location would receive the impression in question.

(8) a. *The garden is swarming with bees.*
b. *The nighttime sky was blazing with forest fires.*
c. *The streets were ringing with church bells.*
d. *My cat is crawling with fleas.*

The construction is sketched in Figure 5.4(a), where the rectangle stands for the location and a solid arrow for the activity going on inside it. The location is focused as trajector and coded as clausal subject. The actors, introduced periphrastically, are not focal participants. As expected given this choice of trajector, the construction highlights the location's role as host for the activity. Solid and dashed arrows represent the location functioning as stimulus with respect to the experiencer (E), who thus perceives the location. However, because this generalized experiencer is implicit and unspecified, I take their perceptual relationship as being unprofiled.

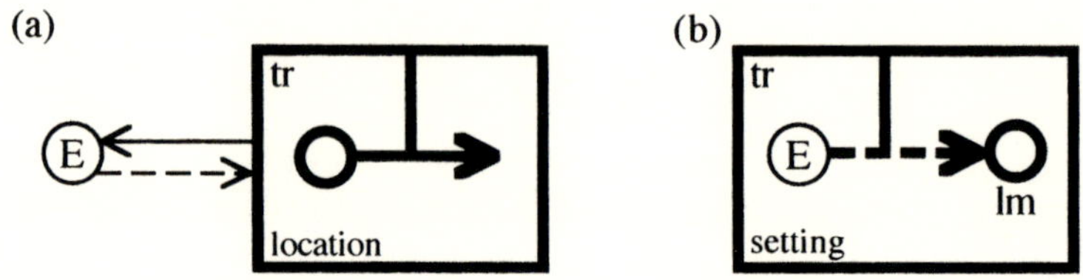

Figure 5.4

While a location is a restricted area, a **setting** is a global expanse within which events unfold (the difference is one of degree). A setting can also function as clausal trajector, as in (9). Whereas a verb like *experience*, *see*, or *witness* normally selects the experiencer as its subject, here the trajector is the spatial or temporal setting hosting the experienced events coded by the object nominal. These predicates do invoke an experiencer, but a generalized one – the import is that the events in question would be observed by anyone found within the setting. The construction is sketched in Figure 5.4(b).

(9) a. *Florida experiences a lot of hurricanes.*
b. *This town has seen a long series of political scandals.*
c. *The last few decades have witnessed amazing scientific progress.*

At least in English, passivizability correlates with transitivity, which in turn involves the interaction of participants, in an **action chain** or something analogous to one (Rice 1987a, 1987b). To the extent that the trajector or landmark is instead construed as a setting, a location, or some other kind of circumstance, the felicity of a passive is diminished (Langacker 1987c, 1991: ch. 7). It is well known that the expressions in (9) do not allow passives, despite the presence of non-oblique subject and object nominals:

(10) a. **A lot of hurricanes are experienced by Florida.*
b. **A long series of political scandals have been seen by this town.*
c. **Amazing scientific progress has been witnessed by the last few decades.*

Observe, now, that impersonals with *it* are analogous, in that they do not passivize, even when they have a nominal in object position:

(11) a. *It's raining big drops.*
b. **Big drops are being rained (by it).*
c. *It seems that the Florida election was rigged.*
d. **That the Florida election was rigged is seemed (by it).*

This parallel behavior is one motivation for my suggestion that impersonal *it* be analyzed as designating an **abstract setting** (Langacker 1993b, 1993d). We will return to this matter after discussing nominal specification and the control cycle.

3. The specification of nominal referents

3.1. Nominal organization

Having reached impersonal *it* through one avenue of approach, pertaining to the external grammar of nominal expressions, we will now approach it along a second avenue, pertaining to their internal semantic and grammatical organization. A nominal expression is one that profiles a thing (abstractly defined). Falling under this heading are both lexical nouns and nominals (full NP's), including pronouns. By itself, a lexical noun (e.g. *pencil*) merely specifies a type of thing. A nominal (e.g. *that pencil*) profiles a grounded instance of some type. The ground comprises the speech event, its participants, and its immediate circumstances (such as the time and place of speaking). Grounding is a grammaticized means of indicating how a profiled thing or process relates to the ground with respect to certain fundamental, "epistemic" notions (like time, reality, and identification). For our purposes, nominal grounding elements are roughly coextensive with what are traditionally called "determiners".[2]

Type specification and grounding work together to single out nominal referents. Consider the phrase *that pencil.* Used successfully in a particular discourse context, this nominal directs attention to one particular thing out of all the conceivable entities in our mental universe that we might possibly wish to refer to. The noun and the demonstrative embody different ways of selecting from this vast range of candidates. The noun describes a type of thing, and thus limits attention to the class of candidates which instantiate this type. Since the type conception is immanent in the conception of all its instances (representing their abstracted commonality), the noun itself fails to choose among them. By

2 For discussion of nominal structure and grounding, see Langacker 1991: Part I, 2002a, 2002d, 2004c (also Chapter 6).

contrast, the demonstrative does single out a particular referent, but irrespective of type. To single out a physical referent in the immediate discourse situation, the demonstrative can stand alone as a full nominal, accompanied by a pointing gesture (*I want that [→]*). I take this as a concrete manifestation of a demonstrative's general conceptual import, which I would characterize (however vaguely and impressionistically) as a kind of mental pointing. In combination with a noun, then, a demonstrative constitutes a mental gesture of pointing to a particular referent selected from the class of candidates delimited by the noun's type specification.

Both definite and indefinite determiners are grounding elements, singling out an instance of the specified type that subsequently functions as a discourse referent:

(12) *Jill needs* ***{the / a} pencil*** *– and she needs* ***it*** *now.*

The difference (as discussed in Chapter 4) is that the referent of an indefinite nominal has a kind of **virtuality** with respect to the range of candidate instances (Langacker 1999d, 2005b). With a definite, the nominal is taken as being sufficient to single out the intended referent, at the current stage of the discourse, **independently** of the clause containing it. It is thus a matter of the speaker directing the hearer's attention to that referent, whose participation in the clause provides supplementary information about it. By itself, on the other hand, an indefinite nominal is merely an instruction for the hearer to "conjure up" (i.e. to imagine) an instance of the type, **pending** the information provided by the clause containing it (Verhagen 1986: 123–124; Langacker 2004c). It is that clause which determines its identity, as well as its status as actual or virtual – that is, the clause may not be sufficient to establish its actuality. In (12), the referent of *a pencil* remains a virtual entity (no particular pencil is singled out).

Nominal structure gives rise to various kinds of impersonal expressions. Most obviously, an indefinite pronoun like *someone* provides an alternative to a specified, personal subject: *Someone broke the glass.* Since the type specification indicates only that the referent is human, and indefinite grounding implies the absence of prior identification, the subject nominal does not itself do anything much by way of singling out a particular individual. The same holds for indefinite nominals like English *one* (e.g. *One never knows*), French *on*, and German *man*, where grounding and type specification are conflated in a single, morphologically unanalyzable form.

Impersonals can also result from using an ungrounded noun (in lieu of a full, grounded nominal) to specify the clausal trajector. This is more familiar in the case of objects, where it is often referred to as "object incorporation". Both are exemplified in (13), from Shoshoni. The noun *ka^{h}ni* 'house' is incorporated in the verb to form a predicate meaning 'house-have', which describes the landmark only in terms of type. This predicate in turn takes the prefix *ta-*, which is schematic even in this regard. In effect, it indicates only that the subject will remain unspecified (Langacker 1976).

(13) *Ta-ka^{h}ni-pai.* '[One] has [a] house.' [Shoshoni]
UNSPEC:SUBJ-house-have

3.2. Definites

It might at first seem contradictory that a definite pronoun, with specific reference, can function as an impersonal subject in a manner comparable to a non-specific indefinite like *one*. For this reason impersonal *it* is generally not attributed any meaning at all, not even that of definiteness, despite its formal identity to the personal pronoun *it*. Recall, however, Bolinger's statement: "Our mistake has been to confuse generality of meaning with lack of meaning."

Let us start with nominals grounded by definite determiners, i.e. demonstratives and definite articles. In contrast to indefinites, a definite nominal identifies its referent independently of the content of the clause containing it. I have further suggested that a demonstrative constitutes a kind of mental pointing (often accompanied by a physical pointing gesture). In using a demonstrative, the speaker performs the act of singling out the intended referent from whatever pool of candidates is eligible given the discourse context and the type specification provided by the nominal it grounds. In lieu of an actual pointing gesture, the singling out is effected by the demonstrative's specification for **proximal** vs. **distal**, whether this is interpreted spatially or with respect to some other dimension, such as discourse proximity or speaker empathy (Kirsner 1993; Janssen 1995). In uttering (14), for instance, the speaker is dividing the relevant scope of discourse into a proximal region and a distal region, where the proximity most likely has spatial, temporal, and attentional components – *this shirt* is the one I am currently examining, *that one* is the shirt I examined previously. Given the partitioning of the scope of discourse into two sectors, using *this* or *that* in reference to the type specification *shirt* amounts to mentally pointing to one or the other instance of that type.

(14) *I like **this shirt** much better than **that one**.*

What about the definite article? At the risk of great oversimplification (cf. Hawkins 1978; Langacker 1991: § 3.1.1; Epstein 2001, 2002), we can say that using the definite article implies that there is only one eligible candidate (only one instance of the specified type) within the relevant scope of consideration. Hence there is no need to single it out from other candidates, either by physical pointing or in terms of proximity. It represents the limiting case of mental pointing, where it suffices to merely **register** unique selection instead of acting to **achieve** it.

Both demonstratives and definite articles co-occur with nouns.[3] Personal pronouns generally do not, despite their close relationship (synchronic and diachronic) to the definite determiners. The type specifications they themselves supply are quite schematic: 'human', 'feminine', etc. Instead they select their referents on the basis of their referential status vis-à-vis the speech event participants, traditionally called **person**, roughly as presented in (15):

(15) Referents of **personal pronouns:**
a. *first person singular:* speaker
b. *first person plural:* group that includes the speaker
c. *second person singular:* hearer
d. *second person plural:* (group that includes the) hearers
e. *third person singular:* individual other than speaker and hearer
f. *third person plural:* group that excludes the speaker and hearer

Though personal pronouns are often used anaphorically, as in (16)a, they do not require any overt linguistic antecedent. A third person pronoun is felicitous when an otherwise unmentioned referent is clearly evident to both interlocutors from the non-linguistic context, as in (16)b (Hankamer and Sag 1976).

(16) a. ***The farmer*** *chased* ***the duckling****, but* ***he*** *couldn't catch* ***it****.*
b. [seeing a farmer chase a duckling] ***He****'ll never catch* ***it****.*

Pronouns like *he* and *it* are comparable to the definite article by presupposing that there is only one eligible candidate within the relevant scope of conception – or **immediate scope** – contextually established by linguistic or non-linguistic means. They differ from a definite article in how the set of eligible candidates is selected. With an article, selection is achieved through the type specification provided by the lexical noun (e.g. *farmer, duckling*). With a pronoun, on the other hand, selection is achieved through the very minimal (highly schematic) type indicated by the pronoun itself (e.g 'human male', 'neuter'). Since there are generally more potential referents in a scene for a form like *he* or *it* than for *farmer* or *duckling*, with a pronoun it is harder to establish a situation where only one eligible candidate is available

3 The definite article does so obligatorily since it does not point, hence cannot single out a referent in the absence of a type specification.

within the scope of consideration. Thus a pronoun requires prior delimitation of the pool of eligible candidates through an explicit antecedent, as in (16)a, or through a particular candidate having sufficient contextual salience to stand out as the only plausible choice (cf. van Hoek 1997). In the case of *I* and singular *you*, uniqueness is normally assured by the very fact of an utterance being produced by just a single speaker and directed at a particular addressee.

We must now confront a basic question: If **personal** pronouns single out a particular referent, how can they function as the subject of **impersonals**? The answer resides in a factor we have not yet considered, namely **delimitation**.

3.3. Delimitation

I have been using terms like **selection** and **singling out** for the process of directing attention to an instance of some type, i.e. establishing the linguistic referent of a nominal. By contrast, I will use the term **delimitation** in regard to how the profiled instance projects to the world (or the relevant universe of discourse). It pertains to how much of the world the instance subsumes (or **delimits**), so that by referring to it we are limiting attention to a certain facet of the world as opposed to all others. As I am using the terms, **selection** and **delimitation** are very similar – both involve restricting attention within the full range of candidates for attention (the world of discourse, everything we might have occasion to think about or refer to with a nominal expression). They are distinguished on functional grounds, as pertaining to different levels of nominal organization. Selection (or singling out) is a matter of **choosing** a profiled instance, while delimitation involves the **size** (or **extension**) of that instance (or the pool of candidates conforming to the type specification).

Although the notion is a general one, we can start with spatial delimitation. Of the two nominal expressions *a pond* and *a lake*, the former projects to a smaller portion of our spatial world than does the latter, just by virtue of lexical semantics. *Pond* implies a higher degree of delimitation than *lake* in terms of size or spatial extension. Observe, however, that the extent of spatial delimitation is sometimes quite flexible. Consider *place*, which profiles a limited region in space. Despite being bounded (since *place* is a count noun), a place has no intrinsic size. What counts as a *place* is functionally determined, reflecting the purpose for invoking it. In terms of actual spatial extension, it ranges from the smallest region imaginable to the largest, as seen in (17). Naturally, increasing the size of the profiled region diminishes the degree of spatial delimitation effected by the nominal.

(17) a. *A zinc atom can be found at several* ***places*** *in this molecule.*
b. *That's a good* ***place*** *to put the vase.*
c. *They're looking for a suitable* ***place*** *to build a shopping mall.*
d. *Dubrovnik is a nice* ***place*** *to visit.*
e. *The world has become a very hostile* ***place****.*
f. *The universe is a very big* ***place****.*

Even a deictic element like *here* varies in its degree of spatial delimitation. If *here* profiles a spatial region that is in some way proximal to the speaker, the actual spatial extent of this region can nonetheless vary without intrinsic limit, as shown in (18). The same holds for *now*, in terms of temporal delimitation, as in (19).

(18) a. *Put the vase right* ***here****.*
b. *We should build the garage right* ***here****.*
c. *It's pleasant* ***here*** *in Dubrovnik.*
d. ***Here*** *in our solar system there is only one habitable planet.*
e. *Everything in the universe has a reason for being* ***here****.*

(19) a. *Hand it to me right* ***now****!*
b. ***Now*** *we can pay our debts.*
c. *The earth is habitable* ***now*** *but won't be much longer.*
d. *The universe is very different* ***now*** *than in its formative stages.*

3.4. Definite impersonals

In (18)-(19), we observed that even a definite nominal can vary greatly in regard to delimitation. *Here* singles out and profiles a bounded, deictically anchored location, but in terms of actual spatial extension it need not effect any significant delimitation – at the extreme, the profiled region is coextensive with whatever spatial expanse we might contemplate. In cases like (18)e, the implied contrast with *there* is essentially vacuous, *here* serving only to indicate the speaker's location within this maximally inclusive spatial region. The temporal expanse profiled by *now* can also be expanded indefinitely. Although the delimitation it effects in time may never be totally vacuous, it can certainly be quite minimal.

We can now understand the impersonal use of plural pronouns. They resemble *here* and *now* in being deictically anchored yet highly variable in their degree of delimitation. But instead of designating a region in space or a span of time, they refer to groups of people.[4] Delimitation thus pertains to the size of

4 I will ignore the application of *they* to non-humans, as this is irrelevant for impersonal expressions.

the profiled group in relation to the set of all people, the **maximal extension** of this type. Each of the plural pronouns can be interpreted as profiling a highly delimited group or one of indefinite size. At least in the case of *we*, the referent can even coincide with the maximal extension.

We profiles a group that includes the speaker. Though its minimal size is two, as in (20)a, there is no intrinsic upper limit. In (20)b, a sentence just employed, *we* referred to a group including myself and a presumed reading audience. In (20)c, a statement of official American economic policy, *we* subsumes the entire US population. And in (20)d it is coextensive with the entire human race.

(20) a. ***We** just had a nice one-on-one conversation.*
b. ***We** can now understand the impersonal use of plural pronouns.*
c. ***We** have the right to exploit the world's resources at the expense of everybody else.*
d. ***We** are not alone.* [I.e. there is other intelligent life in the universe.]

You poses special problems, not only because it neutralizes the singular/plural distinction, but also because its impersonal use involves factors beyond those I am prepared to consider here. Clearly, though, it can designate a group of any size, even everyone in the world other than the speaker. Thus *you* in (21)a refers to either a single reader or an open-ended set of potential readers. In (21)b, a statement of official American foreign policy, *you* refers to all Europeans. Sentence (21)c might conceivably be produced by an individual fugitive terrorist as a threat to everybody else in the world.

(21) a. ***You** should now be looking at example (21)a.*
b. *Why don't **you** Europeans acknowledge our right to rule the world?*
c. ***You**'ll never catch me and **you**'ll never be safe.*

They excludes both the speaker and the addressee. Obviously it can designate a group of two individuals or any larger size. At one extreme, *they* can refer to two specific individuals, as in (22)a. At the opposite extreme, it can be interpreted as referring to everybody in the world except the speaker and addressee – thus (22)d is the plural counterpart of (21)c, the case of two fugitive terrorists alone against the rest of the world. In terms of size, the groups profiled by *they* in (22)b–c are intermediate. In fact, these uses are impersonal in the sense that no specific individuals are identified. The likely import of (22)b is that the grant was denied by whoever is responsible for such matters, the faceless individuals with the power to decide. In (22)c, the claim is not attributed to any specific people, but to generative grammarians collectively (implying that most or all suscribe to it).

(22) a. ***They** met in Istanbul.*
b. ***They** didn't fund my grant.*
c. *In generative grammar,* ***they*** *claim that syntax is autonomous.*
d. ***They**'ll never catch us and* ***they**'ll never be safe.*

The plural pronouns have various uses that would traditionally be considered impersonal. In (23), for instance, no specific individuals are singled out as those who experience the earthquakes, hurricanes, or tornadoes. Instead, the potential for such experience is attributed to "people in general" within the areas mentioned. The subject pronouns do still single out a deictically anchored discourse referent: from (23)a we deduce that the speaker is one of those who live in California; from (23)b we learn that the addressee (but not the speaker) is one of those who live in Florida; and from (23)c we infer that neither lives in Kansas. Still, the only significant delimitation of the nominal referent, serving to distinguish it from the set of all humans, comes from the locative.

(23) a. ***We** have a lot of earthquakes in California.*
b. ***You** have a lot of hurricanes in Florida.*
c. ***They** have a lot of tornadoes in Kansas.*

These sentences refer collectively to the inhabitants of California, Florida, and Kansas, and do not imply that every inhabitant, or any particular inhabitant, has the experience in question. Within the confines of the state, they invoke a generalized experiencer: anyone living there might experience the phenomenon. Hence the only reason for employing a pronominal subject is to indicate whether this undifferentiated mass of people includes the speaker or the hearer. If person is deemed irrelevant – if it is simply desired to make a general comment about natural disasters in these states – we thus have the option of a setting-subject construction, as in (24). These sentences are impersonal in the sense that direct reference to people is totally absent.

(24) a. *California has a lot of earthquakes.*
b. *Florida has a lot of hurricanes.*
c. *Kansas has a lot of tornadoes.*

The plural pronouns *we* and *they* are also used in "full" impersonals, which lack the kind of delimitation imposed by locatives in (23). The pronouns in (25) are definite in the sense that they single out a unique discourse referent, one instance of the type 'people', which could in principle be of any size, representing any proportion of the maximal extension. But since the discourse referent is only characterized intrinsically as a group that includes the speaker (for *we*), or one that excludes the speaker and hearer (for *they*), it is vague in regard to delimitation (how the profiled instance maps onto the world). It is identified by its status vis-à-vis the ground (i.e. person – an essential identification for discourse purposes) independently of the clausal content. At the same time, its identification vis-à-vis the range of eligible candidates in the world is flexibly interpreted. The examples in (25) illustrate two kinds of impersonal interpretations. On the one hand, *we* and *they* refer in generalized fashion to all mankind. Thus (25)a assesses the current state of human knowledge, and (25)b is an item of general human wisdom. On the other hand, (25)c–d pertain to specific events, effected by particular individuals. However, it is not known or not indicated who those individuals might be. One can only surmise that the actions were carried out by relevant authorities or those with the proper expertise, on behalf of the population at large. Note, for example, that (25)c does not imply that the speaker had any personal role in mapping the genome.

(25) a. ***We** know the average global temperature is rising.*
b. ***They** say it's never too late to learn new skills.*
c. ***We**'ve mapped the entire human genome.*
d. ***They** found her body last night.*

When used impersonally, English *you* is singular rather than plural, as witnessed by the reflexive in (26)a. Nevertheless it is fully general in reference, not even excluding the speaker. In fact, (26)c would be a perfectly normal way for the speaker to describe what just happened to him. It is not however a direct description – *you* does not mean *I*. Instead, the statement is given as a general characterization of what can happen, thus portraying the speaker's recent experience as a prime example of the general human condition. While I have not carried out an in-depth analysis, I suspect that singular impersonal *you* involves an elaborate mental construction one component of which is a **virtual dialog**, where the speaker is presenting the facts of life to an imagined interlocutor (Langacker 1999d). As a special case, the speaker is talking to himself.

(26) a. ***You** should never underestimate **yourself**.*
b. ***You** can never be too rich or too thin.*
c. ***You** work hard for years and **you** get rewarded by being fired.*

3.5. Vagueness

We are nearing the end of this long avenue of approach to impersonal *it*. As a final point of interest along the way, we can briefly consider some quasi-pronominal uses of *this* and *that*, where they stand alone as full nominals.

Suppose we take quasi-seriously the notion that a demonstrative singles out its referent by pointing, sometimes physically and always mentally. Even in the case of physical pointing, there is often a certain degree of vagueness in regard to what is being singled out. Imagine that my finger is pointed at a particular rose within a particular bouquet within a larger floral display. If I utter the sentence *I think that [→] is beautiful*, what does *that [→]* refer to? Am I pointing to the rose, to the bouquet, or to the overall display? Or perhaps to a single petal of the rose? The gesture and the sentence are vague in reference. Pointing singles out a target only at a certain level of **granularity**. Moreover, pointing instruments vary as to how fine-grained a specification they can make. A finger is a fairly sharp instrument, so under the right circumstances I can use it to pick out something very small. But if my arm has been amputated and I can only point with the stump that remains, it can only effect a coarse-grained specification – I can indicate the bouquet, but not a particular rose or petal. If I point with a nod of my head, there is less precision still.

When the pointing is only mental, the instrument is blunt indeed. We then rely on just the proximal/distal distinction, by means of which we can only direct attention to one of two broad ranges within the immediate scope. Under appropriate circumstances, a two-way distinction may suffice. If there are just two roses in the room, one near me and one far away, I can single out one or the other by saying *this rose* vs. *that rose*. If it is clear from the discourse context that we are only discussing roses, I can do this with the demonstrative alone, e.g. *This is beautiful*. But if I enter a room filled with diverse objects and merely say *That is beautiful* – with no prior context and without a pointing gesture – my interlocutor can only guess at my intended referent. I am indeed referring to a specific entity, a particular instance of the schematic type 'thing'. Yet, from the listener's standpoint, the expression fails to impose any significant or sufficient delimitation on the range of possible referents. Specific, definite reference does not itself entail actual identifiability in practical terms. Definiteness does not guarantee non-vagueness.

It is not just a matter of uncertainty about which particular referent the speaker intends. One can choose to use a blunt pointing instrument precisely because, within a scene, it may be impossible to delineate precisely what one is pointing to. Years ago, Gensler (1977) called attention to the vagueness of many demonstrative uses, where the reference might be anything within the current discourse frame. In (27)a, *this* refers to some aspect of the current activity, but is vague about which one – it may be the strategy, the manner of execution, the activity itself, the very fact that we are engaging in it, the last few steps, etc. If (27)b is uttered after a carefully reasoned intellectual presentation, neither the speaker nor the academic may be able to say precisely what *that* refers to; the sentence may just register general displeasure with the academic enterprise. In (27)c, *this* alludes quite vaguely to prior information concerning the marriage. Sentence (27)d might be uttered in frustration by somebody losing a game, receiving an order, or learning of an unfortunate development. The speaker may not be able to point to any specific source of the unfairness. It could just be that the situation as a whole, through some unidentifiable convergence of circumstances, is one that the speaker has trouble dealing with. In cases like these, the speaker is verbally and mentally making a referential gesture – it's just that the referent is not a clearly or uniquely delineated entity in the world of discourse. The vagueness is especially great in reference to abstract circumstances.

(27) a. ***This** is getting us nowhere.*
b. ***That**'s the trouble with you academics.*
c. *What's **this** about your getting married?*
d. ***That**'s not fair!*

That brings us to impersonal *it*,[5] which Gensler treats alongside *this* and *that*. Note that *it* alternates with *that* in (27)d: *It's not fair!* At this juncture I will merely suggest that impersonal *it* represents the extreme case of vagueness and non-delimitation. It (or *it*) is not only definite but also referential, given that our mental world includes highly abstract entities. What makes it special, compared to straightforward cases of anaphoric *it*, is that its referent is maximally diffuse, being wholly undelimited within the immediate scope of discourse. Its impersonal uses stem directly from its properties and place in the system of English definites. Of all the English definite nominals, it does the least by way of singling out and identifying a particular, well-delimited referent. As a pronoun it does not occur with a lexical noun providing a type specification. Its own type specification, something like 'neuter' or 'non-human thing', is highly schematic and applicable to the widest possible array of entities. Moreover, it represents an extremely blunt pointing instrument. Neutralizing the proximal/distal distinction, it only points through its person specification, and in this regard third person is maximally general and unmarked (anything other than speaker and hearer). Still, its vagueness or generality of meaning is not the same as meaninglessness.

5 What does *that* refer to, precisely? My last statement? The last paragraph? The last set of examples? Something more abstract, like the flow of ideas?

4. The control cycle

4.1. The general model

The final avenue of approach to impersonal *it* is a general cognitive model applicable to many aspects of human experience. The **control cycle** (Langacker 2002c) has the basic form sketched in Figure 5.5. In the static baseline phase, an **actor** (A) (in a broad sense of the term) controls an array of entities (small circles) which collectively constitute its **dominion** (D). In the next phase, some **target** (T) enters the actor's **field** (F), or scope of potential interaction. This creates a state of tension, for the actor has to deal with the target in some manner. The typical means of dealing with it is by somehow bringing it under the actor's control, i.e. exerting force (double arrow) resulting in its incorporation in the actor's dominion. The result of this action is a modified situation that is once more static (a state of relaxation).

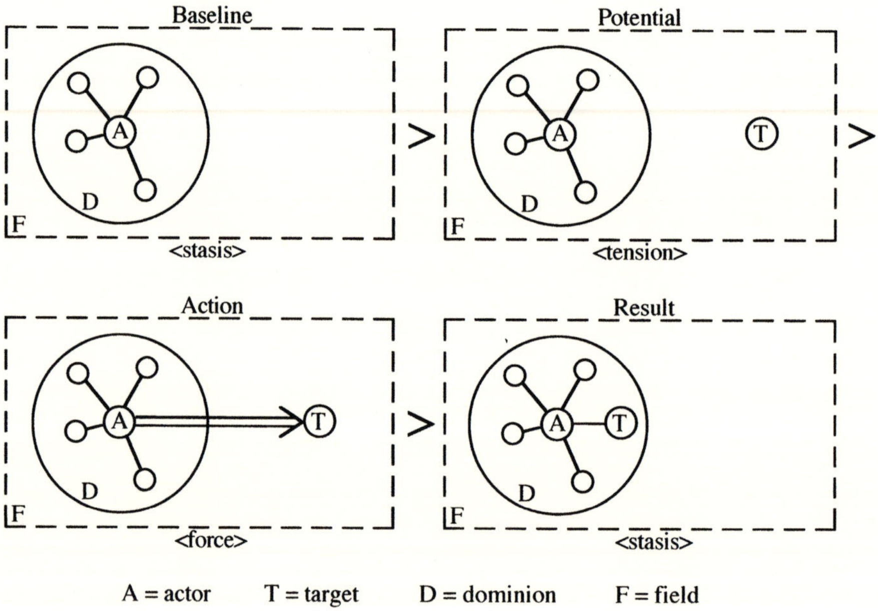

Figure 5.5

Manifestations of the control cycle continuously unfold at the physical, perceptual, mental, and social levels. At the physical level, for instance, a cat (A) catches and controls a mouse (T) that happens to come within reach (F). Seeing or hearing something is a matter of bringing it under perceptual control.

Mentally, we formulate and evaluate propositions, and in some cases we accept them as part of the dominion comprising our view of reality. At the level of social interaction, we encounter new individuals and achieve a kind of social control by establishing stable relationships entailing definite expectations and obligations.

Predicates can be partially characterized semantically in terms of how the profiled relationship maps onto the control cycle. Four typical mappings are shown in Figure 5.6. Some predicates profile bounded actions in which the actor establishes control over the target. Others profile stable situations which result from such actions. Other predicates designate the activity of maintaining control once it has been achieved. Still others indicate preparatory activities which can lead to the act of acquisition.

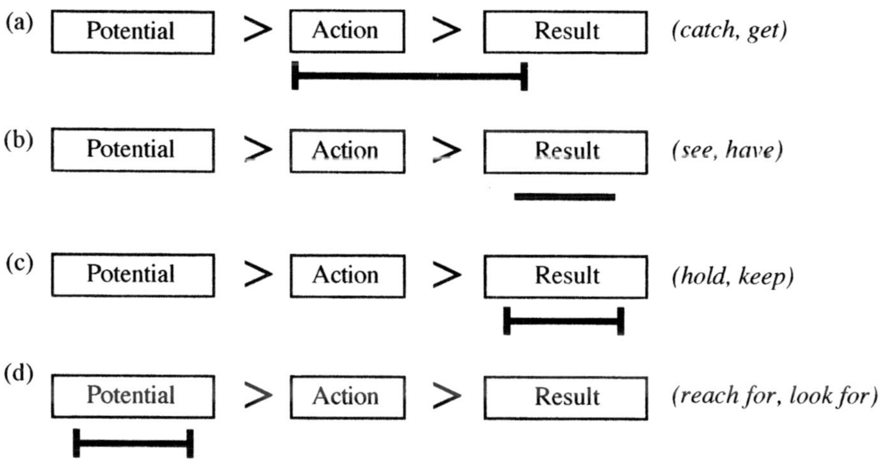

Figure 5.6

4.2. Epistemic level

Our main concern here is with predicates pertaining to the acquisition of propositional knowledge. At this level, the actor is a **conceptualizer**, the target is a **proposition**, and the dominion is the conceptualizer's view of reality (or **epistemic dominion**), i.e. the set of propositions the conceptualizer currently holds to be valid. This level turns out to be extremely rich in terms of lexical coding, even confining our attention to predicates taking finite clauses as complements. There is in fact good reason to break down the potential phase into three successive stages, as shown in Figure 5.7 (Sumnicht 2001; Chapter 9).

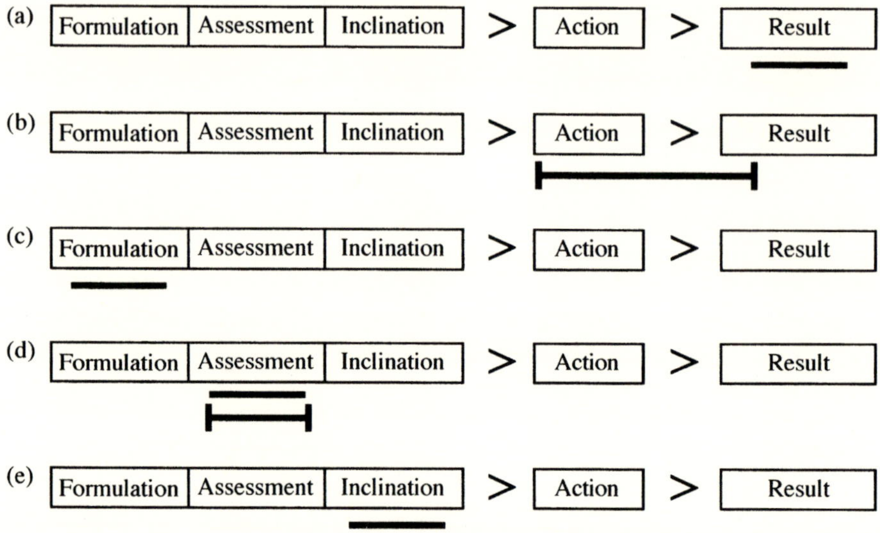

Figure 5.7

These predicate types are exemplified in (28). Result predicates indicate that the proposition is already established in the conceptualizer's epistemic dominion (reality conception).[6] By contrast, action predicates profile the event of accepting it, so that it comes to be established there. The result predicates are analogous to *have*, the action predicates to *get*.

(28) a. **Result:** *He {**knows / believes / thinks / realizes / accepts / is sure / is certain / is convinced**} that Bush is a pacifist.*

b. **Action:** *She {**learned / discovered / decided / concluded / realized / determined / found out / figured out**} that his whole story was a pack of lies.*

c. **Formulation:** *It is {**possible / conceivable / plausible / feasible / imaginable**} that they could be of some use to us.*

d. **Assessment:** *He {**wondered / considered / asked / was unsure / was undecided / was unclear**} whether the effort was worth the bother.*

e. **Inclination:** *I {**suspect / believe / suppose / think / figure / reckon**} they will never agree to my offer.*

The potential phase, preparatory to the action of accepting or rejecting a proposition, breaks down into three successive stages: **formulation**, **assess-**

6 Note that some predicates, e.g. *believe*, have multiple senses distinguished by their position vis-à-vis this model.

ment, and **inclination**. We can speak of formulation when a proposition merely enters the conceptualizer's field of awareness as something that cannot be rejected outright, thus has to be dealt with in some fashion. This can lead to active assessment, signalled grammatically by the use of *whether* in the subordinate clause. Assessment may lead to some preliminary inclination to accept the proposition (or else to reject it). Sumnicht (2001) has shown that so-called "negative raising" pertains to the inclination stage, as seen by the rough equivalence of the expressions in (29) to those in (28)e.

(29) *I don't {**suspect / believe / suppose / think / figure / reckon**} they will ever agree to my offer.*

Let me focus on three kinds of predicates representing stable situations: formulation, inclination, and result. Assessment and action can be thought of as transitions between these steady states. I will adopt the notations in Figure 5.8, where C is the conceptualizer (actor), P is the target proposition, and D is the conceptualizer's current view of reality (his epistemic dominion). In the **formulation** phase, P is merely present in C's field of awareness, as something that needs to be dealt with. Through assessment, C arrives at some sort of **inclination** in regard to P, as represented by the dashed arrow. With varying degrees of force, C inclines either toward accepting P as part of C's view of reality, or else rejecting it (e.g. with *doubt*). Still, no definite decision has been made. I would characterize epistemic modals (*may, will, should, must*, etc.) in this fashion (Chapters 6–7). In the **result** phase, a state of relaxation, P is already established in C's dominion.

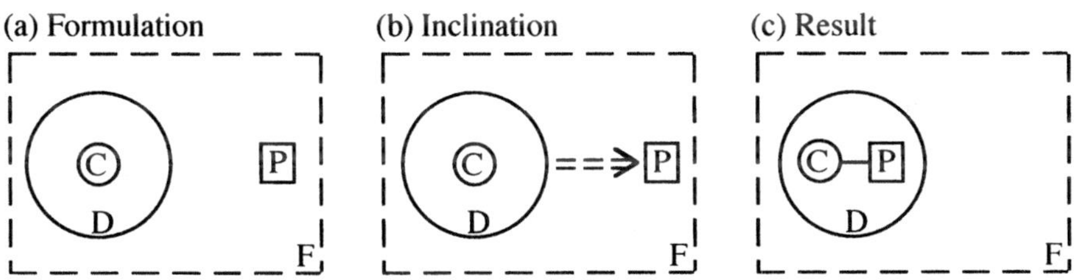

Figure 5.8

Predicates pertaining to epistemic control can either be **personal** or **impersonal**. That is, the trajector (coded as grammatical subject) can either designate the conceptualizer who entertains the proposition expressed by the complement clause, or alternatively, impersonal *it* can fill the subject role.[7] Some

7 I ignore for now the third possibility, quite rare in normal conversation, where the complement clause itself functions as grammatical subject.

predicates allow both options, others just one. The distribution is skewed in interesting ways, reflecting the meanings of the predicates in question. For instance, predicates that profile **actions** (including specific acts of assessment) require personal subjects.[8]

(30) a. ***Albert*** *{learned / decided / discovered} that aliens had stolen his shoes.*
b. ***Albert*** *{wondered / considered / asked} whether aliens had stolen his shoes.*
c. *****It*** *{learned / decided / discovered} that aliens had stolen Albert's shoes.*
d. *****It*** *{wondered / considered / asked} whether aliens had stolen Albert's shoes.*

This makes perfect sense in that mental actions require sentient actors. Conversely, **formulation** predicates seem always to be impersonal, as in (28)c. We do not find corresponding expressions like (31):

(31) *****We*** *are {possible / conceivable / plausible / feasible / imaginable} that they could be of some use to us.*

This too makes sense, for a sentence like this would imply that a conceptualizer consciously entertains a proposition without doing anything by way of initiating its assessment. Though not impossible, merely registering a proposition in consciousness, without any movement toward assessing its possible validity, is not the sort of thing we tend to do or that it is terribly useful to have a lexical item to describe.

Some impersonal predicates allow the option of specifying the conceptualizer by means of a *to*-phrase. Others do not:

(32) a. **Formulation:** *It is {**conceivable / plausible / *possible / *feasible / *imaginable**} to me that we could do it without getting caught.*
b. **Assessment:** *It is {**unclear / *arguable / *uncertain / *unsure / *undecided**} to me whether mosquitoes have souls.*
c. **Inclination:** *It {**seems / appears / *is doubtful / *is likely / *is dubious**} to me that she has enough money to buy Microsoft.*
d. **Result:** *It is {**apparent / evident / obvious / *certain / *definite / *true / *undeniable**} to me that Croatia is destined to be the world's next superpower.*

When possible, however, the *to*-phrase is always optional, and when it occurs, the prepositional object usually refers to the speaker, who is ultimately respon-

8 The *it* in (30)c–d is of course to be taken as impersonal.

sible for the judgment expressed in any case. What this indicates, unsurprisingly, is that impersonal sentences of this sort allow one to characterize the epistemic status of the complement proposition without however attributing the judgment in question to any particular conceptualizer. They instead invoke a **generalized conceptualizer**, implying that the same assessment would be made by anyone in a position to judge. This is not inconsistent with a periphrastic specification, by means of a *to*-phrase, that the speaker (or someone else) identifies with this generalized conceptualizer as one individual – maybe even the primary or the only one – who does in fact view things in this manner. The expressions in (33) support the suggestion that these sentences both evoke a conceptualizer in generalized fashion and also situate the speaker with respect to this general viewpoint.

(33) *It is apparent – **{at least to me / if only to me / to me and doubtless to others}** – that the president has been lying to us about his motivations.*

Consider, then, a minimal contrast like (34), where the same predicate takes either a personal subject or impersonal *it*:

(34) a. ***I** am certain that formalists will someday discover the meaningfulness of grammar.*
b. ***It** is certain that formalists will someday discover the meaningfulness of grammar.*

Choosing *I* as subject highlights the speaker's own responsibility for the epistemic judgment. By using impersonal *it*, the speaker avoids the spotlight, shifting responsibility to the unspecified circumstances on the basis of which **any** conceptualizer would arrive at the same assessment. While it is true that the speaker retains ultimate responsibility, and could not plausibly deny the validity of the proposition said to be *certain*, the speaker's role is nonetheless defocused. The speaker remains offstage, only by implication subscribing to the view claimed to be evident to anyone who might consider the matter.

5. What does *it* mean?

That brings us to our central issues: the meaning of impersonal *it*, and the grammatical structure of expressions that employ it. I have approached these issues from three directions, each providing some important clues about the nature of *it* and *it*-constructions. I will now attempt to fit all the pieces together into a coherent account of the core phenomena.

5.1. Putting the pieces together

I propose that *it* is always meaningful and always referential in the linguistically relevant sense of that term. Its meaning is just as expected given its status as a third person singular neuter definite pronoun. As a pronoun, it profiles a thing characterized schematically in regard to type. Being third person singular neuter, it specifies this type as just non-human and non-plural. As a definite nominal, it singles out a unique instance of that type whose identity is supposedly evident in the discourse context. In anaphoric uses, the referent is identified by virtue of being coreferential to the antecedent nominal. In other cases, its identity may be evident from the non-linguistic context.

Intrinsically, however, *it* imposes few limitations on what it might designate. From the range of possible candidates – everything we might have occasion to refer to – its minimal type specification excludes only those which are human or plural. Since *it* can refer to everything else, it represents a kind of default, employed for anything not covered by other pronouns, which have smaller pools of eligible candidates. In terms of size (the number of eligible candidates), *it* does less to delimit this pool than any other pronoun.

The number of eligible candidates is however only one aspect of delimitation. Other factors include the size or extension of the referent and the possibility of vagueness – imprecision or uncertainty about just what is being singled out. The meaning of *it* is such that these two factors can be exploited to the full extent. For one thing, *it* can be used in reference to certain kinds of entities, such as masses and locations, which can be of any size, and can even be all-encompassing. This is not the case with a pronoun like *he* or *she*, which designates a person. Also, if it is known that the speaker is referring to some facet of a complex situation, *he* or *she* tells the listener just what to look for as its referent – a salient male or female individual. On the other hand, *it* affords no precise guidance concerning what kind of entity to look for – whether it is physical or abstract, discrete or mass-like, etc. The listener cannot even assume that the speaker would be capable of isolating or precisely delineating the intended referent.

The pronoun *it* has numerous non-anaphoric uses where it clearly refers to something but it is hard to say just what. As pointed out by Bolinger (1973), in such uses it sometimes alternates with forms like *things* or *everything*, without however being precisely equivalent to them. In (35)a, *it* is something like the course of one's life, recent experience, or progress toward some goal. In (35)b, *it* can perhaps be identified with a particular social relationship, but may go beyond this to include any potential for association or interaction. In (35)c, *it* might be interpreted as referring to the reason for terminating a conversation, yet it is hardly certain that anything so specific is intended. And in (35)d, I would speculate that *it* alludes to some unidentified entity appearing on the scene, referring either to this entity itself (which turns out to be Harry) or else, more abstractly, to the "path" representing its selection from a range of conceivable alternatives (Langacker 2001d).

(35) a. *How's* ***it*** *going?* [cf. *How are* ***things*** *going?*]
b. ***It's*** *all finished between us.* [cf. ***Everything*** *is finished between us.*]
c. *I don't want to be rude –* ***it's*** *just that I have to go cook dinner.*
d. *Look,* ***it's*** *Harry!*

In such uses, the referent of *it* is abstract yet something we feel we can almost identify. Almost, for it is hard to pin down its referent precisely or with full confidence, due to vagueness or its all-encompassing nature. Owing to these properties, the *it* in such expressions resembles impersonal *it* – indeed, many linguists would deny its meaningfulness. My own position is that impersonal *it* represents the extreme case of vagueness and non-delimitation, the endpoint on the scale, which the examples in (35) approximate but do not quite reach. Within the situation evoked, impersonal *it* is maximally vague and all-encompassing.

Chafe (1970. 101–102) said something similar in describing a sentence like *It's hot* or *It's late* as referring to an "all-encompassing state", and to a sentence like *It's snowing* as referring to an "all-encompassing event". He used the term **ambient** to indicate their maximally inclusive nature. Curiously, however, he ascribed this feature to the verb, treating the pronoun *it* as meaningless. Bolinger (1973) corrected this mistake and demonstrated the continuum between "ambient *it*" and impersonal uses. The notion "ambience" cannot of course be interpreted as referring just to the atmosphere or the physical surroundings. Rather, "it embraces weather, time, circumstance, whatever is obvious by the nature of reality or the implications of context". This characterization is perfectly consistent with the one offered here in terms of extreme non-delimitation within the scene described. It can further be reconciled with the other descriptions that have been offered, in terms of mental space, abstract setting, immediate scope, field, and "mere sceneness"/"general presence or availability".

A key point in coming to grips with impersonal *it* is that it does not refer to a single kind of entity, even if all its instantiations are susceptible to schematic characterization based on maximal non delimitation within a situation. We can speak of many kinds of situations, both physical and abstract, so the referent of *it* varies accordingly.[9]

---

9 To what extent a particular interpretation of *it* constitutes an actual, established meaning – not just a possible way of construing its schematic import – is a matter I will not address, nor is it terribly important from the CG standpoint.

The most obvious interpretations arise with "weather" verbs like *rain*, *snow*, *be foggy*, *be cold*, etc. In expressions like (36), one is tempted to interpret *it* as referring to the surrounding atmosphere which manifests the meteorological phenomenon. While I do not specifically rule this out, in view of the vagueness of *it* we must also consider other possibilities. Instead of the atmosphere per se, we might identify *it* as referring to the atmospheric conditions which generate the phenomenon. It could also be the expanse of space and time encompassing it, i.e. the spatial and temporal setting. More abstractly, *it* might be interpreted as indicating the relevant scope of awareness, i.e. everything evoked in apprehending the situation described. Here too there are alternate possibilities. In particular, who is the relevant conceptualizer? It might the speaker, who reports on a past situation from the more global perspective available at the time of speaking. Alternatively, it might be some implicit viewer observing the scene at the time indicated (*last night*).

(36) ***It*** *was {raining / snowing / foggy / cold} last night.*

Which of these options is the right one? I suspect that none of them is valid to the exclusion of the others. My claim is that the referent of impersonal *it* is maximally vague and undelimited within the situation described. Since the entities mentioned are roughly coextensive with that situation, *it* could be interpreted as referring to any of them, to any combination, or as simply being indeterminate as to which facet(s) of the scene it designates. This does not imply that it is meaningless or that it refers to nothing at all.

To the extent that we identify *it* with the global, all-encompassing surroundings, these surroundings are not always physical, and if physical are not always atmospheric. In (37)a the relevant spatial expanse is the ground. And while the surroundings in (37)b–f have a spatial and/or temporal component, space and time per se do not seem crucial. The emphasis instead is on experiential factors. The experience can occur at the perceptual, mental, emotive, or social level, or any combination of these. The relevant global circumstances are those in which the experience is manifested and which make it possible, whatever their nature: concrete or abstract; physical, psychological, or social. They include the very notion of an experiencer – if only a generalized experiencer – able to apprehend the situation and have the experience in question.

(37) a. *We can't walk through this field –* ***it's*** *oozing oil all over.*
b. ***It's*** *our wedding anniversary.*
c. ***It's*** *quiet in the countryside.*
d. ***It's*** *chaotic in the Middle East.*
e. ***It's*** *fun when old friends get together.*
f. ***It's*** *awkward when your wife meets your lover.*

One kind of mental experience consists in making propositional judgments and constructing an ever-evolving conception of reality. This is the level invoked by classic examples of impersonal *it* supposedly involving "extraposition" of a subject complement clause:

(38) a. ***It's** conceivable that we'll have to buy a new mattress.*
b. ***It's** uncertain whether he can finish the race.*
c. ***It** appears that the epidemic was caused by a virus.*
d. ***It's** very clear that our leaders cannot be trusted.*

What constitutes the relevant circumstances or the total situation at this abstract level? It cannot be limited to a spatio-temporal expanse, or even to any particular domain of experience. What counts as the overall situation for purposes of making an epistemic judgment has to subsume everything evoked by the conceptualizer as the basis for making it. Thus included is any sort of general or particular knowledge required to formulate the proposition as well as any sort of information brought to bear in assessing it. Though it may seem circular, the relevant circumstances can be identified as everything falling with the conceptualizer's scope of awareness for purposes of apprehending the target proposition and dealing with it.

This scope of awareness is what I referred to earlier as the **field**. In general terms, the field was defined as the scope of potential interaction. This can be characterized with respect to different levels of interaction, e.g. physically as the extent of our reach, or perceptually as the maximal field of view. At higher levels of cognition, the field is much harder to delineate, given our extraordinary mental capabilities. But by analogy to the physical and perceptual levels, we can describe the field for higher-level cognitive processes as comprising everything a conceptualizer is capable of apprehending at a given moment, or everything apprehended for a given purpose. Metaphorically, it is the conceptualizer's "mental reach".

I thus propose, as a general characterization, that impersonal *it* profiles the relevant field, i.e. the conceptualizer's scope of awareness for the issue at hand. The conceptualizer may be identified as the speaker or some other specific individual, but – not surprisingly for impersonal constructions – it tends to be a generalized conceptualizer. What constitutes the relevant field varies with purpose and level of experience (e.g. physical, perceptual, social, epistemic), and while *it* evokes the field as an undifferentiated whole, certain facets of it may stand out as being especially relevant or most centrally and directly involved in the relationship profiled by the clause.[10] Such entities offer themselves as

10 These can thus be seen as the active zone of *it* with respect to the clausal relationship (Langacker 1984, 1993b; Chapter 2: § 2).

specific interpretations for the referent of *it*. I suspect, however, that the most schematic value predominates, such that *it* is maximally vague in reference. Imposing no delimitation on the field, in effect its referent is coextensive with it, or at least non-distinct.

5.2. Reconciliation

Highly general notions tend to be the hardest to characterize, and *it* is perhaps the most general of all. To what extent the present effort improves on previous ones is certainly debatable. It seems clear, however, that the various attempts listed earlier are very much in the same spirit, and given our current level of understanding, they are not so precisely formulated that there is any intrinsic conflict among them.

My characterization of impersonal *it* most obviously parallels Bolinger's. First, I emphasize that impersonal *it* represents the limiting case in the range of values consistent with the status of *it* as a third person singular neuter definite pronoun. My statement that it represents the extreme case of non-delimitation mirrors Bolinger's statement that *it* has "the greatest possible generality of meaning, limited only in the sense that it is 'neuter'". I further say that, while impersonal *it* evokes the field as an undifferentiated whole, the reference is vague, and certain facets may stand out as being especially relevant or most saliently and directly involved in the clausal relationship. This mirrors Bolinger's statement that *it* "embraces weather, time, circumstance, whatever is obvious by the nature of reality or the implications of context". What I have added to Bolinger's account is: (i) a more extensive discussion of nominal reference, including the notion of delimitation; (ii) more explicit invocation of a conceptualizer and the conceptualizer's scope of awareness; and (iii) identification of *it*'s referent with a specific construct (the field) central to a basic cognitive model (the control cycle) shown to be important for semantic and grammatical description.

Citing Bolinger and Gensler, Lakoff (1987: 542) mentions *it* in conjunction with existential *there*, proposing that the latter "designates a mental space in which a conceptual entity is to be located". Smith (2000) uses similar language in regard to German *es*, further identifying the mental space as the one introduced by a "space-building" verb like 'know':

(39) a. *Ich weiss* ***es*** *sicher, dass er morgen kommt.* [German]
'I know for sure that he's coming tomorrow.'
b. ***Es*** *ist sicher, dass Inge morgen ankommt.*
'It's certain that Inge will arrive tomorrow.'

He suggests that explicit mention of this space prefigures the introduction of a proposition within it and accentuates its "mental distance" from the conceptualizer. Given how broadly and vaguely the notion mental space is defined (Fauconnier 1985), a field or "scope of awareness" certainly qualifies. Beyond this, Lakoff and Smith indicate that the pronoun prefigures the introduction of an element and establishes the context in which appears. This discourse function, which I have not sufficiently emphasized, is quite compatible with the description of a field, which, as the relevant scope of awareness, provides both the basis for entertaining a proposition and the context in which it emerges.

A space in which a proposition is introduced, or a context in which it emerges, is also reasonably described as an **abstract setting**. A typical setting is an encompassing expanse of space, or analogously an expanse of time, within which the process profiled by a clause unfolds. A setting of this sort is thus the relevant scope of awareness in space, or in time, for apprehending the clausal process. And indeed, for certain instances of impersonal *it*, notably with meteorological predicates, it might indeed be interpreted as referring to the spatio-temporal setting. While this is hardly sufficient for more abstract uses involving the assessment of propositions, there is no inherent reason for limiting the notion of a setting to space and time. A more abstract formulation of this construct along the lines of "scope of awareness" will accommodate both spatio-temporal settings and the epistemic field as special cases.

In CG, an expression's **immediate scope** is defined as the general locus of viewing attention, those facets of the overall situation put "onstage" as being immediately relevant at a given level of organization for a particular purpose. In his analysis of impersonal constructions, Achard (1998: ch. 7) proposes that French *il* profiles the immediate scope for existential predications, with respect to which expressions of propositional judgment represent a natural extension. Thus *il* in (40)a designates the region attended to by the conceptualizer within which the tires are observable. It is not, however, just a spatial region but further subsumes, for instance, knowledge of the state of the art of tire production. Similarly, in (40)b *il* refers to the range of considerations brought to bear in assessing the complement proposition. This is clearly consistent with my characterization of impersonal *it* as indicating the relevant scope of awareness

(40) a. ***Il*** *existe des pneus qu'on a pas besoin de gonfler.* [French]
'There exist tires that don't need inflating.'
b. ***Il*** *est vrai que Jean ne la connait pas.*
'It's true that John doesn't know her.'

Finally, Kirsner's description of Dutch *er* in terms of "low situational deixis" corresponds to my notions of weak pointing (via person only) and minimal delimitation. He further speaks of "general presence or availability", an entity being "on the scene" even though "the identity of that scene is immaterial". These notions can plausibly be equated with vagueness of reference within the scope of awareness.

Is there any conflict between the vagueness and non-delimitation ascribed to impersonal subjects and the CG characterization of subjects in terms of primary focal prominence (trajector status)? I think not. For one thing, this prominence is conferred on some element in a scene by virtue of how one chooses to express it linguistically; it is not a matter of intrinsic cognitive salience. Additionally, focal prominence can itself be characterized in such a way that conferring it on the field (or scope of awareness) seems quite natural.

The characterization I suggest for trajector and landmark is based on **dynamicity**, the notion that the **time course** of a conceptualization – how it develops and unfolds through processing time – is an important dimension of semantic structure (Langacker 2001c, 2005b). A special case of dynamicity is reference point organization (Chapter 2: § 3). This refers to a kind of sequenced mental access, in which one entity – the reference point – is invoked as a way of mentally "reaching" a target associated with it (Langacker 1993c). Trajector and landmark can then be characterized as the **first** and **second reference points** accessed in building up to the full conception of a profiled relationship, which constitutes the target (Langacker 1999c, 2001a, 2008a: § 14.1.5).

On this account, the grammatical subject is a **starting point** vis-à-vis the profiled clausal process, i.e. the initial reference point which anchors its conception (cf. Chafe 1994). Choosing impersonal *it* as subject makes very good sense from this perspective. The immediate scope of awareness is indeed a kind of starting point and point of access for apprehending what is manifested within it. Coding it as the grammatical subject – starting point for apprehending the clausal process – thus conforms to a general strategy of linguistic presentation observed in many other phenomena: that of starting with something large or inclusive, then "zooming in" to something smaller contained in it. Setting-subject constructions, illustrated in (9), are one case. A few others, of diverse sorts, are exemplified in (41): locative inversion, nested locatives, biblical citations, and whole-part compounds.

(41) a. *In the driveway sat a brand new luxury car.*
b. *He's staying in La Jolla, at La Valencia Hotel, on the sixth floor, in room 619.*
c. *the book of Job, chapter 28, verse 17*
d. *fingernail, door handle, tire tread, tree root, jar lid, table leg, mountain top*

6. Impersonal constructions

Determining the meaning of impersonal *it* is only one facet of the overall problem of describing impersonal constructions. Here I can briefly examine only a small number of such constructions, hopefully diverse enough to be representative.

Let me first consider predicates like *hot*, *cold*, *freezing*, and *miserable*, which can take as their subject either an experiencer, impersonal *it*, or a locational expression like *Chicago*:[11]

(42) a. *I'm {hot / cold / freezing / miserable} here in Chicago.*
b. *It's {hot / cold / freezing / miserable} in Chicago.*
c. *Chicago is {hot / cold / freezing / miserable}.*

As shown in Figure 5.9, all three constructions involve the same elements: an experienced sensation (dashed arrow), which implies an experiencer (E); by nature the experiencer has a certain scope of awareness (F), including the ambient environment; something non-specific within this field induces (double arrow) the sensation; and all this occurs in a spatial setting, identified here as Chicago. In each case, the trajector is specified by a nominal which thereby functions as grammatical subject, and a non-trajector setting is specified adverbially in the usual way.

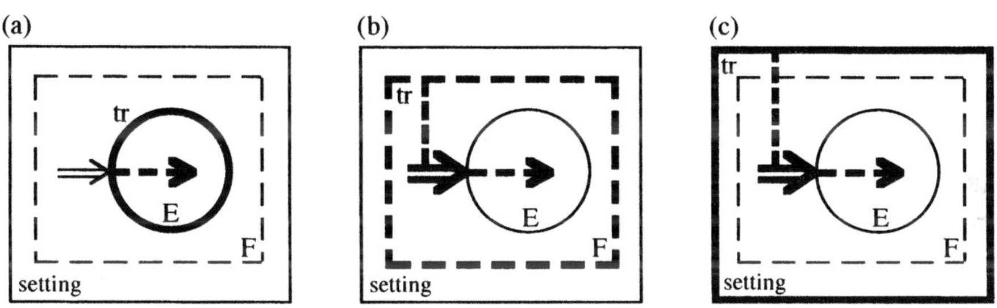

Figure 5.9

The constructions differ primarily in which facets of this situation they highlight through profiling and choice of trajector. The construction in (42)a highlights the experiencer and the experience itself, leaving its cause implicit. Indeed, it does not necessarily imply that the weather in Chicago is responsible – it merely says that the speaker has the sensation, conceivably due to psychosis

11 Of course, not every predicate that can be used in one pattern can be used in the others, e.g. *It's windy in Chicago*, *Chicago is windy*, but **I'm windy in Chicago*; or *I'm happy in Chicago*, but **It's happy in Chicago*, **Chicago is happy*.

or other reasons unrelated to atmospheric conditions. The other constructions shift the primary focus away from the experiencer and place it on either the global field, expressed by *it*, or on the spatial setting, Chicago. Both constructions favor a generalized experiencer, implicit and unidentified. In each case the focus shifts, as expected, to the trajector's role in hosting and possibly being responsible for inducing the experience. The contrast between (42)b and (42)c is a matter of whether the trajector is identified as the experiential field per se or as the spatial setting with which it is largely co-extensive. Because it highlights the scope of awareness, (42)b places slightly more emphasis on subjective experience than does (42)c. Of the two, the latter more easily lends itself to interpretation as an objective statement of scientific fact.

Whereas the predicates in (42) are primarily experiential and only secondarily meteorological, the opposite is true for predicates like *rain*, *snow*, *be foggy*, *be windy*, etc. I suggest, however, that a sentence like *It's raining* does pertain to the nature of environmental experience and thus does invoke an experiencer, abeit one who remains offstage and tends to be construed in generalized fashion. A diagrammatic representation would be analogous to Figure 5.9(b), except that the profiled relationship would be that of water descending through the atmosphere, its apprehension by the experiencer being implicit and unprofiled.

Let us next consider predicates of propositional attitude, which I will exemplify by means of inclination predicates. Once more there are three basic patterns, as seen in (43): a personal subject, impersonal *it* as subject, and a clausal subject.[12] These are respectively diagrammed in Figure 5.10. The epistemic control cycle is in each case an important aspect of their meaning. In the personal construction, the conceptualizer functions as trajector, and the target proposition as landmark. These are respectively spelled out by the subject nominal and the complement clause, in accordance with the regular subject and object constructions.

(43) a. *I {suspect / believe / imagine} that she will be elected.*
b. *It {appears / seems / is likely} that she will be elected.*
c. *That she will be elected is {likely / probable / doubtful}.*

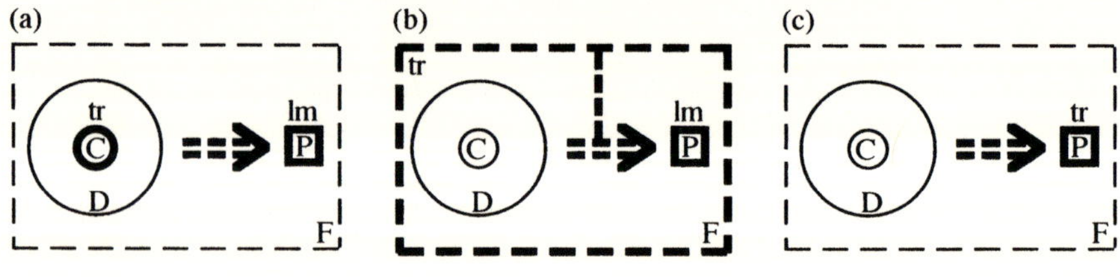

Figure 5.10

12 For so-called "raising" constructions, see Langacker 1995c.

The other two patterns defocus the conceptualizer, which tends to be construed in generalized fashion. *It*-impersonals shift primary focal prominence to the field and therefore highlight the role of the relevant scope of awareness – notably the range of considerations that can be brought to bear for P's assessment – in bringing about the inclination toward accepting P as real. The proposition still functions as landmark. Note, however, that this is not a transitive construction, as it does not profile the interaction between two participants, the trajector being more setting-like. The expressions in (43)b thus cannot be passivized (cf. (11)c–d).

Given that the conceptualizer is not in focus, and that English requires an overt clausal subject, there is one other option besides the field: the complement proposition itself. This results in pattern (c). It simply highlights the role of P as target of inclination, i.e. as something whose validity anybody would incline to (or incline away from, in the case of *doubtful*) under the circumstances (F).

For a final example, consider predicates of emotional reaction, as in (44):

(44) a. *His crude jokes {embarrassed / surprised / amused} me.*
b. *His crude jokes are {embarrassing / surprising / amusing}.*
c. *It's {embarrassing / surprising / amusing} that he tells crude jokes.*
d. *It's {embarrassing / surprising / amusing} when he tells crude jokes.*

Lexical verbs like *embarrass*, *surprise*, and *amuse* profile the process of the trajector inducing this reaction in the experiencer, focused as landmark. This is sketched in Figure 5.11(a). The trajector can be a proposition (e.g. *That he told so many crude jokes embarrassed me*) or some kind of activity or event, but in any case it is something accepted as real, thus included in E's epistemic dominion (D). The field (F) is more inclusive, subsuming such factors as E's sense of propriety, emotional dispositions, and appreciation of social expectations, all relevant to the emotional reaction's emergence. The adjectival predicates in (44)b are parallel to the verbs in (44)a. The difference is that in (44)b the conceptualizer is generalized, hence defocused and usually left implicit. As generalized statements, these sentences ascribe a property to the subject rather than describing specific events of emotional instigation.

In (44)c–d, trajector status shifts to the field, coded by impersonal *it*. In pattern (c), the instigating factor is a proposition accepted as real, while in (d) it is an occurrence. This contrast shows up formally in the use of a *that*-clause vs. a *when*-clause. In the former case, with the field focused as trajector, P has only secondary focal prominence, i.e. landmark status, just as in Figure 5.10(b). This is not a transitive construction (and does not passivize) because it does not profile the interaction of participants. In pattern (d), on the other hand, the instigating occurrence is construed as defining a temporal setting, consisting of the span of time during which the occurrence is manifested. It is thus expressed by means of a *when*-clause, as is usual for temporal settings. The import of (44)d is that, during the time span characterized by his telling jokes, anyone apprehending the total circumstances (F) – including social expectations, a sense of propriety, etc. – would experience embarrassment induced by that occurrence.[13]

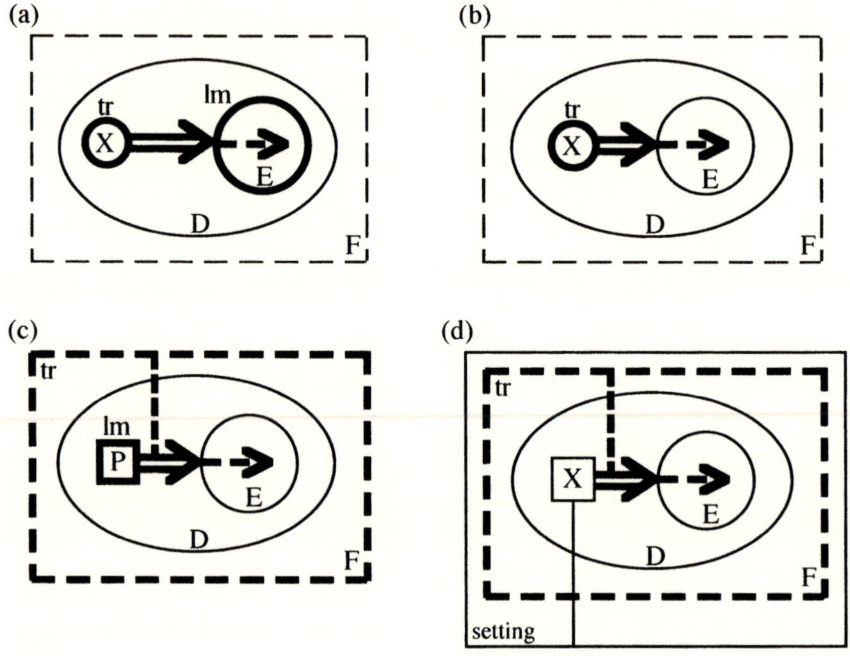

Figure 5.11

7. Further prospects

Numerous topics cry out for further investigation. Let me conclude by mentioning just a few.

13 Since the occurrence has the dual role of both defining the temporal setting and also instigating the emotional reaction, it would be just a short step for this to be reanalyzed as a complement clause construction with *when* as complementizer (analogous to a *that*-clause), rather than an adverbial clause. I would predict that this would show up as an attested path of grammaticization.

First, I have not considered "existential" *there* and how it relates to impersonal *it*. In other languages, the distinction made in English is neutralized, e.g. French *il* translates as *there* in (40)a. At present I can offer only the vague suggestion that *it* tends to be more abstract and more inclusive than *there*.

A second major problem is the analysis of comparable expressions in "pro drop" languages like Spanish and Russian. In particular, how should sentences like (3)c, *Parece que es muy inteligente* 'It seems that she is very intelligent', or those in (45), be analyzed? Is it reasonable to claim, as suggested by the present account, that such sentences have an unexpressed trajector identifiable as the relevant scope of awareness? Smith (1994) has proposed an analysis along these lines for Russian, observing that it neatly accounts for various grammatical properties of these constructions (notably a verb's inflection as third person singular).

(45) a. *Llueve.* 'It's raining.' [Spanish]
b. *Mne xolodno.* 'It's cold to me.'/'I'm cold.' [Russian]

Another matter is the occurrence of *it* in "clefting", e.g. (1)e *It's in April that we go to Japan*. Here I suspect that *it* is more specific than just the relevant scope of awareness. I speculate that *it* designates an abstract "path of selection", whereby one option is chosen from a range of conceivable alternatives. I have previously characterized this notion in the analysis of English WH (Langacker 2001d).

A final problem worth mentioning is the occurrence of *it* in object position, as in (46):

(46) a. *She resents* ***it*** *very much that she hasn't been promoted.*
b. *I love* ***it*** *when you do that.*

Smith 2000 was primarily concerned with the occurrence of German *es* in object position, as in (39)a. Consistent with Smith's analysis, it strikes me as reasonable to say that the attitude (resentment, love, etc.) is directed at the overall situation (scope of awareness), within which the specific occurrence expressed by the subordinate clause stands out as the instigating factor, in the manner of Figure 5.11(c)-(d).

Obviously, all these issues (and many more besides) require extensive investigation, both individually and in relation to one another. I believe, however, that the semantic characterization proposed for *it* and impersonal constructions offers a promising basis for a unified and linguistically revealing account.

Chapter 6
Enunciating the parallelism of nominal and clausal grounding

1. What is at issue?

In various works (especially Langacker 1991), I have noted an extensive parallelism between nominals and finite clauses. It begins with the categories noun and verb, which are polar opposites with respect to both their schematic characterizations and their prototypes. Schematically, each is characterized in terms of basic conceptual abilities: grouping and reification in the case of nouns;[1] and sequentially tracking a relationship in its evolution through time, in the case of verbs. These define the abstract notions thing and process, which in turn define the categories: a noun profiles a thing, and a verb profiles a process. At the prototype level, nouns and verbs are based on the respective conceptual archetypes of a physical object and a forceful interaction involving such objects. Both are central to an idealized cognitive model dubbed the **billiard-ball model**. This is our conception of the world as being populated by discrete physical objects, some of which move around in space, come into contact with others, and affect them through the transmission of energy.

Granted these characterizations of the noun and verb categories, their parallelism continues with their major subcategories: count vs. mass in the case of nouns, and perfective vs. imperfective in the case of verbs. I have argued that the count/mass and perfective/imperfective distinctions are precisely analogous modulo the inherent conceptual difference between a noun and a verb (Langacker 1987a, 1987b, 1991). Most basically, the thing profiled by a count noun and the process profiled by a perfective verb are both construed as being bounded in their domain of instantiation (which for nouns is typically space, and for verbs is always time).[2] By contrast, the referent of a mass noun or an

1 As I define them, **grouping** consists in the co-conception of constitutive entities, and **reification** in their treatment as a unitary entity for some higher-level cognitive purpose. For example, we group a set of dots when we perceive them as a cluster (excluding others), and effect their reification when we observe that this cluster is larger than another.

2 The domain of instantiation is the domain where instances of a type are primarily thought of as residing, being distinguished from one another by their locations.

imperfective verb is **not** inherently conceived as being bounded (although the imposition of bounding is not precluded).

Of more concern here is the parallelism of nouns and verbs at higher levels of grammatical organization. Each corresponds to a higher-level constituent whose universality and grammatical importance is not in question: a nominal and a finite clause. And they do so in parallel fashion. By itself, a lexical noun or verb merely specifies a type of thing or process. On the other hand, a nominal or a finite clause profiles a grounded instance of a thing or process type. What it means for a thing or process instance to be grounded is the topic we will be examining.[3]

Although it could be broadly applied, the term grounding is reserved for particular kinds of relationships that a profiled thing or process bears to the ground. The elements said to have a grounding function share a number of properties. For one thing, they are highly grammaticized, hence they usually belong to small, closed sets of opposing elements. Semantically, they pertain to fundamental properties reasonably considered "epistemic" in nature (e.g. time, reality, existence, identification). Also, they profile the grounded entity rather than the grounding relationship. Concomitantly, the ground itself is **subjectively construed**, i.e. "offstage" and implicit (Langacker 1985, 1990b, 2001e).

The last two properties are represented in Figure 6.1. It shows the interlocutors offstage, as components of the ground, one facet of their interaction being the directing of their attention to the profiled thing or process. By definition, the latter is onstage as the focus of attention.[4] Since only the grounded entity is profiled, and an expression's profile determines its grammatical category, a grounding element is itself a schematic nominal or finite clause. Certain grounding elements can indeed function alone in this capacity. In the case of English, these include demonstratives and certain quantifiers (e.g. *That is incorrect*; *All were defective*). They also include the modals, with the qualification – reflecting a more general syntactic restriction – that a subject is also needed (*She may*; *They should*).

My investigation of grounding and the grounding parallelism has focused on English. I make no claim concerning how much of the analysis carries over to other languages, or precisely how. Even for English I am concentrating on the

3 Grounding has been characterized in numerous works (e.g. Langacker 1991, 2002a, 2002d, 2004c) and is dealt with further in Chapter 7.

4 What I am metaphorically calling the "onstage region" is more technically referred to as an expression's **immediate scope**. For arguments that only the grounded entity is profiled, not the grounding relationship or the ground itself, see Langacker 2002a.

core grounding systems, with no pretense that these are exhaustive or sharply distinguished from other phenomena. For nominals, these core elements include articles, demonstratives, and "relative" quantifiers. The clausal grounding elements are tense and the basic modals.[5]

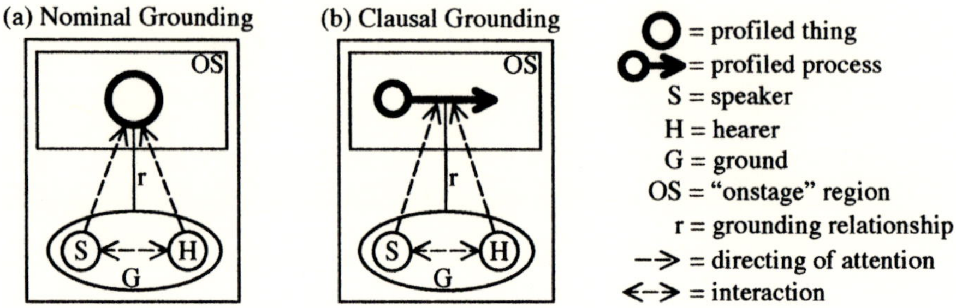

Figure 6.1

In a previous discussion of their parallelism (Langacker 2002d), I pointed out that, due to the inherent nature of nouns and verbs, nominal and clausal grounding are primarily concerned with different issues. Few if any conceptual archetypes are more fundamental than those functioning as the noun and verb prototypes, namely physical objects and events. Objects and events pose different epistemic problems related to how we typically experience them.

In the case of objects, the basic tendency is to **endure**. With obvious qualifications, the default expectation for objects is that they will continue to exist unless and until something happens to change this situation. Another default, in the case of objects, is the simultaneous existence of many instances of a given type. In our daily lives we encounter many people, many birds, many houses, many rocks, many napkins, etc., and further believe that these are only some of the countless instances that exist. With nouns, therefore, the primary epistemic concern is not existence, but rather identification. In learning and talking about the world, what we generally need to know about an object is not "does it exist?", but rather "which one is it?".

In the case of events, just the opposite is true. Instead of enduring, events **occur**, typically in a rather short time span. And while there are many instances of a given event type – e.g. many instances of talking, kicking, designing, crawling, etc. – identification is not a major issue, for several reasons. For one

5 Also included is agreement inflection on the verb, primarily limited to third singular *-s* in the present tense. I will ignore this here. Relative quantifiers are characterized in Langacker 1991: § 3.2.

thing, event instances are transient, and since they do not stick around, they do not develop a permanent identity. Also due to their transience, instances of a type tend not to co-exist in large numbers. At a particular moment, we may well be aware of only one, so distinguishing them is not a major problem. For clauses, then, the primary epistemic concern is not identification, but rather existence – whether the event in question occurs at all.

With events, the problem of identification looms especially small when we factor in a crucial property of event conceptions, as opposed to object conceptions. Events are **conceptually dependent**: their conception inherently invokes and depends on the conception of their participants (even if these are invoked only schematically). By contrast, we can usually conceptualize an object without in any salient way invoking an event it participates in, so objects are **conceptually autonomous**. For this reason nominals are routinely included as part of clauses, but not conversely. And because events are conceptually dependent on their participants, what counts as the event type for purposes of clausal grounding is not simply the **basic type** specified by the lexical verb, but also includes the specifications provided by its nominal complements. For example, the event type grounded by the past tense in *Sheila picked this daffodil* is not just *pick*, but rather the **elaborated type** *Sheila pick this daffodil*. With elaborated types the need to distinguish multiple instances is seldom a pressing concern.

I suggest, then, that a key to grounding parallelism is the realization that the nominal and clausal realms pose different **primary epistemic concerns**. For the two realms there are different answers to the basic question "What is at issue?". In the case of nominals, identification is primarily at issue. In the case of clauses, existence (or occurrence) is primarily at issue. These contrasting primary concerns are reflected in basic aspects of the grammaticized grounding systems. The differences they engender tend to obscure the fundamental parallelism of nominal and clausal grounding – the systems are parallel **modulo** the difference in what is at issue.

2. Control

Nominal and clausal grounding respond to the same imperative: our ongoing effort to achieve what I will call **epistemic control**. While this is really just a fancy term for "knowledge", it highlights what I consider to be a fundamental unity in many aspects of human experience. The abstracted commonality of these experiences constitutes an idealized cognitive model referred to as the **control cycle** (Langacker 2002c). As described in Chapter 5 (§ 4), its essential elements are an actor, the actor's dominion, the field, and a target. The actor's dominion is the set of entities it controls (cf. Langacker 1993c; Chapter 4). The field is its range of potential interaction – when a target enters the actor's field, it has to be dealt with in some way, if only by being avoided or ignored. One basic way for the actor to deal with it is to capture it, bringing it under control as an element in its dominion.

As was shown in Figure 5.5, the control cycle consists in several phases. The first is a static baseline phase, where the actor is at rest. In the next phase a target enters the actor's field, creating the potential for their interaction; this potential phase is one of tension, as the situation has to be resolved in some manner. The action phase consists in the actor resolving it by capturing the target. This yields the result phase, static once more, but with the target now belonging to the actor's dominion. I suggest that this cycle of rest, tension, action, and relaxation is characteristic of many (if not most) experiences, and at different levels: physical, perceptual, mental, and social. My original example involved the physical action of a cat capturing a mouse. Bodily functions like eating and breathing can also be described in these terms (Chapter 10). Perceptually, you can *watch for* something (a state of tension), then *see* it in the active sense of *catching sight* of it, after which you *see* it for a while as a stable perceptual experience (i.e. you *have it in sight* as the focus of your visual attention). An example at the social level is making a new acquaintance: there is first the tension created by meeting a new individual, followed by the action of negotiating a relationship, and then the relaxed state of an established relationship with accepted modes of social control.

Various kinds of linguistic elements can be partially characterized semantically with reference to the control cycle. For instance, the verbs *want*, *get*, and *have* correspond to the potential, action, and result phases. It is probably no accident that these verbs are extended far beyond the domain of physical acquisition and are adapted for varied grammatical purposes. Also reflecting these phases are the aspectual markers *to*, *-ing*, and *-ed* (e.g. *to establish*, *establishing*, *established*). In the case of epistemic control, the phases are reflected in predicates of propositional attitude, like those in (1):

(1) *She {suspected / decided / knew} that her husband was unfaithful.*

Here the actor is a conceptualizer, the target is a proposition, and the dominion is the set of propositions accepted as established knowledge. The predicates *suspect*, *decide*, and *know* respectively profile processes representing the potential, action, and result phases of the **epistemic control cycle**.[6]

6 A finer-grained description of the potential phase (Sumnicht 2001) was presented in Chapter 5: § 4.2. It will be further developed in Chapter 10.

What concerns us here is how the epistemic control cycle is manifested in nominal and clausal grounding. In the case of grounding, the relevant conceptualizers are the speaker and hearer, with the target being the profiled thing or process. The best strategy is to start with clausal grounding, which reflects the cycle more straightforwardly, and then compare it to nominal grounding. However, in using the phrase "more straightforwardly" I am not accusing clausal grounding of being straightforward. To understand it, we must first elucidate other dimensions of the problem.

For one thing, we have to bear in mind that **epistemic** control is not the only kind relevant to the analysis of grounding and finite clauses. Also important is **effective** control. These aspects of linguistic structure reflect not only our constant effort to acquire knowledge about the world, but also our efforts to change it – besides just learning what happens, we try to influence what happens. Thus, in addition to predicates of propositional attitude, like those in (1), we have predicates of desire and influence, like those in (2). These generally have a force-dynamic nature.

(2) a. *She {wants / hopes / aspires} to become an opera diva.*
b. *She {ordered / forced / persuaded} her daughter to end the relationship.*

3. (Inter)Action

Another point to elucidate (one that cognitive linguists have sometimes been accused of ignoring) is that language and speech have a social dimension. Moreover, since speaking is a kind of action, language is dynamic rather than static. Canonically, there is both a speaker and an addressee, engaged in a social interaction.[7] And when these inter-locutors inter-act, they negotiate meanings and the values of linguistic elements.

It is not a matter of choosing between a cognitive and a social-interactive approach – for either to be viable, it has to incorporate the other. Social interaction depends on cognition. It is not carried out by empty heads, but by sentient creatures who apprehend the circumstances, assess the mental state of the other party, and act accordingly. Conversely, apprehension of the speaker-hearer interaction

7 I will limit my attention to the canonical situation of a face-to-face two-participant interaction. There are of course many departures from this canon (e.g. writing, recorded messages, cell-phone conversations, multiple addressees, formal lectures). One major departure is the use of language in thought, which may be its primary use in terms of sheer prevalence. If so, it nonetheless derives from and largely reflects the spoken language of social interaction.

is an essential aspect of the conceptualizations that constitute linguistic meanings. While it figures to some extent in the value of all linguistic elements and expressions, in the case of grounding it is clearly central. As shown in Figure 6.1, grounding elements specifically invoke the speaker, the hearer, and their interaction in a speech event. A more detailed representation would show that each interlocutor attends to the other, makes some assessment of the other's knowledge and intentions, and apprehends the physical, social, cultural, and discourse contexts.

All linguistic units are abstracted from **usage events**: actual instances of language use, in the full detail of their contextual understanding. As units emerge from usage, becoming **entrenched** in the minds of speakers and **conventional** in a speech community, they retain as part of their value any feature which is constant across the events giving rise to them. This includes any facet of the context and the speaker-hearer interaction. Minimally, a unit incorporates the very notion of its being employed by interlocutors in speaking the language in question. Even if quite peripheral, this is part of the conventional import of every linguistic unit (Langacker 2001b). What makes grounding elements special is that the ground has more than just this minimal presence. It is usually specified in more detail. And because its relationship to the profiled thing or process represents the only substantial content of grounding elements, the ground figures more centrally in their meaning.

A usage event is just that – an event, something that happens. More precisely, it is an action carried out by the interlocutors, each of whom apprehends it from their own perspective. Being abstracted from usage events (through the reinforcing of a recurrent commonality they manifest), a linguistic unit resides in a **schematized pattern of action**. It is therefore intrinsically dynamic.[8] Moreover, the action unfolds at different levels: physical, kinesthetic, perceptual, mental, social. These are nonetheless all "cognitive" in the broad sense of being apprehended and/or under neural control. We generally learn these patterns of action from the perspective of both the speaker and the addressee. In the case of a sound, for example, we learn both to articulate it and to perceive it. For many units, e.g. a lexical item or a grammatical construction, it is plausible to suppose that a representation emerges which abstracts away from the difference between the speaker's and hearer's perspective. However, I take no position on how, when, or even whether this occurs.

Be that as it may, the units we abstract are independent of any particular speech event. This is so even for words like *I*, *you*, *here*, and *now*, which refer

8 This dynamicity tends to be obscured by static representations like formulas and diagrams, which are nonetheless useful for analytical purposes if their limitations are kept in mind.

to facets of the ground. Viewed as conventional units – which any English speaker can employ at any time or place – they refer to facets of the ground in **generalized** fashion, i.e. as **roles** within the **speech event scenario**. Representing the reinforced commonality of innumerable usage events, this scenario and its roles retain the notion of indexing a particular speech event without actually doing so. In other words, linguistic units invoke the ground and its various facets schematically, as **virtual** entities (Langacker 1999d) or roles (Fauconnier 1985), by way of generalizing over open-ended sets of particular instances. An actual usage event then constitutes an **enactment** of the speech event scenario, in which the interlocutors and other facets of the ground are **identified** with roles of the scenario. Thus even deictic elements have an abstracted conceptual meaning independent of particular uses. They have both semantic and pragmatic import, the latter arising through particular entities being identified with roles of the scenario whenever it is enacted.

Linguistic units, then, are schematized patterns of **action**, an important aspect of which is **interaction** of the interlocutors. Within a single speech event, the speaker's role is **initiative**, while the hearer's role is **reactive**.[9] Moreover, their interaction invariably has a **force-dynamic** component (Talmy 1988), if only because the very act of speaking calls for the listener's attention. I agree with Harder (1996) that linguistic units are reasonably viewed as instructions for the addressee to follow. In no small measure these instructions pertain to the directing of attention. For instance, the word *elbow* amounts to an instruction to conceptualize an arm, and within that to focus attention on the central part that bends – the profile of *arm*. Using the word constitutes an enactment of the instruction it embodies.

In speaking, the speaker is always striving for effective control at least in the minimal, local sense of getting the addressee to act in a certain way. There are various kinds and levels of hearer response which the speaker may be trying to induce. The minimum response is simply for the hearer to apprehend the expression in accordance with established linguistic convention. For a sentient addressee fluent in the language, this is largely automatic – even without intending to be cooperative, such a person can hardly avoid processing a heard expression in the accustomed manner. If I say *elephant*, you can hardly avoid thinking of an elephant. This minimal level of response is a kind of baseline, prerequisite for higher levels. As sketched in Figure 6.2(a), for the case of *elephant*, the speaker's effort (double arrow) is aimed at inducing the hearer to

9 Naturally, the speaker may be responding to a previous utterance by the current addressee. The speaker's role is nonetheless initiative in local terms, in the context of the current speech event.

access a certain body of conceptual content and direct attention (dashed arrow) to the profiled entity. Similarly, diagram 2(b) shows the hearer directing attention to a profiled process by way of apprehending the clause *She will leave.*

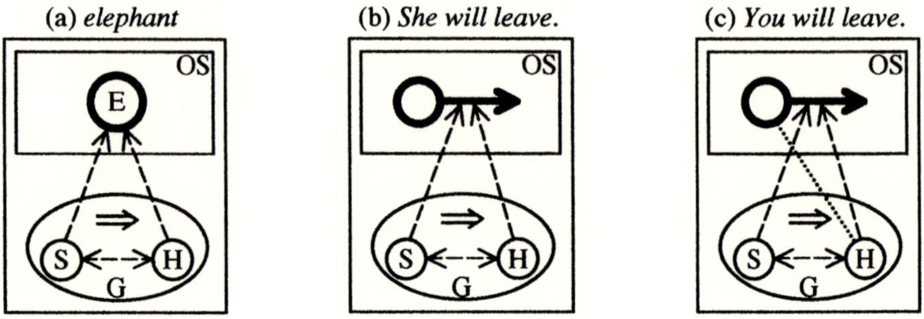

Figure 6.2

Other levels of response correspond to the speech acts of asking, ordering, and asserting. An act of questioning is intended to elicit a **linguistic** response. An order is intended to elicit an **effective** response, in which the hearer carries out some action (typically non-linguistic). An assertion is meant to elicit the **epistemic** response of a proposition being accepted as part of the hearer's conception of reality.

The latter two levels concern us here. Naturally, an order shows most clearly the force-dynamic nature of the speaker-hearer interaction. The intended result is for the hearer to not only apprehend the expression and direct attention to the profiled event, but also to carry out that event. Figure 6.2(c) shows the hearer directing attention to the event profiled by the clause *You will leave*; it differs from 2(b) only in that the hearer is equated with the clausal subject. This much holds whether the clause is construed as an order or merely a description. If we want to represent the distinguishing property of an order, we must therefore add to 2(c) another level of force-dynamic interaction. To keep the diagrams simple, I show this level separately in Figure 6.3(a).[10] Observe that the profiled event is put in the same plane as the force-dynamic arrow directed at the hearer. This notation (admittedly non-optimal) is meant to indicate that the speaker applies social force that will induce the hearer to carry out the profiled action. Except perhaps for intonation, there is no explicit coding of this additional level. As part of the ground, it is however a conventionally sanctioned aspect of the expression's linguistic meaning.

10 Hence the force-dynamic relationship in Figure 6.3(a) is overlaid on that in Figure 6.2(c), instead of being an alternative to it.

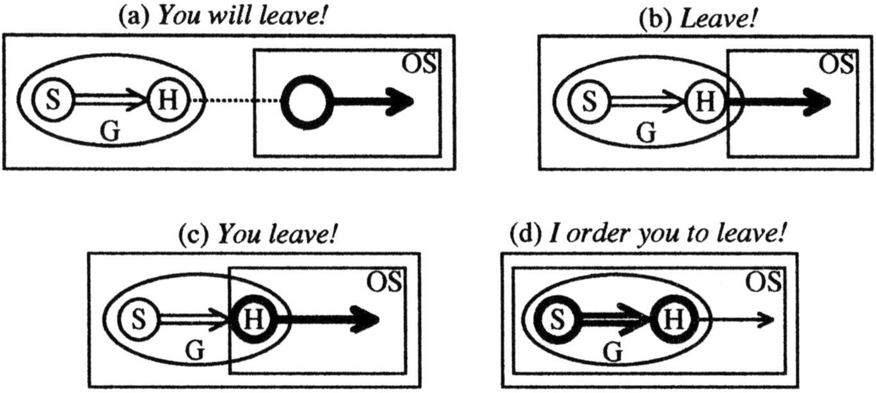

Figure 6.3

The other diagrams in Figure 6.3 represent more explict imperative constructions. What they share is a closer connection between the profiled event and the ground: the imperative force is intrinsic to the clausal construction, rather than being overlaid on a clause that is basically descriptive. The actor is thus inherently identified with the hearer. In (b) and (c), the action to be carried out retains its status as the profiled, onstage event. They differ as to whether the target of the imperative force is coded in its role as hearer – a facet of the ground, hence implicit and subjectively construed – or in its role as agent and clausal subject. Diagram (d) represents a **performative** (Austin 1962), where the profiled event is fully identified with the speech event itself. Because they specify the relationship between the ground and the profiled process, and pertain to a fundamental property (existence, i.e. occurrence), these patterns can be regarded as special grounding constructions.[11]

The force-dynamic interaction depicted in Figure 6.3 represents an abstracted **order scenario**, a special case of the generalized speech event scenario. As a pattern of linguistic interaction established in our culture, it constitutes a conventional unit of English learned from the perspective of both the speaker and the hearer. Analogous scenarios can be posited for other familiar speech acts. These can function as the meanings of speech act verbs (*order*, *ask*, *promise*, etc.), but can also be invoked without being individually symbolized, as in 6.3(a)-(c). When invoked, they are nonetheless part of an expression's lin-

11 Performatives depart from the narrow definition of grounding because the ground is onstage and thus construed objectively. Like the pronouns *I* and *you*, which they incorporate, performatives conflate the functions of grounding and description in a single form.

guistic meaning, one facet of the tacit **conceptual substrate** supporting the interpretation of overtly coded elements and required for the expression to be conceptually coherent (Langacker 2003b). In a particular usage event, the current speaker, hearer, and interaction are identified with those of the scenario invoked. The scenario is thus enacted, i.e. the speech act is performed.

4. Statements and levels of reality

The imperative constructions in Figure 6.3(b)–(c) qualify as a special kind of clausal grounding. Observe that the ground itself is offstage and subjectively construed, as in Figure 6.1. Like other grounding elements, the construction specifies the status of the profiled event vis-à-vis the ground. Note as well that these constructions are mutually exclusive with the other grounding elements – commands like *Leave!* and *You leave!* are not separately marked for tense or modality. In short, these imperative constructions conflate the functions of clausal grounding and illocutionary force.

What about the speech act commonly referred to as "assertion"? Here we can either tell a simple, more or less standard story, or else a more elaborate story that comes closer to being accurate. The simple story – suggested by the very term assertion – is that the speaker performs this act to elicit an epistemic response. On the basis of reasonable evidence, the speaker articulates a proposition that belongs to the speaker's own conception of reality, with the intent of causing the hearer to incorporate that proposition as part of the hearer's conception of reality. If I make the assertion *Dean thought of an elephant*, I am trying to get my interlocutor to accept that proposition as being true.

No doubt this happens on occasion, maybe quite frequently. We may indeed want to posit a speech act of this sort, which can reasonably be called assertion. So characterized, however, assertion is only a special case of how declarative sentences are ordinarily used. They can be used, for example, in stating something the hearer already knows, as in (3)a. They can be used to describe a new situation the speaker and hearer observe simultaneously, as in (3)b. Declaratives can be used to reiterate, and thereby acknowledge, what the hearer has just said, as in (3)c. By describing what is obvious or mundane, as in (3)d, they can serve the purpose of social communion with no real intent to inform. For this reason, the label **statement** is preferable to assertion for the basic speech act typically associated with declaratives. While the **statement scenario** is elaborated in various ways, corresponding to particular standard ways of using declaratives, a general characterization has to be fairly schematic. In terms of the intended hearer response, I suggest that it specifies the minimum: mere apprehension of the expression, so that the hearer directs attention to the profiled occurrence. This response can thus serve a variety of specific purposes.

(3) a. *Take it easy. Remember: you have a heart condition.*
b. *Omigod! Someone's knocking on the door. Get some clothes on!*
c. *Dean thought of an elephant, you say. How about that.*
d. *We're having dinner and it's already dark. The days are getting shorter.*

Does the statement scenario include the specification that the speaker accepts the proposition expressed as being true? Arguably it does. Apparent exceptions could be analyzed as cases where that scenario is embedded as part of a more elaborate scenario which overrides this specification. For example, a statement can be made with ironic intent, as in (4)a. We can analyze this as a **fictive** statement, one interpreted in a larger context which makes it clear that the speaker is only pretending to enact the statement scenario. In (4)b, where the speaker echoes a previous statement but does not subscribe to it, we can likewise posit a higher-level scenario in which the speaker is merely **re-**enacting the hearer's prior act. In such cases, the speaker identifies only partially with the speaker role in the statement scenario, assuming that role only momentarily as part of a larger scenario which indicates that the proposition does not represent the speaker's actual position.

(4) a. *Bush is honest, informed, wise, and intelligent. And I'm the queen of Iraq.*
b. *Dean thought of an elephant, you say. That's ridiculous – George told him not to.*

Thus we have to distinguish several levels of organization at which reference is made to the speaker and hearer. First, the interlocutors are invoked in generalized fashion, i.e. as roles, as part of the abstracted meanings of grounding elements. It is this level that mainly concerns us. Second, the speaker and hearer also figure, again as roles, in the various speech act scenarios. And third, the roles at these two levels have to be distinguished from the actual speaker and hearer in the context of a particular usage event. When a finite clause is actually used to perform a certain speech act, the interlocutors at these three levels are identified: the actual speaker and hearer assume the roles of those in the speech act scenario, which in turn are identified with those invoked by the grounding element. The usage event is then a **true enactment** of the scenario.

To underscore the need to posit these different levels, let me point out that the speech act force is applied to a **proposition**, i.e. the full content of a finite clause, including its grounding. By contrast, the epistemic import of grounding pertains just to the profiled process it grounds – an event or situation per se (not a proposition). We can see this most clearly with modals. Consider the sentence *Alice may* *catch a mouse*. When it is uttered as a genuine statement, the speaker commits to a proposition that includes the modal *may* as part of its characterization. What the speaker accepts as real – part of his conception of reality – is simply the **possibility** of Alice catching a mouse, not the event itself. Thus he is not wrong even if it should turn out later that Alice does not in fact catch a mouse.

In previous discussions of grounding, I generally oversimplified matters by not distinguishing among these levels. I would say, for instance, that *Alice caught a mouse* situates the profiled event in the speaker's conception of reality. But this is so only assuming that the expression constitutes a true enactment of the statement scenario. Grounding obtains at the level of a finite clause, which does not per se have illocutionary force. It can thus be used in many ways which do not imply that the actual speaker accepts the proposition as valid. A few of these are given in (5). To keep things manageable, I will continue to make what I will call the Great Simplification: the assumption that the actual interlocutors are fully identified with those of the ground in the context of making a genuine statement. It is however essential to realize that this is a special case that emerges only in the absence of complicating factors (Chapter 9).

(5) a. *Alice caught a mouse?*
 b. *It's not the case that Alice caught a mouse.*
 c. *Conceivably, Alice caught a mouse.*
 d. *Bill thinks Alice caught a mouse.*

As we strive for epistemic control, we build up a conception of reality that has multiple levels (Achard 1998). At the lowest level are events and situations per se, the prototype being a physical action. With respect to this level, conceived reality (and we are always talking here about **conceived** reality) is simply the set of **realized occurrences**, i.e. what the conceptualizer accepts as having happened or obtained up through the present moment. Let us call this **basic reality**. It roughly corresponds to the direct apprehension of (typically physical) occurrences. A higher level reflects our capacity to **imagine** such occurrences. For example, we can extrapolate from basic reality to envisage a process occurring and thus becoming real, as reflected in modals (e.g. *Alice may catch a mouse*). We can also conceptualize an occurrence as a candidate for inclusion in reality without however accepting it, as with negation (*Alice did not catch a mouse*). This capacity defines what I will call **elaborated reality**. Instead of a set of occurrences per se, it consists of a set of **propositions** pertaining to occurrences, including an assessment of their epistemic status. Elaborated reality can itself be articulated into numerous levels based on our further capacity to conceptualize other conceptualizers as well as the content of their conceptualizations. Thus (5)d represents the higher-level proposition that Bill entertains the lower-level proposition *Alice caught a mouse*. Even if the actual speaker knows that Alice failed to catch one, he may nonetheless accept the higher-level proposition as valid, part of elaborated reality. And of course, there can in principle be any number of such levels (*Chris knows Bill thinks Alice caught a mouse, Dave said Chris knows Bill thinks Alice caught a mouse*, etc.), producing mental space configurations of indefinite complexity.

The epistemic control cycle comes into play at all these levels, with different linguistic manifestations. First, it figures in the meanings of what are traditionally called "predicates of propositional attitude". Here the conceptualizer's epistemic stance vis-à-vis a proposition is put onstage and profiled; the process thus defined can be grounded to form a finite clause (which constitutes a higher-level proposition). Such predicates pertain to different phases of the control cycle, two of which are the potential phase and the result phase. The verb *suspect*, for instance, profiles the state of tension in which the conceptualizer inclines toward accepting the proposition in his conception of reality but has not actually taken this action. By contrast, *know* profiles the state of relaxation resulting from the action: the stable situation where the proposition is an established part of the reality conception.

The epistemic control cycle is further manifested in certain speech act scenarios, where it may remain covert. Most basically, the statement scenario implies that the speaker accepts a proposition as part of reality. But instead of being explicitly coded, this relationship remains offstage and unprofiled, part of the conceptual substrate supporting the interpretation of overt elements. If I make the statement *Alice caught a mouse*, I intimate that the proposition expressed by the finite clause belongs to my conception of elaborated reality. With respect to the speaker, the statement scenario invokes the result phase of the control cycle. With respect to the hearer, the matter is considerably more flexible, as we have seen. A statement may serve to effect the transition between the baseline and potential phases, i.e. it introduces the proposition into the hearer's field of awareness, where it has to be dealt with in some fashion. As a special case, the speaker may intend the statement to induce the action of accepting the proposition into the hearer's reality conception. Or as we saw in (3), it may already be there (the result phase). The question scenario naturally has the general effect of reversing these roles. Canonically, a question implies that the proposition is within the speaker's field of awareness with its status still unresolved (the potential phase).

Finally, and most importantly for our purposes, the epistemic control cycle provides the essential import of clausal grounding. Here, though, the relevant epistemic dominion is the speaker's conception of **basic** reality. That is, the target is simply a profiled **process** (an event or situation), not a proposition (since grounding itself effects the conversion of a process into a proposition).

The grounding relationship (r) pertains to either the cycle's inclination phase or its result phase. But in either case, the ground and the grounding relationship remain offstage and unprofiled, as depicted in Figure 6.1(b).

5. Clausal grounding

With all this background, and by making The Great Simplification, the essentials of English clausal grounding can be briefly stated. Formally, a grounding element has two main components: modality and "tense", which is better described as "distance". Each is iconically organized, with an unmarked "zero" option and a marked option indicating greater removal from the deictic center. For modality, the two basic options are the absence of a modal or its presence, in which case there are five to choose from. For distance there is likewise the option of either the absence of a marker or its presence. Together, then, the modality and distance components define the grounding elements listed in Figure 6.4.[12]

<table>
<tr><td></td><td colspan="2">Modality</td><td></td></tr>
<tr><td rowspan="2">Distance</td><td>Ø</td><td>may, can, will, shall, must</td><td>Immediate</td></tr>
<tr><td>-ed</td><td>might, could, would, should</td><td>Non-Immediate</td></tr>
<tr><td></td><td>Real</td><td>Unreal</td><td></td></tr>
</table>

Figure 6.4

Semantically, I characterize modality in terms of the control cycle: the absence of a modal indicates that the profiled process is accepted by the speaker as real (the result phase), and the presence of a modal, that it is not. More precisely, modals reflect the potential phase by indicating various degrees of inclination to accept the process as real. This basic opposition is sketched in Figure 6.5.

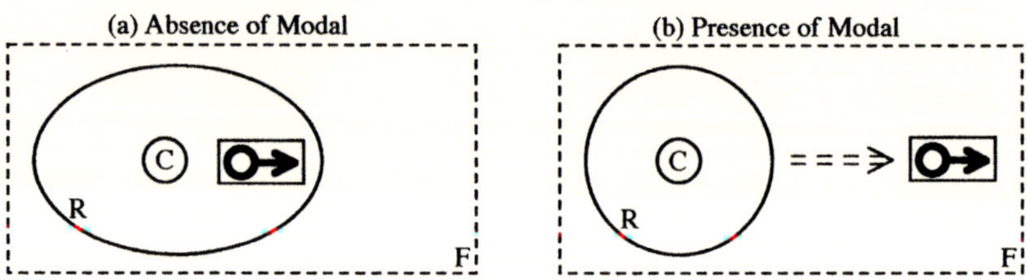

Figure 6.5

12 Verb agreement is omitted. See Langacker 1991 (§ 6.2.2.3) for an argument that *must* simply lacks a non-immediate form.

As for distance, the zero option indicates (iconically) that the profiled occurrence is **immediate** to the ground, while *-ed* specifies **non-immediacy**. These options play out differently depending on whether the grounding element includes a modal. In the absence of a modal, the profiled process is confined to basic reality, roughly describable as the speaker's model of what has happened or obtained up through the present moment – the accepted history of realized occurrences. When interpreted with respect to reality, so defined, immediacy vs. non-immediacy translates into occurrence at the moment of speaking vs. occurrence prior to speaking, i.e. present vs. past. And since reality is the unmarked case, these temporal interpretations constitute the prototypical values of the distance specifications.

On the other hand, a modal places the profiled process outside reality, as a target for potential inclusion.[13] Here the distance inflection is manifested on the modal rather than the verb, both formally – producing the marked forms *might*, *could*, *would*, and *should* – and also semantically. I do not claim that the semantic result is strictly compositional; each form has its semantic idiosyncrasies associated with the particular niche it has carved out for itself in conventional usage. Consistently, however, the non-immediate form conveys a lesser likelihood than the immediate form of the target process being accepted as real. If *Alice* ***may*** *catch a mouse* specifies the possibility of her doing so, *Alice* ***might*** *catch a mouse* specifies a lesser possibility – the speaker is not yet in the position of being able to ground this event using *may*. More drastically, *will* essentially predicts a future occurrence while *would* precludes it. The import of *Alice* ***will*** *catch a mouse* is that the speaker, in extrapolating from his current conception of reality, projects it as "growing" to encompass this event. By contrast, *Alice* ***would*** *catch a mouse* places this development in a counterfactual mental space – it would constitute the projected path of growth only if the starting point were different from what it actually is (e.g. *Alice would catch a mouse if she were not so lazy*).

This view of the epistemic modals follows Talmy (1988) and Sweetser (1982, 1990) in being **force-dynamic**. The modal force manifests the tension inherent in the potential phase of the control cycle, and more specifically the inclination phase. More generally, it reflects our continuous striving for epistemic control, which is simply an aspect of being alive and sentient – something we constantly and automatically engage in. As the essential import of a grounding relationship, the force is subjectively construed, inhering in the conceptualizing process itself rather than the objective situation being talked about (Langacker 1990b, 2006b;

13 Though typically this occurrence is future in time, we can also expand our conception of reality to encompass present or past occurrences that were previously unknown. Hence examples like *They must be home – the lights are on.*

Chapter 4). It is the force we mentally experience in extrapolating our conception of reality in such a way that it comes to encompass the target occurrence.[14]

Intuitively, we recognize *must* as representing the strongest modal force, and *may* the weakest. Accordingly, Sweetser (1990) respectively describes them in terms of compulsion vs. the absence of a barrier. This being so, we cannot directly equate the mentally experienced force with the **effort** required for the extrapolation of reality to encompass the target. That yields the wrong results: imagining something that is necessary requires **less** effort than imagining something that is merely possible. Instead, as Sweetser suggests with the word "compel", we should think of the force as one that "pushes" or "carries" the conceptualizer in the direction of the target: a stronger force aimed at the target implies a greater likelihood of actually reaching it. This motivated my earlier notion of **evolutionary momentum** (Langacker 1991). Our conception of reality continuously evolves as we deal with new occurrences. Based on our model of how things work in general, the history of its evolution up through the present moment gives it a momentum that tends – with varying degrees of strength – to carry its future evolution in certain directions. I regard this notion as quite natural even though, in the last analysis, it is the conceptualizer's mental effort that is actually driving this development. Being constant (like breathing and the force of gravity), our striving for epistemic control easily recedes into the background of awareness. To the extent that it does, reality itself ("the course of events") appears to be striving toward the target.

If Figure 6.5(b) represents an **epistemic** modal (in generalized form), what does a **root** modal look like? The most basic difference is that root modals pertain to **effective** control: they reflect the effort to **influence** what happens, not simply to learn about it. Hence the modal force has a different locus: it inheres in the world itself as opposed to knowledge **of** the world (i.e. in "real" reality as opposed to conceived reality). Typically it is manifested at the social level, where it can often be localized to the interaction of particular individuals. The prototype is for the speaker to direct this force at the hearer, as shown in Figure 6.6(a). The normal interpretation of *You may go now* is thus that the speaker grants the hearer permission to leave, and by saying *You must go to your room right now* the speaker compels the hearer to go there. When the force flows between the interlocutors, it is usual for the hearer to be mentioned explicitly as the clausal subject, as in these examples. The resulting configura-

14 This kind of offstage force-dynamic experience arises as one facet of the mental simulations constituting the apprehension of effortful physical actions, where we imagine what it feels like to carry them out. While they are no longer tied to physical force, the highly grammaticized modals retain a vestige of this experience.

tion, Figure 6.6(a), is quite comparable to the order scenario shown in Figure 6.3(a), for commands like *You will leave!*. Indeed, when the modal force is one of compulsion (rather than something weaker, like permission), it may in fact be equivalent to the order scenario.

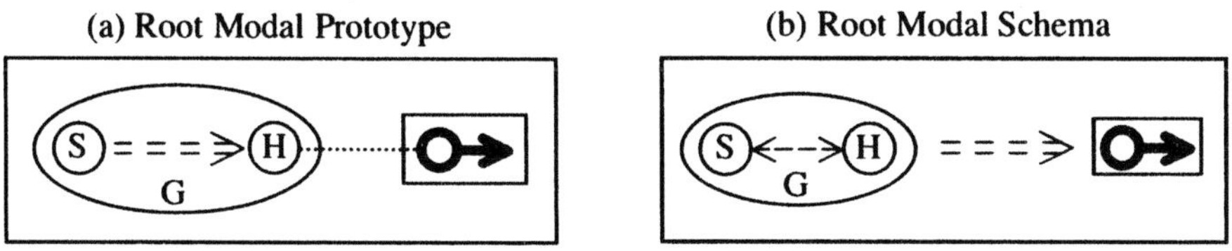

Figure 6.6

However, the configuration in Figure 6.6(a) is at best just prototypical. The origin of the social force is not necessarily the speaker, who may just be reporting it, as in (6)a. Nor is it necessarily directed at the hearer, as seen in (6)b. It is often not possible to localize the force to the interaction of specific individuals. In (6)c, the force originates in general considerations of social practice, and is not directed at anyone in particular. Nor is the force always social in nature. In (6)d, it can be identified as the potential for physical harm, and in (6)e, as a physical and mental capacity. A schematic characterization of root modals, one valid for all instances, must therefore abstract away from the specific nature of the modal force as well as its locus. As shown in Figure 6.6(b), it simply indicates that some kind of force tends toward realization of the target process.[15]

(6) a. *You must go to your room right now – Mom says so.*
b. *Where's Ashcroft? He must cover up those naked statues.*
c. *There must be order in society.*
d. *We really should get out of here – the place is about to explode.*
e. *Ashcroft can recite the Bible backwards without ever pausing.*

6. Grounding and discourse

We come now to the crux of the matter: the putative parallelism between clausal grounding and nominal grounding. It is, to reiterate, a parallelism modulo the

15 In (6)e the force inheres in the clausal subject. It does not however follow that the clause profiles the force itself – instead, it profiles the process *recite*. Only the nature and locus of the force distinguish the capability sense of *can* from other root modals.

inherent difference between nouns and verbs, and modulo the different answers to the question "What is at issue?". Since nouns and verbs are polar opposites in these respects, the similarities are fairly abstract and initially less than obvious. At least at the outset, it will therefore be helpful to make The Great Simplification even Greater by confining attention to a basic range of phenomena that most strongly motivate and most clearly reveal the import of core grounding elements. Thus I will mostly speak of physical (rather than abstract) entities, of objects and events (rather than substances and situations), and of the real world (rather than imaginary worlds and entities created through metaphor and blending). My account of grounding is however a general one not limited to these phenomena.

In the case of objects, the default expectation is for many instances of a given type to exist simultaneously and to continue existing indefinitely. Rather than existence, it is therefore identification that is primarily at issue. For events, the default expectation is just the opposite: they are generally transient, and the simultaneous existence of multiple instances (of an elaborated type) is seldom a significant concern. Instead of identification, it is therefore existence (i.e. occurrence) that is primarily at issue. In both realms the grammaticized grounding system has evolved to deal with the factor at issue.

As living creatures, we are constantly striving for control on numerous levels. Being sentient and intelligent, we strive for control at the epistemic level by constructing and continually updating a conception of reality. If we focus on basic reality, and make The Greater Simplification, we can say that a reality conception comprises objects and relationships. The objects exist indefinitely, and being conceptually autonomous, they are independent of any particular relationship. By contrast, the relationships are conceptually dependent, since they can only be realized via their participant objects. Although some relationships endure through time, the more salient ones are transient events. Objects and enduring relationships give conceived reality a measure of stable organization, providing a frame of reference for apprehending the transient events that occur within it. Together, the objects and relationships – both enduring and transient – constitute a structure that evolves through time as we apprehend new events and learn more about prior ones. Establishing epistemic control is largely a matter of building and evolving this structure.

We build, elaborate, and modify our conception of reality through ongoing experience. An important facet of this experience – the one that concerns us – is discourse. With respect to discourse, we can start by noting a striking asymmetry between nominals and clauses: while it is common for discourse to consist in a series of clauses, hardly ever does it consist in just a series of nominals. There are of course exceptions, e.g. the long list of names read off during a graduation ceremony. But to converse about the world we typically rely on clauses, on the basis of which we extend and refine our conception of reality. This asymmetry does not however count against the parallelism of nominal and clausal grounding. It simply reflects the difference in what is at issue in the nominal and clausal realms. The basic tendency for objects is to endure. Together with enduring relationships, they constitute a stable frame of reference for apprehending events. Their existence being presupposed in this manner, merely naming a series of objects does nothing to extend our conception of reality and thus advance the cause of epistemic control. The basic means of extending our conception of reality is by incorporating new events, thus building on the structure already in place. It is therefore clauses, where the occurrence of events is at issue, that primarily serve this purpose.

As with clauses, nominal grounding relates to both effective and epistemic control. At both levels certain parallels are observable between nominal and clausal grounding, but only modulo what is at issue. Let us start with effective control.

7. Nominal grounding: Effective level

In the case of clauses, the grounding elements employed for purposes of effective control are root modals and the basic imperative constructions of Figure 6.3(b)–(c). Because existence is at issue, these are meant to be effective with respect to the world. If I say *You must leave* or just *Leave!*, I am trying to effect the actual occurrence of your leaving (as part of "real" reality). These are force-dynamic at the social level, involving the exercise of authority, because I am trying to make the hearer actually do something (not just think of it or acknowledge it). And since the profiled event is as yet unrealized, expressions aimed at effective control represent the potential phase of the control cycle rather than its result phase.

So with clauses effective control concerns the **existence** of an **event**. Effective control for nominals should be analogous modulo what is at issue. To arrive at its characterization, we must therefore substitute **object** for **event**, and **identification** for **existence**. Hence effective control pertains to an **object's identification**. Importantly, this substitution has other consequences; *ceteris* is not *paribus*. The main consequence is that the objective is no longer to influence what actually happens "out there" in the world – the speaker is not trying to cause an object to exist. Instead, the effect being sought occurs at the level of the discourse interaction, "in here" in the context of the speech event. The speaker's objective in striving for effective control is the situation where both interlocutors momentarily direct their attention to the same referent. A further consequence is that the social force expended for this purpose is considerably weaker than with root modals or imperatives, and of a different nature. It does not involve the authority or moral suasion needed to influence actions in the world, but is simply a matter of directing the listener's attention. This requires little more than the baseline response of merely apprehending the expression. Moreover, since it is not precluded that the listener may already be attending to the proper referent, a grounding element can represent the result phase of the control cycle as well as the potential phase.

The intended outcome of nominal grounding – the effect of properly apprehending the grounded nominal – is always that the interlocutors momentarily direct their attention to the same discourse referent (Langacker 2001b, 2004c). This outcome was diagrammed in Figure 6.1(a), using dashed arrows for the directing of attention. At this juncture we need a more refined view of attention, hence a more elaborate notation. Let me suggest that the directing and focusing of attention is another manifestation of the control cycle. The basic components of the control cycle are an actor, field, target, and dominion. For attention, the actor is a conceptualizer (C), and the field (F) is C's current scope of awareness. The target (T) is anything that **attracts** our attention and thereby becomes the **focus** of attention. The conceptualizer's dominion (D) is the **focal region**: it is by entering (or being brought into) this region that a target becomes a focus of attention.

As one manifestation of the control cycle, attention is both dynamic and force-dynamic. It is dynamic in the sense that we are constantly shifting our attention from target to target. Each of these shifts amounts to one attentional cycle, sketched in Figure 6.7. The baseline is the momentarily stable situation where a particular target, T_1, is the focus. The potential phase is initiated when some other salient entity, T_2, enters the scope of awareness (F). This is a state of tension, both in the sense that T_2 has to be dealt with in some manner, and also in the sense that, if new and sufficiently noteworthy, T_2 tends to attract our attention. The action then consists in shifting the focal region (D) to encompass or "capture" this new target. C's brief fixation on T_2, as the focus of attention, constitutes the result phase (a new baseline).[16]

In Figure 6.7, C is placed outside of D as an indication that we canonically focus our attention on external entities. In the potential phase, I have made the force-dynamic arrow double-headed, as we can think of the force as flowing in either direction: either the target attracts C's attention; or equivalently, C shifts the focal region in order to capture T. I likewise show two arrows in the action

16 Attention itself occurs on multiple levels. At the level of visual perception, this description applies quite well to saccades. More relevant for nominal grounding is the focusing of attention at the mental or conceptual level.

phase, which we can conceptualize (equivalently) in terms of either T moving into D or else D moving to encompass T. In the following diagrams, I find it most perspicuous to show the dashed arrow pointing toward T, indicating C's effort to achieve attentional control, and to orient the solid arrow in the other direction, to represent T moving into D.

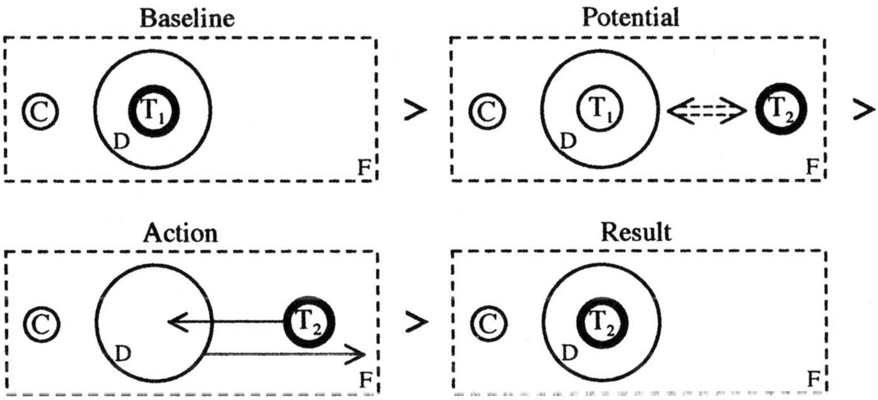

Figure 6.7

By making The Greater Simplification, we limit our initial concern to the nominal grounding elements that occur with singular count nouns designating actual (as opposed to virtual) entities. English has four such elements: the definite article *the*; the indefinite article *a*; and the singular demonstratives *this* and *that*. We can describe a count noun as one that designates a type of thing of which there are many instances. For a given type, t, the set of all instances constitutes a (fictive) entity that I refer to as the **maximal extension** of that type, symbolized as E_t. When a noun functions as a nominal head, therefore, any member of E_t has the potential to be invoked as the intended discourse referent. The problem of identification is thus to single out a particular instance, t_i, as the one being referred to in the current discourse context.

Nominal grounding addresses this problem. The intended outcome, based on proper apprehension of the grounded nominal, is the momentary state of **joint attentional control**, where both interlocutors have their attention fixed on the same instance (t_i) of the specified type (t). This outcome is represented in Figure 6.8, with alternate notations that each reflect certain aspects of the overall conception. Diagram (a) makes explicit the inclusion of t_i in the maximal extension E_t, all of whose members instantiate the type. As in Figure 6.1, it uses dashed arrows for the directing of attention. Diagram (b) employs the notation adopted for the attentional control cycle, as in Figure 6.7. The outcome represents the result phase for both interlocutors. Momentarily, t_i is established in both the speaker's focal region (D_S) and the hearer's (D_H). Another facet of joint attention is the **awareness** of joint attention. Hence the entire configuration – including both interlocutors and their focusing of attention – is included in both the speaker's field of awareness (F_S) and the hearer's (F_H).

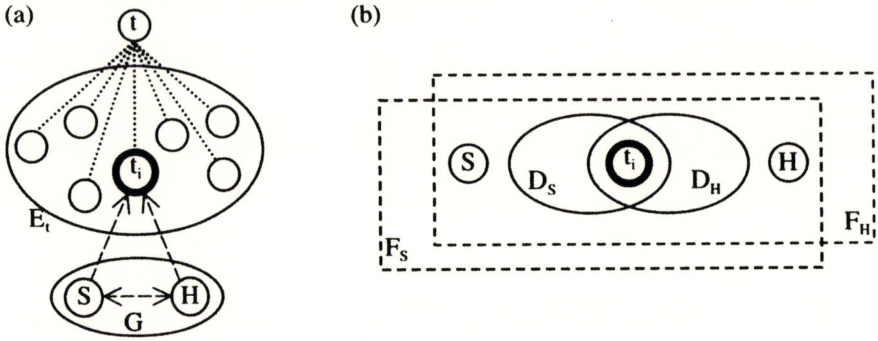

Figure 6.8

What counts as the field of awareness for this purpose is shaped by the ongoing discourse. Out of all the members of E_t that might in principle be the intended referent, those recently mentioned or otherwise invoked in the discourse have the greatest likelihood of being referred to again – their recent activation makes them easily accessible (cf. Ariel 1988; Chafe 1994; Gundel, Hedberg, and Zacharski 1993). Since the outcome is always the same, it is primarily this dimension that distinguishes the basic grounding elements. If we focus on canonical uses of these elements, the differences are discrete and can be precisely characterized in terms of the control cycle. However, when less canonical uses are taken into account their overlapping ranges give the impression of a continuous scale of accessibility.

Their canonical import is sketched in Figure 6.9. For each grounding element, the diagram shows the intended referent, t_i, moving into the hearer's focal region (D_H) by virtue of the speaker referring to it. What distinguishes these elements is the starting point. The definite article *the* represents the degenerate case of zero motion – t_i is already in D_H as a focus of attention. With the demonstratives *this* and *that*, it is presupposed that t_i originates in the hearer's field of awareness (F_H). The choice depends on its position vis-à-vis the speaker: whether or not it is construed as being in the speaker's **proximity** ($PROX_S$). Finally, the indefinite article *a* indicates that t_i originates outside the hearer's field (F_H); it must be brought to awareness for the hearer to focus it.

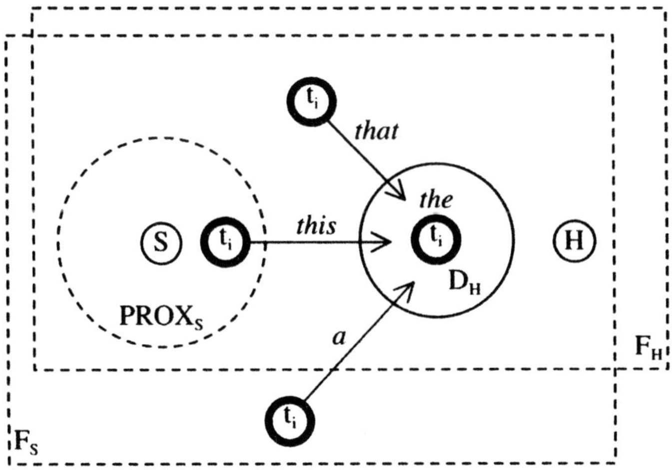

Figure 6.9

Here, obviously, I can offer only the briefest sketch of how these elements are used. I will illustrate both their canonical import, represented in Figure 6.9, as well as certain common but less canonical uses.

The definite article implies that there is only one instance of the specified type in the current field of awareness, and canonically, that it has already been established in the discourse as a focus of attention. A typical example is (7)a. Less canonically, though certainly very frequently, a unique referent is inferrable without having previously been mentioned, as in (7)b. It is then necessary to direct attention to the referent, but since the referent is both inferrable and contextually unique, this requires very little effort – it is essentially automatic given the type specification (in this case *mother*). Hence the definite article represents either the result phase of the hearer's attentional control cycle or at least something very close to it. It is a state of relaxation: no real effort has to be expended, since the target has already been captured (or if not, it is surrounded and has no option but to surrender).

(7) a. *The package contained a letter and some photos.* ***The letter*** *was very brief.*

b. *She comes from an unusual family.* ***The mother*** *has a Ph.D. in theoretical linguistics.*

This is sometimes so with demonstratives, specifically when used anaphorically, as in (8)a. In these uses they are comparable to the definite article, apart from their specification of proximity or distance. Canonically, however, demonstratives are used to direct attention, i.e. not just to register but to establish attentional control. Besides the result phase, they then represent the control cycle's potential and action phases. The effort this requires is sometimes manifested at the physical level, with an actual pointing gesture [→], as in (8) b. In other cases, like (8)c, the choice between the proximal and distal forms (*this* vs. *that*) may be sufficient to single out the intended referent from multiple candidate instances in the field.[17]

(8) a. *He's doing a report on homosexual poodles.* ***This report*** *is bound to be controversial.*

b. *I want* ***that*** *[→]* ***piece****. It's the biggest.*

c. *I like* ***this painting*** *better than all the others.*

d. *Look at* ***that eagle*** *perched on a cactus!*

There are of course demonstrative uses, exemplified in (8)d, which direct attention to something present in the physical context that the hearer was not previously aware of. In this respect their range overlaps with the indefinite article, which is nevertheless quite distinct. Whereas the demonstrative singles out a particular instance of the type, the instance referred to by *a* is either fictive or not uniquely determined. The indefinite article is canonically used to introduce a new participant in the discourse, thereby bringing it into the hearer's field of awareness. In this case it can either be an actual instance of the type, as in (9)a, or else a virtual one, as in (9)b. A virtual instance is "conjured up" for a certain local purpose, existing only in the mental space evoked for that purpose (e.g. to characterize someone's desire). Less canonically, the indefinite article is also employed when the field of awareness holds multiple instances of the type but none has yet been singled out. In (9)c, the speaker is not referring to any particular puppy among those apparent in the context. Instead the hearer is instructed to choose one arbitrarily.

(9) a. *She saw* ***a puppy*** *in the pet store.*

b. *She would really like to have* ***a puppy****.*

c. *We're ready to start the baths – hand me* ***a puppy****.*

At the **effective** level, the most basic parallel between clausal and nominal grounding is their common status as manifestations of the control cycle. Each has a desired outcome: an event's occurrence; a referent's identification. This outcome produces the stable situation – the cycle's result phase – in which the

---

17 Needless to say, this distance specification is not necessarily spatial. It can also pertain to factors like time, affect, and position in the discourse (cf. Janssen 1995; Kirsner 1993).

relevant dominion contains the grounded entity. An event's occurrence makes it "real" in the world, and if apprehended by the speaker and hearer (who typically instigate the action and carry it out, respectively) it is then established as a shared element in their conceptions of reality. Likewise, a referent is identified by virtue of being momentarily established as a joint focus of attention, in the focal regions of both the speaker and the hearer. A further parallel is that each grounding system codes varying degrees of force in "striving" toward the envisaged result: degrees of social force, in the case of root modals; and degrees of effort in directing attention to the target, for determiners. Also, in both systems it is typically the hearer who must act to achieve the result, and the speaker who instigates this action. And finally, both grounding systems incorporate a contrast describable as immediate vs. non-immediate vis-à-vis the speaker.[18]

8. Nominal grounding: Epistemic level

Let us now consider parallels at the epistemic level. For clauses, we achieve epistemic control by incorporating events in our conception of reality. For a given conceptualizer, reality is the accepted history of what has happened up through the present. The key factor is thus existence: out of all conceivable events, reality comprises those accepted as having occurred (i.e. as having been **real**ized). As such, reality is a continuously evolving structure, constantly being updated on the basis of new experience, as well as further thought and inference bearing on the structure already in place.

What should count as epistemic control in the case of objects? What does it mean for an object to be incorporated in a conception of reality? With objects, existence is not primarily at issue. When we first acquire knowledge of an object, and thus incorporate it in our epistemic dominion, it is usually not on the basis of its coming into existence, since that is generally presupposed. Out of all the new objects we come across, most are presumed to have existed prior to the encounter (e.g. we meet new people all the time, but seldom do we see a person born). Thus to accept an object as real is not to accept that it exists – that is taken for granted. If nominal and clausal grounding are parallel modulo what is at issue, it should not be a matter of existence, but rather identification.

18 At the effective level, immediacy corresponds to a stronger modal force (e.g. *shall* vs. *should*). Similarly, Kirsner (1993) argues (for Dutch) that the proximal demonstrative constitutes a "more forceful instruction" to seek out the intended referent.

It is by virtue of being identified that an object is established in the epistemic dominion and accepted as real.

But what exactly constitutes identification at the epistemic level? Unlike **effective identification**, it is not just a matter of momentarily directing attention to an instance of a type for immediate discourse purposes. It is rather a matter of acquiring stable knowledge and building up a conception of reality. While this is often done through discourse, so that both levels are in play simultaneously, **epistemic identification** goes beyond mere attention – it pertains to the actual content and structure of conceived reality.

Crucially, conceived reality is a structure, not merely an inventory of unconnected elements. And while this structure continues to grow and be refined, large portions of it are reasonably constant once established. Basic reality comprises objects and relationships, the latter both transient and enduring. By invoking objects as participants, relationships connect them to form a more or less coherent structure. Objects and enduring relationships provide a stable frame of reference for apprehending more transient events. But once apprehended and accepted as real, even transient occurrences constitute stable aspects of conceived reality – part of the accepted history of occurrences.

An object is **epistemically identified** when it has an **established place** in this structure. Otherwise stated, an identified object is linked to the conceptualizer by a path consisting of relationships accepted as real. In the case of familiar objects, like our personal possessions or the people we know, there are many such paths, representing our interactions with them and the various things we have learned about them. With less familiar objects, the connection can be quite tenuous. I may know, for instance, that my cousin Jane has a pet iguana without knowing anything else about this creature that might distinguish it from other instances of its type. But that single connection is enough: within the set of all iguanas (the maximal extension of this type), I know there is one uniquely identifiable as *Jane's iguana*. Jane's relationship vis-à-vis this creature ties it into the network of relationships constituting my conception of reality. I can therefore "reach" this individual by tracing a mental path through reality, the last segment of which is its connection to Jane. Of course, we can also "reach" individuals through a path that is partly inferential. For example, I have never seen Jane's iguana, so I don't know for sure that it has a tail, but given what I know about iguanas in general I can reasonably infer that it has one. Thus, depending on how we choose to look at things, the specific entity identifiable as *Jane's iguana's tail* is either part of my conception of reality or else directly accessible from it.

Instances identified via inference are intermediate between **basic reality** and **elaborated reality**, the latter reflecting our capacity to imagine objects and occurrences and contemplate their epistemic status. At a basic level, my conception of reality incorporates a certain number of iguanas that have an established place in this structure because I have encountered them individually or otherwise been made aware of them. But at a higher level, I also accept as real the existence of innumerable iguanas that have never had this privilege. As one aspect of elaborated reality, I realize that some previously unknown iguana might emerge from this obscurity at any time, being singled out as an individual and thus incorporated in basic reality as an identified instance. This has just happened to you. You now know, for example, that I have a cousin Jane who has an iguana – this iguana is now identified to you, having a place in your conception of reality.[19]

To summarize, in the nominal realm we achieve epistemic control through identification. An object is identified by virtue of being incorporated in our evolving conception of reality, where it has an established place distinguishing it from other instances of its type. This constitutes the result phase of the epistemic control cycle. As in the case of events, an important means of augmenting conceived reality is discourse, which mainly consists of clauses. As discourse proceeds, both objects and events function as targets – the entities captured and incorporated in the epistemic dominion. The target is either the event profiled by a clause or the object profiled by a nominal it contains.

The incorporation of events and of objects proceed in tandem. Since events are conceptually dependent, they require the support of their object participants. Conversely, events (more generally, relationships) provide the connections giving objects an established place in conceived reality. Thus each depends on the other for what is primarily at issue: events depend on objects for their existence (occurrence); objects depend on events for their identification. This mutual dependence underpins a basic discourse strategy reflected in the canonical alignment of clause structure and information structure. I am hardly the first to observe that subjects tend to be "given", representing "old information", whereas clausal objects are often "new". Conceptually, I characterize a subject as the **starting point** for building up to the full conception of the profiled clausal process (Langacker 1999c; cf. Chafe 1994). As starting point, the subject tends to be given because it is most efficacious to build on the foundation of what has already been established. A known subject can therefore anchor the conception of a relationship which connects it to something new, expressed by the clausal object. Clausal objects are thus a common vehicle for introducing new participants in the discourse (Du Bois 1987), as well as a conception of reality based on that discourse.

19 Just for the record, I do not actually have a cousin named Jane, so the iguana she has doesn't really exist. But it might have been so.

Illustrating this familiar pattern are the discourse sequences in (10). In each case, the first sentence has a definite subject and an indefinite object. The known subject anchors the conception of a profiled relationship by means of which a new participant, expressed by the clausal object, is introduced in the discourse. Once established in this manner, that participant can anchor the next clause in the discourse sequence, where it in turn is expressed by a definite subject. If we assume the canonical situation, where each successive clause updates the conception of reality, the new participant is introduced not only in the discourse but also in the hearer's epistemic dominion.[20]

(10) a. *Jill just bought* ***a car. This machine*** *is much faster than her motorcycle.*
b. *Jill needs* ***a car. It*** *would really help her in her business.*

In this canonical arrangement, a clause uttered by the speaker instructs the hearer to update his conception of reality by incorporating the profiled process. The diagram in Figure 6.10 depicts the updating effected by the first clause in (10)a. Dots and arrows stand for objects and relationships. The ellipse on the left shows the initial configuration, where Jill has an established place in the hearer's epistemic dominion (D_H). The event profiled by the clause (enclosed in a box) is then incorporated in D_H by virtue of their common reference to Jill. This produces the augmented structure shown on the right: the event of Jill buying a car – and hence the car itself – are now part of the hearer's conception of reality.

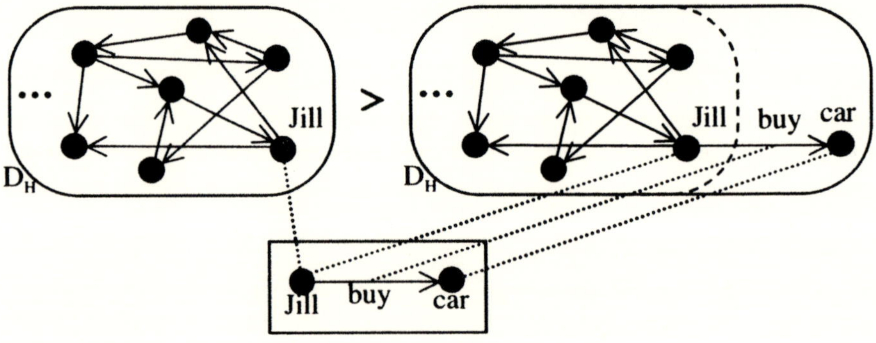

Figure 6.10

What presently concerns us is the object's change in status. What is responsible for the car referred to in (10)a being incorporated in the hearer's reality concep-

20 I emphasize that the canonical situation is not necessarily the most frequent or typical one. It is rather an experientially basic default, the point of departure for characterizing other situations.

tion? It is not simply the fact of being explicitly mentioned. As shown in Figure 6.9, grounding with the indefinite article instructs the hearer to invoke an instance of the specified type as a momentary focus of attention; it is thereby captured and enters the hearer's dominion (D_H). However, Figure 6.9 pertains to effective control, where D_H is merely the hearer's focal region. Directing attention to something is not the same as accepting it as real. The latter pertains to epistemic control, where D_H is the hearer's conception of reality. We can perfectly well bring something into our attentional dominion while excluding it from our epistemic dominion.[21] This happens, for example, in negatives: *Jill doesn't have a car.*

Simply mentioning something is therefore not enough to effect its identification and establish it as real. Instead, its status depends on what is said about it. In cases like (10)a, the object's incorporation in conceived reality is derivative of the event's incorporation. By virtue of its grounding (and other factors previously discussed), *Jill just bought a car* instructs the hearer to accept the profiled event as real, as shown in Figure 6.10. The conception of events includes the conception of their participants, and for many types of events – buying being one of them – the event can only be real if its participants are. If it is in fact the case that Jill bought a car, there is in fact a car that she bought, and the very fact that she bought it serves to identify it. By contrast, verbs like *want*, *need*, and *imagine* do not imply that their objects are real in this sense. If I say that *Jill needs a car* (assuming the default, non-specific interpretation), I cannot continue by saying *She's washing it right now.*

Why, then, is (10)b felicitous? There the pronoun *it* successfully refers to the non-real car introduced by the clause *Jill needs a car.* It is well known that the difference stems from mental space configurations. In the present context, the spaces in question are levels of reality. If *Jill needs a car* fails to establish a car in basic reality – the level of objects and events per se – it does establish one in elaborated reality, which further includes imagined entities as well as the conception of other minds and their conceptualizations. In (10)b, the modal *would* indicates that the second sentence (*It would really help her in her business*) pertains to the same imagined situation that the car inhabits, so *it* can refer to the car without inconsistency.

We can now attempt a characterization of nominal grounding at the epistemic level. I emphasize that we are still making not only The Greater Simplification, but one that is even greater by concentrating on the basic level of reality. At this level, conceived reality comprises **actual** objects and events, as opposed to

21 Analogously, a mouse that attracts a cat's attention may nonetheless escape physical capture. While perceptual control may be prerequisite to achieving physical control, it does not guarantee this result.

the **virtual** ones imagined for a special purpose and thus confined to a special mental space (e.g. the space representing a belief, a desire, or a hypothetical situation). In this respect, it is relevant that one aspect of elaborated reality is the very realization that the identified instances of a type are generally not exhaustive of those which exist. A conceptualized instance which has not yet been identified is virtual in nature pending that development. Further information might establish it as real and actual, connecting it to reality at a particular location in that evolving structure. Or it might not. But unless and until it is captured in this manner, it merely floats unattached as an object of thought.

As we saw in (10), this further information is provided by the larger context in which a nominal appears, in particular by a grounded clause containing it. In and of itself, the indefinite nominal *a car* implies that the instance it profiles is not yet identified (at least to the hearer). Its eventual status is determined by the clause containing it. In (10)a, *Jill just bought a car* provides a connection that serves to incorporate the car in the hearer's epistemic dominion (the speaker, of course, has prior knowledge of it). In (10)b, *Jill needs a car* fails to do so at the level of basic reality – *need* is not a relationship that singles out any particular, actual instance. The profiled instance remains a virtual one.[22] It also remains virtual when the clausal process is not itself accepted as real, e.g. in a negative clause (*Jill didn't buy a car*) or when the clause is grounded with a modal (*Jill may buy a car*). By contrast, a definite nominal presupposes identification, irrespective of the clause containing it. If I say *Jill needs this car, Jill didn't buy this car,* or *Jill may buy this car,* I am in each case referring to a particular, actual car – one identified independently of the clause containing the nominal.

(11) a. *Jill bought a car.* [car established as real]
b. *Jill {needs / didn't buy / may buy} a car.* [car remains virtual]
c. *Jill {bought / needs / didn't buy / may buy} this car.*
[car presupposed as real]

My basic proposal is thus as follows.[23] Assessed at the level of the nominal itself – independently of the clause containing it – definite grounding portrays the nominal referent as being identified to the hearer. Its status as real, with an established place in the hearer's epistemic dominion, does not depend on the information provided by the clause containing it. On the other hand, indefinite grounding instructs the hearer to invoke a previously unidentified instance.

22 It is however established in elaborated reality, which is sufficient for it to function as a discourse referent. Thus *it* refers to it anaphorically in (10)b.

23 This is an elaboration of the description in Chapter 4 (§ 4). See also Verhagen 1986: 123–124.

From the hearer's standpoint the referent is therefore a virtual entity, conjured up just for purposes of apprehending the nominal meaning, **pending** further information from the clause containing it (or the larger context). This additional information can either establish the referent as real, e.g. in (11)a, or confirm its virtuality, as in (11)b. The status provided by the grounding itself, independently of the clause, is thus as shown in Figure 6.11. The two configurations correspond to the result phase and the potential phase of the epistemic control cycle. With definite grounding the profiled instance t_i has an established place in the hearer's conception of reality (R_H). With indefinites, t_i is placed in the hearer's field of awareness (F_H) as something that has to be dealt with. As the focus of attention, it is under the hearer's attentional control, but not yet under epistemic control.

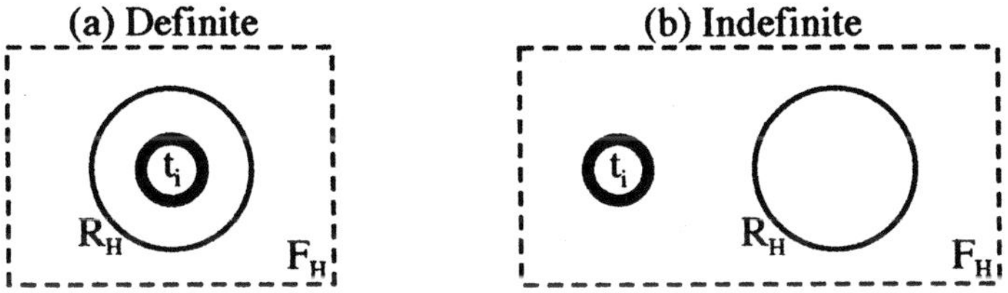

Figure 6.11

Finer distinctions can be made by taking the speaker into account, as shown in Figure 6.12. In particular, indefinites can be interpreted as either specific or non-specific, as in (12). This too is a matter of mental space configuration, the pivotal space being the speaker's epistemic dominion. A specific interpretation is one where t_i is identified to the speaker, independently of the content provided by clause, whereas a non-specific reading is one where the referent is virtual for both interlocutors.

(12) a. *He married* ***the Norwegian.*** [definite]
b. *He wants to marry* ***a Norwegian.*** *She is rich.* [specific indefinite]
c. *He wants to marry* ***a Norwegian.*** *But she has to be rich.* [non-specific indefinite]

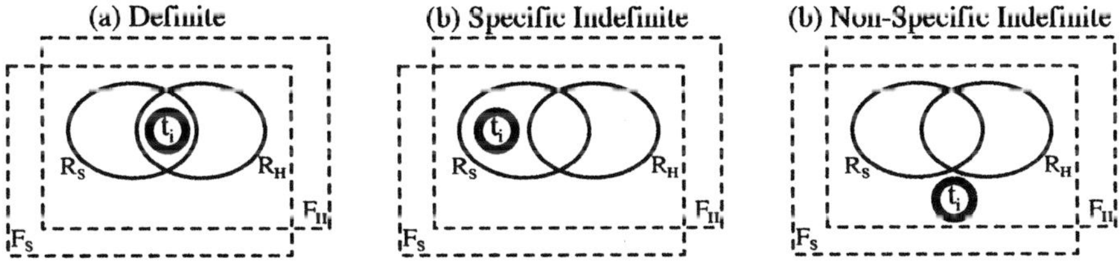

Figure 6.12

By comparing Figures 6.11 and 6.5, we can observe a basic parallelism between nominal and clausal grounding at the epistemic level. Definiteness and the absence of a modal both indicate that the target has been incorporated as part of conceived reality and is therefore under epistemic control. Likewise, indefiniteness and the presence of a modal both indicate that the status of the target has yet to be resolved – it is not yet under epistemic control. One point of difference is that the relevant conceptualizer is the speaker in the case of clausal grounding, the hearer in the case of nominal grounding. This difference does however have an explanation in terms of what is at issue. With respect to future events, and whether they will eventually be realized, the two interlocutors are basically in the same situation: whatever projection they make, they must both await future developments to determine whether an envisaged event will actually occur. It is thus the assessment of the primary conceptualizer, namely the speaker, that is coded by the presence or absence of a modal. On the other hand, nominal grounding pertains to identification and the coordination of reference. Existence being presupposed, it is a matter of the speaker wanting the hearer to focus attention on the same referent the speaker has already singled out. It is thus the hearer's knowledge and attention that are pivotal.

9. Grounding quantifiers

I have concentrated on the grounding of singular count nouns, where some basic features of nominal grounding are most clearly evident, if only due to the absence of complicating factors. I do not believe that extending the account to the full range of grounding elements changes this basic picture in any drastic way. It is worth noting that most of the other grounding elements – all but the plural demonstratives *these* and *those* – are indefinite. In other words, most of the richness of the nominal grounding system pertains to targets not yet under epistemic control, referents whose ultimate status has yet to be determined. This is also true of clausal grounding, where the simple opposition immediate/non-immediate, for events under epistemic control, contrasts with the much wider range of options provided by modals (*may*, *can*, *will*, *shall*, *must*, *might*, *could*, *would*, *should*).[24]

It is further worth noting that most indefinite grounding elements profile entities that are **necessarily virtual**, irrespective of the larger context. Only the

24 I suspect that predicates of propositional attitude follow the same pattern, i.e. that more such predicates pertain to the potential phase of the control cycle than the result phase.

indefinite articles – *a*, *sm*, and *Ø* – offer the possibility of the referent proving to be an actual one, as in (13)a. The remaining elements – the relative quantifiers *all*, *most*, *some*, *no*, *every*, *each*, and *any* – all have inherently virtual referents. I have described these at length in other places (e.g. Langacker 1991, 2004c, 2005b), so here I mention them just in passing.

(13) a. *{A bird / Sm birds / Birds} survived the forest fire.*
[referent proves to be actual]
b. *{All / Most / Some / No} birds survived the forest fire.*
[referent is necessarily virtual]
c. *{Every / Each / Any} bird survived the forest fire.*[25]
[referent is necessarily virtual]

Briefly, the quantifiers in (13)b characterize their referent only as some **proportion** of the contextually relevant extension of the specified type. Hence they do not directly identify any specific individual. Even if we know that most birds survived the forest fire, we do not know which specific birds are still alive. *Most birds* is a virtual entity, not something that actually exists as such.[26] It is perhaps more obvious that the quantifiers in (13)c also have virtual referents. For example, *every bird* cannot be identified as any specific, actual bird. Instead, *every*, *each*, or *any* profiles a fictive entity conceived as being **representative** of some type, in the sense that what is predicated of it (e.g. having survived the forest fire) projects to all members of the relevant extension. These quantifiers contrast semantically in regard to how the members are imagined as being accessed: simultaneously (*every*), sequentially (*each*), or through random choice (*any*).

These quantifiers represent different strategies for achieving a measure of epistemic control. Depending on how one looks at it, the control is either stronger or weaker than can be achieved with specific, actual referents. It is stronger in the sense that the statement made pertains in some fashion to all members of an often open-ended set, not just a single individual. It is weaker in the sense that nothing is directly and definitively specified concerning any particular individual. But obviously, in coping with the world we cannot always deal with specific objects and events. By making generalizations, we achieve a provisional kind of control that may be limited or indirect, but which has the advantage of extending to any number of eventualities.

25 While *any* is possible in this expression, the requisite interpretation is hard to achieve without a fuller context. This can be supplied by a modifier: *Any bird with strength enough to fly survived the forest fire*.

26 To be sure, *all* – as a limiting case – allows the set of birds in question to be identified via inference.

I will conclude by pointing out one additional parallel between the two grounding systems. Examples like (14) reveal a close affinity between particular grounding quantifiers and particular epistemic modals:

(14) a. ***All*** *students pass this test, so Zelda* ***will*** *pass it.*
b. ***Most*** *students pass this test, so Zelda* ***should*** *pass it.*
c. ***Some*** *students pass this test, so Zelda* ***may*** *pass it.*
d. ***No*** *students pass this test, so Zelda* ***will not*** *pass it.*

Evidently, the quantifiers and the modals are comparable in the degree of epistemic control they specify. In fact, the quantifiers cited seem exactly equivalent to the corresponding modals in the degree of confidence they afford in predicting future events. Of course, confidence in predicting occurrences is what modals are all about. But what of nominal quantifiers? These pertain to objects rather than events. What, then, is the basis for their evident correlation with modals?

The answer lies in a previous observation: while events depend on objects for their occurrence, objects depend on events for their identification. Even though the referent of a phrase like *most students* is a virtual entity, hence not identified according to the previous definition, it is still true that identification is what is at issue. And that depends on events, in this case events of the type *student pass this test.* We do not use a nominal like *most students* just for its own sake – if non-elliptic, we would only use it as part of a clause, which specifies some occurrence with respect to which students are being quantified. One facet of the semantic characterization of a quantifier is thus a schematic occurrence representing the one invoked as the basis for assessment. In a particular expression, like (14)b, that occurrence is equated with the one profiled by the clause containing the grounded nominal.

The phrase *most students* is roughly sketched on the right in Figure 6.13(a). The circles indicate students, and the large box represents the contextually relevant extension of this type (possibly the maximal extension). Arrows stand for instances of the occurrence evoked as the basis for quantification. The smaller box, in bold, delimits the plural entity profiled by the nominal: it designates the set of students selected from the relevant extension by virtue of being participants in this type of occurrence; in (14)b, they are the students who pass the test. Overall, this sentence is employed to indicate Zelda's chances of belonging to this group. Hence the diagram shows Zelda (Z) as an actual, identified individual, part of the speaker's conception of reality (R). The dashed arrow in diagram (a) is meant to represent the speaker's effort in assessing how Zelda relates to the fictive students evoked by the phrase *most students.* Will she prove to be one of the profiled set of students, who pass the test, or will she be part of the residue of students who do not? With *most*, the odds are pretty good: in mapping Zelda onto the set of possible targets – students constituting the relevant extension – the targets manifesting the desired occurrence come close to exhausting the set of candidates.

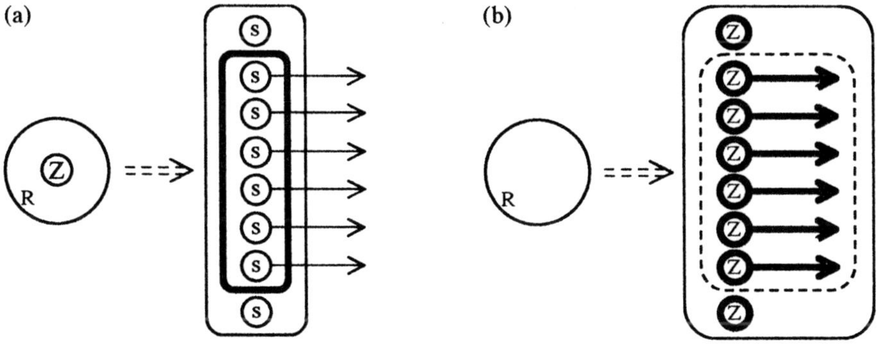

Figure 6.13

Diagram (a) shows the import of *most* in this expression. Diagram (b) depicts the same expression, (14)b, from the standpoint of the epistemic modal *should*. The target is the grounded process *Zelda pass this test*. The presence of a modal indicates that this process is not yet accepted as real, while the choice of modal specifies the likelihood of its realization. As before, the dashed arrow represents the modal force – what the speaker subjectively experiences as the evolutionary momentum of reality in striving to reach the target. The large box stands for the set of **relevant eventualities** involving Zelda, i.e. the paths in the future evolution of reality in which Zelda somehow figures, and which are still possible paths given the current state of reality and its evolutionary momentum. In some of those eventualities, Zelda passes the test; in others she does not. The diagram reflects one way of thinking about the strength of the modal force: the stronger the force tending toward the target, the more the space of eventualities is warped to favor reaching that target. That translates into more of the possible paths of evolution containing the target event. In the case of *should*, it will be much easier for reality to hit the target than to miss it.

Comparing diagrams (a) and (b), their effective equivalence is readily apparent. It makes no difference whether we construe the situation in terms of mapping Zelda onto the contextually relevant set of students, or in terms of extrapolating reality to encompass one of the relevant eventualities. By inspection, we can see that either case yields the same probability of reality incorporating the event of Zelda passing the test.

I have touched on a host of complex and subtle issues. Unavoidably, therefore, the discussion and analysis have been exploratory rather than definitive. By asking different questions I have suggested new ways of looking at much-studied problems. I believe the results have justified the attempt. They should not however be overstated. Just as nominals and clauses are distinct, so are nominal and clausal grounding; a paper could equally well have been written spelling out their non-parallelism. But while the similarities are abstract, they are non-trivial and far from obvious. If valid, they further support the descriptive and theoretical notions required for their explication, all of which were first proposed for other reasons.

Chapter 7
The English present: Temporal coincidence vs. epistemic immediacy

1. Framing the issue

The issue to be addressed is whether the English "present tense" is best described as marking tense or modality. Linguists generally agree that the English present does not mark present time, at least not consistently or exclusively. After all, as seen in (1), the simple present **cannot** be used for present-time events, while it **is** used for events that are past, future, or time-independent.

(1) a. **I read a book right now.* [present]
b. *I get home last night and find a note on my door.* [past ("historical present")]
c. *They leave next week for Darfur.* [future]
d. *Sugar dissolves in water.* [time-independent]

Nevertheless, I have argued (Langacker 1991, 2001 f) that the English present can in fact be analyzed quite successfully as marking present time. I have suggested that its "naïve" characterization, as indicating **coincidence with the time of speaking**, is basically valid. This account has been criticized by Brisard (1999, 2001, 2002), who has argued in general against time-line descriptions of tense, proposing in particular that the English present is best characterized as having a kind of modal import, which I will refer to as **epistemic immediacy**. I think Brisard would agree that it is not really a matter of choosing between these two accounts. In large measure they are interchangeable, representing alternate perspectives on the same basic vision.[1] But while the temporal coincidence account works quite well within its intended scope, i.e. for clauses grounded by "tense" alone, sentences with modals require an epistemic characterization. Thus, if the temporal account is considered prototypical, a schematic (fully general) characterization has to be epistemic. The

1 "... I have not sufficiently emphasized epistemic immediacy, which I see as the flip side of coincidence with the time of speaking ..." (Langacker 2001 f: 271 [fn. 6]). My recognition of the need to develop an epistemic account has been reinforced by numerous discussions over the years with Brisard and with Mariko Higuchi (cf. Higuchi 2008).

basic challenge is then to explicate the notion "epistemic immediacy" and how it applies in a broad range of cases.

Both accounts presuppose some central descriptive proposals of CG (Langacker 1987a, 1987b, 1991, 2008a). Most broadly, they presuppose a conceptualist semantics that recognizes the fundamental importance of construal as well as imaginative capacities (such as metaphor, blending, fictivity, and mental spaces). More specifically, they presuppose that an expression's grammatical category is determined by the nature of its profile (an aspect of construal), and that basic categories – in particular, noun and verb – are susceptible to schematic characterization (Langacker 2008a: chs. 4–5). A noun profiles a thing, defined abstractly as a product of conceptual grouping and reification. A verb profiles a process, defined abstractly as a relationship scanned sequentially through time.

Especially important here is a basic conceptual distinction observable within the noun and verb categories. In the case of nouns, it is manifested in the grammatical opposition **count** vs. **mass**. For verbs, the analogous opposition is "active" vs. "stative", or in my terminology, **perfective** vs. **imperfective**. The verb *throw*, for instance, profiles a perfective process, *resemble* an imperfective one. Once allowance is made for the inherent difference between nouns and verbs, the count/mass and perfective/imperfective oppositions turn out to be exactly the same (Langacker 1987b). For ease of presentation, I will limit my discussion of nouns to the prototypes: physical objects for count nouns, physical substances for mass nouns. We think of these as existing primarily in space – I say that space is their **domain of instantiation**. The account, though, is fully general, accommodating nouns with other domains of instantiation (e.g. time for a noun like *week*). With verbs the domain of instantiation is always time.

The parallelism of count nouns and perfective processes is spelled out in (2). With respect to each property, they are polar opposites of substances and imperfective processes, as described in (3). Let us consider each property in turn, starting with objects and substances.

(2) An object or a perfective process is:

a. conceived as being bounded (in the immediate scope in its domain of instantiation);

b. not conceived as being internally homogeneous;

c. not contractible (an arbitrary subpart is not itself an instance);

d. replicable (combining two instances results in multiple instances).

(3) A substance or an imperfective process is:

a. not conceived as being bounded (in the immediate scope in its domain of instantiation);

b. conceived as being internally homogeneous;
c. contractible (an arbitrary subpart is itself an instance);
d. not replicable (combining two instances results in a single, larger instance).

A physical object, such as a *shoe*, is conceived as being **bounded** in space (its domain of instantiation). The boundary and the shape it defines are inherent in the conception of an instance, so they fall within the immediate scope, i.e. the spatial expanse required to support this conception. This is shown in Figure 7.1(a), where shading represents the material substance constituting the object. Objects in general are not conceived as being internally **homogeneous** – they have distinguishable parts, often consisting of different substances. From these two properties it follows that an object is usually not **contractible**, i.e. a subpart is not itself an instance of the same type (part of a shoe is not itself a shoe). Finally, due to bounding an object is **replicable**: putting two instances together results in multiple instances (not a single, larger instance).

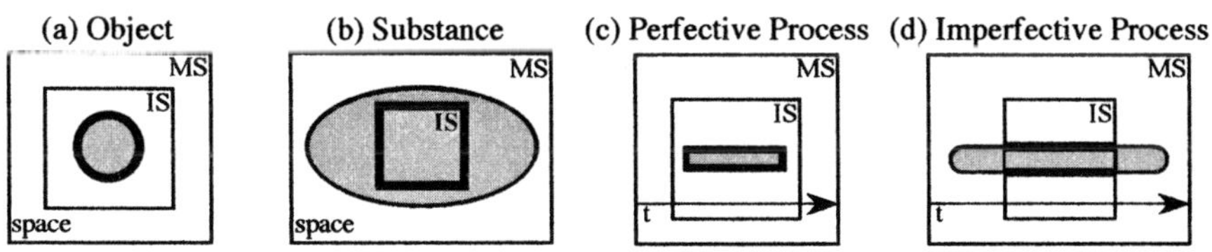

Figure 7.1

Substances, for instance *leather*, exhibit the opposite properties. Though bounding is not precluded, it is not part of the characterization of a substance. Instead, a substance is characterized in qualitative terms (rather than by shape or observation of a spatial boundary). As such it is conceived as being internally homogeneous (the same qualitative properties hold throughout its spatial extension). From these two properties it follows that any portion of a substance is itself an instance of the same type, i.e. a substance is contractible. Hence the configuration in diagram (b): starting from a large expanse of substance, if we "zoom in" and direct attention to just a subpart – which is thus the immediate scope of conception – that portion is itself identifiable (on qualitative grounds) as an instance of the substance in question.[2] Finally, a substance is not replicable, in the sense that combining two instances does not result in multiple instances, but rather a single, larger instance. For example, we talk about *the*

2. Note that only this portion is profiled, since by definition an expression's profile is the focus of attention within its immediate scope.

leather in those two shoes – although the leather and the shoes are spatially coextensive, in terms of their linguistic construal there are two instances of *shoe* but only one instance of *leather* comprising them both.

Turning now to processes, let me first introduce the notational convention of using an elongated box with square corners to represent a perfective process, as in Figure 7.1(c), and one with rounded corners for an imperfective process, as in diagram (d). For either sort of process, the domain of instantiation is time: just as a physical object or substance has spatial extension, a process has temporal extension. To carry the analogy one step further, let us ask what corresponds to the material substance which constitutes a physical thing. With a process, what extends through time (in the same way that substance extends through space) is nothing other than the profiled relationship. And like the material substance of an object, the component states of a process – the relations obtaining at each instant (its "time-slices") – may or may not be the same throughout. That is, a process may consist in either a change through time or the continuation through time of a stable situation.

A perfective process, like *throw*, is conceived as being bounded in time. And since the bounding is part of the characterization of such a process, something required to identify an instance of the type, it falls within the immediate scope in this domain, as seen in Figure 7.1(c). A perfective process is not conceived as being internally homogeneous. For instance, throwing has different phases (swinging of the arm, motion of the projectile), and since even a single phase involves a change through time, the constitutive relations (time-slices) differ from instant to instant. Thus a perfective process is not contractible, e.g. swinging the arm is not itself an instance of throwing. And it is of course replicable: successive acts of throwing constitute two instances of this process type.

By contrast, an imperfective process like *resemble* has indefinite temporal extension, in the sense that bounding is inessential to its characterization. This goes along with its being internally homogeneous: the same relationship holds throughout, thus providing a qualitative means of identification. As a consequence, any portion of the overall process is itself an instance of the same type. If the statement *Bush resembles Putin* is valid throughout their official careers, it is also valid for any part of that time span, e.g. during 2005. So if we limit our attention to that immediate scope, in the manner of Figure 7.1(d), the same statement applies to the profiled segment thus delimited. An imperfective process is also non-replicable, i.e. combining two instances yields a single, longer instance. If Bush resembled Putin all during 2004, and all during 2005 as well, we would not say that *Bush resembled Putin twice*, but rather that he resembled him over the entire period.

2. Temporal coincidence

What is surprising about the account based on temporal coincidence is that it works so well, given the undeniable facts in (1): normally the present **cannot** be used for present-time events, but **can** be used for non-present occurrences (past, future, or time-independent). Nonetheless, I have proposed and defended the following characterization:

(4) The English present tense specifies that an instance of the profiled process occurs and precisely coincides with the time of speaking.

Let us first deal with the problem posed by examples like (1)a, **I read a book right now*, returning later to "non-present" uses of the present.

2.1. Present perfectives

Linguists recognize the need to posit two basic classes of English verbs – perfective (or "active") vs. imperfective (or "stative") – on the basis of grammatical behavior. In particular, perfectives resist occurring in the simple present tense but do take the progressive with *be...-ing*, while imperfectives do the opposite, as seen in (5). In (5)a(i) I include the adverb *right now* to force a "true present" interpretation, as opposed to one of the non-present interpretations (e.g. as habitual). Some linguists might **define** the two classes on the basis of these and other grammatical behaviors. In CG, however, I take such behaviors as being merely **symptomatic** of a conceptual contrast, characterized in (2)-(3). Thus it is not a rigid lexical contrast. Although most verbs have a primary categorization as either perfective or imperfective, numerous factors are capable of inducing an alternate construal resulting in the opposite behavior. I will not attempt to survey these here.

(5) a.	**Perfective:**	(i) **He mows the lawn (right now).*
		(ii) *He is mowing the lawn.*
b.	**Imperfective:**	(i) *He knows Italian.*
		(ii) **He is knowing Italian.*

With respect to the classic aspectual categories described by Vendler (1967), perfective verbs subsume three of the four – achievement, accomplishment, and activity verbs – while imperfectives correspond to stative verbs. Activity verbs, such as *sleep*, *sit*, and *swim*, behave like other perfectives in regard to the present tense and the progressive. While the processes they designate are easily construed as being internally homogeneous, they are nonetheless conceived as occurring in bounded episodes, and bounding is the critical property for the perfective/imperfective contrast. Note that verbs like these – bounded yet internally homogeneous – are directly comparable to count nouns such as *lake*, *board*, or *lawn* (bounded expanses of water, wood, and grass).

Their conceptual characterizations make it possible to explain why perfectives and imperfectives behave grammatically as they do. Why do only perfectives take the progressive? The reason is that the progressive construction serves an imperfectivizing function, so its application to imperfectives would be superfluous. Its effect is sketched in Figure 7.2. On the conception of a perfective process, it imposes an immediate temporal scope internal to its boundaries, thus confining the profiled relationship to the onstage portion so delimited. Since bounding is no longer evident within the immediate scope, the derived process is imperfective. It is further construed as being internally homogeneous (the constitutive relationships are effectively equivalent, being identified only as time-slices of the original perfective process).

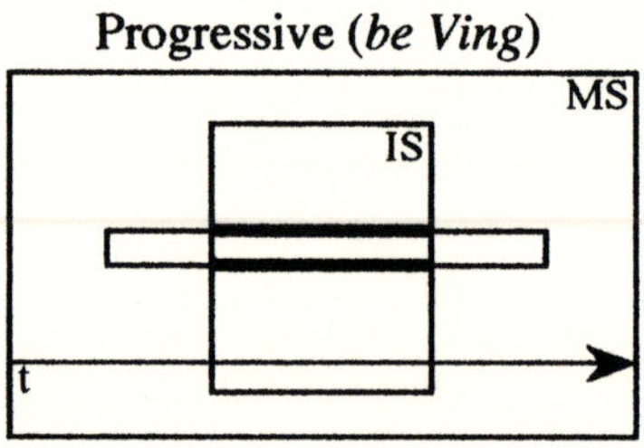

Figure 7.2

Turning now to tense, we observe that the English past tense is compatible with both perfectives and imperfectives (*He mowed the lawn*; *He knew Italian*), and that imperfectives occur in the present (*He knows Italian*). It is only present-tense perfectives that are problematic (**He mows the lawn*). To see why we must first describe the tense morphemes. Like the progressive, they impose an immediate temporal scope, i.e. they direct attention to a particular span of time for purposes of viewing the profiled clausal process. Unlike the progressive, which is aspectual, the present and past are deictic elements which identify this time span relative to the speech event. In diagrams, I will represent the speech event by means of a box with squiggly lines. Obviously, the past morpheme imposes an immediate scope that is prior to the time of speaking, as shown in Figure 7.3(a). The profiled process must appear in this frame. In the case of the present, shown in diagram (b), the immediate temporal scope and the speech event are coextensive. The hypothesis at issue is that the designated process precisely coincides with this time span.

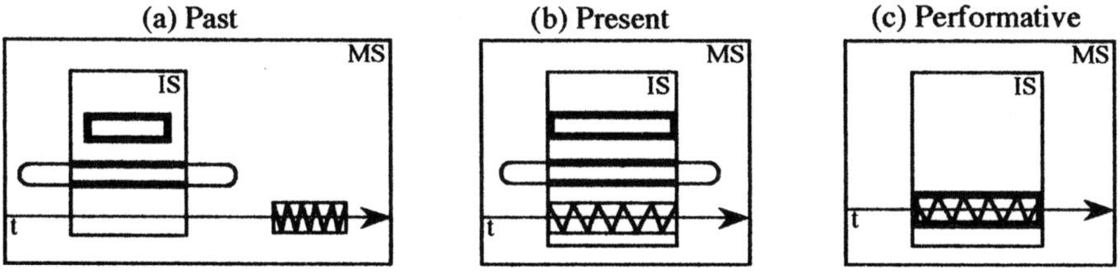

Figure 7.3

Past perfectives are unproblematic because there is no inherent limit on the size of the immediate temporal scope – it need only precede the speech event. Hence it can always be made large enough to encompass a bounded process, as required. Past imperfectives are also unproblematic, but for a different reason. Since they may extend indefinitely, there is no guarantee that a limited immediate scope will always contain them in their entirety. But full inclusion is unnecessary, due to contractibility. Any subpart of an imperfective process is itself a valid instance of its type. Suppose, then, that an imperfective process overflows the limits of the immediate scope, as seen in Figure 7.3(a). The portion subtended by it, and profiled by virtue of being onstage, will itself constitute an instance of the process type, hence the requirements are met. In just the same way, imperfectives work in the present tense because, as seen in diagram (b), the portion of an imperfective process which coincides with the time of speaking itself counts as an instance of its type.

Perfective and imperfective processes are naturally associated with different **modes of apprehension**. Since bounding is inherent in its characterization, a perfective process has to be observed in its entirety to be identified. But with imperfectives this is not an issue, as there may not be any "entirety". For a stable situation that extends indefinitely, the usual mode of apprehension is one of **sampling** some limited portion. A limited sample is sufficient for qualitative identification and may be all that is possible.

Why, it may now be asked, are present perfectives problematic? There is nothing conceptually incoherent about a bounded process being coincident with the speech event. Rather than their being semantically anomalous, I have suggested that present perfectives pose problems of use from the pragmatic standpoint. One problem is **durational**: most bounded events that we might have occasion to talk about happen not to be the same in length as the time required to utter a clause describing them. It takes at most a second to produce the sentence *He mows the lawn*, but the actual mowing is likely to take far longer. There is also an **epistemic** problem: by the time we observe an event to find out what is happening, it is already too late to initiate a description that precisely coincides with it.

Striking confirmation for this explanation comes from a major exception to the non-occurrence of present-tense perfectives, namely **performatives** (Austin 1962):

(6) a. *I order you to destroy those files.*
b. *I hereby sentence you to 30 days in the county jail.*
c. *I promise that I will be more careful.*

Speech-act verbs are perfective (note that they take the progressive when used descriptively, e.g. *She is ordering him to destroy the files*). But when used to actually **perform** the speech act named, they necessarily occur in the present.[3] Performatives represent a special case of language use where the durational and epistemic problems simply do not arise. The durational problem does not arise because, in a performative, the profiled process and the speech event are one and the same, hence necessarily the same in duration, as shown in Figure 7.3(c). The epistemic problem does not arise because the speaker has prior intention to perform the act in question – she does not have to observe the event in order to identify it.

The infelicity of present tense perfectives is therefore not due to inherent semantic anomaly, but rather to the durational and epistemic problems that arise in a particular kind of circumstance. This circumstance does however have default-case status. In the **default viewing arrangement**, the interlocutors are together in a fixed location from which they observe and report on actual occurrences in the world around them. It is on this basis that a sentence like *He mows the lawn* is judged ungrammatical and given a star, even though it is perfectly acceptable assuming a different arrangement (e.g. to describe a habitual practice). The incompatibility stems from the interaction between the default viewing arrangement (involving observation and description) and the meaning of the present tense.

We can therefore predict that present-tense perfectives will also be acceptable in other viewing circumstances where the durational and epistemic problems happen not to arise. This will be so when the event in question has the right duration to be made coincident with the time of speaking, and where the speaker is the actor, acting intentionally and with full awareness. We can

3 I do not consider cases with the progressive, e.g. *I am ordering you to destroy those files*, to be true performatives. Rather, they represent the politeness strategy of indirectness: the speaker avoids the direct assertion of authority, achieving the same effect by merely describing what he is actually doing. Alternatively, the sentence could be used to reinforce an order already made or merely implied, the explicit description leaving no room for ambiguity.

imagine, for example, a friendly game of chess in which a player describes his move as he makes it. The first clause in (7)a would be uttered while moving the rook, and the second clause while removing the opponent's knight. Or, we can imagine a situation where, for some reason, the speaker carries out a series of bodily movements and describes each one as it occurs, as in (7)b. Although the situation may be contrived, use of the present with perfectives is perfectly natural in this context.

(7) a. *I move my rook to QB3, and capture your knight.*
  b. *I raise my hand. I lower my hand. I turn to the left. I turn back to the right.*

A very common use of present-tense perfectives is for the play-by-play description of sporting events, as in (8)a. This would seem to be a clear instance of the default viewing arrangement. Why, then, are present-tense perfectives not just acceptable, but the norm? For one thing, the events described do in fact have just about the right duration. A longer event, like the manager walking from the dugout to the pitcher's mound, would normally not be reported in the simple present. Also, the events in question are highly stereotyped, to the point that they can be identified very quickly and even anticipated. Observe that events which depart from the usual script, like the fight in (8)c, are not reported in the present. There is also a certain amount of tolerance in normal language use. If I say, for instance, that *All politicians are dishonest*, you will not consider me a liar if we both recognize that there are a few exceptions. So given the reality of the situation, we are no doubt prepared to cut the announcer a bit of slack in regard to temporal coincidence. We might also say that the play-by-play style of announcing is based on a **fictive viewing arrangement**, where the fiction of simultaneous reporting is adopted for sake of convenience and "vividness".

(8) a. *He hits it into the hole. Jeter makes a nice stop. He fires to first, and gets him by a step.*
  b. *The manager {is walking / *walks} slowly toward the mound.*
  c. *A fight {has just broken out / *breaks out} in the stands!*

2.2. Non-present uses

Play-by-play reporting represents a transitional case between present and non-present uses of the present. To the extent that it relies on scripting or a fictive viewing arrangement, it resembles the latter. Non-present uses of the present are all based on departures from the default viewing arrangement. When these are properly recognized, an account in terms of temporal coincidence can be rescued.

As another transitional case, imagine a group of detectives watching a surveillance tape which has caught the commission of a crime. One detective, who has previously viewed the tape, narrates what is happening as it happens, in the manner of (9)a, describing each event as it appears on the monitor. In another arrangement, the clerk might recall the same events using the "historical present", as in (9)b. In both cases present tense perfectives are perfectly felicitous.

(9) a. *The suspect enters the store. Now he approaches the counter. He hands the clerk a note. Now he pulls back his coat, and shows her the gun.*
b. *I'm working late last night, just getting ready to close up, when this guy walks in. He comes to the counter and gives me a note. Then he pulls back his coat and I see a gun.*

Why the present, when the events were in the past? What is crucial here is that both situations involve a special viewing arrangement more elaborate than the default one. It is not just a matter of observing and describing actual occurrences. In (9)a, the interlocutors are not observing the events themselves, directly, but are watching a video replay. In (9)b, the events once observed directly are being accessed through recall. The historical present is not unreasonably described as a "mental replay", where previous events are relived by running the tapes of memory.

In both cases, a distinction can be drawn between the **events themselves** and **representations of the events**. A surveillance video represents events. Memory records experience for later access. We must therefore ask which level the expressions in (9) apply to. It seems to me quite evident that they are directly describing the representations rather than the events themselves. When the detective says *He hands the clerk a note*, he is directly describing something that happens in the context of the surveillance video. Of course, since the events on the video are representations of actual events, the expressions also describe the latter – but only indirectly, via the description of the video events representing them. Similarly, the historical present consists in describing events that occur as part of a mental replay; only indirectly, via this replay, do the expressions pertain to the original, actual events.

I propose, then, that the present perfectives in (9) are based on **special viewing arrangements** more elaborate than the default arrangement. As shown in Figure 7.4, these special viewing arrangements involve the distinction between a **represented event**, which may be actual, and a **representing event**, which

– as a representation – is necessarily virtual. In these arrangements, what is being "viewed", and directly described linguistically, is the representing event. However, the entire configuration, including the representing event and the relation it bears to an actual one, is part of an expression's overall meaning. Every expression presupposes a multifaceted **conceptual substrate** which supports the content overtly expressed and renders it coherent. The viewing arrangement is one facet of this substrate.

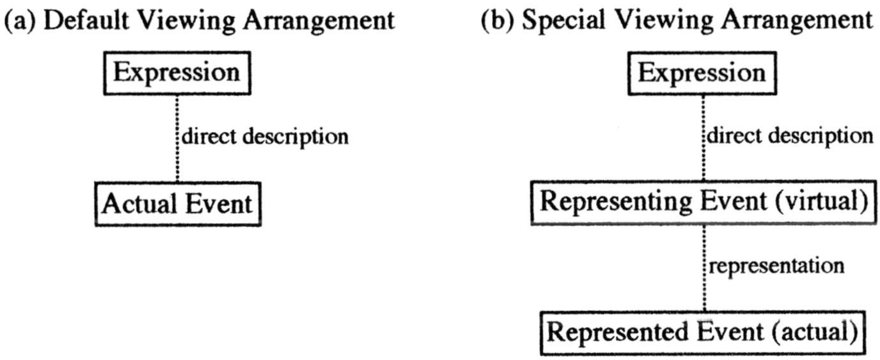

Figure 7.4

On this account the present perfectives in (9) do in fact describe events coincident with the time of speaking. In (9)a, the detective describes each virtual event as it occurs on the monitor. They are all roughly of the proper length. For longer events, the detective would probably resort to the progressive: *Now he's walking around the store to be sure there's no security guard.* Likewise, a speaker using the historical present describes events coincident with their successive recall. Or to put it another way, the speaker relives the events by recounting them. And since they are only being recalled (not actually occurring), duration is not a problem: by adjusting the speed of the replay, the representing events can always be made to coincide with the time of speaking.

I suggest that Figure 7.4(b) represents a general scheme for (so-called) non-present uses of the present. They are all based on mental constructions involving representations of occurrences. It is these **virtual occurrences** – rather than the actual ones they represent – that are directly described linguistically and coincide with the time of speaking. The constructions involved are numerous and varied in nature. I will consider just a few more (representative?) cases.

First is the future use of the present, as in (10)a. I call this the "scheduled future", since it evokes some kind of plan or schedule governing the occurrence of future events. Although it may be physically manifested, in printed form or on a monitor, what matters is the existence of a schedule as a mentally and socially constructed entity – an accepted plan expected to govern the timing and occurrence of future events. Observe that we do not use the scheduled future for events that cannot be planned or controlled, e.g. (10)b. Note further that we have to posit this mental construction and acknowledge its linguistic relevance quite independently of the present tense. In (10)c, for instance, the second clause still describes a scheduled future occurrence, even though the verb is marked for past tense rather than present. In other words, the scheduled future is not just a meaning of the present tense, but arises from the interaction of the present tense with an independent conceptual phenomenon.

(10) a. *We have to hurry. The plane leaves in ten minutes.*
b. **A nuclear accident destroys Seattle next week.*
c. *She was rushing through the airport. The plane left in ten minutes.*

The scheduled future use of the present is sketched in Figure 7.5. A schedule comprises a series of **virtual events**, each the mental representation of an anticipated actual event. While the represented events lie in the future, the virtual representing events are presently available whenever the schedule is known and in effect. In expressions like (10)a, the speaker is not referring directly to the planned future event. What she is doing, instead, is consulting the schedule and "reading off" an entry. Reading off an entry consists in activating or mentally reconstituting the profiled representing event. This virtual occurrence, which is just a matter of the speaker apprehending what she is saying, coincides with the time of speaking.[4]

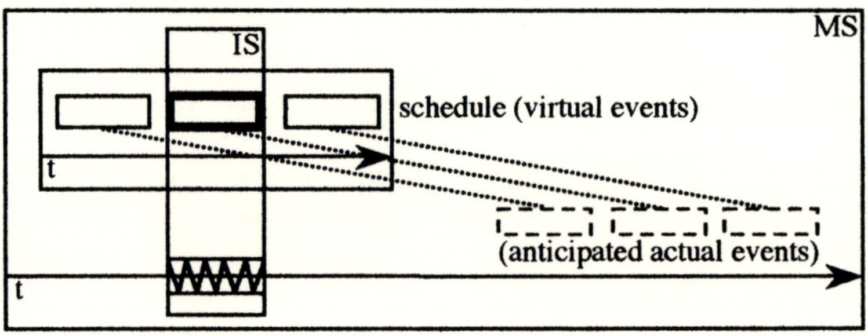

Figure 7.5

4 A diagram for the historical present would be comparable, except that the represented events are prior to the time of speaking, accessible by recall rather than scheduling.

A **script** is something like a schedule, one difference being that the represented events can occur at any time – indeed, any number of times – provided that they all occur in the proper (scripted) sequence. In "reading" a script, the virtual representing events are mentally reconstructed from their descriptions, and interpreted as models to be emulated in producing the actual events constituting a performance.[5]

In the case of scripts, some situations are ambivalent as to whether the events being described are the actual ones of a performance or the virtual ones the performance instantiates. Imagine a cooking show on TV, where the chef describes each step roughly coincident with performing it, as in (11)a. Possibly the chef is directly describing the actions themselves, in the manner of (7). However, the chef is also following a script, so despite the first-person pronoun (which I take as reflecting the actual performance), he might also be describing the virtual representing events which constitute it, doing so in sync with the actual events instantiating them. In another style of narration, the chef describes each action **before** performing it, as in (11)b. If the descriptions pertain directly to the actual events, we have to say that this speech genre allows a generous tolerance in regard to simultaneity (more generous than in the play-by-play mode). What I incline to say, instead, is that the expressions directly describe the virtual events of the script. The chef evokes each successive representing event by way of introducing the actual event that will follow.

(11) a. *First I take an egg. I crack it and empty it into a bowl. Now I take a cup of flour, and put it in the bowl with the egg. I mix them together ...*
b. *First I take six eggs ... I crack them and empty them into a mixing bowl ... Now I measure out two cups of flour ... I put them into the bowl with the eggs ... Next I beat the mixture until it is well blended ...*

As a final example, consider a singular **generic**, as in (12)a. Generics invoke a cultural model in which certain kinds of events are taken as reflecting the world's **essential nature**, which provides a stable **structure** within which other, **incidental** events occur (Goldsmith and Woisetschlaeger 1982; Langacker 1997b). Accordingly, our knowledge of the world includes a set of **structural generalizations**, representing how the world is thought to work. These generalizations are not limited to laws of nature or physical matters; part of what constitutes the structure of our "world" is established social practice. Sentence (12)a describes a structural generalization of this sort. As a generalization, it is necessarily a virtual entity, representing what is common to any number of

5 Of course, these "actual" events may themselves be fictive representations of something that may or may not have happened in reality.

actual occurrences. The process profiled by this clause is thus a virtual event corresponding to an open-ended set of actual ones, as sketched in Figure 7.6. The man and woman referred to by the subject and object nominals are virtual instances of their types rather than actual individuals. In producing a sentence like (12)a, the speaker is "reading off" an entry in this representation of the world's essential structure. So while the represented events have no particular temporal location, this virtual occurrence of the profiled representing event coincides with the time of speaking.

(12) a. *A man proposes to a woman. [That's how it's done.]*
b. *In those days, a man proposed to a woman. [Now anything goes.]*

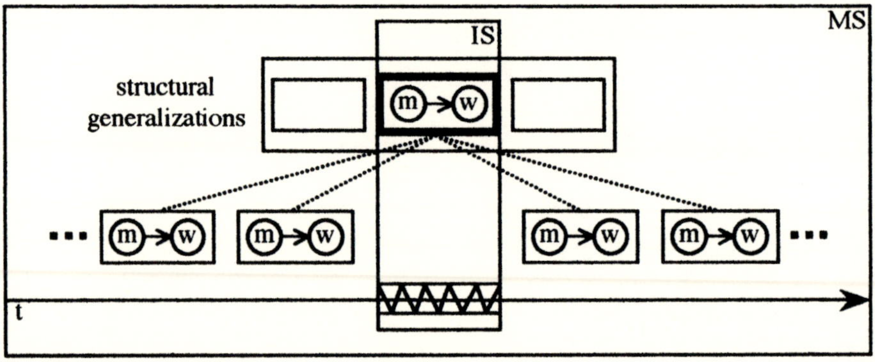

Figure 7.6

Once more, this mental construction – the notion of structural generalizations pertaining to the world's essential nature – is independent of the present tense. It is also invoked in past-tense sentences like (12)b, describing what the world's structure used to be like (before the world went to hell). Thus genericity is not, in and of itself, a meaning of the present tense. Rather, the mental construction provides a particular context in which the present can be used in its normal value.

3. Epistemic immediacy

The temporal coincidence account of the English present enjoys a considerable degree of descriptive success. To compare it with an account based on epistemic immediacy, the latter needs to be formulated with comparable detail and precision. While not the same in all specifics, the following attempt is in the same spirit as the proposals made in Brisard 2002.

3.1. General considerations

In presenting the temporal coincidence account, I spoke of the "virtual occurrence" of events. For the profiled event and the speech event to temporally coincide they have to both occur, and when the former is only virtual, its occurrence must be virtual as well. What it means to say that a virtual event "occurs" depends on its nature and provenance. A taped event occurs in the sense of appearing on a monitor, where it is subject to observation in much the same manner as the original, actual event. A recalled event consists in a **mental simulation**, a partial reactivation of the original experience. In the case of scripts, mental schedules, or generalizations about the world's inherent structure, an virtual event's occurrence may simply be a matter of its apprehension by the speaker as the essential content of a finite clause.[6]

While I take this notion as being both coherent and defensible, it has the drawback that words like *occur* and *occurrence* suggest the actual realization of events. An epistemic approach has the advantage of allowing us to avoid these terms. Instead of saying that an event's occurrence coincides with the time of speaking, we can simply say that the present indicates **epistemic immediacy** of the profiled process. This is what Brisard (2002: 263) is getting at with expressions like "immediate givenness", "present givenness", "epistemic certainty", and "immediate certainty". Of course, I am less concerned with the term than with its import. What does this "immediacy" or "certainty" consist of? And if the profiled clausal process is specified as being immediate, who is it immediate to? And when?

Our concern is limited to English tense and the basic modals. These constitute what is referred to in CG as clausal grounding (Brisard [ed.] 2002; Langacker 2002a, 2002d): grammaticized elements which specify the epistemic status of the profiled process vis-à-vis the ground (the speech event and its participants). To avoid extraneous issues, I will make the standard simplifying assumption that the proposition expressed by a finite clause represents the actual view of the current speaker.[7] Assuming this default, the present indicates epistemic immediacy to the speaker at the time of speaking. So as soon as one tries to be explicit about immediacy, the notion of temporal coincidence re-

6 This too is a kind of mental simulation, granted the view – now prevalent in cognitive semantics – that simulation has a central role in conceptual meaning (e.g. Johnson 1987; Barsalou 1999; Matlock 2004; Bergen 2005).

7 The extent to which this oversimplifies matters, and how to approach the full range of cases (not just this special, albeit privileged case), are spelled out in Chapters 6 (§ 4) and 9.

enters the picture. This should come as no surprise, as temporal and epistemic concerns are closely bound up with one another.

It has often been observed that present, past, and future are not just locations along a line, but differ in essential respects (Brisard 1999; Evans 2004: 186–188). This is sometimes phrased in terms of mental experience and the kind of access we have to occurrences: we access the present through direct experience, the past through memory, and the future through anticipation. Alternatively, it is sometimes phrased more objectively, with no explicit reference to cognition: the past is fixed and the future undetermined, while the present mediates between them as the ongoing transition from potential to realized. But in either case these are fundamentally epistemic notions. I accept the basic validity of these qualitative distinctions. Moreover, I see in them a **motivation** for certain aspects of linguistic structure. In and of themselves, however, they cannot serve as an actual **characterization** of tense.

Obviously, for example, the English present cannot be characterized semantically as indicating that the speaker directly perceives or experiences the profiled occurrence – if only because so much of what we talk about is abstract, mentally and socially constructed, or learned through communication or instruction. We cannot simply describe the past tense as meaning that the profiled occurrence is accessed through memory. After all, much of what we describe in present-tense sentences is also retrieved through memory (e.g. *Lincoln is the capital of Nebraska*). Suppose we base semantic characterizations of tense on the idea that the past is fixed, the present inchoate, and the future undetermined. It would then seem problematic that the present is used for "timeless" statements of general validity, e.g. *A triangle is a three-sided polygon.* And if the relevant notion is "epistemic certainty", why does this not point to the past rather than the present? Something that is fixed would seem to be epistemically more certain that something merely inchoate.

Simple characterizations of this sort – e.g. defining the present tense in terms of direct experience, and the past tense in terms of memory – might be workable if the use of language were limited to personally witnessed physical occurrences (statements like *I see an apple*; *The apple may fall*; *The apple fell*; *The apple is on the ground*). But general characterizations have to be more abstract and broadly applicable. An epistemic account has to accommodate knowledge irrespective of its nature and source. In particular, a general description of the English present requires a notion of epistemic immediacy that is elaborate and less than obvious, being based on cognitive models and mental constructions.

3.2. An epistemic model

My account (Langacker 1991: ch. 6; Chapters 6 and 9) starts from the premise that living creatures are continually striving to gain or maintain control of their circumstances. This striving for control occurs on many levels: physical, perceptual, mental, social. It includes such varied activities as eating, focusing attention, acquiring possessions, and establishing social relationships. And crucially, at the mental level, it includes our ongoing effort to build up a coherent conception of "the world" (in the broadest sense of that term). The result of this activity, for a given conceptualizer at a given time, constitutes what I refer to as a **reality conception.**[8] As life continues, a conceptualizer is constantly engaged in adjusting and augmenting his conception of reality on the basis of new experience.

So reality, for a particular conceptualizer (C), is what C currently accepts as valid or established. At least for the time being, it is a settled matter, as opposed to being merely suspected or simply being considered. It is what C "knows" (rightly or wrongly). Considering an element **p** for inclusion in reality (R) is to some extent a **force-dynamic** activity (Talmy 1988), a manifestation of C's striving for **epistemic control**. But once the issue has been resolved, **p**'s inclusion as part of R represents a locally stable situation, a state of relaxation (rather than mental effort). Note that this abstract characterization makes no reference to the source of knowledge or its means of incorporation in R. It makes no difference whether **p**'s acceptance in R is based on perception, hearsay, inference, instruction, intuition, etc. This much is sketched in Figure 7.7, where a double dashed arrow indicates the striving for epistemic control.

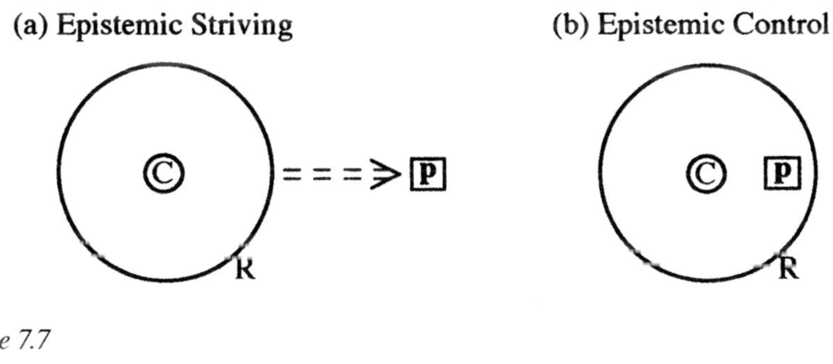

Figure 7.7

8 The word "reality" should not be taken too strictly, since "the world" – in the broadest sense – includes innumerable entities that are not real in any narrow sense, e.g. mental constructions like a schedule or a structural generalization about the world's essential nature.

The English tense-modal system (clausal grounding) is based on this distinction between epistemic striving and epistemic control. The system consists of two binary oppositions: the presence vs. the absence of a modal; and "present" vs. "past", which – as a general characterization – is better described as "proximal" vs. "distal", or **immediate** vs. **non-immediate**. The presence of a modal indicates epistemic striving, in which case the choice of the modal (*may*, *can*, *will*, *shall*, *must*, and their non-immediate counterparts) specifies the degree of force involved (Sweetser 1982; Talmy 1988; Chapter 6). The absence of a modal indicates epistemic control: the profiled process is part of C's conception of reality. We will return to the modals. For now, let us concentrate on cases where a modal is absent.

Part of C's reality conception is C herself, her existence, and her current experience. These are taken for granted as the foundation for cognition. Not only that, but – in a very real sense – C and C's location function as the center of C's mental universe. For linguistic purposes, they define the **deictic center**: the I-here-now from which the world is apprehended, and relative to which other entities are situated.

At a given moment, C's **experience** (E) comprises what C is consciously aware of – internally, through perception, or by thinking about it. Perception (e.g. seeing something) and internal awareness (e.g. feeling pain) are forms of **direct experience**, which provides the epistemic foundation for our mental world. But obviously, the world we inhabit and talk about goes far beyond what we ourselves directly experience. It includes what others have perceived and credibly reported. Much of it is abstract, being mentally, socially, and culturally constructed, but is nonetheless as real and significant to us as the core layers. I accept it as valid, for instance, that Lincoln is the capital of Nebraska, even though this is not something which can be directly perceived. Part of our world, and accepted as part of reality, are mental constructions like schedules, scripts, and structural generalizations about the world's essential nature. Also part of our world are entities like linguistic theories, and while their content may not be accepted as real, their existence certainly is.

As a first approximation, then, our **epistemic landscape** has the configuration shown in Figure 7.8(a). Direct experience accounts for only part of what we accept as real, and what we accept as real is only part of our mental world (W).

For a second approximation, we have to introduce time. We do not experience the world as a series of discrete time-slices, but as something that is continuously developing. One thing we experience is the passage of time itself, and one thing we know is that the world, and our experience of it, are constantly changing through time. We must therefore elaborate our basic epistemic model to incorporate the temporal dimension, as shown in diagram (b). Part of what we know is that our current experience – or **immediate experience** (IE), as I will call it – is just the latest phase in the ongoing process of experiencing. Likewise, the world itself, as well as that portion of the world we know about (R), have a developmental history, of which the current (momentary) phase is only the latest. Those aspects of our knowledge which pertain to the world as presently constituted will be called **immediate reality** (IR). Immediate reality is the locus of immediate experience, i.e. one thing we accept (or take for granted) as valid about the current moment is that we are having our current experience.[9]

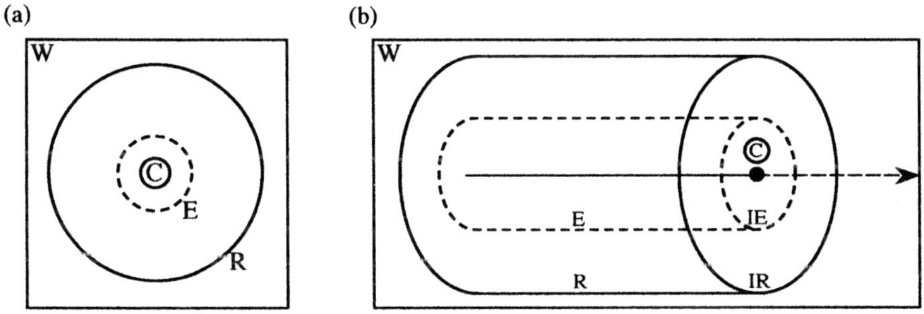

Figure 7.8

At a given moment, most of what C accepts as real is only **latent**, hence not an aspect of immediate experience. I know, for example, that Lincoln is the capital of Nebraska, but this figures in my experience only on those rare occasions when I happen to think about it. The point, of course, is crucial. The distinctive property of the human mental capacity is precisely the fact that immediate experience is not confined to what we currently feel and perceive. We are capable of thinking about anything at all, mentally peering into any corner of our immense conceptual universe, of which reality itself is only a limited portion. When we think about something, we thereby bring it within the scope of awareness, so that – in a sense – it is part of immediate experience. It is not that the object of thought, per se, moves through the epistemic landscape and

9 I should point out a subtle difference in how IR and IE are defined. Whereas IE is the current phase of experience, IR is not the current phase of knowledge – it is rather (what is accepted as) knowledge of the present. At a given moment, we know something about the past as well the present, but we currently experience only what we currently experience. The past figures in IE only to the extent that we recall or apprehend it. The current phase of knowledge includes all of R, of which IR is only a portion.

enters IE; merely thinking about something does not make it real or perceptible. Rather, it is part of IE in the sense that its **apprehension** is an aspect of our conscious awareness, experienced internally. Thus, in and of itself, thinking about something does not make it real or otherwise change its epistemic status. It apprehension **is** however real and directly experienced.

In Figure 7.9(a), the object of thought, X, is shown at an arbitrary location. Its apprehension, X', is internal to C, an aspect of C's conscious awareness. To keep the diagrams simple, I will abbreviate this as shown in diagram (b), where X' is left implicit. Instead, a dashed arrow stands mnemonically for the process we conceptualize metaphorically as C "reaching out" and "apprehending" X.

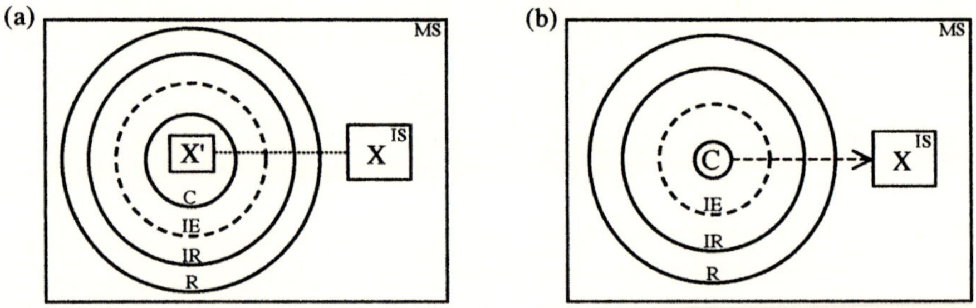

Figure 7.9

As noted, X can be anywhere in the epistemic landscape. It may lie outside reality, e.g. in entertaining future hopes. In thinking about the past, X is real but non-immediate. It may be in immediate reality but outside immediate experience, for instance invoking the knowledge that Lincoln is the capital of Nebraska. In the case of external perception, like seeing a cat on a mat, X – the situation perceived – is part of IE but outside C, X' being the perceptual experience. And in the special case where X is internal to C, e.g. the experience of pain, X and X' effectively collapse – there is no essential difference between apprehending an internal experience and simply having that experience.[10]

I will understand "thinking about X" to mean that we are specifically attending to X, as the focus of our conscious awareness. This does not of course imply that we are aware of nothing else. Even if I am focusing on the fact of Lincoln being the capital of Nebraska, I am still aware to some extent of my

10 Of course, we can also think about the nature of this experience and the fact that we are having it, in which case it also functions as an object of thought, itself being apprehended. I take this as representing another level of conceptual organization.

immediate physical surroundings, of being slightly hungry, etc. In particular, I have some awareness of the overall epistemic landscape and the position of X within it. If I focus attention on a cat being on a mat, I am generally aware as well of the epistemic status of this situation: whether it is purely imaginary, something that happened previously, something I actually see right now, or something I know of by other means (e.g. someone tells me). There are, in short, levels and degrees of awareness. Accordingly, in Figure 7.9 the box containing X is labeled as the immediate scope of conception (IS), i.e. the general locus of attention (the "onstage region"), and the outer box as the maximal scope (MS), the full extent of awareness.[11]

For present purposes, C can be characterized as the **subjective center of consciousness**. We can think of the arrow from C to X as an **epistemic path**, the path C follows in "reaching out" and "apprehending" X. The path is "longer" or "shorter" depending on X's position in the epistemic landscape. In the case of internal experience, where X and X' are the same, the path has a length of zero. Presumably the path is progressively longer as it passes beyond the limits of C, IE, IR, and R. Measured in this way, the path gives a rough estimate of "epistemic distance". These boundaries are all natural places where a language might choose to make a coding distinction. For example, "evidential" markers might indicate whether or not an occurrence is (or was at some stage) part of immediate experience. English makes coding distinctions at IR and R.

This is an **epistemic** model pertaining to facets of cognitive organization. Inclusion in R does not depend on something being true in any objective sense (i.e. true in the world), but rather on C accepting it as being valid with respect to C's mentally constructed world. One difference is that C is truly the center of this mentally constructed world, while probably not enjoying this privileged position objectively (in the "real" world out there). Another difference is that past occurrences accepted as part of R can be modified on the basis of new considerations – our **conception** of previous history is subject to adjustment. We could only wish that the objective course of events were so flexible.

Figure 7.8(b) shows E as the core of a cylinder, suggesting (not unreasonably) that personal experience has a privileged status. But obviously – and obviously essential for language (though not emphasized here) – we accept as real the existence of other conceptualizers each of whom engages in conceptualization and builds up their own conception of reality. We thus have configurations like Figure 7.10, where C_0 accepts as real the proposition that C_1 accepts as real the

11 The latter's apprehension is also an aspect of internal experience. I have not attempted to show this in the diagrams.

proposition that X is accepted as real by C_2.[12] In this case X does figure in C_0's reality conception (R_0), but is only indirectly accessible within it. To "reach" X, C_0 has to trace along a multistep epistemic path leading through other conceptualizers and their own conceptions of reality.

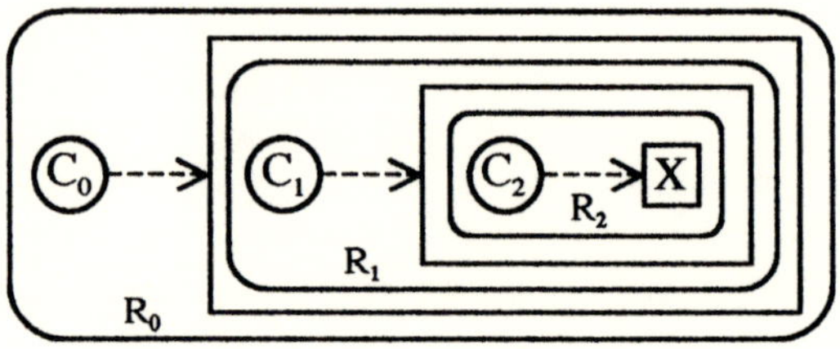

Figure 7.10

Reality, then, is a complex affair involving often elaborate mental space configurations, with any number of hierarchical levels. Among the requisite spaces are those corresponding to mental constructions like schedules, scripts, and structural generalizations. These are virtual entities comprising virtual (representing) events. Their existence as such is nonetheless part of reality, as defined. Being based on accepted validity, real vs. unreal is not the same as actual vs. virtual, since even virtual entities can be accepted as valid (cf. Langacker 1999d).

If R is conceived as a cylinder, as in Figure 7.8(b), we can view it metaphorically as "growing" along the temporal axis as time passes and there is more to know about. On this view, future occurrences per se are not (or not yet) part of R. One could argue this on philosophical or general epistemic grounds – since the future has not yet been determined, it cannot yet be real or known. Actually, though, my basis for this position is linguistic. I am not engaged here in a philosophical exercise. Rather, I trying to explicate the tacit cognitive model underlying English clausal grounding, i.e. its grammaticized tense-modal system. In the basic English system, future is marked by the modal *will.* A fundamental feature of the model I am proposing is precisely that the presence of a modal indicates epistemic striving, as opposed to epistemic control, and R is simply defined as what is under epistemic control. This is not the only possible way to deal with future occurrences – other languages may handle them differently – but it makes sense and appears to be how English is doing it.[13]

---

12 An example would be the sentence *Cheney knows that Rice is convinced that Bush is a genius.*

13 This discussion pertains to the grammaticized tense-modal system. English does have other ways of dealing with the future, e.g. with *gonna, is to,* or *has to,* not to mention the scheduled future use of the present. I consider these to represent dif-

3.3. Non-modal clauses

That brings us back to tense. Let us start with the simplest case: non-modal clauses describing actual occurrences. The absence of a modal indicates that the profiled occurrence (**p**) is accepted as real. What, then, is the import of "present" vs. "past", which I have characterized more generally as immediate vs. non-immediate? Since **p** is confined to R (due to the absence of a modal), the obvious proposal is that immediate vs. non-immediate is a matter of whether **p** is located in immediate reality (IR) or its complement, "non-immediate reality". That is indeed what I propose. This is fundamentally an epistemic characterization, for R is defined as what C (by default, the speaker) accepts as valid (or "knows"). Clearly, though, the distinction is equivalent to a temporal one, since immediate reality consists of those facets of R pertaining to the world at the present time (the locus of current experience). This is the basis for my previous description (Langacker 1991) of present vs. past time as being the **prototypical** values of the more general immediate vs. non-immediate opposition.

The English present and past (for non-modal expressions) are sketched in Figure 7.11. In both cases, the time of speaking delimits what counts as immediate experience and immediate reality for this purpose. For the present tense, the time of speaking also defines the immediate temporal scope for apprehending the profiled clausal process, **p**.[14] The difference between present and past tense is thus a matter of whether **p** is found in immediate reality or non-immediate reality. The past tense involves a slightly greater epistemic distance because the epistemic path crosses an additional boundary (IR).

These configurations are basically equivalent to those in Figure 7.3 and yield the same explanation for the distribution of present and past with perfective and imperfective verbs. A non-immediate perfective is always acceptable because the immediate temporal scope can always be long enough to encompass **p** (e.g. *She drove to Michigan*). An immediate perfective is usually problematic (**She drives to Michigan*) owing to the durational and epistemic problems. Imperfectives can either be immediate (*She is in Michigan*) or non-immediate (*She was in Michigan*) because whatever portion of the overall process is put onstage and profiled itself constitutes a valid instance of the process type. And

---

ferent ways in which constraints on future occurrences are incorporated as part of present reality.

14 Of course, the time of speaking is actually a temporal interval, not just a point, as the diagrams might suggest. If only time is considered, the box enclosing **p** can be eliminated in diagram (a), since IS = IR in this domain. Other domains do however figure in **p**'s conception.

performatives still work, despite being immediate perfectives, because **p** is the speech event itself, hence an aspect of immediate experience.

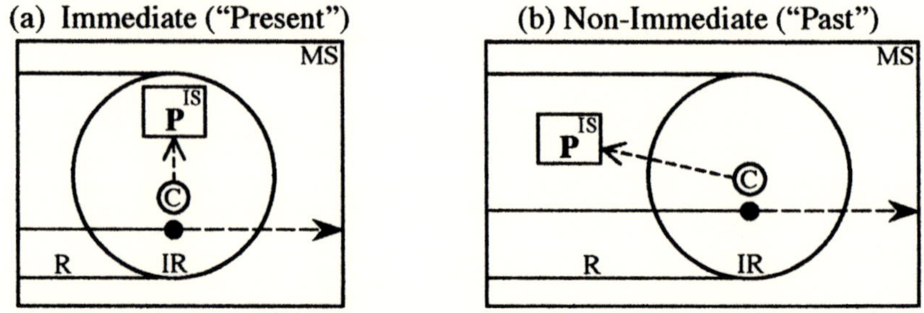

Figure 7.11

With some justice, one might argue that I have merely rephrased the temporal coincidence account in terms of whether **p** is or is not in IR, where IR itself is defined in terms of temporal coincidence with the time of speaking. More charitably, one could say that I have sketched an epistemic approach from which the temporal coincidence account can be derived. Either way, more can be said from an epistemic standpoint.

As noted earlier, the temporal characterization of perfective vs. imperfective processes implies a difference in their typical mode of apprehension. Though flexible in size and scale, subjectively the immediate temporal scope is always bounded (like the visual field) – there is a limit to the temporal expanse we can invoke at one time as the locus for focused viewing. Being temporally bounded itself, a perfective process will always fit within IS just by making this large enough. It is therefore possible for a perfective occurrence to be apprehended in its entirety. And since bounding is inherent in the characterization of a perfective process type, full apprehension – including the endpoints – is required to identify an instance of the type. By contrast, an imperfective process with indefinite temporal extension cannot be apprehended in its entirety, for there is no entirety. All we can do is observe that portion of the overall process which happens to fall within whatever temporal scope we adopt for viewing purposes. In other words, the natural mode of apprehension for imperfectives is one of sampling. But since an imperfective process is conceived as exhibiting qualitative uniformity throughout, a sample is enough to identify it and counts as an instance of the process type.

These contrasting modes of apprehension have different epistemic consequences for what lies outside the immediate temporal scope. Being apprehended in its entirety, within IS, a perfective occurrence tells us nothing about what might occur beyond its limits. On the other hand, since the profiled portion of an imperfective is merely a sample, with no evident bounding, the presumption is that the overall process extends beyond IS in both directions. So at least in local terms, imperfectives correlate with stability both within and beyond the immediate scope of observation. The presumed stability they thereby offer does not necessarily rise to the level suggested by Brisard's term "epistemic certainty". It does however amount to a kind of "givenness" (also his term), a local framework with respect to which more transient occurrences can be assessed. On this basis Brisard (2002) describes all imperfective clauses as being "structural" statements. Even contingent situations, stable only when viewed on a very small time scale, qualify as structural knowledge by this definition (e.g. *I see it now*; *The cat is on the mat*; *He's straightening his tie*). I myself use the term more narrowly, notably for generics, but I acknowledge that we are dealing with a gradation rather than discrete categories (cf. Langacker 1997b). Regardless of terminology, we will see that this notion of "givenness", or "basis for assessment", is relevant to the meaning of the English present.

Let us now extend this epistemic account of the present to so-called "non-present" uses. I have described these as involving the distinction between a representing event and a represented event. In these expressions, I propose, what is directly coded linguistically is the virtual representing event, as opposed to the actual event(s) it represents. These uses of the present all conform to the characterization proposed, i.e. the profiled occurrence (**p**) is found in immediate reality (IR). What differs is the nature of the mental construction in which it figures. I will briefly examine three cases: the scheduled future, singular generics, and the historical present.

The first point to make about the scheduled future, one already noted, is that the mental construction involved is independent of the present tense. Scheduled future expressions are possible for the past, the present, or even the future, as seen in (13). In the last sentence, the intended interpretation – an entirely possible one – is that *will* indicates futurity of the schedule (not the actual event itself), i.e. at 3 it will be appropriate to say *Our plane leaves at 6*.

(13) *First our plane left at noon. Then they rescheduled it, so now it leaves at 3. I'm sure they will reschedule it again, so that when 3 rolls around it will leave at 6.*

Use of the present in this construction therefore does have to do with the time of speaking, in the sense that it indicates that the schedule being consulted is **in effect** at the present moment. While it is in effect, the entire schedule can be consulted at any time. A particular expression, e.g. *Our plane leaves at 3*, is then a matter of "reading off" (or accessing) one schedule entry, whose apprehension is coded linguistically. This is sketched in Figure 7.12(a). The schedule is represented as a box labeled V, to indicate its status as a virtual entity (which is not to deny that some schedules have physical or at least visual instantiation). The boxes inside it stand for schedule entries, i.e. virtual events representing anticipated actual events. Among these virtual events is the one profiled by a particular sentence, like *Our plane leaves at 3.* This situation conforms to the epistemic characterization of the present: that the profiled occurrence (**p**) is located in immediate reality (IR). This despite its virtual nature – recall that the speaker's conception of reality includes many virtual entities, not just actual ones. Here the speaker accepts it as valid that the schedule is currently in effect.[15]

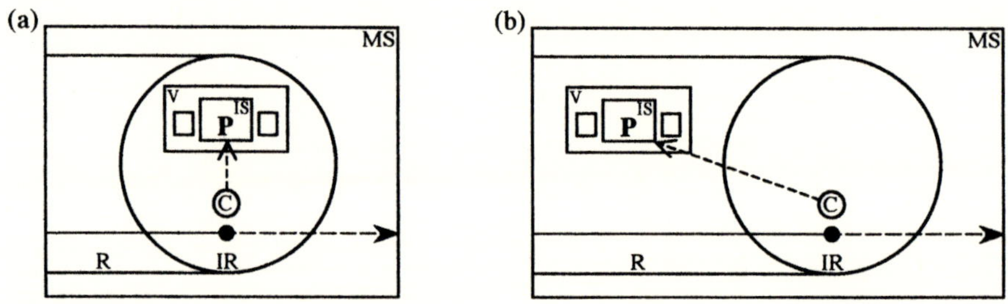

Figure 7.12

The case of a past-tense scheduled future, e.g. *First our plane left at noon*, is shown in diagram (b). It is simply a matter of referring to a mental schedule that was in effect at an earlier time. Granted this conceptual configuration, the expression conforms to the epistemic characterization of past tense: **p** is located in non-immediate reality.[16] What about a future scheduled future, like the last clause in (13)? It simply involves the schedule (hence **p**) being projected as in effect at a future time, in the manner specified by *will* or another modal.

---

15 Does **p** precisely coincide with the time of speaking, as in the temporal account? In this case (as opposed to the situation with actual events), I think the point is moot. **p** is part of a schedule that is in effect throughout the time of speaking, and its apprehension is taken as coinciding with the time of speaking. However, since I am not (in the epistemic approach) talking about a virtual occurrence of **p**, the time of such an occurrence is not at issue.

16 Observe that this does not specify whether the scheduled event was anticipated to occur before or after the time of speaking. It merely has to be subsequent to the time when the schedule was consulted (given the very nature of a schedule). This consequence "falls out" from the characterization proposed.

Singular generics work analogously.[17] The mental construction involved is like a virtual plan or schedule, except that its entries – instead of representing specific actual events – are virtual occurrences taken as representing facets of the world's essential nature. Each of these structural generalizations projects to any number of actual occurrences for as long as it remains valid. We see in (14) that even these "structural statements" may have a limited shelf life, so that we have to specify the span of time when they are in effect. Actually, the diagrams in Figure 7.12 work perfectly well for singular generics in the present and past tense. We simply have to interpret the box labeled V as describing the world's essential structure (i.e. its entries map onto actual events in a different way than with a schedule).

(14) *In the good old days, a woman obeyed her husband. Now things are all messed up: a man obeys his wife. But in the future, when we put all this craziness behind us, a woman will obey her husband again.*

The historical present is sketched in Figure 7.13. It too conforms to the epistemic definition, as it profiles a virtual event located in immediate reality. Here, though, this event is an aspect of C's internal experience, consisting in the recall (or mental replay) of a previous occurrence, given as p'. Observe that p' is shown as part of E, i.e. it is something C previously experienced, though generally not internally. On the other hand, the recall is necessarily internal.[18]

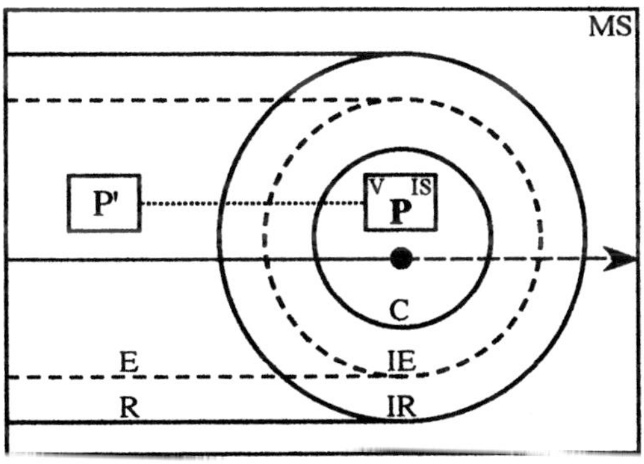

Figure 7.13

17 Singular and plural generics represent different strategies of generalization (Langacker 1997b). To keep things simple, I confine attention to the former.

18 The case of watching a video replay on a monitor is analogous, except that **p** is external to C within IE (being apprehended via perception), and p' need not be part of E (i.e. C may not have witnessed the original event).

I conclude that the epistemic characterization works for both actual and virtual occurrences, given a proper description of the mental constructions in which the latter figure. In all cases, the English present situates **p** in immediate reality, the past in non-immediate reality. But we have not yet considered modals, which specify that **p** has not yet been accepted as real. It is still a target of epistemic striving, the different modals indicating the degree of epistemic force involved. Consideration of modal expressions leads to a more schematic characterization of the immediate/non-immediate opposition.

4. Modals

I am only concerned with the core of the grammaticized modal system: the elements *may*, *can*, *will*, *shall*, and *must*, and their non-immediate counterparts *might*, *could*, *would*, and *should*.[19] Except as necessary, I will not describe these forms individually, the focus here being their common properties. I am not claiming that the non-immediate forms are fully analyzable or derived in a wholly regular fashion from their basic counterparts; each modal has its semantic peculiarities and its own ecological niche in the epistemic landscape. Still, there are general points to be made.

Just a word about the distinction between **root** and **epistemic** senses of the modals, exemplified in (15)a–b. Involving notions like obligation and permission, root modals exhibit more clearly the force-dynamic character of modals (Sweetser 1982; Talmy 1988; Langacker 1991). Ranging in degree from the absence of a barrier (*may*) to compulsion (*must*), the force is generally manifested socially in the case of root modals, mentally with epistemic modals. Both involve what we might call "the evolution of reality", as well as a striving for control, as sketched in Figure 7.7(a). The difference pertains to the level at which this occurs (Chapter 6). Root modals are aimed at **effective** control – determining what happens in the world itself. And obviously, epistemic modals are aimed at **epistemic** control – evolution in our **knowledge** of the world. They register the force subjectively experienced as we mentally simulate reality (R) "growing" in such a way that it comes to encompass the profiled event (i.e. we accept the profiled occurrence as valid). Here we are only concerned with the epistemic modals.

(15) a. **Root modals**: *You {may / should / must} report the theft.*
b. **Epistemic modals:** *It {may / should / must} be hot in Chicago.*

19 In Langacker 1991 (§ 6.2.2.3) I give an argument that *must* simply lacks a non-immediate form.

A key observation is that the morphological distinction immediate vs. non-immediate is manifested on different elements depending on whether or not the clause contains a modal. In the absence of a modal, it is marked on the verb, as present vs. past tense (which I have argued to be a reasonable characterization even in the epistemic approach). With a modal, however, immediate vs. non-immediate is not marked on the verb, but rather by the form of the modal itself: *may* vs. *might*, *will* vs. *would*, etc. Semantically as well, so-called "tense" does not apply directly to the verbal process (**p**), but only indirectly. It is rather the modal, in either its immediate or non-immediate form, which applies to **p** and specifies its epistemic status. This is one respect in which the epistemic approach is advantageous relative to the temporal coincidence approach. With modals, the "temporal" component of grounding does not even apply to **p**, so it can hardly be said to specify **p**'s coincidence or non-coincidence with the time of speaking. And while some modal uses are present-oriented, as in (15)b, very often **p** is future relative to the speech event (e.g. *It {may / might} rain tomorrow*), in which case immediate vs. non-immediate certainly does not indicate temporal coincidence vs. precedence vis-à-vis the time of speaking.

This is not to say that the non-immediate modals are unanalyzable or that the non-immediacy they convey has no connection with past time. They do correlate with past time in the so-called "sequence of tenses" phenomenon, exemplified in (16), where use of an immediate form is subsequently reported with a non-immediate form. Now, English does not actually have a sequence-of-tenses rule (Langacker 1991: § 6.2.2.2). It is however important to understand why the non-immediate form appears in these reports. In the case of (16)a, without a modal, it is simply a matter of the situation described being in the past relative to the time of speaking; the speaker describes the reported situation from her own temporal vantage point. But with a modal, in (16)b–c, the temporal location is indeterminate – from the perspective of the current speaker, the projected time of helping could be in the past or the future. Why, then, is the non-immediate form of the modal employed?[20]

(16) a. Tom says "I **am** tired". Report: *Tom said he* ***was*** *tired.*
b. Tom says "I **may** help". Report: *Tom said he* ***might*** *help.*
c. Tom says "I **will** help". Report: *Tom said he* ***would*** *help.*

20 In all these cases the immediate form can also be used, showing the non-existence of a sequence of tenses rule. The epistemic status thus indicated is always appropriate from the speaker's perspective. For instance, *Tom said he may help* – where *may* indicates future potentiality – can only be used if **p** is still future relative to the current time of speaking.

We must first consider immediate forms of the epistemic modals, e.g. the original use of *may* and *will* in (16)b–c. This is represented in Figure 7.14(a). I have omitted the arrow for time, since with modals time is clearly secondary. When marked by a modal, **p** can be located in the present, as in (15)b; in the future, as when Tom says *I will help*; or even in the past, as in *Tom said he would help yesterday.* The essential factor is that the modal situates **p** outside reality. Hence the single dashed arrow in diagram (a), representing the epistemic path from C to **p**, crosses the boundary of R. The double dashed arrow indicates the nature or degree of the epistemic force, distinguishing one modal from another. Thus *may* specifies that the evolution of reality – as mentally simulated by C – has the potential of it "reaching" and encompassing **p** (there is no barrier to this happening), whereas *will* specifies that R is projected (or predicted) to reach it.

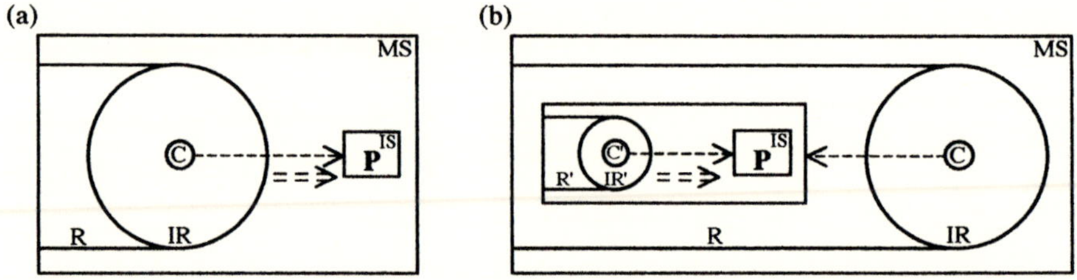

Figure 7.14

Let us now consider non-immediate forms in reported speech, e.g. *might* and *would* in (16)b–c. The key factor, clearly, is that the current speaker (C) does not herself assume responsibility for the epistemic assessment, but is rather reporting on the assessment previously made by another conceptualizer, C'. As shown in Figure 7.14(b), C accepts as real that C' has previously made this assessment, using his own conception of reality (R') as its basis. That assessment placed **p** outside R', its precise status being indicated by the base form of the modal (*may* or *will*). Thus **p** is not per se part of C's conception of reality (R). It figures in R only derivatively: C accepts as real the fact that C' had an epistemic stance in regard to **p**, namely the stance of not accepting it as real. In short, as shown by the arrows, C reaches **p** only via a two-step epistemic path leading through the mind of another conceptualizer (C').

We need to be precise about the modal and how it relates to the situation shown. First, it has to be recognized that **p** is not itself part of R, even though it appears inside R in the diagram, in contrast to Figure 7.12, where **p** is understood as being real (albeit virtual). The difference is that, in Figure 7.12, **p** is an entry on an accepted virtual schedule which C herself accesses directly, while in Figure 7.14(b) C only reaches **p** by apprehending someone else's epistemic judgment. Given the limitations of a two-dimensional representation, to interpret these diagrams properly we have to consider the epistemic path (not just spatial inclusion). In Figure 7.12, the epistemic path leads directly from C to **p** (though it may cross boundaries), whereas in 7.14(b) the path from C only leads to another conceptualizer, C', from which a second epistemic path leads to **p**.

We can go even further and isolate the contributions of each path in determining the modal form. Specifically, the first path – anchored by C – is responsible for the choice of the non-immediate forms, *might* and *would*, instead of *may* and *will*. The choice of *may* or *will*, as the modal base, reflects the second path, anchored by C'. That is, the modal base (*may* or *will*) indicates the epistemic assessment made by C', on the basis of his own conception of immediate reality (IR'). The speaker expresses this assessment with the non-immediate *might* or *would* because the speaker's own conception of immediate reality (IR) does not support the assessment coded by the modal base. In short, the **basis** for the modal assessment (*may* vs. *will*) is IR', and IR' is non-immediate to C. It is non-immediate to C in two respects: first, it is earlier in time; and second, it is the reality conception of another individual.

This apportionment is the key to understanding other uses of the non-immediate modals, as in (17). I suggest that in each case the non-immediacy coded by *might* indicates that IR – the speaker's conception of immediate reality – is **not** the basis invoked for the assessment associated with the modal base, *may*. In each case, the potentiality expressed by *may* is calculated relative to a conception of immediate reality, IR', distinct from the speaker's actual one. Using *might* (in lieu of *may*) indicates the non-immediacy of this presumed basis of modal assessment. As shown in Figure 7.15, the speaker (C) invokes a virtual situation, involving an imagined version of immediate reality (IR'), with respect to which the modal assessment *may* would be appropriate. Just as in Figure 7.14(b), *might* signals the non-immediacy from IR of the assumed basis for modal assessment (IR').

(17) a. *If it weren't so cloudy it {*may / might} get hot.*
b. *When the clouds disperse it {may / might} get hot.*
c. *Even though it's cloudy it {may / might} get hot.*

This is most evident in (17)a, a counterfactual conditional. The counterfactual construction invokes a mental space specifically portrayed as being distinct from reality. The import of (17)a is that the modal assessment *may* would be appropriate given an imagined conception of immediate reality (IR'), namely immediate reality as it would appear to C in the hypothetical situation. There is thus a two-step epistemic path: from IR to IR', and from IR' to **p**. It is further presumed that **p** is **only** accessible via this path, i.e. it would not occur except in the counterfactual situation.[21] For this reason *may* is not a permissible alternative.

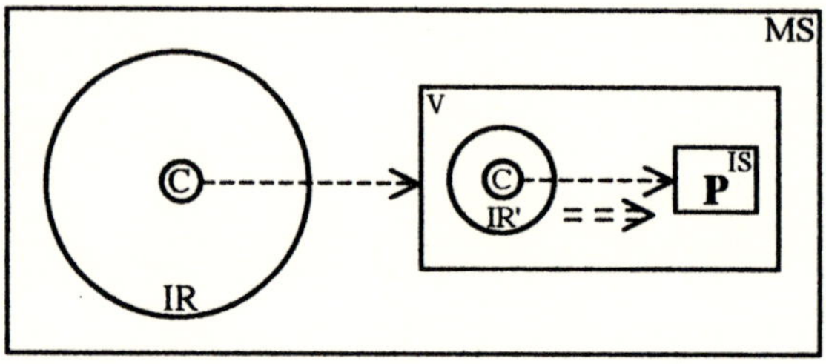

Figure 7.15

In (17)b, the *when*-clause sets up a mental space associated with the specified time (the time when the clouds disperse). Because the situation has not yet been realized, it is still (broadly speaking) a virtual one. Its realization is however anticipated – in contrast to (17)a, where the path of evolving reality excludes both the situation and its consequences. Hence there are two different ways of making the modal assessment. On the one hand, it can proceed as shown in Figure 7.15, resulting in *might.* As the basis for modal assessment, the speaker invokes the imagined conception of immediate reality (IR') expected to obtain at the time specified by the *when*-clause (a reality in which the clouds have dispersed). On the other hand, because that situation is projected as occurring, the potentiality expressed by *may* is equally appropriate whether IR' or IR itself is taken as the basis for assessment. With *may*, in other words, **p** (it getting hot) is directly accessed from IR via a one-step epistemic path, just as in a single-clause expression (*It may get hot*). In this case the function of the *when*-clause is simply to specify **p**'s temporal location.

Finally, in (17)c the adverbial clause does not itself invoke a virtual situation, but merely describes an aspect of IR. The adverbial has no direct bearing on the choice of *may* vs. *might*, since either would be appropriate even without it. With *may*, IR itself is the basis for modal assessment, as in Figure 7.14(a). What about *might*? Does it still imply a virtual basis for assessment, as in Figure 7.15, despite the absence of a clause that explicitly introduces it? I suggest that

---

21 This feature of the counterfactual construction can however be overridden: *If it weren't so cloudy, it might get hot – but it may get hot anyway.* Note that *but* and *anyway* indicate the suspension of this feature.

it does. Choosing the non-immediate form (*might* instead of *may*) itself signals that the potentiality normally conveyed by *may* is not an appropriate assessment from IR as presently constituted. No other mental space being indicated, the basis for assessment may simply be an alternative to IR that differs from it in relatively minor respects. In (17)c, for instance, the alternative IR' could be just like IR except for there being fewer clouds. The assessment *It may get hot* would then be supported, but since that situation does not in fact obtain, *might* is used instead to register its non-immediacy. This is essentially equivalent to saying that *might* expresses a more tenuous potentiality than does *may*.

In (18), I summarize the proposed epistemic description of the immediate/non-immediate opposition in English. In the absence of a modal, where **p** is confined to reality (R), immediacy implies that **p** is in IR. Obviously, then, non-immediacy indicates that **p** is not in IR. We can take this as being the default situation (the prototype), in which immediate vs. non-immediate is largely equivalent to present vs. past in time. In combination with a modal, where **p** is excluded from R, immediacy implies that IR is the direct basis for the modal assessment of **p**. Here non-immediacy indicates that some other basis (IR') must be found. These two characterizations clearly have a lot in common. From them we can abstract the schematic description in (18)c, which covers both modal and non-modal clauses. In both cases, immediacy implies that IR is the direct basis for **p**'s epistemic assessment – either containing **p** or providing direct access to it (via a one-step epistemic path).

(18) a. In the absence of a modal, where **p** is confined to R, (non-)immediacy implies that **p** is (not) in IR. [prototype]
b. In combination with a modal, where **p** is excluded from R, (non-)immediacy implies that IR is (not) the direct basis for the modal assessment of **p**.
c. In either case, (non-)immediacy implies that IR is (not) the direct basis for the epistemic assessment of **p**. [schema]

5. Summing up

This has been a preliminary attempt at pinning down the specifics of an epistemic account of the English present. While fairly comprehensive, it is certainly not exhaustive. I have not, for instance, considered the use of the present in adverbial clauses, e.g. the initial clause in (17)b.[22]

22 An analysis of this use that conforms to (18) is proposed in Langacker 2007.

Two possible advantages over the temporal coincidence account have come to light. First, it avoids the need to talk about the "virtual occurrence" of events, a notion that may be defensible but might be considered dubious. Second, it is readily extended to clauses with modals, whereas temporal coincidence cannot be. That the epistemic approach would prove advantageous is hardly a surprise. My time-based account of the English present (Langacker 2001 f) was limited to non-modal clauses, where the label "tense" is not altogether inappropriate. Here immediate vs. non-immediate is essentially equivalent to present vs. past. With modals, however, immediacy vs. non-immediacy requires a non-temporal characterization. Thus, in my overall description of English clausal grounding (Langacker 1991: ch. 6), I characterized it schematically as a "proximal"/"distal" contrast, with present and past tense representing prototypical values.

I conclude that the English present is reasonably described as having "present time" (coincidence with the time of speaking) for its prototypical value, and "epistemic immediacy" as its schematic characterization (valid for all instances). It thus exemplifies a general finding of CG concerning the meanings of grammatical elements: many such elements have both prototypical and schematic semantic values, the latter consisting in some mental experience inherent in the former. For instance, the schematic import of possessives – that of invoking one element as a reference point to mentally access another – is immanent in the possessive prototypes of ownership, kinship, and whole/part relations (Langacker 1993c; Chapter 4). More controversially, I have claimed that nouns are characterized schematically in terms of mental operations inherent in the conception of physical objects, the category prototype (Langacker 1987b). The English present can be seen as another instance of this general pattern: epistemic immediacy is an aspect of the mental experience inherent in the apprehension of present-time occurrences.

Chapter 8
A functional account of the English auxiliary

Chomsky's classic analysis of the English auxiliary was instrumental in the widespread acceptance of transformational grammar and autonomous syntax. It appears to demonstrate that this central and prominent feature of English grammar, replete with apparent idiosyncrasies, is nonetheless handled quite neatly in a purely formal syntactic description making no reference to meaning or function. Proponents of a cognitive-functional approach thus face the challenge of providing an account that does at least as well. Here I will try to indicate what such an account might look like.

1. The formalist account

The essential features of the classic account (Chomsky 1957) are presented in (1). Just to facilitate discussion, I have made some minor adjustments, which do not affect the points at issue. For one thing, I am using *-en* and *-ed* to distinguish the perfect and the passive participial endings.[1] Also, I show *be* + *-ed* as being introduced by the phrase structure rule in (1)a, whereas Chomsky introduced it via the passive transformation. Rule (1)a captures some basic regularities of the auxiliary system, even though the elements it introduces are not in their surface position. The proper ordering is effected by transformations, primarily those in (1)b–d. The derivations in (2) are illustrative.

(1) a. Phrase structure rule: AUX → TNS (M) (*have* + *-en*) (*be* + *-ing*) (*be* + *-ed*)
b. Subject-Auxiliary Inversion [SAI]: NP TNS ({M, *have*, *be*})
⇒ TNS ({M, *have*, *be*}) NP
c. Affix Hopping [AH]: *Af v* ⇒ *v-Af#*
d. *Do* Support [DS]: *#Af* ⇒ *#do-Af*

(2) a. NP TNS V ⇒ NP V-TNS [AH] (*She waited.*)
b. NP TNS V ⇒ TNS NP V ⇒ *do*-TNS NP V [SAI; DS] (*Did she wait?*)
c. NP TNS M V ⇒ TNS M NP V ⇒ M-TNS NP V [SAI; AH] (*Could she wait?*)
d. NP TNS *have -en be -ing* V ⇒ NP *have* TNS *be-en* V*-ing* [AH]
(*She has been waiting.*)

---

1 These are of course morphologically identical, with varied realizations. They represent two semantic variants of the past participial morpheme (Langacker 1982).

Despite the manifest insight of this analysis, from a broader perspective it has major shortcomings (Langacker 1991: 197–198). We can start by noting some mechanical problems that detract from its formal elegance. For one thing, tense and the participial inflections have varied morphological realizations (including zero, ablaut, etc.); only as a special case do they follow the verb they combine with in the linear (i.e. temporal) sequence. And if considered suffixal, tense inflection is handled differently for *do* and the other auxiliary verbs, as seen in (2)b: instead of the placement of TNS being effected by Affix Hopping, *do* is simply inserted to bear it. More seriously, the phrase structure description provides no basis for identifying the elements affected by certain transformations (Chomsky merely lists them). The elements fronted by Subject-Auxiliary Inversion are TNS + M, TNS + *have*, TNS + *be*, and TNS alone (in the absence of M, *have*, and *be*). In addition to this listing being awkward, the fronted elements are not even constituents on this account. In the case of Affix Hopping, *v* is adopted as an ad hoc label for *have*, *be*, any M (modal), or any V (main verb). Likewise, *Af* is simply defined as *-en/-ed*, *-ing*, or a tense marker. No semantic, functional, or formal rationale is offered that would make these lists of elements non-arbitrary.[2]

An even more serious problem is that there is no evidence whatever for the elements grouped under AUX being a syntactic constituent. Whereas constituency has fundamental importance in generative theory, in CG it is seen as being non-essential, flexible, and often variable (Langacker 1995a, 1997a). The English auxiliary does in fact show quite nicely that the same elements can sometimes participate in alternate constituency groupings. But if any grouping is fundamental, it is not the one in (3)a, as implied by Chomsky's analysis, but rather that in (3)b, where auxiliary elements are split between two main constituents.

(3) a. [NP] [[TNS M *have -en be -ing be -ed*] [V]]
    b. [NP TNS M] [*have -en be -ing be -ed* V]

One manifestation of this basic division is the placement of sentence-level adverbials, as in (4):

(4) a. *?*She may have been, unfortunately, waiting.*
    b. *She may, unfortunately, have been waiting.*

The grouping [NP TNS M] is further evident in both ellipsis and tag questions, as in (5):[3]

2 Without such a rationale, labeling these elements with syntactic features like [+V] and [+Af] would only serve to disguise the difficulty.

3 This is not the only possibility (note, for instance, *She has been, hasn't she?*). The fact remains, however, that the grouping [NP TNS M] represents a primary option in

(5) *I hope she will be waiting for us. She will, won't she?*

On the other hand, we see in (6) that the grouping [*have -en be -ing be -ed* V] appears in non-finite complement clauses, where TNS and M are excluded:

(6) a. *She is likely [to have been being criticized].*
b. *She dislikes [having been being criticized].*

I am unaware of any syntactic phenomenon where the putative auxiliary constituent functions as such.

From the CG perspective, the most basic shortcoming of Chomsky's original account is the absence of any attempt to deal with meaning.[4] This is not a sin (and might even be considered a virtue) if one assumes the autonomy of syntax. I suggest, however, that this omission has negative consequences for the grammatical description itself. Without considering the meanings involved, one cannot characterize certain sets of elements that behave alike, and some basic organizational features of the auxiliary system remain mysterious.

For example, tense and modality are precisely the elements characterized semantically as serving the function of clausal grounding. Since grounding is a defining property of finite clauses, tense and modals are naturally excluded from non-finite complements, as in (6), in contrast to all the other auxiliary elements. A striking feature of the latter is their occurrence in pairs: the perfect *have* + *-en*, the progressive *be* + *-ing*, and the passive *be* + *-ed*. Why should this be the case? And why these particular elements? I have argued elsewhere (e.g. Langacker 1991: ch. 5) that each of these elements is meaningful, and that the perfect, progressive, and passive meanings are largely compositional with respect to their parts. Moreover, *have* and *be* are highly schematic verbs (they profile processes), while *-en/-ed* and *-ing* are deprocessualizing elements that impose a particular perspective on the verbal processes they apply to. Though based on verbs, the resulting participles are themselves non-processual and can thus be used to modify nouns (e.g. *crying baby*; *nation destroyed by civil war*).[5] But since a finite clause designates a process, when used to head such a clause they have to combine with *have* or *be*, which impose their processual nature on the composite expression.

---

these constructions, whereas the putative auxiliary constituent, in its entirety, does not appear in it (e.g. **She doesn't like being criticized, but she must have been being (-ed), mustn't she have been being (-ed)?*).

4 By contrast, the account in Langacker 1991 describes the meanings of all the auxiliary elements.

5 A past participle used to modify a noun is interpreted as passive. For perfects, noun modifiers employ a present participial construction incorporating *have*: *any student having finished his assignment.*

In the CG analysis, the various elements that inflect as verbs – through tense or participial morphology – all have a common semantic characterization: they are simply verbs, i.e. they designate processes.[6] Included are lexical verbs (V), *have*, *be*, *do* (considered later), and the modals (M). The elements fronted by Subject-Auxiliary Inversion can likewise be characterized in a principled way (not just by listing them). As a first approximation, we can say that the fronted structure is a grounded auxiliary verb, which as such designates the process profiled by the clause as a whole. It is an "auxiliary" verb in the sense of being highly schematic (in contrast to "lexical" verbs).[7] I will later suggest another dimension to the conceptual characterization of the fronted element.

As for any grammatical phenomenon, a full account of the English auxiliary system has to combine a semantic and functional characterization with an explicit description of the constructions, one that captures the distributional regularities and imposes the proper restrictions. I will try to indicate that the CG framework makes it possible to accomplish this. The present description is however just a preliminary sketch, both partial and exploratory – especially so because the English auxiliary system is not a separate or self-contained entity, but consists in overlapping, highly grammaticized portions of larger families of constructions.

2. Functions and systems

Language has both a semiological function – allowing the symbolization of conceptualizations – and a multifaceted interactive function. To this end, each language makes available a vast array of conventional units for constructing expressions. One dimension to the characterization of expressions pertains to more specific conceptual and interactive functions served by particular aspects of their structure (cf. Croft 2007). To some extent the units of a language are organized into systems comprising alternate means of fulfilling these functions.

For example, nominals (i.e. "noun phrases") serve the function of nominal reference – the directing of attention to particular facets of our world (real or mentally constructed) conceived as things. One strategy for achieving this is

---

6 They are further characterized as being phonologically **autonomous**, i.e. stems (whereas affixes and other inflections are phonologically **dependent**, requiring an autonomous element to support their manifestation). This distinguishes them from the tense inflections, which also designate processes and thus satisfy the most general definition of a verb.

7 Modals represent the special case where the verb itself is a grounding element (further grounded by TNS).

through a combination of type specification and grounding, each of which can also be regarded as a function. Often such functions are directly reflected in grammatical structure. Thus it is usual for the elements effecting nominal reference to form a continuous linear sequence (a classical constituent). Perhaps the most basic structural pattern, moreover, is for a nominal to consist of a determiner plus a noun. What linguists call a "determiner system" is (roughly at least) a set of alternative grounding elements. The lexical nouns they combine with can likewise be regarded as a system of options for making a type specification. But structure and function do not always dovetail in this fashion. There may be alternate strategies subserving the same global function (as with proper names). Or the same strategy may have different means of morphosyntactic expression (e.g. *those with several wives*, where a prepositional phrase is used to specify a non-standard type). So while function motivates grammatical structure, there is no strict correlation between them.

The **systemic** view of language – its organization into sets of elements defined in opposition to one another – is not exactly new, of course. It is pivotal to the structuralist view of language, most familiar from the classic definition of a phoneme, and enjoys a comparable position in certain modern approaches, e.g. the Columbia School (Diver 1995). This is not the place to explore either the history of this notion or the full range of its linguistic applications. I will limit myself to a few remarks concerning its status and treatment in CG.

Though it has not much been emphasized, systemic organization is subsumed under the CG definition of a language as a **structured** inventory of conventional linguistic units (Langacker 1987a: § 2.1). It is a structured inventory because the units of a language, rather than being separate and wholly distinct, relate to one another in various ways: through overlap or inclusion, and by participation in relationships of symbolization, integration, composition, and categorization. Broadly speaking, systemic organization falls under the rubric of categorization. The elements of a system constitute a category at least in the sense that its members are treated as being equivalent for some purpose, namely for fulfilling the function in question. Conversely, the members of a category constitute a system to the extent that they are mutually exclusive as ways of fulfilling the function. The units comprising a system thus compete with one another for the privilege of being selected or activated for this purpose (Langacker 2000). Presumably they are mutually inhibitory at the level of neural implementation.

Thus the systemic view has never been absent from CG.[8] It has not, however, been given the attention it deserves. Its importance becomes apparent through

8 It appears explicitly, for instance, in discussion of the opposition in Cora between the locative elements *u* 'inside' and *a* 'outside' (Casad and Langacker 1985).

investigation of the English auxiliary. I do not yet know the **extent** to which the units of a language are organized into systems. Nor do I accept the structuralist notion that linguistic elements derive their value solely from their position in a system of oppositions. This is at best one factor in their characterization. The meaning of a lexical item, for example, is not revealingly described just by indicating the systemic relations it bears to others (i.e. its participation in relationships of antonymy, hyponymy, and so on). At least as important – and arguably more fundamental – is the task of providing a positive characterization in terms of conceptual content and construal. Without a specification of content a system of oppositions is just an empty shell.

To the extent that grammar is organized systemically, we need some notation to represent this. While any simple notation has severe limitations, it is helpful to start with tabular representations, as in Figure 8.1. Functions are indicated at the top, and elements serving those functions at the bottom. A global function can often be resolved into more specific functions, each subserved by a different system of elements. Recall, for instance, that the global function of nominal reference comprises the local functions of grounding and type specification, respectively corresponding to the determiner system and the set of lexical nouns. A local function may in turn be resolvable into others (e.g. clausal grounding involves both deixis and modality). In this notation, each column represents a system of mutually exclusive elements fulfilling the function in question. Thus A and B constitute a system corresponding to function 4; C and D another, for function 5; and E, F, G, and H another, for function 3. Dashed horizontal lines indicate that elements in a column are interchangeable with respect to their combination with elements in other columns. Thus either A or B occurs with either C or D, and any combination of these occurs with E, F, G, or H. All the expressions to the right of the table are therefore available to fulfill the global function 1 as well as the local ones it subsumes.

<table>
<tr><th colspan="3">Function 1</th></tr>
<tr><th colspan="2">Function 2</th><th rowspan="2">Function 3</th></tr>
<tr><th>Function 4</th><th>Function 5</th></tr>
<tr><td rowspan="2">A</td><td rowspan="2">C</td><td>E</td></tr>
<tr><td>F</td></tr>
<tr><td rowspan="2">B</td><td rowspan="2">D</td><td>G</td></tr>
<tr><td>H</td></tr>
</table>

ACE	ADE	BCE	BDE
ACF	ADF	BCF	BDF
ACG	ADG	BCG	BDG
ACH	ADH	BCH	BDH

Figure 8.1

Figure 8.1 represents the situation of maximal regularity and transparency in regard to function, with a one-to-one correspondence between functions and overtly occurring elements. Usually, however, linguistic structure falls considerably short of this ideal. It need not be the case, for instance, that the elements of a given system always occupy the same position in the linear sequence, as suggested in the tabular array. Suppose the table is perfectly correct as an indication of functions, their hierarchical arrangement, and the elements that fulfill them. It might still be the case, say, that C and D occur in different positions, with C preceding the exponent of function 3 and D following it. That is, the common function of C and D and their divergent positions cannot both be represented in a single table of this sort.

Let me briefly note some other complexities that arise and introduce some notations for handling them. First, one member of a system may be zero, as I cleverly show in Figure 8.2(a) by leaving one cell blank. Along with *a* and *sm*, for instance, zero is one exponent of the English system of indefinite articles: *He caught {a / sm / Ø} fish*. Second, a complex form subserving multiple functions may be only partially analyzable. An example is a past-tense form like *caught*, where any precise segmentation corresponding to type specification (stem) and deixis (past tense) is problematic. In 8.2(b) this is indicated by the vertical dashed line between B and D. At the extreme, multiple functions can be fulfilled by a single, wholly unanalyzable form. A case in point is English *am*, where *be*, present tense, first person, and singular are all conflated in a single, indivisible form. In 8.2(c), B is shown as conflating the functions individually served by A and C.

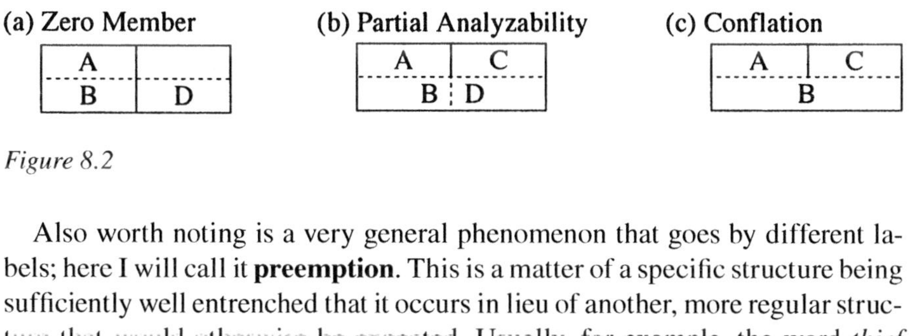

Figure 8.2

Also worth noting is a very general phenomenon that goes by different labels; here I will call it **preemption**. This is a matter of a specific structure being sufficiently well entrenched that it occurs in lieu of another, more regular structure that would otherwise be expected. Usually, for example, the word *thief* preempts the regular, morphologically more transparent *stealer*, constructed in accordance with the general *V-er* derivational pattern. In systemic terms, preemption can disrupt a regular paradigm by obscuring the neat correspondence between form and function that it otherwise exhibits.

Consider the transparent arrangement in Figure 8.3(a), where there are two systems with three members each, which can occur in any combination. These define a regular paradigm, which for this purpose is best represented as in

8.3(b): the functions correspond to the dimensions of a 3x3 matrix, each cell containing a composite form representing one way to fulfill both functions. The effect of preemption is shown in 8.3(c): in lieu of the expected CE, we find the single, unanalyzable expression G.[9]

(a) Systemic View

Function 1	Function 2
A	D
B	E
C	F

(b) Regular Paradigm

	Function 1		
Function 2	AD	BD	CD
	AE	BE	CE
	AF	BF	CF

(c) Preemption

	Function 1		
Function 2	AD	BD	CD
	AE	BE	**G**
	AF	BF	CF

Figure 8.3

3. Global organization

When properly analyzed, the English auxiliary provides an elegant example of the functional motivation of grammar. Its apparent complexity and idiosyncrasy stem from the fact that multiple levels and dimensions of systemic organization figure in its characterization. An initial survey of these factors should thus prove helpful.

3.1. Nominals and finite clauses

Nominals and finite clauses are parallel in many respects (Langacker 1991, 2008a). Just as a nominal profiles a grounded instance of a thing type, a finite clause profiles a grounded instance of a process type.[10] In both cases we can thus make a global functional distinction between grounding and specification of the grounded entity. In both cases, moreover, the grounding function is effected by two subsystems, one pertaining to deixis and one to epistemic status.

9 In cases like this it may not be necessary to make any explicit specification that CE does not occur. It may just be a matter of structure G being so well entrenched that, when the occasion arises for using CE, G imposes itself as an unavoidable alternative (it wins the competition for activation as the means of expressing the notion corresponding to that cell of the matrix). In a sense, then, the systemic arrangement may be left intact, with one option simply not being exploited.

10 I will henceforth just speak of "clauses", since non-finite clauses will not be dealt with here.

Likewise, specification of the grounded entity in each case starts with a type specification effected by a basic lexical category (noun or verb).

As noted in Chapter 6, the parallels are even more extensive when we make due allowance for the fact that nominals and clauses contrast in regard to **what is primarily at issue**. For nominals, where there are usually many instances of a given type and they generally have a measure of permanence, the primary issue is identification. A pivotal factor in nominal grounding is therefore definiteness, pertaining to whether the intended nominal referent is identified by both interlocutors. But unlike objects (the prototype for things), events (the prototype for processes) are transient and we seldom have to deal at once with multiple instances of a type. For clauses, then, the primary issue is existence, i.e. whether the event occurs at all. A pivotal factor in clausal grounding is thus reality, defined as the established history of occurrences. At issue is whether the speaker accepts the profiled process as having been realized. The **epistemic status** central to grounding is therefore primarily **identificational** in the case of nominals, **existential** in the case of clauses.

What does it mean, precisely, to say that a relationship "exists"? Or, using a term more commonly applied to events, to say that it "occurs"? In speaking of "existence", I am drawing an analogy to physical objects, the prototype for nouns. For objects, space usually functions as what I call the **domain of instantiation**: the domain where instances of a type are primarily thought of as residing and are distinguished by their locations.[11] In the case of objects, then, existence can be described as realization in space. For events, on the other hand, the domain of instantiation is always time: events are primarily thought of as residing in time, and instances of an event type are distinguished by their temporal locations. Existence for events can thus be described, analogously, as realization in time. Hence the CG characterization of a process as a relationship followed in its evolution through time.

3.2. Grounding and grounded structure

A finite clause thus predicates the existence of some relationship – i.e. its occurrence, or realization through time – and specifies the epistemic status of that predication. How does this relate to the English auxiliary? Underscoring the fact that "the auxiliary" is not a syntactic constituent, we can first note that cer-

11 It is also the domain where the presence or absence of bounding determines the count/mass distinction for nouns, and the perfective/imperfective distinction for verbs (Langacker 1991, 2008a).

tain auxiliary elements specify the status of the existential predication, while others help specify the relationship whose existence is at issue.[12] The role of specifying existential status falls to the grounding elements: tense and modality. The perfect, progressive, and passive elements contribute to specifying the relationship whose existence is predicated. The lexical verb specifies a basic process type. Starting from this type, the perfect, progressive, and passive allow the derivation of higher-level processes in which the basic one is viewed from different **perspectives**. These perspectival adjustments are optional, but when all are chosen they exhibit the following layering: [Perfect [Progressive [Passive [Lexical Verb]]]]. This entire configuration constitutes the **grounded structure**.[13]

These different semantic functions are reflected in different semantic properties. Naturally, the role of the ground is far more central and crucial in the case of the grounding elements. Tense and modality specifically relate the profiled occurrence to the deictic center it defines: the time of speaking and the speaker's conception of reality, respectively.[14] By contrast, the other auxiliary elements do not themselves invoke the ground in any salient way. While the perspective they impose on the lexically specified process does imply some vantage point, this is not specifically or directly identified with the deictic center. The passive merely imposes an alternate choice of trajector on the designated process, and the progressive restricts the profile to some internal portion of it. Even the perfect, which indicates the "current relevance" of a prior occurrence, does not itself identify the locus of relevance with the ground in particular – whether the vantage point can be identified with the ground is specified only indirectly, through the grounding of *have*.

A concomitant semantic difference is that only the non-grounding elements effect a shift in profile. Correlating with their distance from the lexical verb in the maximal sequence, the passive, progressive, and perfect form higher-level structures whose profiles are successively more divergent from those of the structures they apply to. The processes designated by a lexical verb and its passive are referentially the same, but they have different profiles in the sense that

12 Note that **predicating** existence is not the same as **asserting** existence. A predication of existence merely incorporates the **notion** of a relationship extending through time, hence the need to also specify existential status.

13 The grounded structure also includes complements and various modifiers, which further specify the grounded process type, but the focus here is on verbal elements.

14 By default, the speech event and the interlocutors are included in "reality" (i.e. the speaker presupposes that they are real).

the focal prominence of profiling is centered on different participants (alternate trajectors). The progressive derives an imperfective process consisting of just a portion of the perfective process it applies to. The divergence is even greater with the perfect, which designates a relationship of temporal anteriority and current relevance vis-à-vis the original process.

Grounding continues this iconic pattern whereby elements farther from the lexical verb (in the maximal sequence) introduce relationships that are more extrinsic to it. The grammatical evidence clearly shows, however, that tense and the modals do not effect a shift in profile (Langacker 2002a). Instead of being profiled, the grounding relationship (position vis-à-vis the deictic center) is "offstage" (subjectively construed). What the grounding elements profile (put onstage as the objectively construed focus of attention) is the grounded process itself: a schematic representation of the process whose status they specify.

3.3. Existential verbs

To understand the English auxiliary, we need to make some subtle but crucial terminological distinctions. The **grounded structure** consists of all those elements which help to specify the grounded process type. These include the lexical verb, perspectival elements, complements, and certain modifiers. Within the grounded structure, the **grounded verb** is the one introduced at the highest level of grammatical organization. Depending on which perspectival elements are chosen (if any), this can be the perfect *have*, the progressive *be*, the passive *be*, or the lexical verb (v). The **grounded process** is the one profiled by the grounded verb, which imposes its profile on the grounded structure as a whole. Since grounding does not effect a change in profile, the grounded process is the one profiled by the full, finite clause.

I follow tradition in referring to the modals, *have*, and *be* as **auxiliary verbs**. They differ from lexical verbs by virtue of being highly grammaticized and profiling a maximally schematic process. The auxiliary *do*, which conforms to this description, will be treated separately because it has a special place in the overall system. Finally, within a clause the **existential verb** is the one marked for tense (or deixis). This is a modal (if present), the auxiliary *do*, or the grounded verb (*have*, *be*, or V). It can thus be either an auxiliary or a lexical verb, and either a grounding or a non-grounding element. It is striking that tense is manifested on elements that are grammatically and functionally so divergent. While this is neatly handled mechanically in Chomsky's original formulation, it suggests that something deeper is involved. I propose that it concerns the pivotal role of existence in finite clauses, as being what is primarily at issue.

Describing the tense-bearing verb as "existential" seems quite plausible when things are looked at in the proper manner. Note first that, cross-linguistically, *have-* and *be*-type verbs are commonly used for predications of existence (e.g. French *il y a*; English *there is*). In the case of the English auxiliary, the relationship they extend through time – thus effecting its realization or existence – is the one profiled by their complement: an adjective, prepositional phrase, or participle. Also quite evident is the existential import of the modals. Modals profile a schematized representation of the grounded process, and while they specify that this process is **not** yet accepted as being realized, its realization is precisely what is at issue; they indicate some kind of force or potency tending toward its realization (Sweetser 1982; Talmy 1988; Langacker 1991: § 6.3). I will describe this by saying that modals make a **qualified** predication of existence.

Modals therefore conflate the functions of grounding and existential predication, but offer only a schematic characterization of the relationship whose occurrence is at issue. *Have* and *be* serve only the existential function, but are likewise schematic in regard to the relationship they extend through time. What about lexical verbs? These are specific in regard to the relationship tracked through time. But are they existential? They are, granted the conceptual characterization of verbs adopted in CG. A verb profiles a **process**, defined schematically as a relationship followed (scanned sequentially) in its evolution through time. In other words, the schematic characterization of a verb in CG turns out to be equivalent to the notion of existence as it applies to relationships: realization through time (occurrence). And since schemas are **immanent** in their instantiations, existence is inherent in the conception of a process, constituting its schematic conceptual core. Thus a lexical verb conflates the functions accomplished separately in the case of *have* and *be*, namely existential predication and specification of the profiled relationship.

What about the auxiliary verb *do*? We have yet to consider this predicate, which is central to the auxiliary system and strengthens the case for its basically existential nature. In CG terms, *do* is analyzed as designating a maximally schematic process (Langacker 1987a: 354–356). Semantically, then, it is equivalent to the verb-class schema, residing in the abstracted commonality of all class members. For this reason it gives the impression of being semantically vacuous (hence the initial plausibility of a rule like *Do* Support): when *do* combines with a lexical verb, the composite structure appears to have the same meaning as the latter. But while it does not supply any additional conceptual content, *do* does make a semantic contribution. As the schematic characterization of a process, it separately expresses the existential core of the process specified by the lexical verb and thereby reinforces the very notion of its existence. Observe that *do* is employed in precisely those situations where its occurrence is specifically at issue. It is well known that *do* appears in questions (*Did she wait?*), with negation (*She didn't wait*), and in affirmative statements in cases where occurrence needs to be made explicit (*She* DID *wait*). It fails to appear in matter-of-fact descriptions where the profiled occurrence is simply presented as something to be accepted. In this case the lexical verb itself fulfills the existential function (*She waited*).

3.4. The interactive system

A **predication** of existence is not the same as an **assertion** of existence. While an existential predicate incorporates the **notion** of a relationship extending through time, it does not – in and of itself – imply that the speaker actually accepts its occurrence as part of her own conception of reality. Even the qualified existence expressed by a modal need not represent the speaker's own epistemic assessment. Note, for example, that a finite clause can be used as a complement, so that the epistemic stance expressed by grounding is attributed to someone else (often the matrix subject), as in (7)a. Or an adverb, such as *conceivably*, might indicate that the speaker merely contemplates the stance expressed by clausal grounding, without necessarily subscribing to it (Chapter 9). To talk about grounding exclusively in relation to the speaker (as I have done so far) is thus an oversimplification.

(7) a. *Jack says [that <u>Jill **may** be waiting for us</u>] – but I know for a fact that she isn't.*

b. *Conceivably <u>Jill **is** waiting for us</u> – but I really doubt it.*

c. *<u>Jill is waiting for us</u>. Well, you can say that, but I don't believe it.*

Clearly, we have to distinguish between the essential elements of a finite clause and how such a clause is further elaborated and put to use at higher levels of organization. I will thus distinguish between a **basic clause**, consisting of grounding plus grounded structure, and a finite clause in its entirety. The underscores in (7)a–b identify two basic clauses which belong to finite clauses also containing non-basic elements. In different ways, *that* and *conceivably* both indicate that the proposition expressed by the basic clause is not purported to represent the speaker's actual position. Instead, it is merely introduced as something to be considered, its validity being subject to negotiation or determination at higher levels.

I will say, then, that a basic clause expresses a **negotiable proposition**. The basic grounding elements – tense and modality – are **internal** to that proposition. They specify the epistemic status of the grounded process with respect to a deictic center and a conception of reality. Usually the deictic center is the one defined by the actual speech event (Langacker 1991: 255–256). Crucially, however, the conceptualizer need not be the actual speaker. In (7)a, the assessment of potentiality conveyed by *may* is not ascribed to the speaker, but to Jack. And in (7)b, the speaker merely imagines (allows as being *conceivable*) the situation of the proposition (*Jill is waiting for us*) being valid. The speaker does not now **identify** with the conceptualizer who accepts the waiting as being real (as reflected in clausal grounding).

In short, the conceptualizer invoked by clausal grounding has no particular identity. It is thus a virtual (or imagined) conceptualizer unless and until it comes to be identified with a specific individual. By default, the actual speaker assumes this role. That, however, is a matter of how a basic clause is used and interpreted at higher levels of organization. Even when a basic clause stands alone as a complete sentence its grounding need not reflect the speaker's actual conception of reality. For instance, it might just be echoic, as in (7)c. The default – where the speaker fully identifies with the stance implied by clausal grounding – represents a particular way of embedding the basic clause in a more elaborate interactive situation involving evaluation and negotiation of the proposition expressed.

An **elaborated clause** is one that incorporates elements pertaining to this higher level of interactive evaluation. Among these elements are *that*, as in (7)a, and adverbs like *conceivably*, in (7)b. Also included are indications of **polarity** and **illocutionary force**. These in particular concern us, since they are closely bound up with auxiliaries. For instance, almost all the English auxiliaries have contracted negative forms (e.g. *Jill **isn't** waiting*), and they all invert with the subject in forming questions (***Is** Jill waiting?*).

Polarity and illocutionary force can be seen as constituting an **interactive system** representing one dimension in the characterization of finite clauses.[15] The interactive system concerns the validity of the proposition expressed by the basic clause. For our purposes, it can be described as having four basic values: **question** (Q), **negative** (NEG), **affirmative** (AFF), and neutral (non-affirmative) **positive** (POS). The affirmative/positive contrast is indicated by whether the existential verb bears a secondary degree of stress (represented

15 As discussed in Verstraete 2002, there is some similarity here to the "interpersonal" system in Halliday's Systemic Functional Grammar. Verhagen (2005: ch. 2) discusses the interactive nature of negation. To keep things manageable, I must leave aside imperatives and negative questions, which pose special problems but can nonetheless be accommodated in this framework.

here by small caps) or is wholly unaccented (and possibly contracted).[16] In combination with auxiliary verbs, we thus have the paradigm in Figure 8.4.

	Q	NEG	AFF	POS
M	*Will she wait?*	*She will not wait.*	*She* WILL *wait.*	*She will wait.*
have	*Has she waited?*	*She has not waited.*	*She* HAS *waited.*	*She has waited.*
be	*Is she waiting?*	*She is not waiting.*	*She* IS *waiting.*	*She is waiting.*
do	*Did she wait?*	*She did not wait.*	*She* DID *wait.*	**She did wait.*

Figure 8.4

The striking feature of this table is the ungrammaticality of the entry in the lower right-hand corner, i.e. expressions like **She did wait*, where *do* is unstressed. This gap in the system is the key to characterizing *do* and provides evidence for its existential nature. Observe, first, that *do* is mutually exclusive with the other auxiliary verbs: we say *Was she waiting?* or *Did she wait?*, but not things like **Was she doing wait?* or **Did she be waiting?*. This mutual exclusivity is indication that *do* shares with the modals, *have*, and *be* the property of being fundamentally existential – they constitute a system of opposing elements with this value. Moreover, as noted earlier, *do* occurs in just those situations where occurrence rises to the level of explicit concern: in cases of questioning, negation, and affirmation, which all involve the consideration of alternatives. It fails to appear in the unmarked situation where the speaker merely directs attention to the clausal proposition, with no felt need to negotiate its validity. In other words, *do* indicates that existence (occurrence of the profiled relationship) is somehow **being negotiated**. Instead of just being presented, it is specifically being viewed in relation to other options.

The gap in Figure 8.4 corresponds to the maximally unmarked situation where neither a modal, *have*, or *be* is warranted, and where existence is merely being presented rather than being negotiated. Filling this gap, of course, is a lexical verb bearing tense, as shown in Figure 8.5. That is, the expected sequence *do* + v is **preempted** by v itself in simple positive statements. When existence is being negotiated, *do* gives separate expression to this notion, thereby reinforcing it. But in the absence of negotiation, there is no real need for such reinforcement. We make do with the lexical verb itself, which incorporates the notion of existence as its own schematic core. v itself then functions as the existential verb marked for tense.

16 We are not dealing here with **contrastive** stress, which is primary (e.g. *She hás waited – despite what you say*), but a lower level of stress which merely indicates that the existential predication must be attended to (*She hàs wáited, after all – you should take that into consideration*).

	Q	NEG	AFF	POS
M	*Will she wait?*	*She will not wait.*	*She* WILL *wait.*	*She will wait.*
have	*Has she waited?*	*She has not waited.*	*She* HAS *waited.*	*She has waited.*
be	*Is she waiting?*	*She is not waiting.*	*She* IS *waiting.*	*She is waiting.*
do	*Did she wait?*	*She did not wait.*	*She* DID *wait.*	*She waited.*

Figure 8.5

3.5. Levels of clausal organization

Let me now attempt an interim summary. In functional terms, an English finite clause is organized as shown in Figure 8.6. There are three main systems: **basic grounding** (tense and modality); specification of the **grounded process** (including the lexical verb and perspectival factors); and an **interactive system** (involving polarity and illocutionary force). Together, basic grounding and grounded process constitute a **basic clause**, which expresses a **negotiable proposition**. Internally, this proposition involves an epistemic assessment – on the part of a virtual conceptualizer – concerning the existence (realization through time) of the profiled relationship. Whether the speaker **identifies** with this conceptualizer and **subscribes** to this assessment depends on how the basic clause is used and interpreted at higher levels. As one facet of this higher-level organization, the proposition expressed is subject to negotiation and evaluation concerning its possible validity. Polarity and illocutionary force represent interactions at this level. Their incorporation in a basic clause results in an **elaborated clause** reflecting the speaker's epistemic stance in regard to the proposition.[17]

I have often characterized grounding as relating the profiled clausal process to the ground, defined as the speech event, its participants, and their immediate circumstances. While this is useful as a first approximation, for certain descriptive purposes, it oversimplifies matters by conflating distinct levels of functional organization. In more nuanced presentations (e.g. Langacker 2008a; Chapter 9), I therefore distinguish different levels of conceptualization and epistemic assessment. Minimally, we have to distinguish between the conceptualizer invoked by the basic grounding elements, clause-internally, and the

17 I emphasize that these are **functional** groupings, which need not correspond to grammatical constituents in any direct or simple manner. Functional organization **motivates** grammatical structure, and helps shape it in various ways, but is not isomorphic to that structure (which consists in assemblies of symbolic structures). The grammatical conventions of a language are determined by numerous interacting factors that are often at odds with one another.

actual speaker, who uses the finite clause for a certain higher-level purpose and may or may not identify with the clause-internal conceptualizer. They coincide in the default-case situation where the speaker uses a finite clause without qualification as a statement of her own, actual epistemic assessment. But in general, clause-internal grounding invokes a virtual conceptualizer, perhaps to be thought of as an imagined speaker in an imagined speech event. Relating the profiled occurrence to the actual speaker, as part of an actual speech event, requires additional specifications at higher levels of organization.

<table>
<tr><td colspan="3">Elaborated Clause</td></tr>
<tr><td rowspan="2">Interactive Grounding</td><td colspan="2">Basic Clause</td></tr>
<tr><td>Basic Grounding</td><td>Grounded Process</td></tr>
<tr><td rowspan="2">polarity
illocutionary force
actual speaker
elaborated reality</td><td>tense
modality
virtual conceptualizer
basic reality</td><td>lexical verb
perspectival elements
complements</td></tr>
<tr><td colspan="2">Negotiable Proposition</td></tr>
<tr><td colspan="3">Negotiated Proposition</td></tr>
</table>

Figure 8.6

Relevant here are levels corresponding to a basic clause and an elaborated clause. In many respects the levels are analogous. Each involves a conceptualizer, a profiled occurrence, and an assessment by the former of the latter's epistemic status. Both assessments are facets of grounding as originally defined: together they serve to relate the profiled occurrence to the actual speaker and speech event. Grounding in this global sense can thus be factored into **basic grounding** (tense and modality) plus **interactive grounding** (polarity and illocutionary force), respectively associated with a basic clause and an elaborated clause.

The analogy runs as follows. A **basic clause** expresses a **negotiable proposition**, consisting of grounding plus grounded structure. The conceptualizer is a **virtual** entity: the speaker in an imagined speech event. The grounded structure is a **process**. The basic grounding elements, **tense** and **modality**, specify its status vis-à-vis **basic reality**, i.e. what the conceptualizer accepts as the established history of occurrences (Chapter 6: § 4).

Analogously, an **elaborated clause** expresses a **negotiated proposition**, the conceptualizer (and chief negotiator) being the **actual speaker**. The grounded structure – the one whose epistemic status is at issue – is the **proposition** expressed by the basic clause. Grounding at this level is a matter of its status being negotiated interactively, as reflected in the specifications of **polarity** and **illocutionary force**. Reality at this level consists of the set of **propositions** the speaker accepts as valid, i.e. **elaborated reality**.

4. Basic clauses

Having surveyed the global organization of finite clauses, we must now look in more detail at the various systems it comprises. Let us start with basic clauses, turning subsequently to interactive factors.

4.1. The grounded structure

The grounded structure comprises perspectival elements (perfect, progressive, passive), the lexical verb, its complements, and various kinds of adverbs. Collectively these specify a process type an instance of which is grounded and profiled by the clause as a whole. While this grouping has clear functional significance, it varies in the extent to which it emerges as a discrete structural unit. In questions with modals, like (8)a, all but the subject forms a continuous linear sequence plausibly treated as a constituent. In the absence of a modal, the grouping emerges less distinctly, since the grounded verb (the highest-level auxiliary) precedes the subject as part of a clause-initial grouping that serves an interactive function (to be considered later).[18]

(8) a. *Will she, perhaps, be waiting for us impatiently?*
  b. *Has she, perhaps, been waiting for us impatiently?*

Irrespective of its grammatical realization, we can recognize the grounded structure as a conceptual grouping with a definite semantic function: it specifies a process type whose grounding produces a finite clause. This can either be the basic type designated by the lexical verb (as further specified by complements and modifiers, which we can ignore for present purposes), or else a higher-order type derived by viewing it from a certain perspective. The perspectival elements are the perfect, progressive, and passive constructions. Since these affect

18 This is quite analogous to the alternate syntactic realizations of a complex lexical item, e.g. *keep tabs on*, some of which are discontinuous (e.g. ***Tabs*** *were* ***kept on*** *all vocal critics of the Bush administration*). Despite these varied manifestations, the lexical components form a coherent conceptual grouping based on correspondences established by the constructions employed.

the viewing of a process in non-commensurate ways, they are not mutually exclusive but occur in any combination.[19] They are however constrained to occur in a certain order. How can these patterns and restrictions be described in CG?

Their description takes the form of constructions, i.e. symbolic assemblies of various sizes. To facilitate discussion, I will represent each minimal construction in the format [**D** [A]], where D and A are component elements integrated to form a composite expression. The labels indicate that A is **autonomous** and D is **dependent** on it: D requires A for its full manifestation. D requires A in the sense that it "operates on" A (has A "in its scope"), hence A elaborates a salient substructure of D; this is the import of the bracketing. Finally, D is in bold to show that it functions as profile determinant, i.e. it imposes its profile on the composite structure. The constructions in (9) all exhibit this organization.

(9) a. Participial constructions:
(i) [***-en*** [v]] (ii) [***-ing*** [v]] (iii) [***-ed*** [v]]
b. Perspectival constructions:
(i) [***have*** [*-en* [v]]] (ii) [***be*** [*-ing* [v]]] (iii) [***be*** [*-ed* [v]]]

We can start with the individual participial constructions, given formulaically in (9)a. The elements I represent as *-en*, *-ing*, and *-ed* operate on a verb to derive a perfect, active, or passive participle. The perfect, progressive, and passive constructions are then as shown in (9)b. These are more complex symbolic assemblies, where in each case a schematic existential verb imposes its processual profile on a participle.[20]

As roughly described so far, this array of constructions sanctions all the occurring sequences, including the maximal one. The reason, quite simply, is that each construction in (9)b profiles a process at the composite structure level, so by the CG definition the composite expressions thus derived qualify as (complex) verbs. Thus any such expression, as a whole, can function as v in one of these same constructions. For instance, the passive *be discussed*, a product of construction (9)b(iii), can function as the verb in (9)b(ii), resulting in *be being discussed*. This in turn is a complex verb, hence able to instantiate the v slot in (9)b(i), producing *have been being discussed*. The problem, of course, is that these constructions would seem to allow as well an open-ended set of

19 If they form a system, it is thus a loose-knit one.

20 Obviously, these formulas drastically abbreviate the full CG description of these elements and constructions (Langacker 1987a, 1990a, 1991). They do not show the internal structure of the components, the correspondences effecting their integration, or the composite structure that results. And of course, the past participial morpheme (be it perfect or passive) has varied morphological realizations.

non-occurring combinations, e.g. *be been having discussed* (the passive of the progressive of a perfect), or *be had been discussing* (the passive of the perfect of a progressive). What, then, is responsible for imposing the observed restrictions? I can think of four general approaches to such questions. They may not always be clearly distinct. Nor is it a matter of choosing, as they all have a valid role to play, their relative importance depending on the phenomenon.

One approach is to seek a functional explanation. Here iconicity suggests itself as a basis for the sequencing of auxiliary elements. It seems evident that their closeness to the verb correlates with how intrinsically they relate to it, whether viewed in terms of linear ordering or the grammatical layering it reflects: [Perfect [Progressive [Passive [v]]]]. Passive affects the choice of trajector, the central participant and primary focus of attention. The progressive relates to a process more globally; starting from a bounded process overall, it selects for profiling a portion that excludes the endpoints. And the perfect is quite extrinsic to a process, as it sets up a posterior vantage point for viewing it. I believe such factors are very real and have a significant shaping influence on language structure. One might question, however, whether they alone are sufficient to impose and enforce the rather inflexible restrictions of a grammaticized system like the English auxiliary. While they motivate the system, they do not themselves predict its specific form or effect its full implementation.

A second approach is to rule out non-occurring sequences through a finer-grained semantic characterization of the constructions and their elements. In the case at hand two small adjustments are sufficient. First, the English passive is only applicable to lexical two-participant verbs construed as transitive. Using v_T to represent such verbs, the passive constructional schema can thus be revised as follows: [***be*** [-*ed* [v_T]]]. This eliminates the passive of a perfect or progressive, since *have* and *be* are incompatible with v_T. Also, the progressive construction as a whole (though not -*ing* individually) requires that the verb be perfective: [***be*** [-*ing* [v_P]]]. This eliminates the progressive of a perfect, since *have* is imperfective.[21]

A third option is simply to state the distributional facts as such. In a usage-based approach, it is recognized that symbolic assemblies of indefinite complexity have the potential to be established as conventional units. There can be no doubt that, due to their frequent occurrence, particular combinations of auxiliary elements are well entrenched and easily elicited. Collectively these amount to a positive specification of permitted sequences. Given the CG treat-

21 A progressive passive is allowed because the passive *be* is neutral in regard to perfectivity (a passive inherits its aspect from v_T). The progressive coerces a perfective construal (e.g. in *She was being admired*).

ment of well-formedness (Langacker 2000, 2008a: ch. 8), such well established units will consistently be invoked to categorize non-conforming sequences, which will thereby be judged ill-formed.

Surely speakers of English are often enough exposed to progressive passives (e.g. *It was being discussed*) that the complex assembly in (10)a constitutes a well-rehearsed unit. It is simply a matter of the passive schema instantiating the verb slot in the progressive schema. Likewise, perfect progressives (*She has been waiting*) and perfect passives (*It has been discussed*) give rise to the entrenched assemblies in (10)b–c. Moreover, it is not implausible to suppose that even the maximal sequence (as in *It had been being discussed*) achieves the status of a unit. Given in (10)d, it represents the special case of (10)b where v_P is instantiated by the passive constructional schema. Note that this last assembly is tantamount to a formula summarizing the maximal grounded structure. In CG, of course, this formulaic representation is merely abbreviatory. It stands for a multilevel structure comprising meaningful elements connected via correspondences in very specific ways.[22]

(10) a. [***be*** [*-ing* [*be* [*-ed* [v_T]]]]]
b. [***have*** [*-en* [*be* [*-ing* [v_P]]]]]
c. [***have*** [*-en* [*be* [*-ed* [v_T]]]]]
d. [***have*** [*-en* [*be* [*-ing* [*be* [*-ed* [v_T]]]]]]]

A fourth and final approach involves the organization of symbolic assemblies into systems constituting alternate ways of fulfilling semantic functions. I have suggested that the perfect, progressive, and passive constructions collectively serve a perspectival function but represent three more specific functions that are not really commensurate, hence they co-occur. We can reasonably posit three subsystems: voice (pertaining to focused participants), perfective/imperfective (pertaining to whether an event is viewed as a bounded whole), and a reference point system (pertaining to whether an event is viewed directly, in its own terms, or in terms of the trace it leaves in the apprehension of a later situation). Since the perfect, progressive, and passive are optional, at the very least each alternates with its absence.[23] Though quite minimal, a system of this

22 The bracketing indicates semantic and functional relationships but does not necessarily dovetail with grammatical constituency, which in CG is seen as flexible and variable (Langacker 1995a, 1997a, 2008a). The same semantic relationships can often be realized in symbolic assemblies with different configurations.

23 This can be considered a minimal or degenerate system. With the passive there are more evident options, such as the **setting-subject construction** with *see* and *witness*: *The following day {saw / witnessed} another surprising turn of events.*

sort – representing conventionally sanctioned means of fulfilling the function in question – implicitly precludes further options that might otherwise be allowed. Note in particular that nothing presented so far rules out the perfect of a perfect (e.g. **She has had waited*).[24] As a complex reference point relationship, however, a double perfect would have to be analyzed as belonging to the perspectival system. But once established, a structured, highly grammaticized system of this sort simply has no place for new exponents.

Limiting our attention to auxiliary elements, the various possibilities for the grounded structure are thus as shown in Figure 8.7(a). The sequences listed constitute an integrated system of well-entrenched alternatives for the role of grounded structure. In the absence of perspectival adjustments, the lexical verb itself functions as the grounded verb. Its schematic processual core then fulfills the existential function served by *have* or *be* in the other constructions. For subsequent purposes, the nature of the complement will not concern us. The table in 8.7(a) can thus be collapsed as shown in 8.7(b).

(a)

Grounded Structure	
Grounded Verb	Complement
be	(*-ed* (v))
be	(*-ing* (v))
have	(*-en* (v))
be	(*-ing* (*be* (*-ed* (v))))
have	(*-en* (*be* (*-ing* (v))))
have	(*-en* (*be* (*-ed* (v))))
have	(*-en* (*be* (*-ing* (*be* (*-ed* (v))))))
v	

(b)

Grounded Structure	
Grounded Verb	Complement
have	*X*
be	
v	

Figure 8.7

4.2. The grounding system

The English grounding system, a defining feature of finite clauses, serves to locate a grounded process (**p**) with respect to the deictic center. At the center is a conceptualizer (C), by default the actual speaker, who apprehends the process

Their systemic alternation is responsible for the passive and setting-subject constructions being mutually exclusive: **Another surprising turn of events was {seen / witnessed} by the following day.* (Cf. Langacker 2006a.)

24 The refinements made above, involving v_P and v_T, rule out the progressive of a progressive and the passive of a passive.

and makes an assessment concerning its existential status. The close-knit grounding system comprises two binary oppositions, each of which has an unmarked member with zero coding. The "tense" opposition, where "present" is the zero member,[25] more generally indicates whether the profiled occurrence is **immediate** or **non-immediate** with respect to the center. The other basic opposition is the absence vs. the presence of a modal. With the absence of a modal, C makes an **unqualified** existential predication, thereby portraying the profiled process as part of reality (the established history of occurrences). The function of modals is to **qualify** the existential predication. With the different modals, realization of the grounded process is described as having various shades of potentiality.

The core grounding system specifies the configurations shown in Figure 8.8. Since one member of each opposition is always chosen, every finite clause makes a specification in regard to both immediacy and reality. Immediacy plays out differently depending on the latter. Reality being what C accepts as the history of occurrences – up through the current moment, where C and the ground are located – immediacy vs. non-immediacy amounts to present vs. past in time. These are the two basic positions **within** reality. But with modals the grounded process lies **outside** reality, where "location" is construed as a matter of (typically future) potentiality. Here the import of immediacy vs. non-immediacy is that reality – as presently constituted – functions either directly or only indirectly as the basis for modal assessment (Chapter 7). For instance, *might* attenuates the force of *may* by indicating that the current conception of reality is not quite sufficient to support the degree of potentiality it expresses: *She may wait for us* vs. *She might wait for us.* More blatantly, *would* cancels the predictive force of *will* by basing the prediction on a fictive (or counterfactual) version of reality: *She will wait* vs. *She would wait (if she could).*

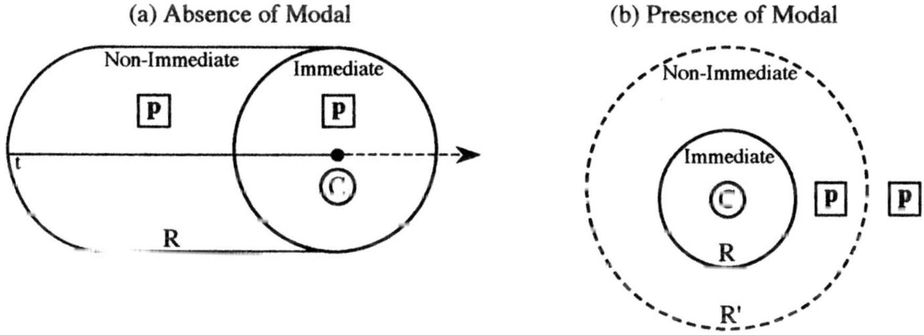

Figure 8.8

25 Third-singular *-s* will be dealt with shortly.

A paradigmatic view of the core grounding system is given in Figure 8.9(a). The paradigm is not quite regular morphologically, since the non-immediate modal forms involve stem modification as well as suffixation, and are not really perceived as being suffixal. The system is also less than fully regular and analyzable semantically. Each modal form has developed and specialized in its own way and carved out its own niche in usage. A certain amount of polysemy has to be acknowledged. Besides its general predictive force, for instance, *will* has a well-entrenched variant that specifically indicates future time. Moreover, the non-immediate modals are considerably less than fully analyzable and compositional (a case in point being the counterfactuality of *would*).[26] Further complicating the basic system is the use of modals for both **effective** and **epistemic** purposes, as part of a broad pattern of duality in English grammar (Langacker To appear f). Both involve a striving for control, the difference residing in whether the modal force is aimed at influencing the course of events (the root or deontic senses) or at gaining knowledge of events (the epistemic senses).

(a) Basic Paradigm

	Reality	Non-Reality
Immediate		*may, can, will, shall, must*
Non-Immediate	*-d*	*might, could, would, should*

(b) Preemption

Person: 3s	Reality	Non-Reality
Immediate	*-s*	*may, can, will, shall, must*
Non-Immediate	*-d*	*might, could, would, should*

Figure 8.9

An additional complicating factor is third-person singular inflection, which I will represent as *-s*. I think it is best analyzed as an extra-systemic element which conflates the function of immediacy, modality, and person. It specifically indicates the default value for all three parameters: immediate, real, and third singular. Given its availability to mark this cluster of properties, *-s* **preempts** zero for the grounding of clauses with third-person singular subjects, as shown in Figure 8.9(b).

These diagrams offer a paradigmatic view of clausal grounding. A systemic view is given in Figure 8.10, in two formats, because a single table cannot represent all the relevant details. Table (a) analyzes the non-immediate modals into their systemic components, and is thus inaccurate in regard to their composite morphological shapes. Table (b) shows their actual forms, but does not reflect their partial analyzability. Effectively it treats the grounding ele-

26 An additional point is that *must* lacks a non-immediate form (Langacker 1991: § 6.2.2.3).

ments as unanalyzable wholes conflating specifications regarding immediacy and reality.

(a) Systemic View (analytic)

<table>
<tr><th colspan="2">Grounding</th></tr>
<tr><th>Immediacy</th><th>Reality</th></tr>
<tr><td rowspan="3"></td><td></td></tr>
<tr><td>may</td></tr>
<tr><td>can</td></tr>
<tr><td rowspan="3">-d</td><td>will</td></tr>
<tr><td>shall</td></tr>
<tr><td>must</td></tr>
</table>

(b) Systemic View (synthetic)

<table>
<tr><th colspan="2">Grounding</th></tr>
<tr><th>Immediacy</th><th>Reality</th></tr>
<tr><td colspan="2"></td></tr>
<tr><td>-d</td><td></td></tr>
<tr><td></td><td>may, will, ...</td></tr>
<tr><td colspan="2">might, would, ...</td></tr>
</table>

Figure 8.10

Having examined both grounding and grounded structure, we can now consider the systemic organization of the basic clause as a whole. This is shown in Figure 8.11, which is simply the combination of Figures 8.10(a) and 8.7(b).

<table>
<tr><th colspan="2">Grounding</th><th colspan="2">Grounded Structure</th></tr>
<tr><th>Immediacy</th><th>Reality</th><th>Grounded Verb</th><th>Complement</th></tr>
<tr><td rowspan="3"></td><td></td><td rowspan="2">have</td><td rowspan="4">X</td></tr>
<tr><td>may</td></tr>
<tr><td>can</td><td rowspan="2">be</td></tr>
<tr><td rowspan="3">-d</td><td>will</td></tr>
<tr><td>shall</td><td colspan="2" rowspan="2">V</td></tr>
<tr><td>must</td></tr>
</table>

Figure 8.11

4.3. The role of *do*

Let us now turn to auxiliary *do*, which has several basic properties.[27] First, it is primarily existential in its import, being comparable to the verb-class schema (the schematic existential core of lexical verbs). Second, it is mutually exclusive

27 *Do* also functions as a lexical verb. For detailed comparison, see Langacker 2005a.

with other auxiliaries: **She does have waited*; **She has done wait*; **She does be waiting*; **She is doing wait*; **She does may wait*; **She may do wait*. Third, *do* indicates that existence is being negotiated, occurring in questions, with negation, and in affirmative statements, but not in simple positive statements (where v preempts it).

Do, then, does not fit neatly into the general system of grounding plus grounded structure. It is rather a partial alternative to the general scheme, representing a different strategy for giving certain functions formal expression. *Do* actually plays a role in all three basic systems: grounding, grounded structure, and the interactive system. With respect to the former two, it conflates the functions of reality specification and grounded verb, as shown in Figure 8.12. Effectively, then, it is one member of the modal system – like the zero member, it indicates unqualified existence (the occurrence is accepted as being real). As such, it bears tense but does not occur with other modals. *Do* can also be regarded as a member of the perspectival system, where it indicates neutral perspective: the profiled occurrence is viewed in the manner specified by the lexical verb (without adjustment for voice or aspect). But since *do* itself profiles that occurrence (in schematized form), in effect it serves as the grounded verb, relegating v to the role of complement. Beyond this, *do* has the interactive import of indicating that existence is subject to negotiation.

<table>
<tr><th colspan="2">Grounding</th><th colspan="2">Grounded Structure</th></tr>
<tr><th>Immediacy</th><th>Reality</th><th>Grounded Verb</th><th>Complement</th></tr>
<tr><td rowspan="2"></td><td>may</td><td>have</td><td rowspan="3">X</td></tr>
<tr><td>can</td><td rowspan="2">be</td></tr>
<tr><td rowspan="4">-d</td><td>will</td></tr>
<tr><td>shall</td><td colspan="2" rowspan="2">v</td></tr>
<tr><td>must</td></tr>
<tr><td colspan="2">do</td><td>v</td></tr>
</table>

Figure 8.12

We can summarize by saying that *do* represents the default or unmarked value with respect to reality and perspective: unqualified existence, neutral perspective. With respect to interaction, it represents a departure from the baseline situation of non-negotiation, where the speaker merely presents a statement for acceptance. It is in this maximally unmarked circumstance (involving unqualified existence, neutral perspective, and non-negotiation) that the sequence *do* + v is preempted by the lexical verb.

5. Interaction

Turning now to interactive factors, two main topics need to be examined. We will first consider the interactive grounding of the proposition expressed by the basic clause. Also relevant to the auxiliary are matters involving word order and information structure.

5.1. Existential verb

A finite clause expresses a negotiable proposition which specifies the epistemic status of an existential predication (as assessed by a virtual conceptualizer). Both structurally and semantically, it pivots on an **existential verb** ($V_{\exists}$), which I have identified as the one bearing tense (or more generally, a specification for immediacy). This can be the tense-marked form of a modal, *have*, *be*, *do*, or a lexical verb, which are quite diverse as regards their role in the systems of grounding and grounded structure. Their functional unity pertains instead to the interactive system: the existential verb is the one whose status is specifically being negotiated. This shows up grammatically in at least a couple of ways. First, the existential verb attracts the marking for polarity (e.g. *She* ***won't*** *wait; She* DID *wait*). And second, it is the verb that inverts with the subject in questions (***Is*** *she waiting?*). Since we are dealing here with word order, the existential verb has to be identified as the full **verb word** rather than just the stem.

Presented in Figure 8.13(a) is the existential verb's systemic organization. There are three systems: immediacy, the alternate stems, and polarity (negative, affirmative, and positive). With certain qualifications, all combinations of values are permitted and manifested in a single word – a contracted form in the case of negation. One qualification is that not every modal has a negative form.[28] Also, since v preempts *do* in (non-affirmative) positive statements, it only appears with positive polarity, while *do* is limited to negative and affirmative. Representative forms are given paradigmatically in 8.13(b), the modal *will* being chosen for illustration. Only the non-immediate (or past-tense) forms are shown; the immediate forms constitute an analogous paradigm.

Table (b) also gives an indication of markedness. With respect to polarity, positive is clearly the neutral (default-case) value, affirmative and negative being marked. Along the other axis, *do* and v represent the unmarked value: they indicate neutral perspective (in contrast to *have* and *be*) as well as unquali-

---

28 *May* does not (**mayn't*), and in my speech both *mightn't* and *shan't* are very marginal.

fied existence (in contrast to M). Within the mini-system comprising *do* and V, the latter is the unmarked member, since it further indicates non-negotiation. When it functions as the existential verb (bearing tense), V is thus unmarked in regard to the reality system (an aspect of grounding), the perspectival system (an aspect of the grounded structure), as well as both dimensions of the interactive system (polarity and illocutionary force). *Do* is neutral in regard to reality and perspective, but takes over for V when negotiation is involved. As an indication of non-negotiation, a lexical verb does not attract negation and does not appear in questions. There is, in short, functional and systemic motivation for these apparent idiosyncrasies.

(a) Systemic View

Existential Verb ($V_\exists$)		
Immediacy	**Stem**	**Polarity**
	M	NEG
	have	
	be	AFF
-*d*	*do*	
	V	

(b) Paradigmatic View

	NEG	AFF	POS	
M	*wouldn't*	*WOULD*	*would*	Marked
have	*hadn't*	*HAD*	*had*	Marked
be	*wasn't*	*WAS*	*was*	Marked
do	*didn't*	*DID*		Neutral
V			*vd*	Neutral
	Marked	Marked	Neutral	

Figure 8.13

Polarity, of course, is just one dimension of interactive grounding, the other being illocutionary force. Here we will only be concerned with questions. Unlike polarity, questions are not marked on the verb in English, but by its position relative to the subject. To deal with this properly, we must first address some other issues affording a broader perspective.

5.2. Existential core

English finite clauses give evidence of a functional grouping that I will refer to as the **existential core**. While it is not necessarily a grammatical constituent, the existential core does have structural significance. And while it may be fuzzily bounded and flexible in membership, its central members include the existential verb, the clausal subject, as well as indications of polarity and illocutionary force.

As evidence of its structural significance, note the common pattern in (11), where the existential core is separated from the remainder of the clause by an adverb or a parenthetical insertion. Especially natural in this position are expressions pertaining to judgment and epistemic assessment.

(11) a. *You will, I think, be pleased with the results.*
b. *She has, it seems, been working hard all afternoon.*
c. *Are they, perhaps, less trustworthy than we thought?*
d. *He did not, apparently, notice that anything was wrong.*

More clearly indicating its functional and structural signficance is the existential core's anaphoric use, exemplified in (12). The core can either be appended as a "tag", or it can stand alone as a separate utterance. While the specifics of these constructions cannot be dealt with here, several points are worth noting. First, the core is appropriate for anaphoric use because the auxiliary verb and pronominal subject provide a schematic representation of the proposition being negotiated. Second, these constructions are obviously shaped and motivated by discourse function and information structure. And third, they are strongly interactive, serving to ground or establish a negotiated proposition.

(12) a. **A:** *The president shouldn't be lying to us, should he?*
B: *No, he shouldn't.*
b. **A:** *You've finished your homework, have you?* **B:** *Yes, I have.*
c. **A:** *The students are still complaining, aren't they?* **B:** *Yes, they are.*
d. **A:** *He* DID *fix the computer, didn't he?* **B:** *No, he didn't, actually.*

The elements considered so far constitute the **basic** existential core, a close-knit system having three exponents for polarity (positive, affirmative, and negative) and two for illocutionary force (statement vs. question). We can also recognize an **elaborated** existential core allowing more nuanced epistemic assessments. The elaborated core is at best a loose-knit system not amenable to precise delimitation. As the basis for its recognition, observe that a limited set of elements occur in close proximity to the basic core and either refine or reinforce its existential import. Just a few elements commonly occur within the basic core, between the subject and existential verb, as in (13)a. These clearly pertain to epistemic assessment. A somewhat larger group of elements seem natural directly following the existential verb in sentences like (11). The ones listed in (13)b have basically negative import, while those in (13)c reinforce a positive assessment.

(13) a. *He* ***{never / always / really / surely / probably / most likely}*** *has been a problem.*
b. *He has* ***{never / hardly ever / seldom / barely / not}****, it seems, reached his potential.*

c. *He has* ***{always / often / really / certainly / clearly / definitely / undoubtedly}****, it would seem, been difficult to deal with.*

Here I will focus on elements that precede the basic core. As evidence that such elements serve to elaborate the existential core, and are thus a peripheral part of it, I will rely on their ability to trigger Subject-Auxiliary Inversion. Not every preposed element does so, as we see in (14). Some that do are exemplified in (15).

(14) a. ***Me*** *she would never wait for.*
b. ***There*** *she waited for several hours.*
c. ***Finally*** *she got tired of waiting.*
d. ***For several hours*** *she waited patiently.*
e. ***With her iPod*** *she didn't mind waiting.*

(15) a. ***Who*** *was she waiting for?*
b. ***Never*** *will she wait for her sister.*
c. ***Seldom*** *has she waited for me.*
d. ***Thus*** *was she willing to wait.*
e. ***Only with her iPod*** *does she not mind waiting.*

The elements well established in this role fall into several semantically coherent classes, listed in (16): question words; negatives; adverbials and quantifiers that restrict some specification to a minimal value; and more marginally, a few basically positive expressions.[29] What unifies these classes, and motivates their inclusion in the existential core, is that they all bear directly on the existential predication. The interrogative and negative elements are alternatives to those in the basic core. The restrictive adverbials and quantifiers have weakly negative existential import by virtue of excluding the profiled occurrence from almost the entire range of options. Though positive in nature, the deictic expressions *thus* and *there* achieve a comparable restriction. *So* (as in *So will I*) is in effect the positive counterpart of *nor* and *neither*, indicating that multiple events are parallel in terms of their existential status. *Truly* (as in *Truly are we fortunate!*) functions as an emphatic in regard to existence.

(16) a. **Question words:** *who*, *what*, *why*, *where*, *when*, *how*, etc.
b. **Negatives:** *never, nor, neither, in no way*
c. **Restrictives:** *seldom, hardly ever, only, few, barely, scarcely*
d. **Positives:** *thus, there, so, truly*

From a systemic perspective, the fact that these elements are mutually exclusive with the subject in initial position suggests that they and the subject fulfill a com-

29 The effect of *only* can be seen by comparing (14)e and (15)e.

mon function. I propose that this function pertains to **information structure**, in a broad sense of the term. To understand it, we need to consider two dimensions of functional organization within a clause. One involves successive **layers**. Here we start with the **core** and work our way outward, layer by layer, until we reach the whole. The other dimension is linear order, where we start with the **initial element**, which serves as a kind of **anchor** for presenting the clausal content.

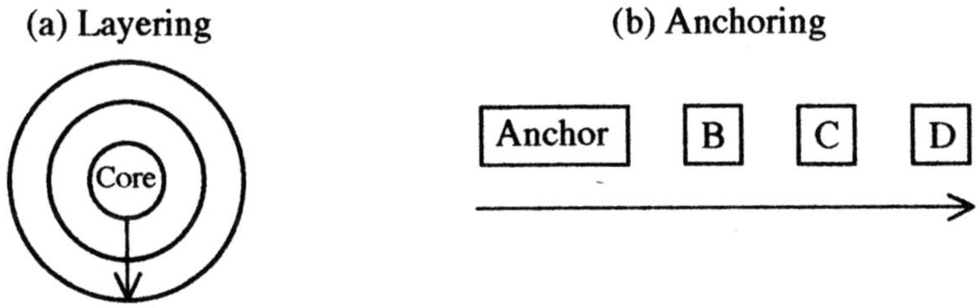

Figure 8.14

5.3. Layering

I have been suggesting that the basic function of a clause is to predicate the existence of some relationship, i.e. its occurrence or realization through time. With respect to this function, an existential predicate is thus the pivotal element of a finite clause, a kind of core which other elements elaborate in various ways to form more specific existential predications at successively higher levels of organization. We can distinguish at least the layers shown in Figure 8.15. I leave open the question of whether all these functional groupings should also be recognized as grammatical constituents. They do however all have some structural significance.

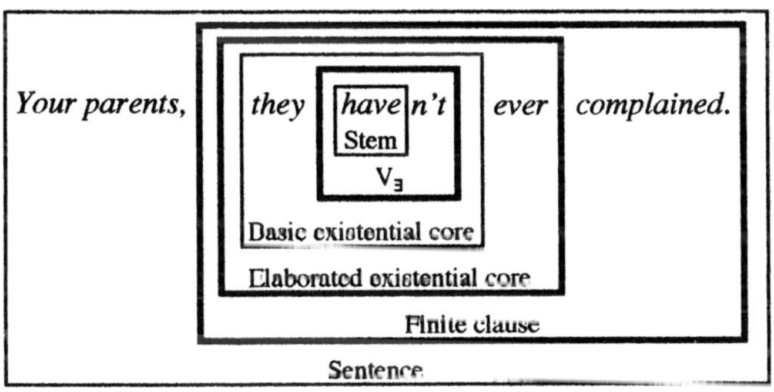

Figure 8.15

By way of brief review, we can start with the **existential stem**, in this example *have*. It can be identified structurally as the verb stem inflected for tense (here zero). The **existential verb** ($V_\exists$) is the **word** based on this stem; it incorporates specifications for tense (immediacy) and polarity. This is the word that inverts with the subject in questions and other constructions, as in (15). The **basic existential core** was defined as including the existential verb, the subject, polarity, and illocutionary force (statement vs. question). This is the structure that appears in tags (e.g. *They haven't ever complained, **have they**?*). The **elaborated existential core** incorporates additional elements like the ones in (13) and (16). This structure is used anaphorically (e.g. *No, **they hardly ever have***). The existential core of a **finite clause** is a schematic representation of the clause as a whole, which is more specific in regard to what is predicated as occurring. Lastly, a finite clause can itself be thought of as the existential core of a larger expression, as in 8.15.

Of particular relevance here are the levels highlighted in Figure 8.15. I will be drawing the following parallel: the role of the existential verb within the (elaborated) existential core is analogous to the role of the core within a finite clause. To see the significance of this analogy, we must first consider the **anchoring** function.

5.4. Anchoring

The sentence in Figure 8.15 represents a clause-external **topic** construction. While the term topic is usually limited to nominal expressions, other kinds of elements – broadly adverbial in nature – can occur in what appears to be the same structural position: preposed to a finite clause, and set off from the clause by "comma intonation", as in (17). I propose that these elements all serve an **anchoring** function vis-à-vis the following clause. A topic (as usually understood) is thus a particular kind of anchor. Being more abstract, the notion "anchor" is even harder to characterize conceptually than is "topic". Impressionistically and metaphorically, an anchor might be described as "framing" the clausal proposition: an instruction to interpret it with respect to a particular domain of knowledge or a certain aspect of the situation described. In a general sense it is also a kind of **reference point** (Langacker 1993c), selected for discourse reasons as the initial point of access for presenting or apprehending that situation.

(17) ***{Last night / in her study / with a fine brush / carefully},*** *she was painting Easter eggs.*

I will focus here on just three basic kinds of anchors, exemplified in (18). The anchor can be a **participant** in the clausal process; this is what is traditionally known as a topic. The anchor can also be a **location** in a broad sense of the term (subsuming both spatial and temporal locations, as well as global **settings**). The third case might be described as the **absence** of an anchor. There is however another way to look at it. I suggest that we can reasonably describe it as involving an **existential** anchor.

(18) a. Participant anchor: ***Easter eggs,*** *she was painting them last night.*
b. Locational anchor: ***Last night,*** *she was painting Easter eggs.*
c. Existential anchor: ***She was painting Easter eggs last night.***

In sentences consisting of an anchor plus a finite clause, the latter constitutes the existential core, in that it predicates the existence of a relationship (its realization through time). Suppose a finite clause stands alone as a full sentence, without a separate anchor. Instead of saying that it lacks an anchor altogether, we can perfectly well say that the clause itself assumes the anchor function, making it an existential anchor. The anchor constitutes an instruction to interpret the clausal proposition with respect to a certain aspect of the situation described. Thus an existential anchor represents the special case where no particular aspect is singled out for this purpose – this is the **neutral** case where the proposition as a whole functions as point of access at the sentence level. In systemic terms, we can say that the existential (or clausal) element **conflates** the functions of **anchor** and **anchored structure** (in much the same way that v conflates the functions of existential verb and lexical verb when used preemptively).

This is at the sentence level. But the same can be observed at two lower levels (or inner layers): within a finite clause, and within its elaborated existential core. For finite clauses, the three kinds of anchoring are exemplified in (19). In (19)a, the preposed object serving as anchor is what is usually described as a clause-internal topic. This is a blended construction in which *her sister* conflates the functions of anchor and clausal object. What I identify in (19)c as the existential anchor is simply the clause's (elaborated) existential core. *She was* conflates the functions of anchor and existential core.

(19) a. Participant anchor: ***Her sister*** *she was waiting for all morning.*
b. Locational anchor: ***All morning*** *she was waiting for her sister.*
c. Existential anchor: ***She was*** *waiting for her sister all morning.*

In Figure 8.16 I give a systemic view of these expressions. For subsequent purposes, it suffices to show a (finite) clause as comprising three functional elements: **anchor**, (elaborated) **existential core**, and the **remainder**.

Clause		
Anchor	Existential Core	Remainder
Her sister	*she was*	*waiting for all morning.*
All morning	*she was*	*waiting for her sister.*
She was		*waiting for her sister all morning.*

Figure 8.16

Let us now consider the existential core itself. In (20), the existential core is the portion outside the brackets. The default anchor within the core is the subject, *she* in (20)a. But other elements, such as *never*, can also appear in anchor position, before the existential verb, in which case the subject follows it instead. Included are all the elements in (16), which were in fact identified by this very property. These can be considered "locational" in a suitably broad sense of the term. Finally, at this level too it is possible for the existential element itself to be chosen as anchor. Here this element is the existential verb (*hasn't*), which then conflates the functions of anchor and existential core.

(20) a. Participant anchor: ***She*** *hasn't ever [waited for you].*
b. Locational anchor: ***Never*** *has she [waited for you].*
c. Existential anchor: ***Hasn't*** *she ever [waited for you]?*

A systemic view of these expressions is given in Figure 8.17. Comparison of 8.16 and 8.17 reveals the parallelism alluded to earlier: the role of the existential verb within the existential core is analogous to that of the core within a finite clause. Moreover, the two levels exhibit analogous functional organization, consisting of an anchor, an existential core, and the remainder, occurring in that specific linear sequence.

Existential Core		
Anchor	$V_\exists$	Remainder
she	*hasn't*	*ever*
never	*has*	*she*
hasn't		*she ever*

Figure 8.17

5.5. Inversion

Earlier I gave a systemic account of *Do* Support. It is actually not a matter of *do* being "inserted"; rather, the sequence *do* + v is preempted by the lexical verb in simple, positive statements (where negotiation is not a factor). Here we likewise have a systemic account of Subject-Auxiliary Inversion. Nothing actually changes position: it is just a matter of some other element supplanting the subject in its default role as anchor within the existential core.

Why should the subject be the default anchor within the existential core? Indeed, why should the subject be part of the existential core at all? Its role as anchor makes sense given that a topic is one kind of anchor (a participant anchor) and that the notions topic and subject are closely related (Li and Thompson 1976; Langacker 2001a). I agree with Chafe (1994), who describes the subject in discourse terms as a **starting point** for the presentation of clausal material. In CG, a subject is defined as specifying the trajector of the profiled clausal process, and the trajector in turn is characterized as starting point – initial reference point – for purposes of building up to the full conception of that process (Langacker 2008a). Though at different levels of organization, topic, subject, and trajector all serve as reference points providing access to a profiled relationship. Thus they anchor the conception of that relationship.

Why should the subject be part of the existential core? The core is a schematic representation of the clause as a whole (hence its anaphoric function), so it profiles the same relationship and has the same trajector. Relationships are conceptually dependent on their participants, especially their trajector, which is the primary focal participant and initial reference point for their conception. The trajector thus has to be invoked even for the core's schematic depiction of the profiled relationship. And the subject, which specifies the trajector, is the natural choice of anchor for the core and the clause overall.

In Figures 8.16 and 8.17, organization in terms of anchor, existential core, and remainder is viewed separately at the level of the clause and that of the core itself. The next step is to view these levels in relation to one another. This is done in Figure 8.18, where the clause-level existential core is broken down into its own component functions (which mirror those of the clause as a whole). The first example, *Me she has seldom waited for*, represents the case where distinct elements manifest each function at both levels. In this case there is both a clause-level anchor (*me*) and a core-level anchor (*she*). The remaining examples represent the unmarked situation, where there is no separate clause-level anchor. Instead, the existential core itself assumes this function, thus conflating the roles of core and anchor. Or more precisely, the table indicates that the **existential anchor** in particular conflates two roles: clause-level and core-level anchor. The element in question is usually the clausal subject, but when the core has a non-default anchor, like *never* in the last example, it supplants the subject in both roles.

I first indicated – in (19) and Figure 8.16 – that the existential core functions as clause-level anchor in such expressions. In Figure 8.18, I show the core-level anchor, in particular, as serving this function. This apparent inconsistency is really only due to the limitations in what a tabular array can represent. We get a clearer idea of what is going on by shifting to a representation that directly indicates layering (not just linear sequence). In Figure 8.19 we see the functional layering inherent in maximally differentiated expressions, where all the functions are separately realized. It should be self-explanatory.

<table>
<tr><th colspan="5">Clause</th></tr>
<tr><th rowspan="2">Anchor</th><th colspan="3">Existential Core</th><th rowspan="2">Remainder</th></tr>
<tr><th>Anchor</th><th>$V_\exists$</th><th>Remainder</th></tr>
<tr><td>Me</td><td>she</td><td>has</td><td>seldom</td><td>waited for.</td></tr>
<tr><td colspan="2">She</td><td>will</td><td>seldom</td><td>wait for me.</td></tr>
<tr><td colspan="2">She</td><td>didn't</td><td></td><td>wait for me.</td></tr>
<tr><td colspan="2">She</td><td>may</td><td>not</td><td>wait for me.</td></tr>
<tr><td colspan="2">She</td><td>hasn't</td><td>ever</td><td>waited for me.</td></tr>
<tr><td colspan="2">She</td><td>has</td><td>never</td><td>waited for me.</td></tr>
<tr><td colspan="2">She</td><td>is</td><td>not</td><td>waiting for me.</td></tr>
<tr><td colspan="2">Never</td><td>has</td><td>she</td><td>waited for me.</td></tr>
</table>

Figure 8.18

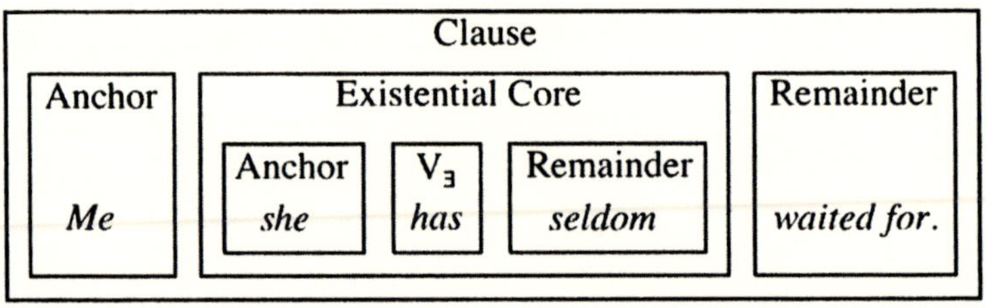

Figure 8.19

The more interesting case is represented in Figure 8.20, where the existential core functions as clause-level anchor, thus conflating those two functions. This would seem to be the unmarked configuration for a finite clause in English. Noteworthy here is the special status of the clausal subject, which anchors the core, which in turn anchors the clause. Derivatively, then, the subject – as anchor within the anchor – has an anchoring function for the clause as a whole. We can also say that the clause simultaneously accommodates two anchoring functions: it has both a participant anchor (the subject) and an existential anchor, the latter providing a schematic representation of the clause as a whole. In different ways, both are natural points of access for presenting the clausal content.

Subject-Auxiliary Inversion represents a special case of structures like these, in which the existential core functions as clause-level anchor: the case where the core has a non-default anchor. The subject then has to follow the existential verb, as in the last example in Figure 8.18 [*Never has she waited for me*]. Note that inversion is mutually exclusive with a clause-internal topic, as shown by the examples in (21). In other words, it **only** occurs when the existential anchor is also the clausal anchor, as in Figure 8.20. The reason is that the motivation for inversion stems from discourse and interactive factors, pertaining to how a clause is used at higher levels of organization.[30] This is quite evident in the most typical use of inversion, namely in questions.

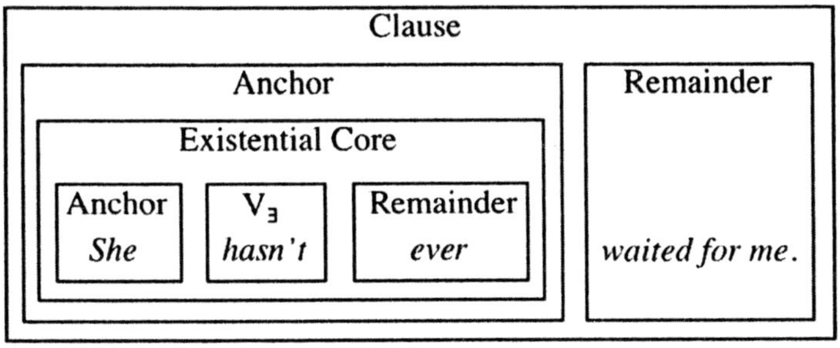

Figure 8.20

(21) a. *Me she has seldom waited for.*
b. *Seldom has she waited for me.*
c. **Me seldom has she waited for.*

5.6. Questions

Though it has sometimes been described as the question-forming rule of English, Subject-Auxiliary Inversion is neither limited to questions nor observed in all types of them. Its appearance in questions manifests a broader pattern of non-default anchoring in expressions with the basic configuration in Figure 8.20. There are two main options: the non-default anchor can either be a question word, based on the formative WH,[31] or else the existential verb itself. I will refer to these two general types as **content** questions and **polarity** questions.

A content question has the layered systemic organization shown in Figure 8.21. The only difference from 8.20 is that the anchor at both the core and clause levels (the anchor within the anchor) is the question word *where* rather than the subject. This makes perfect sense given the characterization of an

---

30 Hence this account is quite consistent with Goldberg's characterization of inversion as a radial category with "non-prototypical sentence" as its prototype, a prototypical sentence being positive, declarative, and assertive (Goldberg 2006: ch. 8).

31 For the meaning of WH, see Langacker 2001d.

anchor: an instruction to interpret the clausal proposition with respect to a certain aspect of the situation described. In this case it is viewed in relation to the event's location and is interpreted as a request to specify that location.

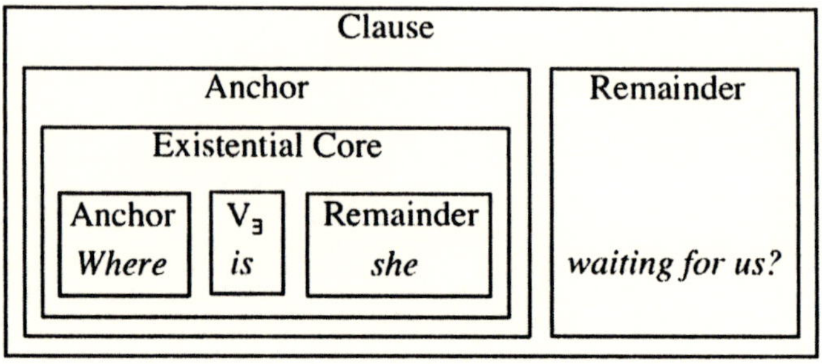

Figure 8.21

Of course, inversion does not occur in content questions when the question word happens to be the subject, as in Figure 8.22. The reason should be obvious: this is precisely the case where the question word assuming the role of anchor has that role in any case by virtue of being the subject. That is, *who* in 8.22 is both the default anchor (in its guise as subject) and the special anchor characteristic of content questions (the focus of interest which frames the clausal proposition). The question word's occurrence in anchor position is therefore doubly motivated. Or to put it another way, the question word's appearance in anchor position does not result in the subject being displaced when the question word itself is the subject.

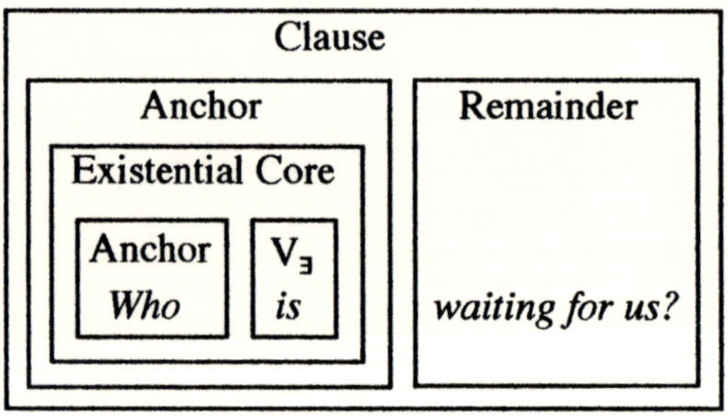

Figure 8.22

That leaves us with polarity ("yes/no") questions. In this case the subject follows the existential verb even though it is not preceded by an alternate anchor. The reason, I suggest, is that the existential verb is itself the anchor, as shown in Figure 8.23. Just as the existential core functions as clause-level anchor, the existential verb functions as core-level anchor. Derivatively, it is thus the clause-level anchor as well (anchor within the anchor). This makes perfect sense semantically. In polarity questions, the main concern is with existence per se. It is thus the existential predication that frames the proposition and serves as natural point of access for presenting the situation described.

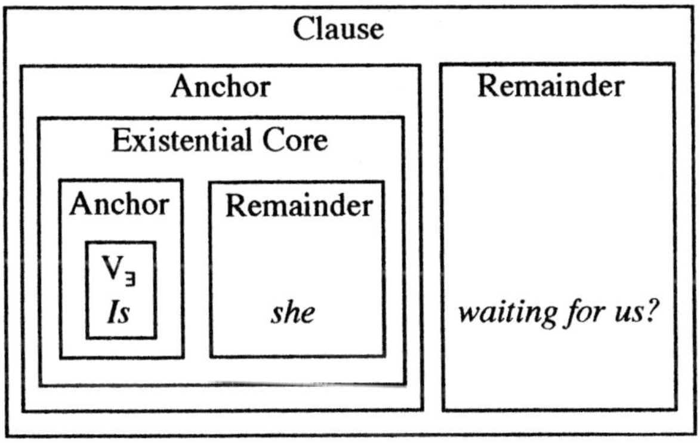

Figure 8.23

A final matter to consider is the occurrence of auxiliary *do* in questions. Because questions involve negotiation, *do* is expected to appear in them, given its characterization as indicating negotiation (as well as unqualified existence and neutral perspective). And it does, as we see in (22)a. Moreover, it has to used in such expressions – the lexical verb cannot be used alone, as (22)b is ungrammatical in modern English. The lexical verb can indeed function as the existential verb bearing tense, but only in neutral statements (e.g. *She waited for us*), where negotiation is not involved.

(22) a. *Did she wait for us?*
b. **Waited she for us?*
c. *Who waited for us?*
d. **Who did wait for us?*
e. *Who didn't wait for us?*
f. *Who* DID *wait for us?*
g. *Where did she wait for us?*
h. **Where waited she for us?*

But it is not true that the lexical verb never functions as the existential verb in questions. It has this function in subject questions, as in (22)c. Is this consistent with the earlier description, according to which v assumes existential function just in cases of non-negotiation? Actually it is, because in content questions existence per se is not the main concern. A question like (22)c **presupposes** the existence of the clausal process – to the effect that someone waited for us – and merely requests that the subject be identified. Thus existence is not itself being negotiated. But questioning is not the only factor in negotiation: there is also polarity. So even a subject question involves negotiation when the polarity is negative or affirmative (rather than simple positive). In this case *do* does appear, as (22)e–f.

However, the lexical verb only functions as the existential verb in **subject** questions, not any other sort of content question. We thus have (22)g, with *do*; (22)h is ungrammatical. I take this as reflecting the limited scope of the preemptive pattern whereby v assumes existential function. As stated earlier, the preemption is narrowly defined as affecting the expected sequence *do* + v in the absence of negotiation. That is, preemption by v is limited to one particular place in the auxiliary system, in cases of neutral polarity (positive) where *do* and v would otherwise be adjacent. This is the case in both statements and subject questions, with the consequence that *She waited* and *Who waited?* occur in lieu of **She did wait* and **Who did wait?*. But it is not the case in other kinds of questions, where the subject follows the existential verb, as in (22)g. We do not then expect the sequence *do* + v because the subject intervenes.[32]

This is obviously neither a complete nor a definitive analysis of the English auxiliary. I consider it exploratory, from both the theoretical and the descriptive standpoint. Theoretically, it represents a first extensive attempt to explore the systemic aspect of language and how to deal with it. Descriptively, I think it shows the potential insight of a systemic approach. I have tried to demonstrate that – despite its complexity and many idiosyncrasies – the auxiliary system is actually both natural and very reasonable. Its complexity is due to the fact that many factors come into play simultaneously. But when these are examined individually, in each case we find clear systemic organization and functional motivation. As for the auxiliary's many idiosyncrasies, I have argued that these too have a definite functional basis. While they are not predictable in any absolute sense, neither are they arbitrary: each has a cogent rationale in terms of the overall system and the functions served. In sum, I have come to appreciate that the English auxiliary performs its functions with elegance and efficiency.

32 Thus we may not want to say that negotiation is inherent in the meaning of *do* per se. Rather, the occurrence of *do* merely **indicates** negotiation by virtue of its preeemption being limited to cases of non-negotiation.

Chapter 9
Aspects of the grammar of finite clauses

This chapter considers relationships between the internal structure of finite clauses, especially in regard to grounding, and their external grammar, where they function as complements to predicates of propositional attitude. Relevant at both levels is a general cognitive model fundamental to embodied experience: the control cycle, first introduced in Chapter 5 (§ 4). In particular, the striving for **epistemic control** is pivotal to the semantics and grammar of clauses and clause combinations.

1. Finite clauses and the control cycle

As was shown in Figure 5.5, the control cycle comprises a number of elements and a number of phases. The elements are an actor, its dominion (the region over which it exercises control), a target, and the field (the region of potential interaction). There are four basic phases: baseline, potential, action, and result. The baseline situation is static. The actor is in control of various entities, each of which has some established place in its dominion. When the target appears within the actor's field, it creates the potential for their interaction. In force-dynamic terms, this is a situation of tension, as opposed to the stasis of the baseline. Since the target impinges on the actor's field, it has to be dealt with in some manner. The action phase consists of the actor effecting its interaction with the target through the exertion of force. The result is that the target is now in the actor's dominion, subject to its control. The situation is once more static, but different from the baseline.

In suitably abstracted form, we can see the control cycle as being utterly ubiquitous in our own experience. It occurs at the level of bodily functions (where the relevant dominion is the actor's own body). For instance, getting hungry and seeing an apple creates a state of tension, resolved by taking and eating it; the result is a full belly and the cessation of hunger. Externally, at the physical level, we respond to needs and opportunities by acquiring objects and assigning them a particular place in the structure of our daily lives. For example, I might buy a new shirt, hang it in the closet, and wear it on appropriate occasions. Socially, we encounter new individuals and achieve a kind of control by establishing a stable relationship entailing definite expectations and obligations (i.e. we incorporate and situate individuals in our social dominion). At the cognitive level, we entertain new ideas, assess them for their possible validity, and resolve the matter by either accepting them in our conception of reality or else excluding them. It is not an exaggeration to say that being *alive* is to function as actor in control cycles, interacting with the environment to gain control over certain facets of it. By its very nature, life is force-dynamic (Talmy 1988). We use the term *life force* in reference to organisms expending energy to acquire resources, minimally for growth, renewal, and self-maintenance. Life is inherently dynamic. Permanent stasis is *death*.

We have seen that the control cycle has broad linguistic applicability. The characterization of possessives in terms of reference point, target, and dominion (Chapter 4) can be seen as a special case. Chapter 6 examined the cycle's role in nominal and clausal grounding, at both the effective and epistemic levels. It also figures in the semantic description of a wide and varied range of lexical items. In regard to possession, for example, *want*, *get*, and *have* pertain respectively to the potential, action, and result phases. With perception verbs, the phases provide a basis for distinguishing subtly different senses. The five basic verbs – *see*, *hear*, *feel*, *taste*, *smell* – can all be used for either the action of achieving perceptual contact (e.g. *I finally managed to see it*) or the stable experience that results (*I see it very clearly*). Additionally, representing the potential phase, *feel*, *taste*, and *smell* can describe activity preparatory to achieving perceptual contact (e.g. *I smelled the liquid, but it was completely odorless*).

Here our interest lies in epistemic control, i.e. the knowledge of events and propositions. In this case the actor is a conceptualizer (C) and the dominion is C's conception of reality. The epistemic control cycle is manifested both **within** a clause, as an aspect of grounding, and **between** clauses, as an aspect of complementation. Though it is basically similar at these two levels, there are also some crucial differences, one of which is the nature of the target. For grounding, the target is the profiled clausal **process** (an event or situation), represented here as **p**. With complementation, on the other hand, the target is the **proposition** (P) expressed by a finite complement clause (including its grounding). This contrast implies a difference in the nature of the epistemic dominion. For grounding, "reality" is the established history of events and situations: what C accepts as having occurred, up through the present moment. But with complementation, "reality" is the set of propositions accepted as being valid.[1] The interaction between these two levels of epistemic assessment is a major focus in what follows.

---

1 This is the distinction between **basic** and **elaborated reality**, discussed in Chapter 6 (§ 4) and Chapter 8 (§ 3.5).

With complementation, the epistemic control cycle is central to the semantic description of matrix predicates. The predicates in (1) represent the result phase. They indicate that the complement proposition has already been established and accepted as part of the subject's conception of reality, i.e. they are under the subject's epistemic control. Because they describe a stable situation, they function as imperfectives, hence occur in the simple present tense, as in (1) a–b. They differ as to "factivity" (the speaker's acceptance of the proposition), how the subject came to accept the proposition as true (e.g. via persuasion), and the subject's degree of commitment to it. For instance, *believe* and *think* imply a lower level of commitment than *sure* and *certain*, as shown in (1) c–d. The latter have a certain force-dynamic component, since they indicate that the present attitude would be hard to change. Nonetheless, they describe a constant situation where the proposition is already part of accepted reality – they do not specify any current struggle for resolution or maintenance.

(1) a. *He {knows / believes / thinks / realizes / accepts} that the earth is round.*
b. *He is {sure / certain / persuaded / convinced} that wealth implies virtue.*
c. *He definitely {believes / thinks} the earth is round, but he isn't absolutely {sure / certain} – you might be able to change his mind.*
d. **He is {sure / certain} the earth is round, but it's not definitely the case that he {believes / thinks} it is.*

The verbs in (2) pertain to the action phase, describing what the subject does by way of achieving epistemic control. While they vary as to the degree of volition and effort exerted, all these verbs designate mental activity resulting in the complement proposition being brought into the subject's conception of reality. Consequently they are perfective.

(2) *She {learned / discovered / decided / concluded / realized / determined / found out / figured out} that his whole story was a pack of lies.*

As noted in Chapter 5 (§ 4.2), predicates representing the potential phase give evidence for dividing it into three successive stages: the initial **formulation** of a proposition, as a potential object of consideration; the **assessment** stage, where its status vis-à-vis reality becomes an active issue; and an **inclination** stage, where the subject inclines toward a positive or negative judgment without yet being able to definitely resolve the matter. Overall, these stages involve the tension of entertaining a proposition whose status is uncertain, as well as preparation for the mental act of finally accepting or rejecting it.

(3) a. *It is {possible / conceivable / feasible / imaginable} that a politician might occasionally distort the truth.* [formulation]

b. *She {wondered / considered / asked / was unsure / was undecided / was unclear} whether anything could be done to alleviate the situation.* [assessment]

c. *He {suspects / believes / supposes / thinks / figures / reckons} the judge will never agree to reduce his sentence.* [inclination]

We need to distinguish between alternate senses of the same verb that pertain to different phases. The most obvious example is *believe*, which has well-established uses corresponding to the inclination, action, and result phases. These are respectively exemplified in (4). *Believe* exhibits distinct grammatical behavior in these three senses. When pertaining to the inclination and result phases, as in (4)a and (4)c, it behaves imperfectively, whereas the action sense in (4)b is perfective, designating admission into the subject's reality conception. Distinguishing the inclination and result phases is the contrast between *believe so* and *believe it* (Lindholm 1969). In (4)a, *believe* is interchangeable with verbs like *suspect* and *imagine* (which also occur with *so*). Despite the inclination (which may be quite strong), a decision has not yet been made. It has been made in (4)c, where *believe* is interchangeable with predicates like *be sure* and *be convinced.*

(4) a. *She believes he should retire, and I believe so too.* [inclination]
b. *I told him that whisky is good for you, and he believed it.* [action]
c. *He firmly believes that God is female, but I don't believe it.* [result]

Reinforcing the importance of these stages in the overall assessment process is "negative raising", where negation in the main clause yields a meaning quite comparable to that of a corresponding sentence with negation in the subordinate clause instead. The sentences in (5)a, for example, are roughly the same in meaning. Lindholm (1969) noted that negative raising is characteristic of *believe so*, but not *believe it*. On the latter interpretation (indicating acceptance of a proposition rather than inclination), the corresponding sentences are not at all equivalent, as seen in (5)b. Sumnicht (2001) argues persuasively that negative raising is only found with the inclination stage, where the matter is still at issue. In (5)c we observe that the action stage precludes it. On Sumnicht's account, it occurs when the matter is still in doubt, the existence of an inclination is presupposed, and the absence of other salient content causes the force of negation to be focused on the polarity of the inclination. It is thus analogous to (5)d, where negation would generally be construed as reversing the polarity of the affect – from liking to disliking – rather than simply denying the liking. Under this construal the negation is comparable to the polarity reversing prefix *dis-*.

(5) a. *I don't believe she has any children.* [inclination]
= I believe she doesn't have any children.
b. *I don't believe (the theory) that God is female.* [result]
≠ I believe (the theory) that God isn't female.
c. *I didn't believe (his story) that he had to work late.* [action]
≠ I believed (his story) that he didn't have to work late.
d. *He doesn't like it. = He dislikes it.*

The postulation of these various stages is thus supported by both semantic and grammatical evidence. As shown in Figure 9.1, the epistemic control cycle is also usefully viewed as consisting in three locally stable phases – formulation, inclination, and result – connected by two transition phases. In the formulation phase, P is merely in the field of C's awareness, as something to be dealt with. A process of assessment leads to some degree of inclination to admit P into C's conception of reality (or else to specifically exclude it). This inclination, represented by a double dashed arrow, represents a kind of provisional judgment. It is locally stable (note that the predicates in (3)c are imperfective), yet force-dynamic in the sense that the status of P vis-à-vis reality is still at issue and has yet to be resolved. Metaphorically, we can think of the inclination stage as a kind of plateau in the climb toward certain knowledge (a place to pause while searching for a path to the summit). The action phase constitutes the final judgment, leading to the result of P being either established in D or excluded from it.

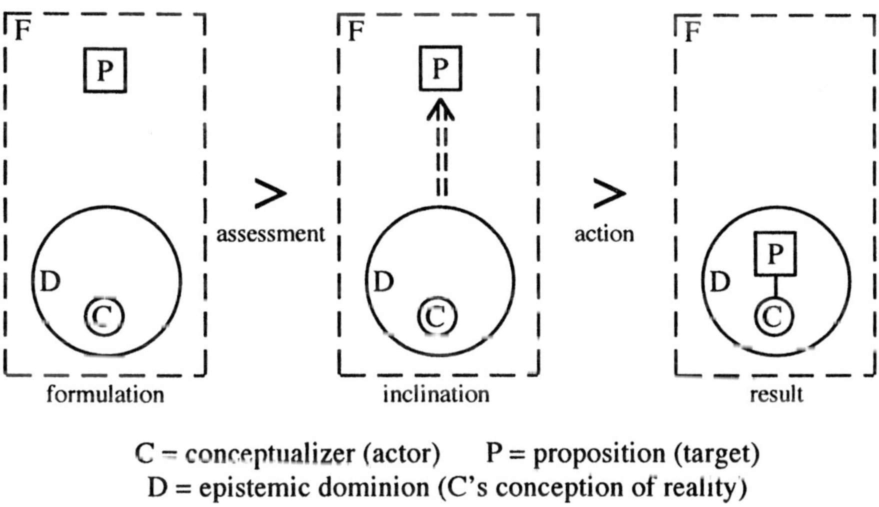

Figure 9.1

Typical inclination predicates (like *think*, *believe (so)*, *suppose*, *suspect*, *imagine*, *figure*) and result predicates (like *know*, *believe (it)*, *realize*, *sure*, *certain*, *convinced*) are represented in Figure 9.2. An inclination predicate profiles a provisional judgment about P characterized in terms of the manner and degree of inclination to accept P into C's epistemic dominion. C is the trajector, coded by the subject. P is the landmark, expressed by the subordinate clause. The double arrow indicates a force-dynamic relationship, yet the situation is locally stable in that the force is only latent or potential (hence the arrow is dashed rather than solid) – it is not currently being expended to bring about a final judgment. If I say that *A suspects B*, I am describing a stable attitude (one item in A's inventory of provisional opinions), not anything A is doing at the moment; indeed, A is probably not even thinking about B right now.

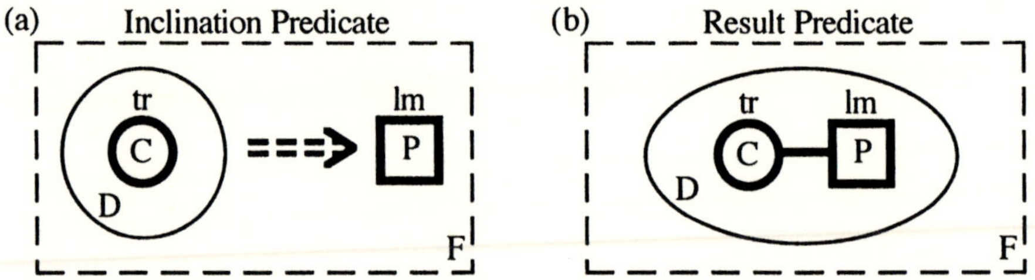

Figure 9.2

Even from this very partial survey, it is evident that verbs taking finite complements are numerous and varied, allowing fine-grained distinctions pertaining to any phase in the epistemic control cycle.[2] They contrast in these respects with the options permitted clause-internally as part of the grammaticized grounding system. Of the five phases in Figure 9.1, just two are represented here: inclination and result, as indicated by the presence vs. the absence of a modal. Only with the former is there any appreciable semantic differentiation, as the modals specify various kinds and degrees of inclination.

(6) a. *She {may / might / could / should / will / must} be upset.* [inclination]
b. *She {is / was} upset.* [result]

Modals can thus be characterized as a special sort of inclination predicate. As Sumnicht observes, the epistemic modals all behave like inclination predicates with respect to the "negative raising" phenomenon. That is, although negation combines grammatically with a modal (as indicated by intonational

2 These fine-grained distinctions are further discussed in Chapter 10.

grouping, as well as contractions), negating the modal is effectively equivalent to negating its verbal complement:

(7) a. *She might not / be finished. = She might / not be finished.*
b. *You shouldn't / have any problem. = You should / not have any problem.*
c. *They must not / be at home. = They must / not be at home.*

The two basic options are shown in Figure 9.3. Comparison with Figure 9.2 reveals the similarity to the corresponding lexical predicates but also some important differences. The first is the nature of the target: a proposition (P) for lexical predicates, a process (**p**) for grounding elements. There is also a difference in profiling. Whereas a lexical process profiles the epistemic assessment, with a grounding element this is offstage and subjectively construed – it is **p** that is profiled as the onstage focus of attention. Finally, they differ in regard to the conceptualizer. While C of course varies with lexical predicates, it is typically the trajector (as in Figure 9.2) or another clausal participant. But with grounding, on the other hand, the relevant conceptualizer is typically identified with the speaker. We have seen, however, that their identification is only a special case, albeit the default.[3] The following discussion examines this matter more carefully.

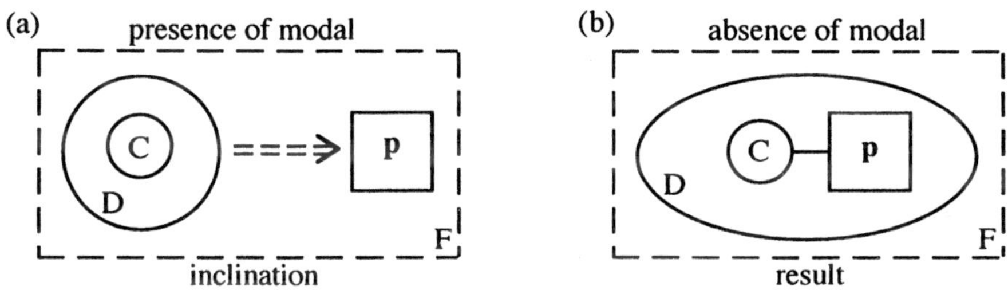

Figure 9.3

2. The virtuality of clausal grounding

Clause internally, the target of grounding is simply a process – an event or situation. Clausal grounding not only presupposes our ability to apprehend a process, but further reflects the capacity to assume an epistemic stance in regard to it: viewing it as immediate or non-immediate, real or unreal. It indicates a measure of independence from the here and now of present circumstances. In

3 In Chapter 6 (§ 4), this was referred to as the Great Simplification.

addition to what is real and immediate, our mental world comprises processes that are non-immediate and/or unreal. Still, the targets at this level are simply events and situations, and reality (D) is just the history of events that have occurred and situations that have obtained, up through the moment of speaking.

Of course, if a conceptualizer adopts an epistemic stance toward an event or situation, that itself constitutes an event or situation at a higher level of organization. Pivotal to human intelligence is our capacity to operate at this higher level. That is, the situation of a conceptualizer adopting an epistemic stance toward a process can itself function as an object of conception toward which an epistemic stance can be adopted. And that itself is a situation subject to epistemic assessment at a higher level, and so on. The external grammar of finite clauses pertains to these higher levels of organization, where the targets of assessment are not just events or situations, but the propositions expressed by such clauses. Thus, as shown in Figure 9.2, a result or inclination predicate profiles an epistemic stance toward a complement proposition (P), which itself incorporates an epistemic stance toward a process (**p**), as in Figure 9.3. At this higher level, a conception of reality (D) consists of a set of propositions.

This leads us to an essential point. Namely, a finite clause and its grounding do not, in and of themselves, specify the speaker's actual epistemic stance in regard to the grounded process, **p**. They define a proposition, in which the process has a certain epistemic status, but they do not establish the epistemic status of the proposition itself, as a higher-order object of conception. As Achard (1998) has correctly noted, a finite clause merely presents a proposition as a **candidate** for incorporation in a view of reality. It does not per se assert or establish its inclusion in the speaker's actual conception of reality. Listed in (8) are a few examples where the speaker produces a finite clause – *they will finish the project on time* – while making no commitment to the validity (the reality) of the proposition it expresses.

(8) a. *Perhaps they will finish the project on time.*
b. *It's not the case that they will finish the project on time.*
c. *They will finish the project on time?*
d. *Joe believes they will finish the project on time.*
e. *They will finish the project on time. And I will be elected pope.*

To put it another way, in and of themselves a finite clause and its grounding evoke the epistemic configurations in Figure 9.3 as **virtual** entities, as objects of contemplation. In forming a finite clause, the speaker imagines or conjures up the situation of the profiled process having the epistemic status depicted in diagram 3(a) or 3(b), without however identifying that situation as being the speaker's **actual** one. In (8)a, for instance, the speaker conjures up the situation where the prediction that *they will finish the project on time* is appropriate, reflecting the speaker's true assessment; however the adverb *perhaps* indicates that this situation itself is **only** an imagined one, possible but not yet realized. Similarly, (8)b specifically denies the actuality of the situation where saying *they will finish the project on time* is a valid description of the speaker's epistemic judgment. And so on.

Let me point out that the evocation of **virtual** or **fictive** entities is extremely prevalent in language, even for purposes of describing **actuality** (Dapremont 2001; Langacker 1999d, 2005b; Matsumoto 1996, 1997; Sweetser 1997; Talmy 1996). Some examples are given in (9). The Norwegian mentioned in (9)a is virtual (non-referential), being conjured up just to characterize the nature of Phil's desire. In (9)b, the profiled situation *I have a dog* is fictively invoked just for purposes of negating it, i.e. excluding it from actuality. The three cars referred to in (9)c are fictive, conjured up to characterize a type of event – the event type *own three cars* – one instance of which is ascribed to a small number of people, themselves fictive. No actual people are referred to, even though the sentence purports to describe what the world is actually like. The generic statement in (9)d profiles a virtual event involving a virtual kitten, being conjured up as a generalization about the world's inherent structure. Sentence (9)e likewise makes a generalization, but not a generic (or "structural") one. Instead, it makes a local generalization over contingent occurrences, specifying something they all have in common. The profiled event, *a heckler shouted out an insult*, expresses the abstract commonality of four such occurrences – the occurrences were actual, hence the generalization pertains to actuality, yet the profiled event and its participants are fictive.[4]

(9) a. *Phil wants to marry a Norwegian – provided that she is thin, rich, sexy, and blonde.*
b. *I don't have a dog.*
c. *Few people own three cars.*
d. *A kitten is born with blue eyes.*
e. *Four times during the speech, a heckler shouted out an insult.*

Since reference to virtual entities is commonplace and well-established on independent grounds, invoking it for the characterization of grounding elements should not be considered inherently suspicious or in any way problematic. Indeed, it is necessary, as already indicated. A finite clause – through its grounding elements – does ascribe an epistemic status to the profiled situation vis-à-vis a conceptualizer and a conception of reality, thereby defining a

4 Observe that even though there might have been four hecklers and four insults, the nominals describing them are singular.

proposition. However, as shown in (8), it evokes C and C's epistemic dominion as virtual entities, not necessarily identified with the actual speaker and the speaker's actual conception of reality. We can relate this to the notion that propositions are thought of as objective entities, independent of any particular conceptualizer. According to this idealized cognitive model, the same proposition is available for inspection by different conceptualizers, such that each, from his own perspective, can assess its validity.

We need to spell this out with greater technical precision. A finite clause profiles a process – indicated by boldface **p** – and specifies its epistemic status vis-à-vis a conceptualizer (C). Internally, the clause does not specify any particular conceptualizer, but rather invokes C as a virtual entity by way of generalizing over all potential conceptualizers. We can say that **p** is **virtually grounded**. The process **p** is **actually grounded** when C is identified with an **actual** conceptualizer, by default the actual speaker. This produces a **proposition**. Since the process **p** is now situated in time and reality with reference to a particular conceptualizer, it has an **address** which distinguishes it from other instances of the same process type. This address makes it possible to assess the proposition's validity. Crucially, however, such assessment is still required. Knowing the address – knowing where **p** is supposedly located in relation to the speaker's epistemic dominion – is not the same as knowing whether the speaker accepts the proposition as conforming to his actual view of the world. As we saw in (8), the production of a finite clause does not per se indicate that the speaker subscribes to its contents.

To accept a candidate proposition as valid requires a further judgment, representing another level of conceptual organization. We **formulate** propositions all the time, for myriad purposes. But formulating a proposition is not the same as **embracing** or **asserting** it. When it is merely formulated, a proposition itself (despite its actual grounding) has a kind of virtuality, being conjured up for any purpose whatever. The further act of embracing the proposition is needed to incorporate it as part of how the speaker actually views the world. This process of formulation, assessment, and acceptance is of course another manifestation of the epistemic control cycle. It operates at a level of organization pertaining to the external grammar of a finite clause – how it is put to use in larger contexts, as in (8). Grounding predications also manifest the epistemic control cycle, but at a lower level of conceptual organization, pertaining to the internal structure of a finite clause. The grounding of a process creates a proposition by giving it a virtual epistemic status. The proposition can then be evaluated to determine whether this virtual epistemic status should be accepted as its actual one.

We can describe the difference between formulating and embracing a proposition in terms of how strongly the actual speaker identifies with the virtual conceptualizer, C, invoked by a grounding element. In **weak identification**, the virtual ground – including C, D, and F (the field) – is assimilated to the actual ground just for purposes of giving the profiled process, **p**, an address (thereby creating a proposition), without however losing its virtuality. I show this in Figure 9.4(a), where C_0, D_0, and F_0 stand for the actual speaker (the initial conceptualizer), the speaker's actual conception of reality, and the relevant field. For the correspondences involved in weak identification I will use single dotted lines. **Strong identification** will be indicated by double correspondence lines, as in Figure 9.4(b). Here the virtual ground loses its virtuality, being fully assimilated to the actual ground. They can therefore be collapsed, as shown in 9.4(c). Diagrams (b) and (c) are notational variants, "exploded" and "compacted" representations of the same configuration. Strong identification has the consequence that the epistemic status of the profiled process **p**, as specified by the grounding element, constitutes the status which the speaker actually ascribes to it.

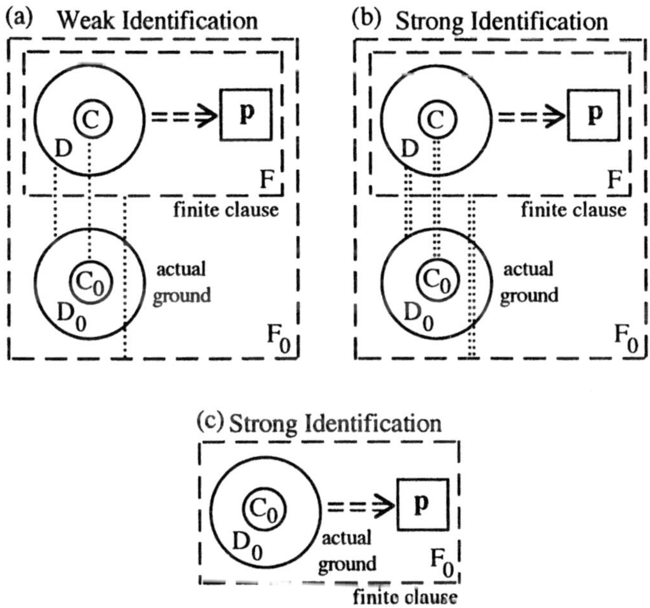

Figure 9.4

Let us work through an example. Suppose I say *They will finish the project on time* and mean it – I am making an actual prediction of the event's occurrence. The profiled event (**p**) is coded by the finite clause minus its grounding element, *will*. At this level of organization, summarized in (10)a, the process description (*they finish the project on time*) merely indicates a **type** of event. In the absence of grounding (which specifies a temporal and epistemic location), it is compatible with any number of **instances** of the type.

(10) a. *they finish the project on time* **[p]**
profiled process (type)
ungrounded

b. *they will finish the project on time* [C [**p**]]
finite clause
generalized (virtual) C
virtually grounded process (instance)

c. *they will finish the project on time* C_0---[-C [**p**]]
finite clause
actual C (by default, the actual speaker)
actually grounded process (instance)
proposition (formulated)
weak identification of C with C_0
virtual epistemic status of **p**

d. *they will finish the project on time* C_0==[=C [**p**]] = [C_0 [**p**]]
finite clause
actual C (by default, the actual speaker)
actually grounded process (instance)
proposition (embraced)
strong identification of C with C_0
actual epistemic status of **p**

By adding grounding, in this case the proximal modal *will*, we obtain a full finite clause, as summarized in (10)b. In and of itself, the grounding element evokes the ground – including the conceptualizer, C – only in generalized fashion, as a virtual entity. That is, grounding is deictic in nature, and as for any such element, the deictic center it invokes is only virtual (or "floating") until it is anchored to the here and now of a specific conceptualizer. Another way to say this is that (10)b corresponds to a finite clause as a purely linguistic object, independent of any particular use.

When a finite clause is actually used in discourse, the virtual conceptualizer is at least weakly identified with an actual one, by default the actual speaker, C_0. This does not entail any change in form, but nonetheless has the consequences described in (10)c. The address provided by the deictic anchoring produces a proposition capable of being evaluated for its possible validity. Still, so long as C is only weakly identified with the actual speaker, the proposition is only formulated (not embraced), so the epistemic status ascribed to **p** is only virtual. *They will finish the project on time* expresses a proposition of this sort – formulated but not embraced – in all the examples in (8).

Finally, strong identification of C with C_0 produces the situation characterized in (10)d. The speaker not only formulates the proposition but embraces it, so the epistemic status ascribed to **p** by the clausal grounding is presented by the speaker as its actual status. This is the situation portrayed in Figure 9.4(c). I say *They will finish the project on time* and actually mean it. In the diagram, **p** is the profiled event (*they finish the project on time*), and the double dashed arrow represents the inclination expressed by *will*.

The speaker's strong identification with C, as in Figure 9.4(c), is perhaps a kind of default. Still, it is not automatic, and a long series of factors are capable of blocking it, so that the grounding effected by the finite clause remains wholly or partially virtual. For the default to fully emerge, the finite clause must be the main clause, not presented as the view of another conceptualizer. The clause must be positive, and must not be qualified by an adverb (e.g. *perhaps*) that removes it from actuality. The utterance of the clause has to be embedded in a speech act of assertion, not (say) one of questioning. Moreover, it must be an actual act of assertion, not a virtual one, as in (8)e, where the speaker only pretends to assert the initial clause. And so on.

Let us contrast this actual assertion of the clause with the qualified assertion in (8)a, *Perhaps they will finish the project on time.* The adverb *perhaps* indicates that the speaker is not quite ready to make the straightforward prediction that they will finish on time. *Perhaps* is itself a kind of modal expressing a degree of inclination. It is not however grammaticized as an inherent part of the characterization of English finite clauses; instead it is external or at least peripheral to a clause, hence optional. Its effect is to add a layer of epistemic insulation, shielding the speaker from the full implications of making a bald assertion.

We can treat this as a case of weakly identifying the virtual and actual grounds, as shown in Figure 9.5. On the default interpretation of a sentence like this, the conceptualizer, C, is identified with the actual speaker – it is the speaker whose conception of reality is at issue. Also, the temporal location of **p** (in this case, future) is calculated with respect to the speaker's actual temporal location. Nevertheless, the reality conception, D, with respect to which **p** constitutes a prediction (prediction being coded by modal *will*) is prevented by *perhaps* from being fully identified with the speaker's actual one. The sentence indicates that the speaker can envisage a situation where, on the basis of all relevant considerations (F), **p** can be projected from D. But it is not now actually the case that, on the basis of all relevant considerations (F_0), **p** can be projected in this manner from D_0.

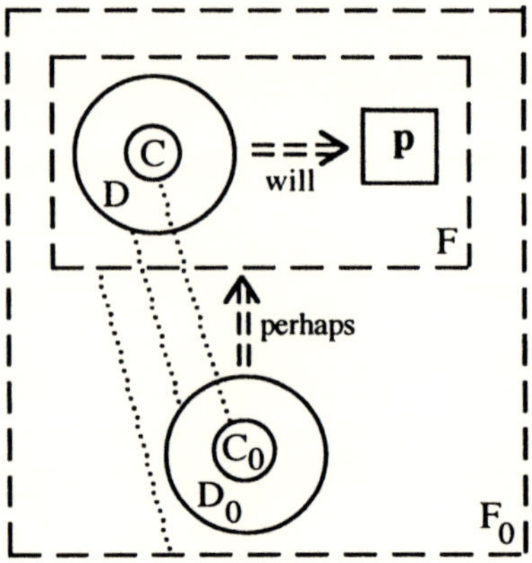

Figure 9.5

3. Finite clause complements

The need to distinguish weak and strong identification is especially apparent in the description of finite clause complements. Still confining our attention to predicates of propositional attitude with personal subjects, we can start with an observation by Achard (1998): that the speaker's role in conceptualizing the main clause proposition is parallel to the subject's role in conceptualizing the subordinate clause proposition. This is shown in Figure 9.6, where P_0 and P_1 represent the propositions expressed by the main and subordinate clauses, respectively. Just as the main clause subject, C_1, is a conceptualizer with respect to proposition P_1, so the speaker, C_0, is a conceptualizer with respect to P_0. They differ in that C_1 and the relationship it bears to P_1 are onstage as focused objects of conception, whereas C_0, in its apprehension of P_0, remains offstage as the implicit subject of conception.

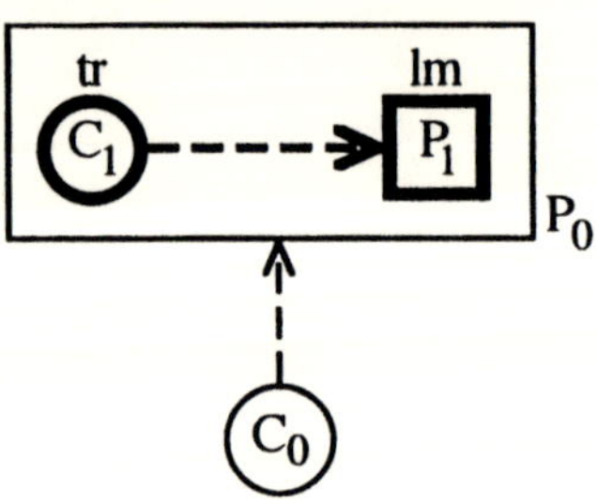

Figure 9.6

In (11), for example, P_1 is the proposition *Alice is unhappy*, while P_0 is the proposition that *Joe suspects P_1*. The onstage relationship profiled by the main clause consists of its subject, *Joe*, entertaining a propositional attitude in regard to P_1. Analogously, the speaker entertains a propositional attitude in regard to P_0, but one that is offstage and subjectively construed.

(11) *Joe suspects Alice is unhappy.*

However, the main clause subject, C_1, is not the only one who entertains proposition P_1 – the speaker also does, in his role as offstage conceptualizer for the meaning of the entire sentence. This leads to a crucial observation in regard to clausal grounding: for the most part (at least in English), a finite clause describes the proposition it expresses from the vantage point of the speaker, even when it represents the proposition entertained by another conceptualizer. The matter is complex and cannot be explored here in any detail (see Langacker 1991: § 6.2.2). A few examples will have to suffice.

With a perfective complement, such as *help* in (12), a modal is future oriented. Suppose that on Monday Jack says "I may help you Wednesday". On Tuesday I can then report this with the statement *Jack said he may help us tomorrow*, since the helping is still future with respect to the time of my utterance. On Thursday, however, I cannot use the statement *Jack said he may help us yesterday*, since *yesterday* is necessarily past relative to the actual time of speaking. Even though the event grounded by *may* is future relative to Jack, who first put forth the proposition, it is past relative to actual speaker. The temporal vantage point of the actual speaker is the one that counts in determining the import of *may* in the report of Jack's utterance.

(12) Context: On Monday Jack says "I may help you Wednesday."
a. On Tuesday: *Jack said he may help us tomorrow.*
b. On Thursday: **Jack said he may help us yesterday.*

In (13), Jill says at noon: "I'm hungry. Let's get some lunch." In the evening I can report this with the statement *Jill said she was hungry*, since the hunger in question is past relative to the time of my utterance I am describing the proposition Jill expressed, but have to do so relative to my own vantage point. I cannot report it instead with the statement *Jill said she is hungry*, since the proposition Jill put forth only covered a brief time span.

(13) Context: At noon Jill says "I'm hungry. Let's get some lunch."
a. In the evening: *Jill said she was hungry*
b. In the evening: **Jill said she is hungry.*

Note, however, that if *hungry* is changed to *pregnant*, as in (14), then either tense can be used in my later report of what Jill said. Jill being pregnant is a situation long enough to endure through both the time of the original statement and the time of the later report. If I report it as in (14)a, I am taking Jill's earlier vantage point into account, and describing the situation obtaining at the moment of her utterance, but I use the past tense because the situation at that moment is in the past from my vantage point. On the other hand, in (14)b I describe the same ongoing situation as it currently appears from my own vantage point.

(14) Context: On Monday Jill says "I'm pregnant."
a. On Tuesday: *Jill said she was pregnant.*
b. On Tuesday: *Jill said she is pregnant.*

Returning now to (11), we can note that unhappiness is a situation that has the potential to endure indefinitely, so even if Joe voiced his suspicion on Monday, I can report it on Tuesday by saying *Joe suspects Alice is unhappy.* The proposition entertained by Joe ascribes to Alice a mental state that is present from my current vantage point as actual speaker.

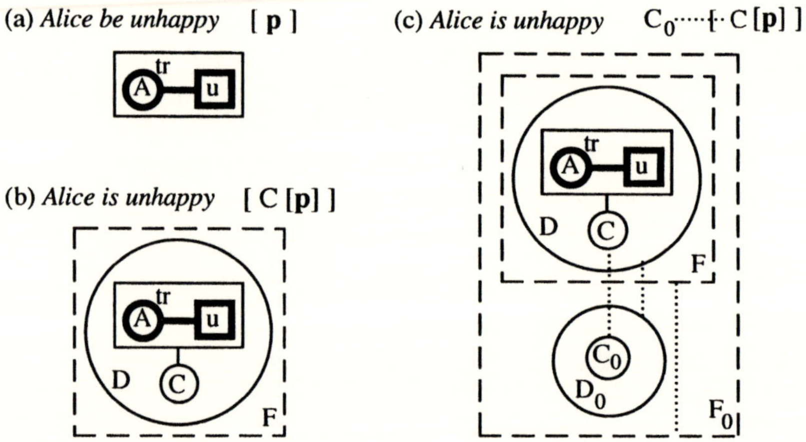

Figure 9.7

Let us work through this example step by step, starting with the subordinate finite clause, *Alice is unhappy.* As shown in Figure 9.7(a), it profiles the relationship of Alice (A) exhibiting a certain property, in this case the mental state of being unhappy (u). This relationship, viewed as enduring through time, constitutes the profiled process (**p**). Since the clause is finite, the process is grounded, so in generalized terms it invokes a conceptualizer (C), C's epistemic dominion (D), and the field (F). This is shown in diagram (b). The grounding consists of present tense (or epistemic immediacy), the absence of a modal, and also the third-person singular inflection of *is*. Diagrammatically, I have only represented the absence of a modal; its effect is to indicate that **p** is part of C's conception of reality (D). Lastly, as shown in diagram (c), the virtual ground abstractly invoked by the finite clause is weakly identified in discourse with the actual ground. The proposition expressed is one that the speaker **formulates**, and it is characterized from the vantage point of the actual ground. However, the speaker does not necessarily **embrace** this proposition. In (11), it is only put forth as something toward which the main clause subject (*Joe*) inclines. In asserting (11), the speaker takes no actual position regarding its validity.

The point is subtle yet fundamental, so it bears reiteration. In a sentence like (11), there are two conceptualizers with respect to the proposition P_1 expressed by the complement clause. On one level, it constitutes the proposition toward which the main clause subject (C_1) inclines. It is C_1's conceptualization of P_1 that the main clause profiles. At the same time, the speaker (C_0) also apprehends P_1 as an inherent part of conceptualizing C_1's propositional attitude toward it. This is not at all problematic. Recall that our idealized cognitive model for a proposition includes the notion that it is sufficiently autonomous to be viewed by different conceptualizers, each of whom can assess it from his own vantage point. While a sentence like (11) describes the assessment made by the main clause subject, the speaker also apprehends the proposition from his own vantage point in the actual ground. The speaker's apprehension is the one explicitly coded in the finite clause. However, the actual speaker, C_0, only weakly identifies with the virtual conceptualizer, C. While C_0 formulates the proposition entertained by C_1, he does not necessarily embrace this proposition.

Thus, Figure 9.7(c) represents P_1 – the proposition entertained by the main clause subject, C_1 – as viewed from the standpoint of the actual speaker, C_0 (who only entertains it via the conception of C_1 entertaining it). We must now consider C_1's apprehension of P_1. It is Joe who originally formulates the proposition, and (11) describes Joe's inclination toward it. For our purposes it is sufficient to represent *suspect* as shown in Figure 9.8(a). It profiles C_1's inclination toward accepting the proposition expressed by the complement clause. C_1 is thus the trajector, and the complement clause specifies its landmark.

If Figure 9.8(a) is taken as representing the main clause without its grounding, i.e. *Joe suspect* P_1, we may next consider the result of elaborating the schematic landmark P_1 with the specific structure *Alice is unhappy*, diagrammed in Figure 9.7(c). The result is shown in Figure 9.8(b). Observe that the content of Joe's suspicion is limited to the situation of Alice being unhappy – it does not include the fact that the actual speaker apprehends it from the speaker's own vantage point. Thus, I have excluded the weak identification of the virtual ground with the actual ground from the box representing the landmark of *suspect*. That is, the complement clause *Alice is unhappy* describes P_1 from the speaker's perspective, but we understand the sentence as meaning that Joe apprehends P_1 from his own perspective. C_1's apprehension of what is taken as being the same proposition is indicated by the correspondence lines equating C_1 with C, D_1 with D, and F_1 with F. This is only weak identification, since Joe merely formulates and inclines toward proposition P_1 but does not embrace it.

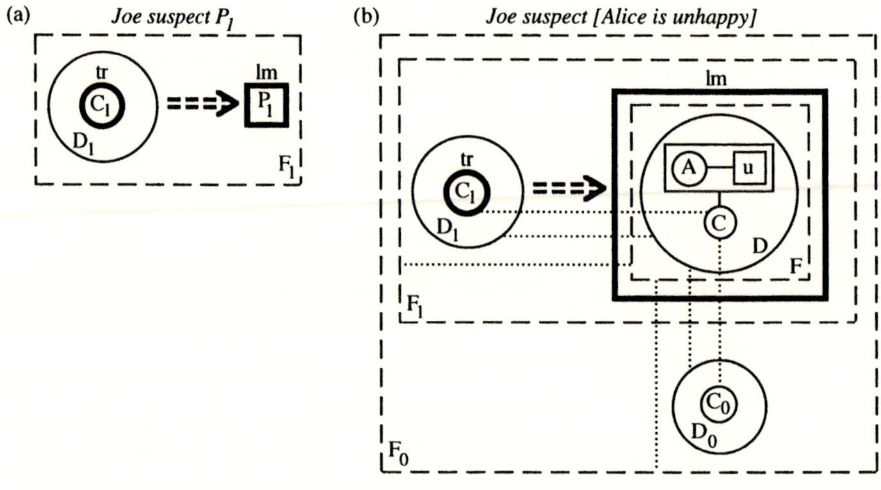

Figure 9.8

The last facet of (11) we need to examine is the grounding of the main clause. It consists of the absence of a modal, plus the inflectional ending *-s* on *suspect*, marking immediacy to the ground (specifically interpreted as present time) as well as the trajector's status as third person (non-ground) and singular. Here we are only concerned with the absence of a modal, which indicates that the profiled process, **p**, is accepted as real. Thus, in Figure 9.9(a) the profiled process, *suspect*, is represented as being established in the epistemic dominion (D) of a conceptualizer (C). We are assuming the default interpretation, where the speaker utters (11) and really means it, as an actual, sincere assertion. Thus, in the manner of Figure 9.4(b), the actual ground is strongly identified with the virtual ground evoked by the grounding element. Since they are strongly identified, they can be collapsed notationally, as shown in Figure 9.9(b). The proposition P_0 – namely, *Joe suspects P_1* – is part of the actual speaker's conception of reality.

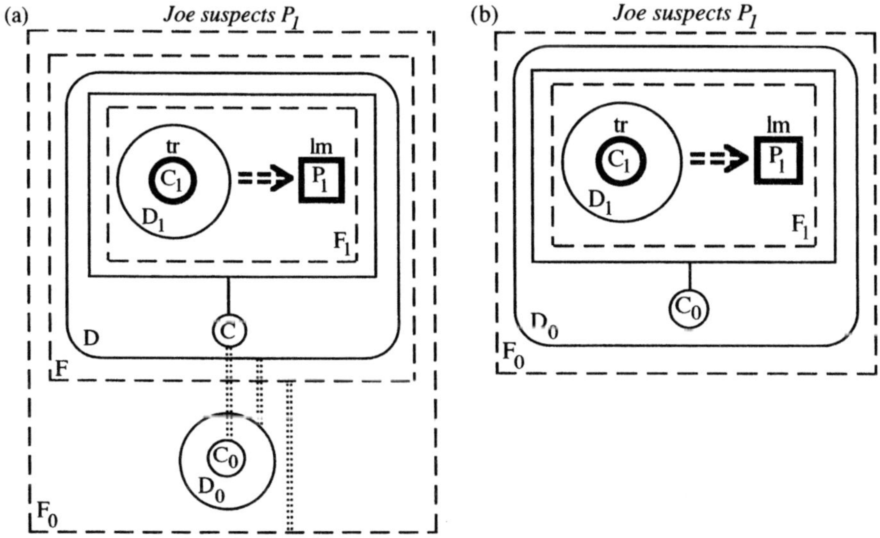

Figure 9.9

Individually, we have now examined the complement clause (Figure 9.7(c)), how the complement clause elaborates the landmark of the main clause (Figure 9.8), and how the main clause is grounded (Figure 9.9). The final step is to put this all together, showing the grounding of the main clause and the elaboration of its landmark simultaneously. This is done in Figure 9.10. Observe that the actual speaker, C_0, embraces the proposition expressed by the main clause, but merely formulates the one expressed by the subordinate clause for purposes of characterizing Joe's suspicion. P_1 does figure in the speaker's conception of reality, but only indirectly, as a characterization of what Joe suspects – it is only the profiled relationship of Joe suspecting it that is directly portrayed as being real. Still, in terms of their grounding, both propositions are described linguistically from C_0's vantage point.

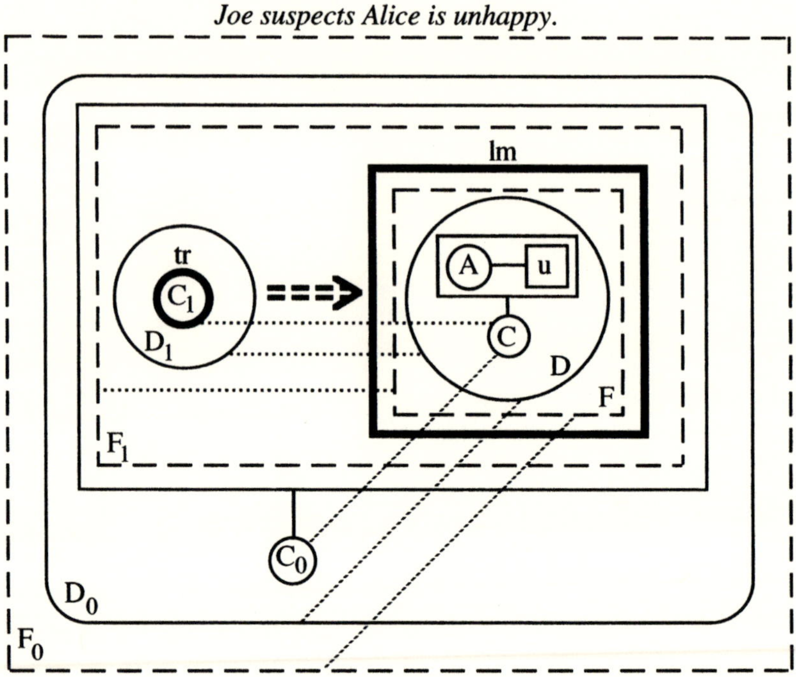

Figure 9.10

4. Factivity

Things are really not this simple. In particular, (11) does not necessarily have the meaning shown in Figure 9.10. It might in some circumstances be interpreted differently, with the speaker directly accepting P_1, *Alice is unhappy*, as part of his own conception of reality. Suppose that you and I both know that Alice has been unhappy for some time, but we don't want her brother Joe to find out about it, since knowing that Alice is unhappy would make Joe unhappy. In this circumstance, (15)a would indicate that we are still being successful in keeping Joe in the dark, while (15)b (= (11)) would indicate that our plot is starting to fail. But in either case I presuppose the validity of P_1. That is, in both cases the virtual ground evoked by the subordinate clause is not just weakly but strongly identified with the actual ground. Diagrammatically, this could be shown in Figure 9.10 merely by replacing the single correspondence lines equating them with double correspondence lines.

(15) a. *Joe doesn't suspect Alice is unhappy.* [Continuation: *He's still in the dark.*]
b. *Joe suspects Alice is unhappy.* [Continuation: *What tipped him off?*]

In other words, *suspect* is susceptible to a **quasi-factive** interpretation. **Factive** predicates are generally characterized as presupposing the truth of their complements (Kiparsky and Kiparsky 1970). To demonstrate this property it is noted that the status of the subordinate-clause proposition is unchanged when the main clause is negated. Thus, with a factive verb like *regret*, the subordinate proposition is accepted as true in both (16)a and (16)b. However, with a non-factive predicate like *certain*, the speaker is committed to its truth only when the main clause is positive, i.e. in (16)c but not in (16)d.

(16) a. *I* ***regret*** *that your dog is ill.* [factive; the dog is ill]
b. *I don't* ***regret*** *that your dog is ill.* [factive; the dog is ill]
c. *I'm* ***certain*** *that your dog is ill.* [non-factive; the dog is ill]
d. *I'm not* ***certain*** *that your dog is ill.* [non-factive; the dog may not be ill]

I suspect that a lot of predicates usually not considered factive are nonetheless susceptible to a factive construal under particular circumstances, as shown in regard to (15). But whether factivity is lexically or contextually determined, it can be characterized in terms of strong identification of the actual ground with the virtual ground invoked by a finite clause. Let us see this by comparing the meanings of *certain* and *regret*. To facilitate description, I introduce the notation in Figure 9.11. It is intended as a schematic representation of finite clauses. It shows the profiled process, **p**, as having some status vis-à-vis C and C's epistemic dominion, D, without however specifying just what that status is. The diagram should thus be understood as neutralizing the contrast between inclination and result (signaled by the presence or absence of a modal).

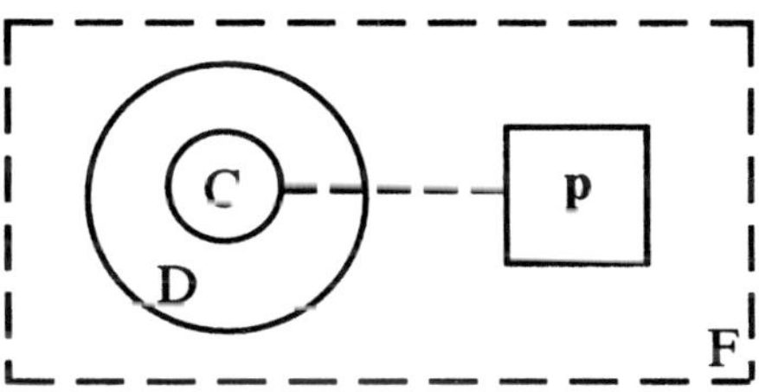

Figure 9.11

Being a predicate of propositional attitude, *certain* makes schematic reference to a proposition as an inherent part of its meaning. As shown in Figure 9.12(a), it profiles the stable situation of a conceptualizer, C_1, controlling a proposition, i.e. having it in his epistemic dominion (D_1). I have added to this a double dashed arrow as a rather inadequate way of representing the predicate's force-dynamic component. In contrast to *know*, which is neutral in this respect, *certain* specifies the strength of C_1's attachment to the landmark proposition. It is stronger, for instance, than with *sure*: it is felicitous to say *I'm sure, but I'm not absolutely certain*, but not the converse. We can think of the dashed arrow in diagram (a) as indicating the degree of force which would have to be applied to sever C_1's link to the proposition, removing it from C_1's conception of accepted reality. The force is only latent, since there is no implication of any current struggle to maintain the conviction.

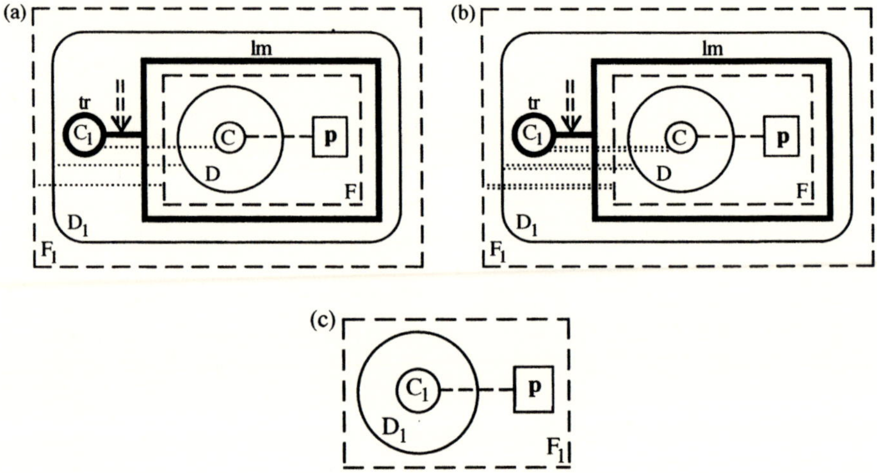

Figure 9.12

The correspondence lines in Figure 9.12(a) indicate that C_1 weakly identifies with C, thus apprehending the proposition from C_1's own standpoint. However, for result predicates the question arises whether C_1 should be described as identifying with C not just weakly but strongly, as shown in diagram (b), which collapses into (c). With strong identification, C_1 views the proposition from a position internal to it, as shown in diagram (c). From this internal vantage point, only the process **p** is onstage and objectively construed. The issue, then, is whether a sentence like *Joe is certain Alice is unhappy* specifies Joe's stance in regard to a full proposition (coded linguistically by the full finite clause, *Alice is unhappy*) or just to the grounded process (*Alice be unhappy*).

I believe that *certain* is indeed a predicate of "propositional attitude", so that Figure 9.12(a) is the proper representation. However, its meaning, so represented, allows 9.12(b) as an inference. *Certain* thus implies the configuration in 9.12(c), where C_1 plays the role of C in grounding the complement clause, but does not directly portray C_1 in this role. If Joe should say "I am certain Alice is unhappy", explicitly commenting on his attitude toward the expressed proposition "Alice is unhappy", the speaker could report this with the sentence *Joe is certain Alice is unhappy.* From this it follows – as an inference – that Joe could also say "Alice is unhappy", where Joe occupies the position of C in the ground. But that is not what Joe actually said, nor what the sentence directly portrays. In terms of what it directly describes, *Joe is certain Alice is unhappy* objectifies and profiles Joe's attitude toward the full proposition.

Unlike *certain*, *regret* is a factive predicate, sketched in Figure 9.13. Both are result predicates, situating the landmark proposition in the trajector's epistemic dominion (D_1). Some differences are however apparent from a comparison of Figures 9.12(a) and 9.13. For one thing, *regret* lacks the force dynamic element of *certain*, there being no specification of how strongly C_1 holds to the landmark proposition. Indeed, its inclusion in C_1's dominion is not necessarily even profiled – thus in Figure 9.13 the line connecting C_1 with the landmark is not in bold. While *regret* includes this link as part of its meaning, as a kind of presupposition, what it profiles is the associated attitude, respresented by a single dashed arrow. *Regret* focuses on the trajector's negative reaction to the supposed reality of the landmark proposition, the wish that things had turned out otherwise.

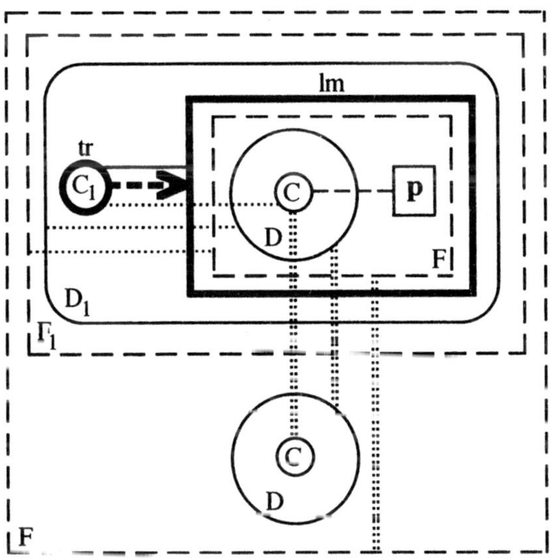

Figure 9.13

Factivity can be characterized as a particular manifestation of strong identification. As part of its lexical meaning, *regret* specifies that the conceptualizer implied by the grounding of the landmark proposition is strongly identified with some other conceptualizer apparent in the discourse context, by default the actual speaker. Thus, the speaker has direct access to the complement proposition, and assumes the role of conceptualizer for its grounding, in addition to the access afforded by apprehending C_1 and C_1's acceptance of the proposition. Consider, then, the sentences in (17). It doesn't matter whether Joe regrets or doesn't regret the circumstance described by the complement proposition, *Alice is unhappy.* Either way, the speaker has independent access to this proposition, strongly identifying with the conceptualizer who anchors its grounding. Because the speaker assumes the role of that conceptualizer – seeing the profiled relationship (Alice being unhappy) from that vantage point – the speaker could in either case say "Alice is unhappy".

(17) a. *Joe regrets that Alice is unhappy.* ⊃ C_0 could say: "Alice is unhappy."
b. *Joe doesn't regret that Alice is unhappy.* ⊃ C_0 could say: "Alice is unhappy."

The attentive reader will have noticed that in Figure 9.13 the conceptualizer external to the complement proposition was given just as C, not as C_0. I have been using C_0 to represent the actual speaker in a particular discourse context, while Figure 9.13 depicts the abstracted meaning of *regret*, independent of any particular context. Moreover, factivity is not invariably defined in relation to the actual speaker. Consider (18)a, which strikes me as being quite acceptable. Here the external conceptualizer who identifies with the complement proposition is the father, not the actual speaker, who explicitly rejects it. Indeed, the external conceptualizer might even be identified with the main clause subject, C_1, as in (18)b. This would traditionally be described in terms of the factive presupposition being defeasible.

(18) a. *According to his father, Joe regrets that Alice is unhappy. But I know for a fact that she's really not unhappy at all.*
b. *?Joe regrets that Alice is unhappy, but I know she really isn't.*

I will briefly mention two other possible manifestations of strong identification. The first pertains to interactions between the main clause predicate and a modal in the complement clause. In general, the main and complement clauses involve distinct conceptualizations, each with its own status in regard to the epistemic control cycle. We see in (19), for instance, that the result predicate *certain* in the main clause allows a complement clause of either inclination (marked by a modal) or control (absence of a modal). These conceptualizations are not however totally independent. The main clause predicate no doubt interacts semantically in numerous subtle ways with the subordinate clause grounding.

(19) a. *Jill is certain that she {may / could / should} be promoted, but not that she will be.*
b. *I am certain that Jill {is / was} the best qualified candidate.*

Illustrating one such interaction is (20):

(20) *Jack suspects Jill may be pregnant.*
a. Jack inclines to the proposition "Jill may be pregnant."
b. Jack inclines to the proposition "Jill is pregnant."

The sentence is ambiguous. On one interpretation, Jack inclines to the proposition that Jill **may be** pregnant, i.e. to the proposition that her pregnancy is a possibility. On the other, more likely interpretation, Jack inclines to the proposition that she **is** pregnant. What should be noted is that the modal *may* appears in the complement clause even when the potentiality it indicates does not figure in the proposition that Jack entertains.

Impressionistically, we can describe this as a kind of "leakage", where the inclination coded by *suspect* seeps into the subordinate clause and manifests itself as the modal *may*. A bit more technically, we can describe it in terms of strong identification. As shown in Figure 9.14, the main clause subject, C_1, does not just weakly identify with C, by way of formulating the complement proposition, but does so quite strongly, in that the modal inclination expressed by *may* (anchored by C) is taken as being referentially the same as the inclination profiled by the main clause predicate. Thus Jack inclines toward a proposition which – as seen by the speaker – characterizes the target situation (Jill being pregnant) as being only potential. Yet, by adopting an internal perspective, Jack views the proposition from the standpoint of C, with the consequence that the target of Jack's inclination is merely the situation of Jill being pregnant, not "Jill may be pregnant".

One further manifestation of strong identification is **performative** sentences, as in (21). For instance, (21)c might be uttered by our Attorney General, whose duty is to protect the civil liberties of all Americans.

(21) a. *I promise to stop drinking.*
b. *I order you to shred those documents!*
c. *As part of our war against terrorism, fought to ensure the enduring freedom of all Americans, I hereby inform you that your civil liberties are suspended.*

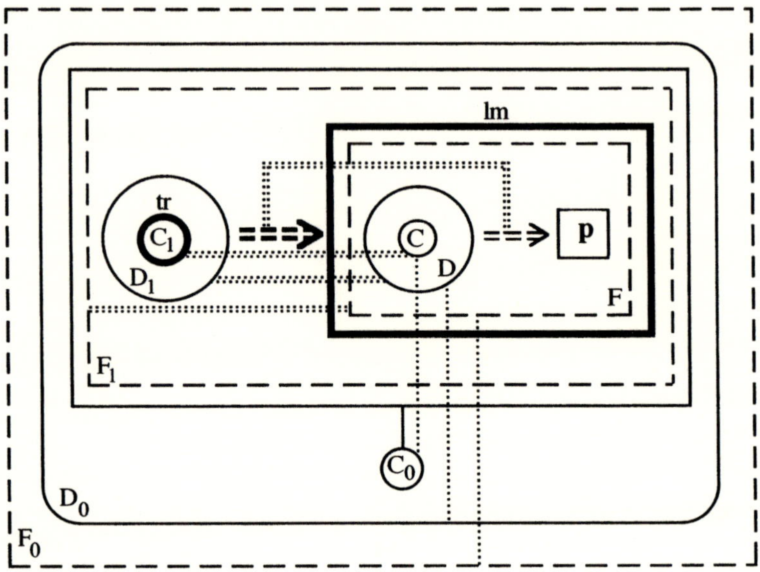

Figure 9.14

A performative both describes an action and performs that action when uttered under appropriate circumstances. A statement is not a performative by virtue of its form alone. For instance, (21)a might be said in response to the question *What do you do every time I find you drunk?*, in which case it is merely a description, not a promise. A speech act description becomes a speech act performance when the profiled event is strongly identified with the actual ground. The overtly stated action (e.g. *I promise*) is fully assimilated to the speaker/hearer interaction. Usually offstage (subjectively construed), in performatives this interaction goes onstage as the profiled event. The speaker thus views this event from the internal perspective he has by virtue of actually performing it.

This notion of strong identification provides a way of handling **embedded performatives**, as in (22):

(22) a. *I regret that I must hereby inform you that your civil liberties are suspended.*
b. *It gives me great pleasure to inform you that your civil liberties are hereby suspended.*

Here the description of an act of informing functions as the content of a subordinate clause. In terms of its overt grammatical form, the description (in this case *I inform you that X*) need not be fully contiguous or wholly explicit: in

(22)a, it is interrupted by *must hereby*; and in (22)b the speaker's role as subject is implicit. Still, nothing prevents the actual speaker, the actual hearer, and their actual interaction constituting the ground from being strongly identified with the corresponding conceptual elements of the complement clause, thus imbuing it with the action they embody.

5. Impersonals

We have so far confined our attention to predicates with personal subjects. As a final topic, let us briefly look at impersonals, where the subject is either the so-called "dummy" *it*, or else the finite complement clause itself:

(23) a. *It's just plain false that celery causes warts.*
b. *That celery causes warts is just plain false.*

An initial observation is that impersonal epistemic predicates can be found representing all five phases previously distinguished for the epistemic control cycle:

(24) a. **Formulation:** *possible, conceivable, feasible, plausible, imaginable*
b. **Assessment:** *uncertain, unsure, unclear, undecided, doubtful, arguable, debatable*
c. **Inclination:** *seem, appear, likely, unlikely, doubtful, dubious*
d. **Action:** *strike, hit, dawn on, become apparent*
e. **Result:** *certain, clear, evident, obvious, apparent, definite, true, undeniable*

However, they are not evenly distributed. The action predicates are small in number and rather marginal, being either metaphorical or periphrastic. Moreover, most of the predicates are adjectival. Note in particular that assessment verbs like *wonder, consider*, and *ask* are absent from the list, as they require personal subjects. This skewing suggests that the meaning of impersonal constructions is hard to reconcile with the notion of a mental action, which strongly invokes a sentient actor.[5]

Of the predicates in (24), only the action verbs *strike, hit*, and *dawn on* require the overt specification of a conceptualizer – but as an object rather than a subject. Among the remaining predicates, some allow its specification, nor-

5 The meanings of impersonal predicates are examined more closely in Chapter 10. There it is argued that the predicates in (24)d are actually alternatives to semantic characterization based on the epistemic control cycle.

mally via a *to*-phrase, while others do not. Predicates that most readily allow a *to*-phrase include *unclear, seem, appear, become apparent, clear, evident*, and *obvious*. This is not a usual option with *possible, feasible, unsure, undecided, certain, definite*, or *true*.

I therefore suggest the following as a general characterization of these impersonals. They pertain to epistemic control, each invoking a particular phase of the control cycle at the epistemic level. Hence they do invoke a conceptualizer, the actor whose conception of reality is at issue. However, these predicates are impersonal precisely because they **defocus** the mental activity of any particular conceptualizer (cf. Shibatani 1985). Some (notably *strike, hit*, and *dawn on*) do this by focusing instead on some outside influence impinging on the conceptualizer. More commonly, they defocus the conceptualizer by evoking it only in generalized fashion – rather than designating a particular judgment by a particular individual, they specify a property, such that the judgment in question will occur to any conceptualizer who considers the matter.[6] Evoking the conceptualizer in generalized fashion, abstracting away from any particular individual, gives C the status of a **virtual** entity. All the predicates which follow this defocusing strategy can therefore be used without the specification of any actual conceptualizer, as pure impersonals. Of course, it is not precluded that a particular conceptualizer might identify with the virtual C implied by the predicate. There is always some way to effect this, if only periphrastically:

(25) *{In my view / As I see it / For me} it is possible that the Cubs will win the World Series.*

Consider, then, the contrast between a personal statement like (26)a and the corresponding impersonal, (26)b:

(26) a. *I am certain that beer prevents cancer.*
b. *It is certain that beer prevents cancer.*

Although the speaker is ultimately responsible in both cases for the proposition expressed in the complement clause, the statements differ as to the nature and degree of the speaker's responsibility. In (26)a the speaker directly and explicitly portrays the proposition as being part of his own conception of reality. Its inclusion in the speaker's epistemic dominion constitutes the relationship profiled by the main clause. On the other hand, in (26)b the speaker merely presents the complement proposition as part of the epistemic dominion of a virtual conceptualizer (C). In the absence of contextual restrictions, C is effec-

6 This relates to the idealized cognitive model of propositions as objective entities accessible to different viewers.

tively a generalized conceptualizer, so the certainty is portrayed as being characteristic of anyone who might have occasion to assess the proposition. In the default situation, a speaker who sincerely asserts (26)b must therefore suscribe to the proposition's validity, but that is a matter of inference, not something that is directly stated per se.

It was argued in Chapter 5 that impersonal *it* can be characterized in reference to the control cycle: it designates the **field** (F), which for epistemic predicates comprises the relevant scope of awareness. The contrast between personal and impersonal *certain*, as in (26), is thus as shown in Figure 9.15. By choosing the conceptualizer (C) as trajector, the personal *certain* profiles the relationship between C and the target proposition P. On the other hand, the impersonal *certain* defocuses the conceptualizer by construing it in generalized fashion, so that trajector status falls instead on the field (interpretable as the array of knowledge brought to bear in assessing P). As a consequence, the profiled relationship centers on the role of this knowledge in causing P to be incorporated in the epistemic dominion, D: given the overall circumstances, any conceptualizer would incorporate P as part of his conception of reality. There is no difference in the overall content, only in which facets of it are singled out for focal prominence (profiling and trajector status).

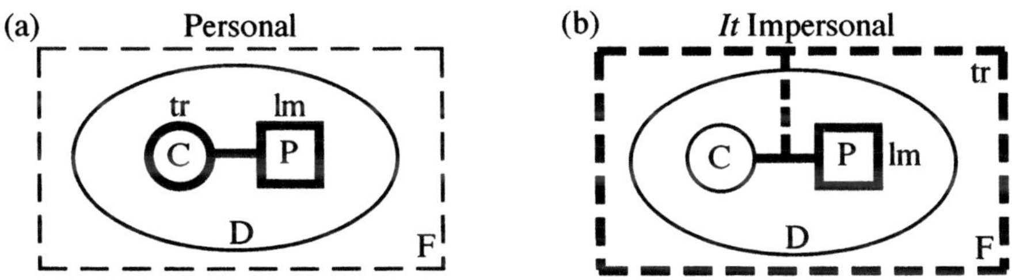

Figure 9.15

There is of course a third option, namely for the complement proposition to be chosen as trajector and coded as subject, as in (27).

(27) *That beer prevents cancer is certain.*

However infrequent such expressions may be in spoken discourse, they still need to be described. This variant of *certain* also defocuses the conceptualizer, making it impersonal, but it does so without conferring any special prominence on the field or its contribution to the assessment. Instead, P itself functions as trajector, there being no salient landmark. The semantic effect is to view the proposition and its epistemic status essentially in isolation, i.e. to simply present P as having that status. This is sketched in Figure 9.16.

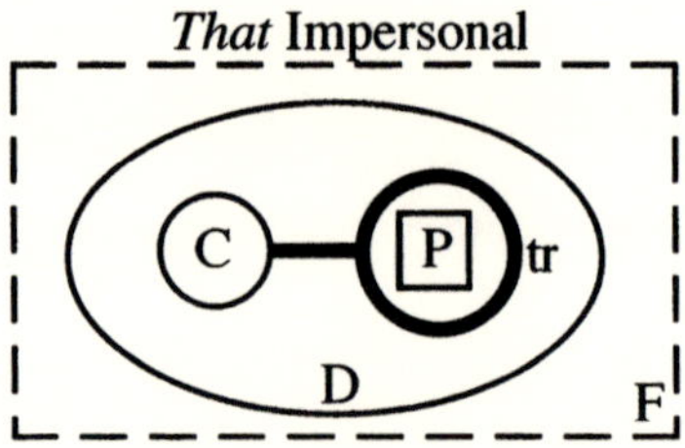

Figure 9.16

In Figure 9.16, P is enclosed in a heavy-line circle. This is the notation I use for a profiled **thing**. I am thus suggesting that P is nominalized, i.e. it undergoes conceptual reification, producing an abstract thing which is profiled by the *that*-clause and functions as trajector of *certain*. Because the trajector is construed with maximal objectivity, P's selection as trajector strongly encourages its nominalization. Conceptual reification resides in viewing something as a unitary entity for higher-order cognitive purposes. Thus, to the extent that a proposition functions as an object of conception, saliently portrayed as participating in a higher-order relationship, a nominal construal tends to emerge. I have not shown P as being reified in the case of personals and *it* impersonals (Figure 9.15), since there it functions as landmark (secondary focus), not as the primary object of conception.

As a final point, let me note the existence of what amount to **impersonal adverbs** of propositional attitude corresponding to the three stable phases of the control cycle. Some commonly used adverbs of this sort are listed in (28) and illustrated in (29).

(28) a. **Formulation:** *possibly, conceivably*
b. **Inclination:** *apparently, seemingly, evidently*
c. **Result:** *certainly, clearly, obviously, definitely, undeniably*

(29) *{Possibly / Apparently / Certainly} a discarded cigarette started the fire.*

Though I am not prepared to offer a full account of such adverbs or adverbial modifying constructions, it at least seems evident that the notions I have introduced provide a basis for approaching this range of problems.

As described in CG, an adverb profiles an atemporal relation whose trajector is itself relational, and which has no focused landmark (Langacker 1987a: ch. 6). Its trajector corresponds to the adverbially modified element, so for the adverbs in (28)–(29) the trajector is characterized in schematic terms as a proposition (i.e. a grounded process). Thus, as seen in Figure 9.17, these adverbs are comparable in their trajector choice to *that* impersonals. In the case of a formulation adverb, the profiled relationship merely consists of P occurring in a conceptualizer's field.

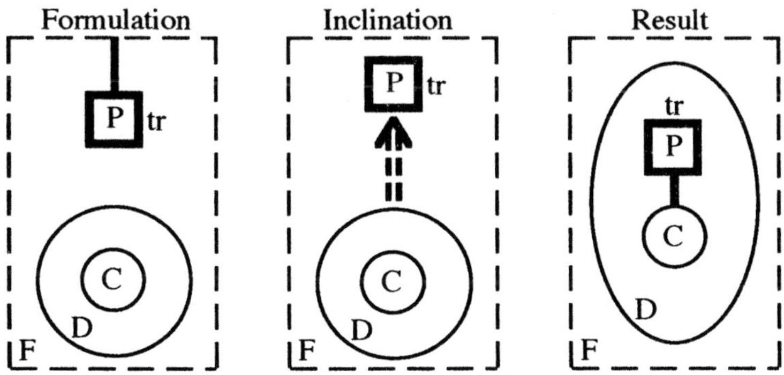

Figure 9.17

By comparing Figures 9.16 and 9.17, it is seen that an impersonal adverb (e.g. *certainly*) differs from the corresponding impersonal predicate (*certain*) in that the proposition focused as trajector retains its relational character rather than being conceptually reified. The reason for the difference is that the relationship profiled by an adverb is never focused as a clausal profile. Because its trajector is therefore less salient than a clausal trajector, it does not stand out to the same extent as an object of conception participating in a higher-order relationship. It is thus the clausal subject – not the adverbial trajector – that more saliently functions as a unitary entity for higher-order cognitive purposes (the basis for conceptual reification).

Naturally, the virtual conceptualizer evoked by the adverb tends to be identified in discourse with an external one, by default the actual speaker. When it is the speaker, the meaning of a formulation or inclination adverb prevents the speaker from strongly identifying with the conceptualizer grounding the finite clause. We saw this for *perhaps* in Figure 9.5. Conversely, a result adverb lets one infer their strong identification, as we saw for *certain* in Figure 9.12.

Chapter 10
Finite complements in English

This chapter continues the examination of finite clauses and their combination in complement constructions, with special attention to some basic cognitive models underpinning the epistemic control cycle. Further articulation of this cycle allows a finer-grained semantic characterization of complement-taking predicates.

1. Conceptions of reality

At least in English, clausal grounding locates a process in relation to **reality**. As I use it, the term reality relates to a general and very basic cognitive model, which I will call the Reality Model. This is the notion that, in our world (which is not just physical, but also has mental and social aspects), matters have developed in a particular way, out of all those ways conceivable. There is a certain course of events, whereby some events and situations have occurred, while countless others have not. Reality (R) consists of the events and situations that have occurred up through the present moment. This course of events cannot be changed – what has happened has happened. The future, however, has yet to be determined. As reality continues to evolve through time, there are many future paths it can take, some more likely than others given the world's essential nature and what has happened so far. With respect to this basic cognitive model, reality is defined as the history of what has happened up through the present moment, the **established** course of events.[1]

Another aspect of the Reality Model is that our knowledge of reality is partial and imperfect. Moreover, as shown in Figure 10.1, every individual has a different view of it, a different "take" on reality. As living and sentient creatures, we are constantly engaged in building up a **conception** of reality (RC), what we ourselves accept as real. And one thing we accept as real is that there are other conceptualizers engaged in this task, each with their own reality conception. While they

1 For sake of convenience, I will usually just speak of **events**, but reality also includes occurring situations (or states). I also use the term **occurrence**, for both events and situations. It is roughly equivalent to **process**, employed in CG as a technical term for the entity profiled by a verb: a relationship viewed in its evolution through time. Additionally, since the Reality Model is now being considered in more detail, RC (reality conception) is used here for what was simply labeled R in earlier chapters.

overlap, these reality conceptions diverge in what they cover and differ in specifics, hence they are subject to negotiation. This is one major reason why we talk. Of course, the Reality Model specifies that reality is the way it is regardless of whether anybody knows it, i.e. it is independent of particular reality conceptions.

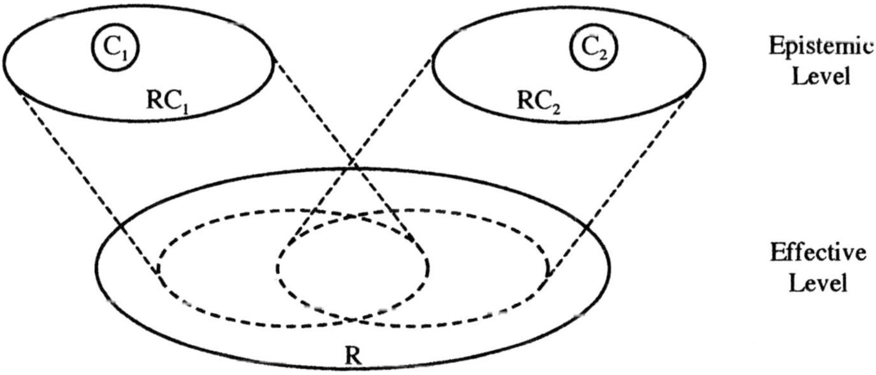

Figure 10.1

We can make a broad distinction between **epistemic** and **effective** relations. Epistemic relations are those which hold at the level of **knowledge**, and thus involve **conceptions** of reality. By contrast, **effective** relations hold at the level of reality per se. A systematic opposition between epistemic and effective relations, evident at multiple levels of structural organization, is an important feature of English grammar (Langacker To appear f). One of its manifestations, briefly noted in Chapter 6 (§ 5), is the distinction between root and epistemic senses of the modals. Both sorts of modals indicate that the grounded process, **p**, is not yet accepted by C as being real. The difference is whether the striving or inclination toward its **realization** obtains at the effective or the epistemic level. With a root modal (e.g. *You must see this movie!*), it is aimed at influencing the course of reality itself (R). But with an epistemic modal (e.g. *He might retire early*), it pertains to the evolution of C's reality conception (RC).

Normally modals pertain to future events, since the future has not yet been determined. But epistemic modals can also pertain to present situations: *She must be angry.* At the level of reality itself, the issue of whether or not she is angry has already been resolved. Either she is or she isn't. However, it has not been resolved at the level of RC – what the conceptualizer presumes to **know** about reality. This distinction between future and present orientation is shown in Figure 10.2(a)-(b), where dashed arrows represent the modal **force** (Sweetser 1982; Talmy 1988; Langacker 1991: § 6.3); this force is the "strength" of the tendency toward **p** being realized (e.g. the strong force of prediction, or the weak force of mere possibility). At issue in both (a) and (b) is the likelihood of **p** being incorporated in RC (as something C **knows**). The difference is that, in diagram (a), incorporation in RC depends on what happens in R (how reality itself evolves), whereas in (b) incorporation in RC depends solely on the evolution of C's **knowledge** (since the matter has been decided at the level of reality). But under either interpretation, epistemic modals contrast with root modals in the locus of the modal force. The latter are basically future oriented because, as shown in diagram (c), the force applies to the evolution of reality itself.

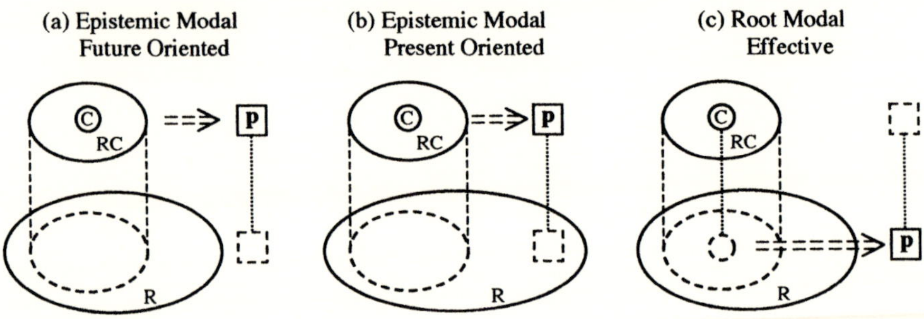

Figure 10.2

As discussed in Chapter 9, the identity of C is a subtle but crucial matter. While typical, identification of C with the actual speaker is only a special case. It corresponds to a particular way of **using** a finite clause, in which the speaker makes a simple, unqualified statement directly expressing something the speaker believes to be true. There are however many kinds of situations where the speaker uses a finite clause without presenting it as a representation of what the speaker himself actually believes. Some examples are given in (1). The clause may be used as a question rather than a statement. It may include an adverb, such as *perhaps*, which indicates that it does not necessarily reflect the speaker's conception of reality. The speaker may merely be repeating what the hearer has said, without accepting it, as in (1)c. Or the clause can be used as a complement, in which case the matrix predicate may indicate that it is not accepted as valid, as with *doubt*, or the matrix subject may be someone other than the speaker, as in (1)e.

(1) a. *Her father is very rich?*
b. *Perhaps her father is very rich.*
c. *Her father is very rich, you say. That's ridiculous.*
d. *I doubt that her father is very rich.*
e. *My brother suspects that her father is very rich.*

None of the expressions in (1) implies that the situation of her father being very rich is accepted by the actual speaker as part of the speaker's conception of reality. The clause *her father is very rich* is however grounded through present tense and the absence of a modal, which locate the situation within RC, as part of immediate reality. What this shows is that the conceptualizer invoked by a grounding element has no particular identity. C is rather a **generalized** or **virtual** conceptualizer, i.e. one that is simply imagined as a way of representing the **idea** of a conceptualizer assessing **p** with respect to C's conception of reality (Langacker 1999d; Chapter 9). It is natural for the speaker to assume the role of C; this happens when the speaker wishes to describe his own, actual view of reality. But C can also be identified with the hearer, as in (1)c, with somebody else, as in (1)e, or with no one at all – sentences (1)b and (1)d do not portray anybody as believing that the father is rich. In such examples the conceptualizer whose assessment is reflected in clausal grounding retains its virtual character.

Thus, as shown in Figure 10.3(a), use of a finite clause involves at least two conceptualizers and two levels of conception. There is first the actual speaker, the initial conceptualizer, which I will represent as C_0. A dashed arrow indicates that the speaker **apprehends** the clause, i.e. understands it or grasps its content. As part of its meaning, this clause invokes a conceptualizer, C, who apprehends the profiled occurrence, **p**, and adopts some **epistemic stance** in regard to it; the diagram shows the special case where C accepts **p** as belonging to C's conception of reality, RC. This much holds for all uses of a finite clause, including those in (1). As a special case, the actual speaker (C_0) may **identify** with C, assuming the role of C in making the judgment expressed by the clausal grounding. Showing this (strong) identification is the dotted correspondence line in diagram (b). As a result, C_0 occupies the role of C in the grounding relationship, so that RC is the reality conception of the actual speaker, labeled RC_0 in the third diagram. This happens when the speaker uses the finite clause to make a statement that honestly reflects his own view of reality.

(a) Use of a finite clause **(b) Identification** **(c) Result of identification**

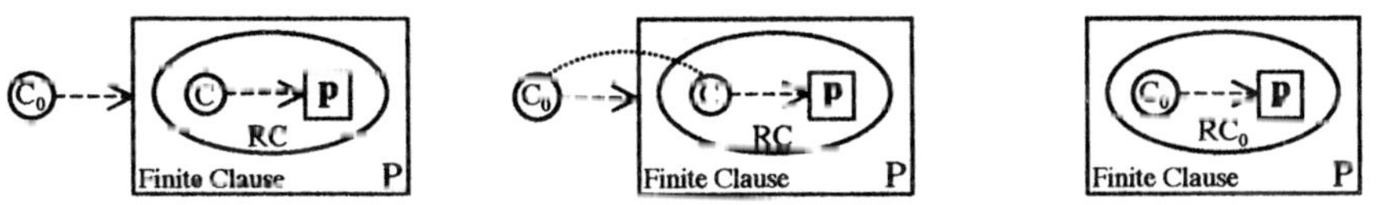

Figure 10.3

A finite clause expresses a **proposition**. A proposition (P) is thus defined as a grounded process. P = [G--->**p**]. It consists of both a process (**p**) and its epistemic assessment by a conceptualizer, as indicated by the grounding element. So when a speaker, C_0, uses and apprehends a finite clause, the speaker is conceptualizing not only the profiled process, **p**, but also the apprehension of that process by another conceptualizer, as shown in Figure 10.3(a). We may not be aware that there are two conceptualizer roles, either because the speaker identifies with C, as shown in diagrams (b) and (c), or else because C is only a virtual conceptualizer and is left implicit. But there **are** two roles: only as a special case is the conceptualizer implied by clausal grounding identified with the actual speaker.

This point is quite important. The fact that we can use a finite clause for something other than the direct expression of our own actual view indicates that we recognize the existence of other conceptualizers and other conceptions of reality, as in Figure 10.1. Not only do we recognize their existence, to some extent we apprehend the content of their conceptualization and their epistemic stance in regard to it. Furthermore, since we are able to conceptualize propositions without assuming the role of C, they have a kind of **autonomy**, being independent of any particular conceptualizer. Thus it is possible for different conceptualizers to entertain the same proposition, each apprehending it from his own vantage point.

This is the basis for complementation. In a sentence like (1)e, both the speaker and the matrix subject, *my brother*, apprehend the proposition expressed by the finite clause *her father is very rich*. But neither conceptualizer necessarily identifies with the role of C in the grounding element – neither the speaker nor the brother is prepared to say *her father is very rich* as a true reflection of his own conception of reality. The brother merely suspects that the father is rich but does not know it, and the speaker merely describes the brother's attitude. The grounding expressed by *is*, locating the father's being rich in immediate reality, is that of a virtual conceptualizer C internal to the proposition. The speaker and the brother are both external to this proposition – neither identifies with C.

With finite complements, an epistemic stance analogous to those grammatically expressed by grounding elements is lexically expressed instead by the matrix predicate. Inside a finite clause, C and the grounding relationship are offstage and unprofiled – what a finite clause profiles is the grounded process, **p**, not its relation to the ground (however important that is). But in a complement construction, such as (1)e, the epistemic stance is profiled by the matrix predicate, like *sure* or *suspect*, and the conceptualizer is often made explicit as a focused participant, typically the subject. Of course, the matrix clause itself is grounded, and the entire sentence is apprehended by the speaker. Thus a sentence of this sort involves no less than four conceptualizers and levels of conception.

Let us see in detail how this works, taking as our example the following commonplace sentence: *My wife is sure the dog will bite her friend*. Shown at the lower right in Figure 10.4 is the grounding by *will* of the process *the dog bite her friend* to form the complement clause *the dog will bite her friend.*[2] The essential point is that the profiled process **p** lies outside C's conception of reality, as the target of modal force (prediction in the case of *will*). Shown at the lower left is the grounding of the matrix clause *my wife is sure*. The grounding locates the profiled relationship in immediate reality, as part of RC. Here the profiled relationship is one in which a conceptualizer – identified as *my wife* – has an epistemic stance in regard to a proposition. In particular, *sure* specifies that the wife accepts this proposition as part of her conception of reality (RC_w).

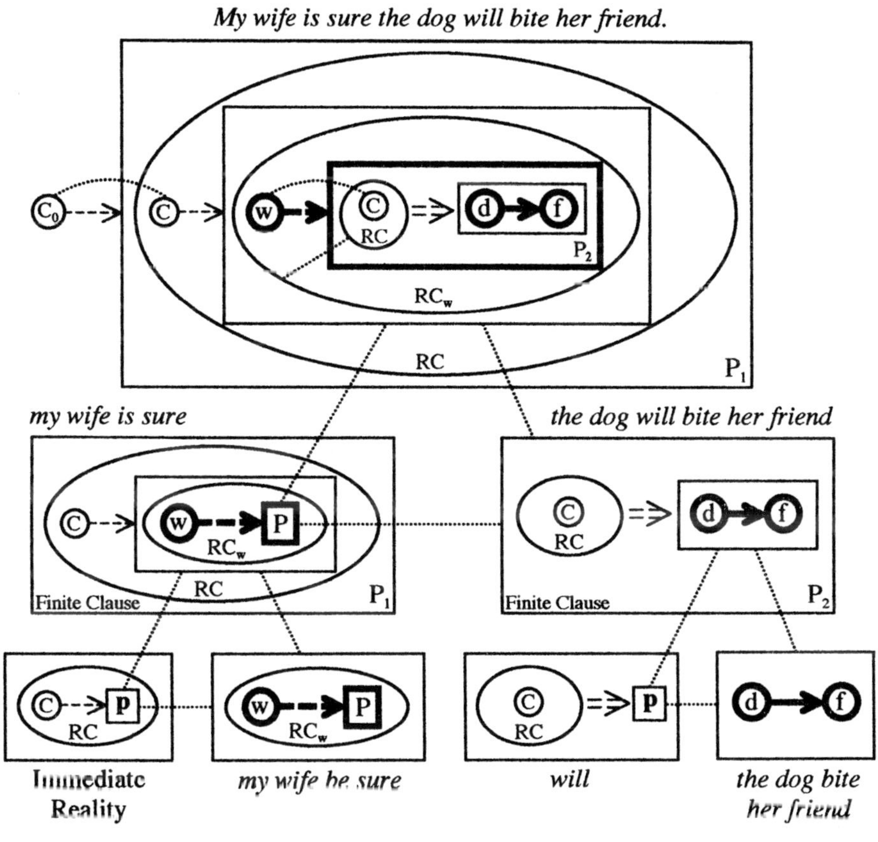

Figure 10.4

2 I am not necessarily claiming that this is the actual grammatical constituency, but it is convenient for discussing the points at issue. In CG, constituency has only secondary importance (Langacker 1997a). More essential to grammar are semantic factors like correspondences and profiling.

The composite structures produced by these grounding constructions are the finite clauses *my wife is sure* and *the dog will bite her friend*. Each expresses a proposition; these are labeled P_1 and P_2. Putting these two clauses together produces a complement construction. How do they combine? As shown in the middle level of the diagram, they are connected by a correspondence between P_2 (*the dog will bite her friend*) and the schematic proposition (P) evoked by *sure* (the proposition accepted as real). So by superimposing these corresponding elements, we obtain the overall composite structure shown at the top, where what the wife is sure of is that the dog will bite her friend.[3]

Also shown at the topmost level are the identifications made between conceptualizers. Assuming that the sentence is offered as a true statement, the speaker (C_0) identifies with the virtual conceptualizer invoked by the grounding of the matrix clause. Hence the wife being sure is part of the speaker's conception of reality ($RC = RC_0$). Moreover, the predicate *sure* implies that the wife identifies with the conceptualizer invoked by the grounding of the complement clause. If the wife accepts the validity of the proposition *the dog will bite her friend*, the wife – like C – must be predicting the future occurrence of the process *the dog bite her friend*. Thus W identifies with C, and RC_w is equated with RC. So although there are four conceptualizer roles, in the composite conception there are only two actual conceptualizers.

As this example illustrates, the essential feature of a finite complement construction is that the proposition expressed by one clause – the complement – specifies a schematic proposition invoked by the other clause (the matrix). This proposition can be the trajector of the matrix clause, as in (2)a, the primary landmark, as in (2)b, or a secondary landmark, as in (2)c. Likewise, the conceptualizer who entertains the proposition – C_1 – can be a subject (trajector), as in (2)b, an object (landmark), as in (2)c, or a prepositional object, as in (2)d. The conceptualizer may also remain implicit, being a virtual or generalized conceptualizer. The predicate *true*, for instance, does not make reference to any particular conceptualizing individual. Nonetheless, *true* is based on the Reality Model, sketched in Figure 10.1. By its very nature, it evokes the notion of conceptualizers who formulate propositions and try to determine whether they conform to reality. Though it lies in the background, a (generalized) conceptualizer who apprehends the proposition is still part of the meaning of such predicates.

(2) a. *That the polar ice is melting is true.* [P = tr; generalized C]
b. *We know that the polar ice is melting.* [P = lm; C_1 = tr (subject)]

3 I have shown both clausal processes as being profiled at the composite structure level. The issue of profiling in complex sentences is discussed in detail in Chapter 11.

c. *She persuaded him that the polar ice is melting.*
[$P = lm_2$; $C_1 = lm_1$ (object)]

d. *It seems to me that the polar ice is melting.*
[$P = lm$; C_1 = prepositional object]

So despite their abstract similarity, complement constructions are quite varied in terms of the grammatical role of the proposition (P) and the conceptualizer (C_1). The differences are largely ascribable to the meaning of the matrix predicate. As shown in Figure 10.4, a predicate like *sure* implies that its subject identifies with the conceptualizer of the complement proposition. If you accept P as valid, you must be adopting the epistemic stance P expresses in regard to the profiled occurrence. *Know* is another such predicate: (2)b implies that *we* "embrace" the proposition that the polar ice is melting – we assume the epistemic stance expressed by its grounding. But the matrix subject is not always the relevant conceptualizer. With *persuade*, in (2)c, it is the object, *him*, that identifies with C in the complement. If she persuaded him that the polar ice is melting, then **he** is the one who accepts that it is. The sentence does not actually imply that **she** does; it is possible that she does not believe it herself, but simply wants to mislead him. For a particular matrix predicate there is thus a particular relational participant (C_1) whose attitude toward the complement proposition is the one that counts. In the case of *persuade*, this is the landmark, expressed by the clausal object. As shown in Figure 10.5(a), the trajector exerts argumentative force on the landmark, who thereby comes to accept the proposition as valid, hence part of RC_1. Thus C_1 identifies with C.

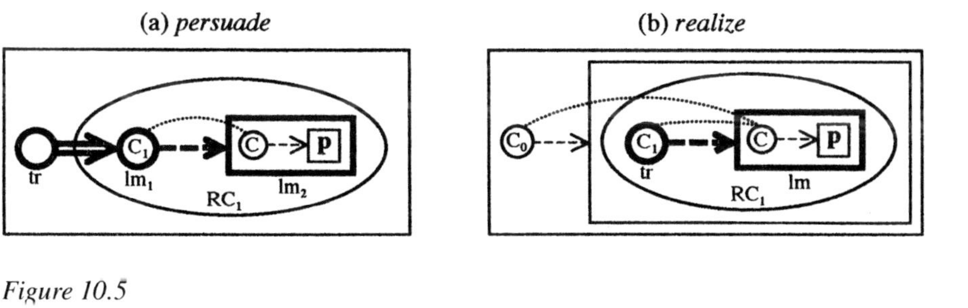

Figure 10.5

However, this individual does not necessarily identify with the conceptualizer of the complement proposition – that depends on the meaning of the matrix predicate or the entire matrix clause. With a predicate like *doubt*, as in (3) a, the matrix subject specifically does **not** identify with the complement conceptualizer. Even a predicate like *seem* fails to ensure identification. As we see in (3) b, *seem* merely indicates an inclination to accept the proposition as valid, not necessarily actual acceptance. Moreover, negation can block identification, as in (3) c, where the object *him* does not accept that the ice is melting. Whether or not the matrix conceptualizer identifies with the complement conceptualizer therefore depends on the interaction of various factors.

(3) a. *Bush doubts that the polar ice is melting.*
b. *It seems to me that the polar ice is melting – but I'm not sure.*
c. *She couldn't persuade him that the polar ice is melting.*
d. *She {realizes / doesn't realize} that the polar ice is melting.* [**factive** predicate]
e. **She realizes that the polar ice is melting – but it isn't.*

But matters are even more complex. Certain predicates – said to be **factive** (Kiparsky and Kiparsky 1970) – carry with them the notion that the speaker (C_0) identifies with the conceptualizer of the complement proposition. One such predicate is *realize*, sketched in Figure 10.5(b). Not only does the trajector (C_1) accept the proposition as valid, and thus identify with C, but the speaker does as well. In fact, the speaker accepts it as valid even when *realize* is negated, so that the subject does not accept it. So in (3)d, whether the subject *she* identifies with C depends on whether the matrix clause is positive (with *realizes*) or negative (*doesn't realize*), but either way the speaker agrees that the ice is melting. A sentence like (3)e is therefore semantically inconsistent.

2. Grammatical marking

Usually a finite complement is optionally introduced by the complementizer *that*: *My wife is sure (that) the dog will bite her friend.* Though related to the demonstrative *that* (as in *that dog*), the subordinating *that* is now a distinct element. It is not limited to complements, but also appears in relative clauses (e.g. *the dog that she bit*) and certain other constructions (e.g. "clefting": *It's you that I dislike*). In some cases its occurrence is strongly preferred if not obligatory. With subject complements, as in (2)a, it cannot be omitted: **The polar ice is melting is true.* With *persuade*, as in (2)c, its omission is questionable: *?She persuaded him the polar ice is melting.* But there are also cases where its use is quite unnatural: *?I think that she's angry.* And when the matrix clause is postposed and phonologically reduced, it does not appear: **That she's angry, I think.*

I make the following tentative proposal: *that* marks a proposition as an **object of conception**. I have suggested that a proposition, by its very nature, has a certain autonomy – being independent of any particular conceptualizer – and can thus be apprehended by different conceptualizers, each from his own perspective. I have further suggested that its use in a finite complement construction always implies its apprehension by some conceptualizer (if only a generalized one). By nature, then, a complement proposition functions as an object of conception, even when *that* does not appear. The effect of including *that* is to reinforce this function and make it salient by marking it explicitly.

This proposal helps make sense of the complex data. *That* is usually optional because it merely reinforces an aspect of a complement construction's inherent meaning. And as one might expect, the likelihood of its appearance correlates with the extent to which the proposition functions as an object of conception, being apprehended by external conceptualizers. For instance, two places where *that* is required is when the complement is the matrix clause subject, or when it combines with a noun like *fact, idea, claim*, etc. to specify what the fact, idea, or claim consists of. A subject complement specifies the matrix clause trajector, which is the primary focal participant in the profiled relationship. As the primary focus within the profile, which itself is a focus of attention, a subject is the most salient clausal element: onstage as the central, most focused element. So when a proposition serves in this capacity, its status as an object of conception is maximized. When it occurs with nouns like *fact*, *idea*, and *claim*, its status as an **object** is maximized. Since *fact*, *idea*, *claim*, etc. are nouns, they profile abstract things. And in this construction, the thing profiled by the noun is equated with the proposition: in *his claim that the polar ice is melting*, the claim in question simply **is** the one expressed by the clause. The proposition has to be marked with *that* because the construction specifically portrays it as an object of thought.

Conversely, constructions where *that* is disfavored or not allowed are those which minimize its status as an object of conception. Note that it does not occur with a finite clause which stands alone as a complete sentence: **That she's angry.* Since there is no matrix predicate with respect to which the proposition is a participant, it has no explicit role as object of conception. It is of course apprehended by the speaker and hearer, but their ever-present conceptualizing role is offstage and thus non-salient. Moreover, when there is a matrix predicate, the likelihood of *that* appearing is reduced by a number of factors: the speaker functioning as C_1, present tense, the expression being short, and informality. These factors are all observed in a sentence like *I think she's angry*, where *that* is strongly disfavored. They all lessen the extent to which the complement is independent of the speaker, hence they diminish its status as an autonomous proposition apprehended by multiple conceptualizers.

The semantic contribution of *that* is shown in Figure 10.6(a). It indicates that the proposition (P) is construed as an abstract thing (circle), which – taken as a whole – functions as an object of conception, being apprehended by an external conceptualizer (C_1). By introducing the notion of P being conceptualized, it provides a connection to the matrix clause, which usually specifies C_1 and profiles the process of C_1 conceptualizing P. *That*, however, is only one of the grammatical markings used in English to indicate the connection between a matrix and a complement clause. These "complementizers" have been a major and problematic topic of linguistic investigation. They are sometimes considered meaningless, but that of course is incorrect. In simplified form, and without attempting detailed justification, let me briefly sketch their meanings.

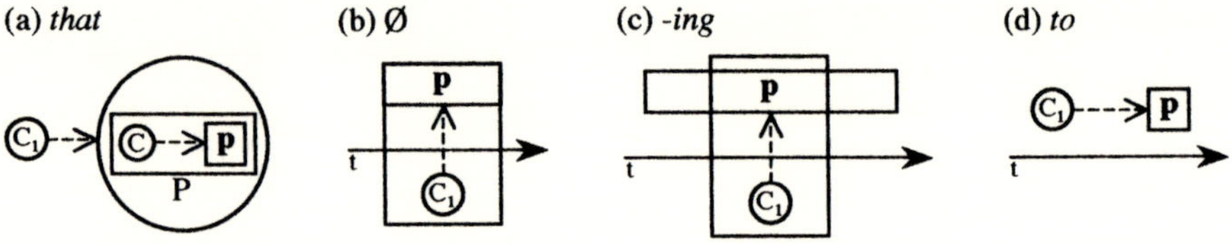

Figure 10.6

Three alternatives to *that* are zero (Ø), *-ing*, and *to*. In contrast to *that*, these do not combine with a full, finite clause, but rather with a partial clause lacking grounding – instead of a proposition (P), they mark an ungrounded process (**p**). Zero is used primarily with verbs of perception, like *see*, *hear*, and *feel*. Like the present tense, it indicates **immediacy**, i.e. **p** is temporally coincident with (occurs at the same time as) another process. In the case of the present tense, **p** coincides with the time of speaking. But in a complement construction, **p** coincides with the duration of the matrix process, the perceptual experience of witnessing the occurrence. So in Figure 10.6(b) the box representing C_1's apprehension of **p** is shown as being coextensive with **p** along the time axis. That is, the event's perception occurs during precisely the same span of time as the event itself.

(4) a. *We {saw / heard / felt} the bomb explode.*
[Ø; immediacy; full temporal coincidence]
b. *We {saw / heard / felt} the bombs exploding.*
[*-ing*; immediacy; partial coincidence]
c. *We {want / expect / would like} the bombs to explode.*
[*to*; non-immediacy]

Zero contrasts with *-ing* in this respect (Kirsner and Thompson 1976; Langacker 1995d). Like the progressive *-ing*, the complementizing *-ing* restricts the scope of perception to some internal portion of the overall event. Whereas in (4)a we perceive the entire event of a single bomb exploding, in (4)b we perceive only part of the ongoing process of multiple bombs exploding. That portion constitutes the profiled process **p**. So *-ing* also indicates a kind of immediacy, but only partial temporal coincidence with the overall event. On the other hand, *to* indicates **non-immediacy** with respect to the time of the matrix process and apprehension by C_1. Typically **p** lies in the future, relative to the matrix process, and can thus be apprehended as a whole (Wierzbicka 1988: ch. 1).

I want to emphasize that these diagrams and examples greatly oversimplify the well-known problem of *to* vs. *-ing*, though I do believe they represent their central values (the starting point for a full analysis). Note that the matrix predicates in (4) all describe mental processes. With zero and *-ing*, these are basically perceptual in nature; since perception requires temporal coincidence, their meanings are compatible. With *to*, which is not based on immediacy, the connection is less direct and the apprehension of **p** is non-perceptual. But in all three cases, the target of apprehension is the complement process, **p**, and not a full proposition (as with *that*). The connections specified by zero, *-ing*, and *to* are thus **effective**: they hold between mental and physical **events** (e.g. the event of seeing and the event of exploding). By contrast, with *that* the connection between matrix and complement is usually **epistemic** – in one way or another, the matrix predicate pertains to **knowledge** of events. A proposition is not the sort of thing we perceive, expect, or desire. A proposition does of course **refer** to an event, but it is not itself part of **reality** (in the narrow sense defined earlier). Basically all we can do with a proposition per se is to consider it for inclusion in our **conception** of reality.

The effective relationships in (4) are mental in nature, involving either perception or non-perceptual apprehension. Another basic kind of effective relationship is **causation**, which is often mental or social but may be purely physical. Zero, *-ing*, and *to* all have causal uses largely consistent with their characterizations in Figure 10.6. With zero and *-ing* the matrix and complement events (the causing and its effect) are temporally immediate. With zero, the two can sometimes be temporally coincident, as in (5)a. But since cause usually precedes effect, the strict coincidence inherent in perception is not required. It is however implied that the connection is direct, so that if the effect follows the cause, it follows it immediately (or with a very short time lag). With *-ing*, the matrix verbs *get* and *have* involve not only the causation of the fire burning but also the experience that results. This is either the experience engendered by successfully initiating the burning, or what is experienced in the midst of the process, as in Figure 10.6(c). And with *to*, there is no implication of immediacy (Fodor 1970; Wierzbicka 1975). It is quite possible that something which occurs at one moment – either doing something (like opening a window) or failing to do something (like putting another log on the fire) – causes the fire to go out at a later time.

(5) a. *I {made / let} the fire go out.* [Ø; immediacy; temporal coincidence or adjacency]
b. *I {got / have} the fire going.* [*-ing*; immediacy; partial coincidence]
c. *I {caused / allowed} the fire to go out.* [*to*; non-immediacy]

Since causation is a prime example of something which happens at the effective level, there is no basic causal predicate taking a *that*-complement. Strictly speaking, one cannot cause a proposition, only an event.[4] If we limit our attention to *that* and *to* (which do not imply immediacy), a general picture thus emerges: predicates taking finite complements designate relationships at the epistemic level, while those taking infinitival complements designate relationships at the effective level. I believe this is basically correct. If we want to maintain this generalization, however, these notions need to be clarified and certain problems need to be addressed. I will mention just two.

First, infinitival clauses (those marked with *to*) occur in various expressions with what is usually considered to be epistemic import. Indeed, the same matrix predicate sometimes takes either a finite or a non-finite complement:

(6) a. (i) *They expect that she will be late.* (ii) *They expect* **her** *to be late.*
b. (i) *It is likely that she will be late.* (ii) ***She*** *is likely to be late.*

These turn out to be the predicates generally analyzed in terms of a nominal (shown in bold) being "raised" out of the complement clause into the complement's position in the matrix clause. From the CG perspective, this is not a matter of raising, but of the predicate having variants making different choices of trajector or landmark (Langacker 1995c). While the "raised" nominal participates only minimally in the matrix process, it does have a valid semantic role, namely it specifies the topic with respect to which an assessment is made. And since this assessment pertains to the likelihood of the complement event's occurrence (as with the epistemic modals), it might be characterized as epistemic.

But we can still make the distinction, subtle though it may be, between estimating the **likelihood** of an **event** and judging the **validity** of a **proposition**. Effective relations (those holding between events) are not limited to causation or the physical level: they can perfectly well be mental, one event involving the apprehension of another. The first event may, for example, consist in having an

4 Of course, we can use a finite clause to describe an event whose causation is specified by other means: *I brought it about that the fire went out.* The object of the complex causal predicate *bring about* is not the finite clause but rather the pronoun *it*, which refers to the general circumstances in which the event is realized (Achard 1998; Chapter 5). I do not analyze the predicate as indicating that a proposition per se is caused.

attitude in regard to another (*want, prefer, be afraid*), being able to mentally access it (*remember, forget*), or – as a special case – projecting or estimating the likelihood of its occurrence. By the same token, projecting the future course of events is only a special case of epistemic relationships. Note, for instance, that a proposition assessed for validity is not limited to describing future occurrences; it can perfectly well pertain to the present, as in (3), or to the past, as in (7). So in (6), it is really due to the modal *will* – which grounds the complement clause internally – that the judgment expressed by the matrix pertains to a future event. Strictly speaking, what is described as being likely or anticipated is the validity of a proposition – its eventual acceptance as part of a conception of reality. This seems fairly clear for past occurrences, as in (7), and I suggest that it also holds for future events, as in (6). Of course, in practical terms the sentences in (6)(i) and (ii) are equivalent. In terms of predicting what might happen, there is no real difference between projecting a future event and projecting the acceptance of a proposition describing a future event.

(7) a. *They expect that she was late.*
  b. *It is likely that she was late.*

The sentences in (8) illustrate a second apparent problem for the correlation of finite complements with epistemic relationships: while the complement clauses are marked by *that*, the relations profiled by the matrix predicates are **effective** rather than epistemic. They represent actions or assessments aimed at determining what actually happens (instead of just knowing about it). Observe, however, that the complement clauses are not really finite. Although they do have overt subjects, they do not display the usual pattern of clausal grounding – for the most part, the verb appears as an uninflected stem, with no marking for tense or modality (**She demanded that I {am / will be / would be} there on time*). Here I will only say that this construction is closely related to imperatives (cf. *You be there on time!*) and are comparable to infinitives, as represented in Figure 10.6(d), in terms of the connection they establish between matrix and complement events.[5]

(8) a. *She {demanded / required / asked / requested} that I be there on time.*
  b. *It is {important / essential / crucial / advisable} that you be there on time.*

In short, not every clause marked by *that* is truly finite, nor is every finite clause marked by *that*. We have already seen that *that* is sometimes optional with a finite clause, or even impermissible. Furthermore, as seen in (9), certain

5 They are also comparable to **subjunctive** complements in a language like French. These are intermediate between finite and non-finite clauses.

complement-taking predicates occur with *whether* instead of *that.*[6] Just as the sentences in (8) are closely related to imperatives, these are closely related to interrogatives; the complements are often called "embedded questions". For our purposes, we can analyze *whether* as shown in Figure 10.7. It indicates that a conceptualizer (C_1) who is attempting to augment his conception of reality has reached a "branching" point where he has to make a decision: from a range of candidate propositions, he has to choose just one to include in RC_1 (Langacker 2001d).

(9) *I wonder whether I lost my passport (or whether someone stole it).*

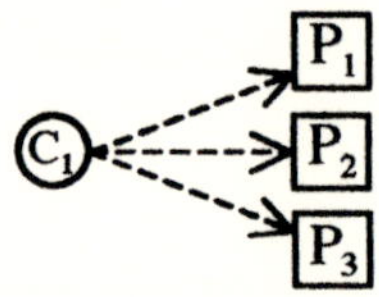

Figure 10.7

3. Cognitive models

By now it should be evident that certain general **cognitive models** are relevant for the semantic and grammatical description of complement constructions. In particular, we have seen the relevance of the Reality Model for clausal grounding as well as the distinction between finite and non-finite complements. This is just one of the cognitive models supporting the semantic characterization of complement-taking predicates.

Despite its generality, the Reality Model pertains to a particular aspect of human experience. A number of relevant models are applicable to most any domain of experience and are thus quite abstract when formulated to cover the full range of cases. Perhaps the most general involves the detection of some **bounded entity** which contrasts with a broader expanse that includes it. In perception, this is the basis for figure/ground organization, e.g. observing a star in the sky, or a noise which interrupts a span of silence. It is the basis for apprehending physical objects (bounded entities in space) and events (bounded occurrences in time). It is hard to imagine any aspect of our experience which does not exhibit this type of organization.

---

6 More generally, they require an interrogative element, as in *I wonder what I should wear.* Infinitival clauses can also be interrogative: *I wonder what to wear.*

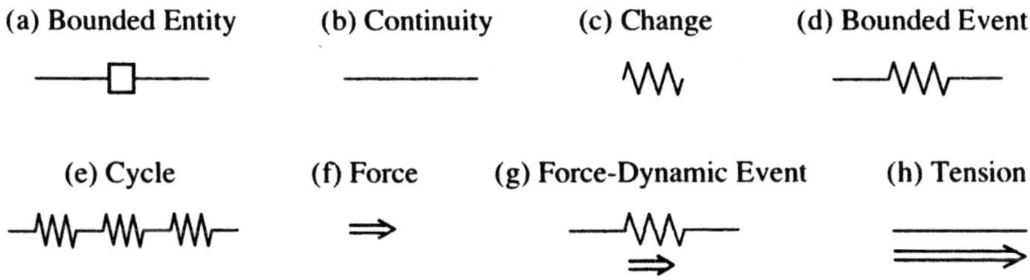

Figure 10.8

Equally fundamental (if not more so) is the notion of **continuity** vs. **change**. Indeed, from the processing standpoint the detection of a contrast can be regarded as a kind of change. Here, though, we are mostly concerned with continuity vs. change **through time**. Change tends to occur in episodes of limited duration, with a period of continuity on either end. This gives rise to a special case of a bounded entity, namely a **bounded event**. This in turn makes possible the observation of a **cycle**, where the same phenomenon occurs at different locations in time, separated by periods of its absence. Numerous cycles are fundamental to both our bodily functioning and the world we live in: breathing; sleeping and being awake; the alternation of day and night; the phases of the moon; the seasons; calendrical cycles; etc.

Also fundamental, with many linguistic manifestations, is the notion of **force** and the conception of basic kinds of force-dynamic interactions (Talmy 1988). We are generally most cognizant of force when it occurs in bounded episodes and causes an observable change. This correlation of force and change yields the notion of a bounded, force-dynamic event, which is arguably the prototype for verbs and clauses. Less typical, but still quite common in our experience, is the combination of force with continuity. These are cases where there is no observable change becauses the forces involved are in balance or are too weak to have an effect. Notably, the stable structure of our physical environment depends on forces which counteract the constant force of gravity: we keep ourselves upright, a table supports an object placed on it, posts and beams keep a roof from caving in. Because these forces are constant, we tend to notice them only when the balance is disrupted and something happens: we fall down, an object falls off a table, a roof collapses. Steady force that does not lead to change is what we refer to as **tension**.

As we have already seen, these basic notions combine in various ways into more elaborate cognitive models that are also reflected in many aspects of everyday experience. One such model, the Tension Cycle, consists of four successive stages: an initial stage of relaxation (i.e. non-force-dynamic continuity); next a stage of increasing tension; then a force-dynamic event which has the effect of releasing the built-up pressure; and finally, resulting from the event, another stage of relaxation. An obvious example is the explosion of a volcano. Another is what we describe metaphorically as a person "erupting" or "exploding" due to anger (Kövecses 1990: ch. 4). Still another is the release of sexual tension through intercourse.

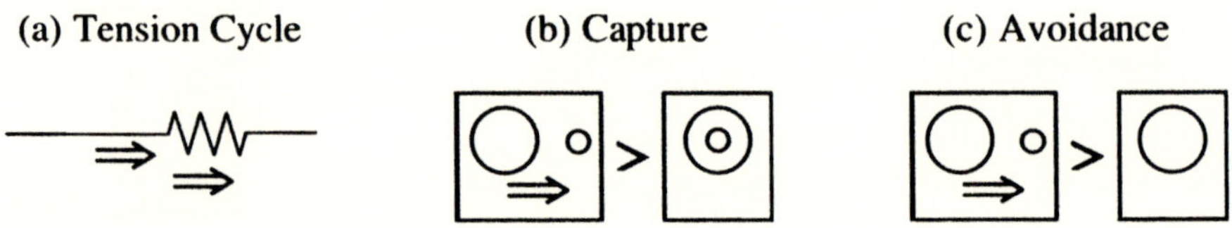

Figure 10.9

Often a state of tension is created when something comes close enough to us that we can interact with it; I will say that it enters our **field**, or region of potential interaction. This potential for interaction creates a state of tension – we have to deal with the situation in some manner (if only by ignoring it). One basic way of resolving the tension is by **capture**: taking control of the intruding entity, or **target**. We might, for example, see a piece of candy that we want very much to taste, and resolve this tension by eating it. Or if I use a book and leave it lying on my desk, I feel the tension of it being out of place until I dispel the tension by putting it back on the bookshelf where it belongs. The opposite way of resolving tension is by **avoidance**, i.e. acting in such a manner that the target is no longer in the field. For instance, instead of putting the book away I could simply leave the room, so that I no longer see it lying there on my desk.

These examples illustrate the general cognitive model referred to as the Control Cycle (Langacker 2002c; Chapter 9), represented in Figure 5.5. The Control Cycle combines the Tension Cycle with the notion of capture (or alternatively, avoidance). Its basic elements are some kind of actor; the actor's dominion, i.e. the set of entities under the actor's control; the field, defined by the potential for interaction; and the target, an entity that appears in the actor's field. The Control Cycle has a number of phases, starting with the baseline, a state of relaxation. When a target enters the actor's field, it creates a state of tension, for it has to be dealt with in some manner; this is the potential phase. This leads to the action phase, where the potential for interaction is realized, typically by capture. In the result phase, where the target is under the actor's control, the tension has been resolved, and the actor is once more in a state of relaxation.

The prototype would be an instance of physical capture, as when a cat catches a mouse. A cat is normally in a state of relaxation (resting). But if a mouse should wander into its field of view, this creates a state of tension, in which the cat intends to catch it and physically prepares to do so (by creeping up on it and getting ready to spring). The cat releases the tension by pouncing on the mouse and biting it. If the cat is successful, the mouse is then under its control, to be played with and finally eaten.

However, physical capture and control are special cases. Abstractly formulated, the Control Cycle applies to a wide range of phenomena. Consider visual perception. In this case the actor is a perceiver, the field is the visual field, the dominion is the focal region, and the target is the object of perception. Suppose a salient target, e.g. a moving object, appears in the field of view – not in the center, but at the periphery of the visual field. This creates a state of tension, for objects at the periphery cannot be perceived with any acuity. We resolve this tension by shifting our gaze, so that the target appears in the focal region, where we can see it in clear detail. This amounts to perceptual capture – the target is brought under perceptual control. The situation is stable until we have reason to shift our gaze once more, thereby focusing on another target.

Living creatures are continually engaged in activity in the effort to achieve and maintain control of their circumstances. Bodily functions like breathing, eating, and drinking instantiate the Control Cycle. So does the directing and focusing of attention, at the perceptual and mental levels. At the social level, we experience a state of tension when meeting someone new; the tension is resolved through interactions which establish a stable relationship providing social control. To satisfy our needs and desires, we go through life acquiring possessions which we then control. Viewed abstractly, the Control Cycle represents a fundamental pattern inherent in many aspects of living and functioning in the world.

A complex event may involve multiple instances of the Control Cycle, or be analyzable in more than one way with respect to it. Consider breathing. A number of phases can be discerned in a single breathing cycle: after completing one cycle, for just a moment we feel OK (relaxation); then we feel the need for air (tension); in the next phase we contract our abdominal muscle (force) to let air in; for a brief span of time we keep the air in, with increasing effort required the longer we do so (growing tension); we then relax the abdominal muscle (suspension of force) and let the air rush out; after which we are momentarily OK once more (relaxation).

<table>
<tr><td rowspan="2">OK</td><td rowspan="2">need air</td><td colspan="3">breathe/take a breath</td><td rowspan="2">OK</td></tr>
<tr><td>inhale/breathe in</td><td>hold breath</td><td>exhale/breathe out</td></tr>
<tr><td>relaxation</td><td>tension</td><td>force</td><td>tension</td><td>force</td><td>relaxation</td></tr>
<tr><td>Baseline</td><td>Potential</td><td colspan="3">Action</td><td>Result</td></tr>
<tr><td>Baseline</td><td colspan="3">Potential</td><td>Action</td><td>Result</td></tr>
<tr><td rowspan="2">Baseline</td><td rowspan="2">Potential</td><td rowspan="2">Action</td><td>Result</td><td rowspan="2">Action</td><td rowspan="2">Result</td></tr>
<tr><td>Potential</td></tr>
</table>

Figure 10.10

As shown in Figure 10.10, the overall event can be analyzed in several ways. Viewed in global terms, it constitutes one instance of the Control Cycle, where the felt need for air functions as the potential phase, and the action phase consists in a single act of breathing (taking air in and letting it out). Alternatively, we could analyze the potential phase as including the intake of air and the growing pressure we feel to release it; the action phase is then limited to letting it out. But in a finer-grained view we can see the overall event as comprising two overlapping instances of the Control Cycle. The first mini-cycle involves the action of breathing in, which relieves the tension of feeling the need for air. However, the situation that results from this capture of air is itself a state of tension and building pressure, which is relieved by letting the air flow out, to complete the second mini-cycle. It should not be thought that any particular analysis is necessarily "right" or "wrong". The important point is that so many aspects of our ongoing experience instantiate fundamental patterns susceptible to abstract characterization.

These patterns provide a partial basis for semantic description. For instance, *hungry* describes a state of tension relieved by the action of *eating*, which results in being *full*. The verbs *need*, *get*, and *have* describe a parallel cycle. You can resolve the tension of *wanting* something by *picking* it *up*, which results in your *holding* it. But since holding requires the steady exertion of force, this is also a state of tension, which can be relieved by *putting* the object *down*. In a similar case of overlapping cycles, the cat which *catches* a mouse then *has* it, a steady-state result. However, if the mouse tries to escape, the cat must exert energy to *keep* it, a state of tension relieved if the cat decides to *let* it *go*. Or in regard to Figure 10.10, you *need* air and relieve this state of tension by *taking* a breath. Once you breathe in – also describable as *taking* a breath – you can *hold* your breath until you decide to *release* it.

(10) a. *hungry* (potential) > *eat* (action) > *full* (result)
b. *need* (potential) > *get* (action) > *have* (result)
c. *want* (potential) > *pick up* (action) > *hold* (result/potential) > *put down* (action)
d. *want* (potential) > *catch* (action) > *have* (result) > *keep* (potential) > *let go* (action)

I suggest that these notions are quite relevant to the semantic description of complement-taking predicates. In this case, as shown in Figure 10.11, the actor is a conceptualizer (C), the dominion is C's conception of reality (RC), and the target is a proposition (P). Predicates like *suspect*, *learn*, and *know* then represent successive phases of the Control Cycle, wherein C gains control of P in the sense of incorporating it in RC. I will try to show that the Control Cycle is pivotal to the semantic characterization of English predicates taking finite complements.

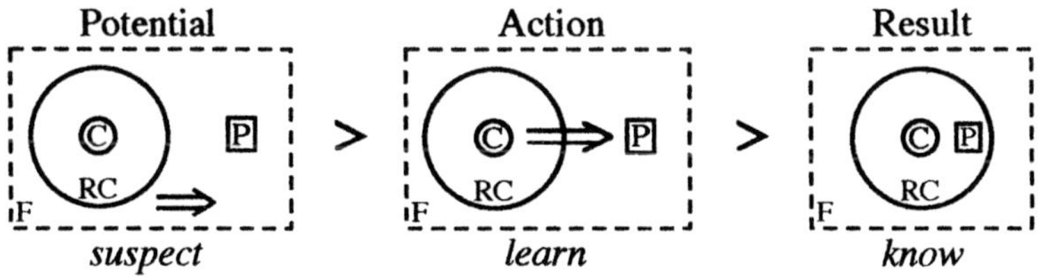

Figure 10.11

Like grounding elements (tense and the modals), these predicates specify the status of occurrences with respect to a conception of reality (RC). There is however an important difference. At the grounding level (internal to a finite clause), the target of assessment is a process (**p**), i.e. an event or situation. Reality (R) is the history of occurrences up through the present, and at the clause level RC is a particular conceptualizer's version of this history. By contrast, at the level of complex sentences and complementation the target is a proposition (P), as expressed by a finite clause (that itself incorporates grounding). At this level a reality conception (RC) is a **set of propositions**, not just the history of occurrences. While they pertain to occurrences – events and situations – propositions are more abstract, for they also include an indication of their epistemic status. We can still define **reality** as the history of events and situations, but for propositions RC is not just C's version of this history. Note that propositions accepted as valid (part of RC) are not limited to those describing past and present occurrences. As seen in (11), they can also describe future occurrences, things which did not happen, or situations whose status is uncertain. That is, what we purport to **know** (accept as real or valid) includes not only reality in the narrow sense – the established course of events – but how the path it has followed relates to other conceivable paths (both past and future).

(11) a. *I know that she will be angry.*
b. *It's true that we did not get the grant.*
c. *They realize that the lost climbers may already be dead.*

In Figure 10.12 I show the difference between these two levels of reality conception.[7] In the case of grounding, C's conception of reality corresponds

7 These are the levels referred to as **basic** vs. **elaborated reality** in Chapter 6 (§ 4) and in Chapter 8 (§ 3.5).

to some portion of R. A process (**p**) accepted as real (part of RC) is therefore viewed as belonging to the history of occurrences constituting R. On the other hand, since complementation pertains to propositions (not just processes), the perspective is much broader. A proposition (P) incorporates not only **p** (the profiled occurrence), but also **p**'s position in relation to R – whether it is in R or excluded from R, as in (11). So at this level a reality conception (RC_1) includes not only the course of events that constitute R, but also the alternative evolutionary paths it might have followed instead and the various paths it might follow in the future. In Figure 10.12(b) I show the case of a proposition whose grounding locates the profiled process (**p**) outside of R. Although the **process** is then not real (part of RC), the **proposition** is still accepted as valid (part of RC_1) by virtue of making an accurate assessment of **p**'s location in regard to R.

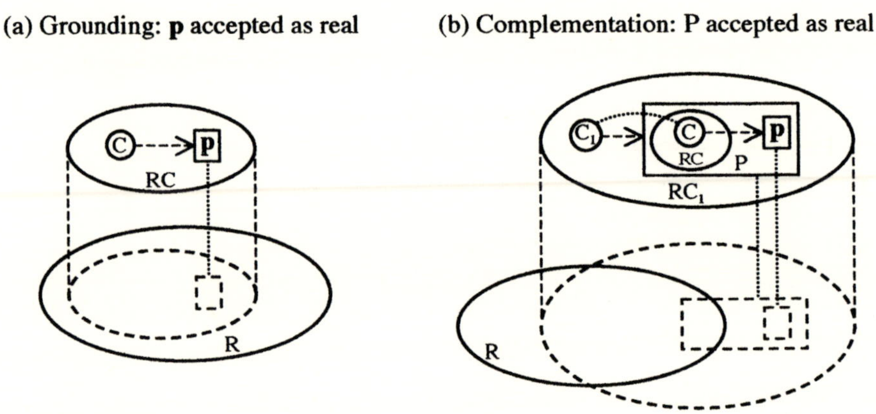

Figure 10.12

An example is (11)a, where the profiled occurrence (**p**) is the situation of her being angry. Because it lies in the future, that process is not yet real. However, the proposition expressed by the complement – *she will be angry* – is nonetheless accepted as real (or valid), i.e. as part of RC_1. RC_1 is still a conception of reality, not in the narrow sense of being **confined to** R, but in the broader sense of indicating how occurrences **relate to** R, whether they are part of R or excluded from it.

4. Personal predicates

Let us now consider the predicates that occur with finite complements. We will first examine **personal** predicates, where the subject is the person who functions as conceptualizer (C). Afterwards we will look at **impersonal** predicates, where the grammatical subject is the pronoun *it* (e.g. *It's true that she is angry*). For the most part I will confine my attention to single-word predicates, as opposed to periphrastic expressions like *take it for granted* (e.g. *I take it for granted that she is angry*).

Even limiting our attention to personal subjects, a large number of predicates take finite complements. In one way or another, most if not all of them involve the Epistemic Control Cycle (ECC), partially shown in Figure 10.11. The density of the lexical coding in this domain indicates the importance in our lives of propositional judgment and epistemic control. Some predicates, like *suspect*, *learn*, and *know* in Figure 10.11, refer specifically to phases of the ECC. With others, this cycle is more in the background. While P does have some position with respect to the ECC, the semantic focus of such predicates is on other realms of experience.

One large class, sampled in (12)a, consists of **affective** predicates expressing some attitude or emotional reaction to a proposition. These involve the result phase of the ECC, in that the conceptualizer (C_1) accepts the proposition as being valid (established in RC_1). Expressions like (12)b indicate that P is part of RC_1: if Steve (C_1) is *happy* that his wife is pregnant, he must know that she is. These predicates tend to be factive, i.e. the speaker also accepts the validity of P. Though not impossible, (12)c is therefore somewhat odd. However, P's epistemic status – its acceptance by both the subject (C_1) and the speaker (C_0) – lies in the background, being **presupposed** rather than **asserted**. In CG terms, it is part of the **base** rather than being **profiled**. What these predicates profile (put onstage as the focus of attention) is the affective relationship, the subject's positive or negative feeling about the proposition. So when the matrix predicate is negated, as in (12)d, the negation bears on C_1's attitude toward P, not its validity. It is not denied that she knew her husband was unfaithful (or that he was), but only that this surprised her.

(12) a. **Affective Predicates:** *happy, sad, elated, thrilled, disappointed, devastated, regret, pleased, displeased, annoyed, disturbed, offended, appalled, disappointed, shocked, surprised, devastated, like it, love it, hate it, resent it, dislike it, detest it*
b. *Steve is happy that his wife is pregnant (*but he doesn't know it).*
c. *Alice resents it that her husband is unfaithful (??but he isn't).*
d. *She wasn't surprised that her husband was unfaithful.*

Another large class of predicates pertain to communication and verbal interaction. Being interactive, these imply two conceptualizers, each with his own conception of reality. In describing these predicates, one must therefore consider P's epistemic assessment by each conceptualizer in relation to their own (and each other's) conception of reality. In (13)b, *ask* indicates that for Alice the assessment of P (*he was unfaithful*) is only in the potential phase, whereas for Steve it is presumably in the result phase – Steve either knows that P is valid or knows that it is not. In (13)c, Steve's denial implies that P is excluded from his conception of reality; this represents the result phase, based on avoidance rather than capture. It may further be intended to induce his interlocutor, who was considering P for inclusion in her reality conception (potential phase), to reject it instead (action phase avoidance). As for *persuade* in (13)d, it suggests that Steve accepts P as valid (result phase) and profiles a successful effort in getting Alice to accept it (action phase).

(13) a. **Interactive Predicates:** *say, tell, inform, state, ask, suggest, propose, hint, persuade, convince, admit, confess, hear, argue, claim, maintain, agree, disagree, deny*
b. *Alice asked Steve whether he was unfaithful.*
c. *Steve denied that he was unfaithful.*
d. *Steve persuaded Alice that he was faithful.*

We see, then, that interactive predicates invoke the ECC in varied and complex ways. Here we will concentrate on the simpler case of predicates reflecting the epistemic efforts of a single conceptualizer. As a first step in their analysis, we can assign them to one of the three main phases of the ECC, as in Figure 10.11: result, action, or potential. The lists in (14) give an indication of their nature and variety, but are certainly not exhaustive.[8] Since each class has numerous members, it is evident that their position in regard to the ECC represents only a partial characterization of their meanings (though certainly a very basic one). Much can be learned from a fine-grained description of their differences. Here, though, I can only make a few brief comments on each group.

(14) a. **Result Phase:** *know, sure, certain, believe, understand, realize, accept, acknowledge, convinced, persuaded, recognize, remember, recall, forget*
b. **Action Phase:** *learn, figure out, calculate, ascertain, determine, realize, recognize, notice, see, observe, find out, discover, decide*

8 Due to polysemy, some predicates are listed in more than one category.

c. **Potential Phase:** *believe, think, suppose, imagine, suspect, figure, reckon, expect, doubt, consider, ponder, wonder, unsure, unclear, undecided, uncertain*

Among the result phase predicates, *know* is the neutral term (and doubtless the most frequent). *Sure* and *certain* emphasize the strength of C_1's commitment, hence the unlikelihood of C_1 "changing his mind" in regard to P. When used as a result predicate, as in (15)a, *believe* retains a vestige of its more basic use for the potential phase, as in (15)b, indicating that the knowledge derives more from faith or authority than from solid evidence. *Understand* suggests that P is part of a broader system of knowledge. Predicates like *realize, accept, acknowledge, convinced, persuaded*, and *recognize* convey some information about the process which led to P's incorporation in C_1's conception of reality. *Remember, recall*, and *forget* pertain to the process of mentally accessing a proposition already established there.

(15) a. *He firmly believes that the earth is flat.* [result]
b. *He believes the earth is flat, but he really doesn't know.* [potential]
c. *By accident she learned that Steve was unfaithful.* [action]
d. *Through great effort she learned that Steve was unfaithful.* [action]

Unsurprisingly, the action phase predicates differ primarily in the nature of the process leading to P's acceptance as being valid. The neutral expression is *learn*, which suggests passivity, as in (15)c, but does not require it, as seen in (15)d. With *figure out, calculate, ascertain*, and *determine*, P's acceptance results from effortful activity. *Realize* indicates the absence of such activity: P's validity simply became apparent to C_1. *Recognize, notice, see*, and *observe* are also non-effortful but specify that the realization is based on observation (whether perceptual or purely mental). *Find out* and *discover* highlight P's prior status as something not known or observable. *Decide* emphasizes that C_1 faced a choice in accepting P as real.

While the distinction between the result and action phases was made on semantic grounds, there is grammatical evidence for its correctness. In English, predicates describing stable situations – imperfectives – comfortably occur in the present tense with true, present-time meaning, and resist the progressive; predicates describing bounded events – perfectives – do the opposite (Langacker 1987b, 2001 f). This behavior is exemplified in (16)a–b. From the semantic analysis, we can therefore predict that result predicates should behave like imperfectives, and action predicates like perfectives. This proves to be the case, as exemplified in (16)c–d. It is further predicted that a predicate which can be used in either way will be interpreted as indicating result or action depending on whether it occurs in the simple present or in the progressive. This prediction is also borne out, as seen in (16)e–f: in (16)e, where the present tense indicates the imperfective meaning, Alice already knows that Steve is unfaithful, whereas in (16)f, where the progressive indicates the perfective meaning, she is in the process of learning this.

(16) a. *Alice {is tall / *is being tall}.* [imperfective; stable situation]
b. *Alice {*gets fat / is getting fat}.* [perfective; bounded event]
c. *Alice {knows / *is knowing} that Steve is unfaithful.* [result; imperfective]
d. *Alice {*learns / is learning} that Steve is unfaithful.* [action; perfective]
e. *Alice recognizes that Steve is unfaithful.* [result; imperfective]
f. *Alice is recognizing that Steve is unfaithful.* [action; perfective]

Turning now to the potential phase, we find that predicates exhibit mixed behavior. Most, like *believe*, behave as imperfectives. However, *consider* and *ponder* behave as perfectives, and *wonder* goes both ways. Also, a number of these predicates occur with *whether* instead of *that*. So we have the three-way split illustrated in (17). This is grammatical indication that the potential phase of the ECC is complex and ought to be divided into smaller subphases.

(17) a. *She {believes / *is believing} that he is unfaithful.* [imperfective; *that*]
b. *She {*considers / is considering} whether he is unfaithful.* [perfective; *whether*]
c. *She {is unsure / *is being unsure} whether he is unfaithful.* [imperfective; *whether*]

I propose that these subphases represent a **mini-cycle** comprising an **action** phase and a **result** phase, as shown in Figure 10.13. The action phase of this mini-cycle consists in a process of **assessment**, i.e. actively considering the proposition in order to determine its possible validity. The result phase of the mini-cycle is some kind of **inclination** with respect to P – some initial but still tentative judgment concerning it. This is the final stage preparatory to making a definite decision on whether to accept P as real or to reject it.[9] The inclination stage is one of tension, for although it represents a locally stable situation, the ultimate status of P has still not been resolved. The final decision is still pending.

9 It is analogous to the stage where a cat has decided to catch a mouse, and is in a crouching posture (a state of tension), but has not yet sprung.

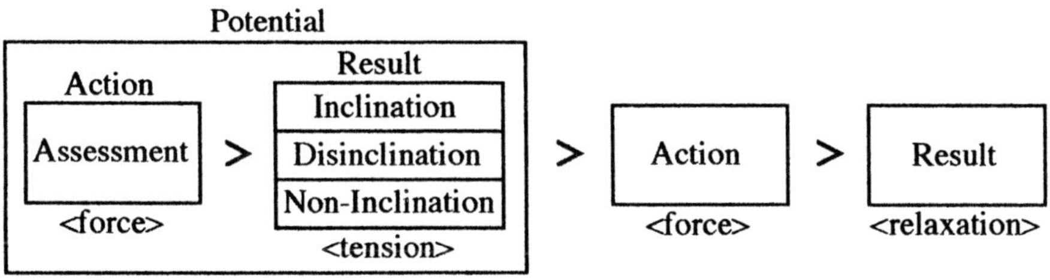

Figure 10.13

These mini-phases are sketched in Figure 10.14. In the assessment phase, C_1 faces the task of deciding between two options: either P is valid or it is not (~P). C_1 assesses this matter by **projecting** the extension of RC_1, with P as the **target** of extension. By taking account of RC_1 as it is presently constituted, C_1 tries to anticipate whether its future development (based on additional evidence) will follow a path that results in P being incorporated in RC_1. The double arrow in diagram (a) represents C_1's effort in making this projection. This is an active process involving mental force. Being force-dynamic, it is construed as occurring in bounded episodes, so assessment predicates like *consider* function grammatically as perfectives.

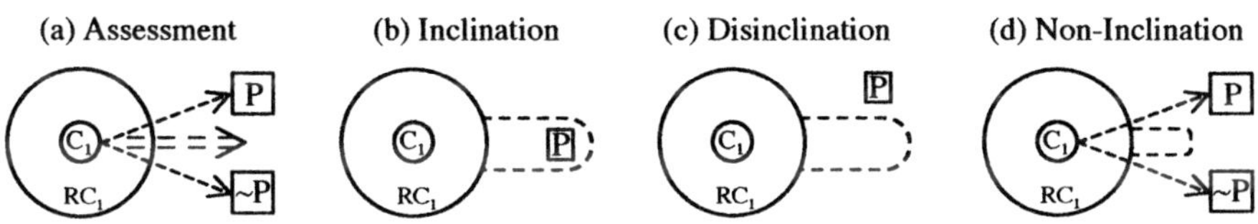

Figure 10.14

This activity has different possible outcomes, each a kind of inclination with respect to P's acceptance in RC_1. These are only inclinations, not final decisions, since they only reflect C_1's projection, which (on the basis of further evidence) may or may not prove accurate. And since the matter has not yet been resolved, this represents a state of tension with respect to the global ECC. Locally, however, it is a stable situation resulting from the action of assessment. One possible outcome is a **positive inclination** (which I will simply call **inclination**). As shown in diagram (b), this results when C_1's projection of RC_1 (dashed-line ellipse) leads to P's incorporation. The opposite outcome, labeled **disinclination**, is when the projection specifically does not include P. These two possibilities, illustrated by *believe* and *doubt*, are of course instances of capture and avoidance. There is however a third outcome, where mental projection does not result in either. With a predicate like *unsure*, the assessment process has failed to establish either inclination or disinclination with respect to P's inclusion in RC_1. I will call this **non-inclination**.

(18) a. **Assessment:** *consider, ponder, wonder*
b. **Inclination:** *believe, think, suppose, imagine, suspect, figure, reckon, expect*
c. **Disinclination:** *doubt, don't {believe / think / suppose / imagine /...}*
d. **Non-inclination:** *unsure, unclear, undecided, uncertain, wonder*

I believe these characterizations are justified on purely semantic grounds. I want to emphasize, however, that they are supported by grammatical evidence. First, the distinction between action (i.e. assessment) and result (the various kinds of inclination) accounts for why the predicates in (18)a behave as perfectives, and those in (18)b–d as imperfectives. The contrast shows up nicely with *wonder*, which behaves in either fashion. In (19)a, the perfective *wonder* designates a bounded episode in which Alice actively considers the issue of Steve's possible unfaithfulness. On the other hand, the imperfective use in (19)b does not imply that Alice is thinking about the matter right now. It merely indicates that the matter is unresolved in her mind, i.e. that the projection she is able to make (whenever she does think about it) does not result in either a positive or a negative inclination.

(19) a. *At this very moment Alice is wondering whether Steve is unfaithful.*
b. *Since men are so untrustworthy, Alice wonders whether Steve is unfaithful.*

Also accounted for is the distribution of *that* and *whether*. Note that *whether* is used in the two circumstances where C_1 still faces an option, namely assessment and non-inclination. Both involve the configuration in Figure 10.7. On the other hand, *that* is used for both inclination and disinclination, the two cases where – in local terms – the issue has been resolved: the extension of RC_1 either includes P or it does not. So at least within this mini-cycle, C_1 no longer faces an option.

As is generally the case, there are more predicates describing the positive situation than the negative one. There are numerous simple predicates describing inclination, but few describing **dis**inclination *Doubt* is the only one that readily comes to mind.[10] Observe that *doubt* can sometimes occur with *whether* as well as *that*, especially when P itself involves potentiality:

10 While *skeptical* and *dubious* are similar, they are not so strongly negative in regard to P. Instead of **dis**inclination, they indicate that a high or higher level of justification

(20) a. *I doubt very much {that / whether} she can trust him.*
b. *I doubt {that / *whether} he has been unfaithful.*

It seems, then, that the combination of *doubt* and *whether* is used for something intermediate between disinclination and non-inclination: while it does express disinclination, the content of P itself invokes the multiple options coded by *whether.*

Be that as it may, there are indeed alternatives to *doubt* for expressing disinclination. As noted in (18)c, disinclination can also be conveyed through the negation of certain inclination predicates. In the generative era, expressions like (21)a were sometimes analyzed by positing a transformation which "raised" the negative from the complement clause into the matrix clause. This rule accounted for the apparent semantic equivalence of (21)a–b. Although the negation appears in the matrix clause in (21)a, semantically it seems to affect the complement, just as in (21)b.

(21) a. *I don't {believe / think / suppose /...} she can trust him.*
b. *I {believe / think / suppose /...} she can't trust him.*

Because CG does not allow transformations or derivations from underlying structures, some other analysis must be found. The conceptual characterizations in Figure 10.14 suggest a straightforward account based on the **focus** of negation, i.e. what it applies to (Sumnicht 2004). One possible interpretation of sentences like (21)a is that the force of negation applies to the matrix predicate itself, bearing on some facet of the predicate's meaning. To account for the rough equivalence of (21)a–b, all we need say is that the negation in (21)a affects the polarity of the inclination, changing it from (positive) **inclination** (capture) to **dis**inclination (avoidance). That is, it affects the direction of C_1's mental projection of RC_1, the result being that it does not reach P (the case of inclination) but instead reaches its alternative (~P). On that interpretation (21)a is "logically" equivalent to (21)b, which specifies a positive inclination toward ~P. The expressions represent alternate ways of **construing** (i.e. conceiving and portraying) the same situation.

Finally, I will mention just in passing some other predicates that do not fit neatly into any of the above categories. *Wish* and *hope* have special properties that presumably reflect their basis in **imagination**. *Wish* is basically counterfactual, and thus requires a non-immediate form of the complement verb. The complement of *hope* can be past, present, or future. I have no good explanation

is needed for a **positive** inclination. They may also be interactive, indicating C_1's reluctance to accept as valid the proposition offered by an interlocutor.

for why, with future events, the complement favors the present tense (rather than *will*). In any case, *wish* and *hope* are not based on the ECC, i.e. they do not refer to stages in the striving for knowledge.

(22) a. *I wish he {were / would be} more considerate.*
b. *I hope she {won the award / is happy / wins the award / ?will win the award}.*

Sharing this feature are such predicates as *promise*, *guarantee*, *vow*, and *determined*. In a broad sense these are **effective**, since they have to do with ensuring the occurrence of events.[11] The relation, however, is indirect – the matrix predicates merely indicate a **commitment** to bring about the complement event, not any actual effort to do so (let alone causation or success). So in contrast to predicates like *make*, *cause*, and *try*, they are not effective in the narrow sense of a relation between events at the level of reality itself. But neither are they epistemic in the narrow sense of pertaining to knowledge, as expressed by propositions. Hence the complement, though finite, is not a fully autonomous proposition. For the most part, it can only describe **future** occurrences that the subject is able to control. With a past event, as in (23)b, what the subject promises or guarantees is that **future knowledge** will include the complement occurrence (it will turn out to be the case that Alice got the award). In this case the predicates do indeed have epistemic import.

(23) a. *I {promise / guarantee / vow / am determined} that Alice will get the award.*
b. *I {?promise / ?guarantee / *vow / *am determined} that Alice got the award.*

These exemplify predicates which either require or prefer complements describing future events. Among these **future oriented** predicates are some with affective value:

(24) a. *I {fear / anticipate / am afraid / am optimistic} that the judge will find him guilty.*
b. *?I {fear / anticipate / am afraid / am optimistic} that the judge found him guilty.*

Their future orientation distinguishes these from the affective predicates in (12), involving reaction to something already known. Here the attitude pertains to the **prospect** of the event described in the complement occurring, in which case the proposition expressed by the complement will be valid. Once more,

11 In this respect they resemble root modals, sketched in Figure 10.2(c).

the proposition – largely being restricted to future occurrences – is less than fully autonomous. With non-future events, as in (24)b, the expression is once again more clearly epistemic. The affect is not directed at the complement event per se, but rather at the possibility of the proposition proving valid in the future.[12]

5. Impersonal predicates

With impersonal predicates the matrix subject is the pronoun *it*, which is often considered meaningless. Alternatively, the complement clause can itself function as matrix subject. And in some cases such expressions seem equivalent to an infinitival construction with a personal subject, the so-called "raising" construction:

(25) a. *It is likely that your daughter will fail the examination.* [impersonal]
b. *That your daughter will fail the examination is likely.* [subject complement clause]
c. *Your daughter is likely to fail the examination.* ["raised" subject]

In classic transformational grammar (e.g. Rosenbaum 1967; Postal 1974), such expressions were derived from the same or very similar underlying structures. This is not permitted in CG. Instead, the differences in form are taken as indicating subtly different meanings.

The three constructions differ in their choice of matrix subject. Semantically, the subject functions as trajector, the element accorded primary focus within the profiled relationship. This is a matter of emphasis, or prominence, not a matter of "logic" – we are quite capable of choosing alternate facets of a situation to highlight in this fashion. In different ways, the options chosen in (25) each represent a natural choice. The complement is a natural choice of subject, as in (25)b, because the event it profiles is what is actually being assessed for likelihood. The scale invoked by *likely* ranks events for their probability of occurrence, so in a narrow, technical sense only an event can be directly positioned with respect to it.

12 *Fear* and *afraid* have another use, in which the affect does not pertain to the event, but rather to the prospect of having to report the event, e.g. *I'm afraid the news is bad*. In this use the predicates are not future oriented: *I'm afraid your cat has died* [= *I'm {sorry / reluctant to tell you} that your cat has died*].

However, languages show a general tendency to avoid clausal subjects. It is people – not events or propositions – that most commonly serve as the focus of interest and topic of conversation. It is therefore quite natural for primary focal prominence to be conferred on an event's major participant, as in (25)c, even when the event itself is the entity being situated on the scale.[13] This alternate focusing produces the "raising" construction (Langacker 1995c). I have already discussed the rough equivalence of expressions like (25)b, with a finite complement, and (25)c, with an infinitival complement. In practical terms, there is no real difference between estimating the likelihood of an event (one kind of effective relationship) and judging the validity of a proposition which designates that event (an epistemic relationship). These notions are nonetheless distinct, as witnessed in (26). Events *occur* or *happen*; propositions are *true* or *valid*.

(26) a. *That she will fail the exam is likely to {be true / prove valid / *happen / *occur}.*
b. *Is she likely to fail the exam? It might well {happen / occur / ??be true / *prove valid}.*

What about (25)a? Why is *it* a natural choice of subject? An answer was proposed in Chapter 5. The *it* that appears in complement constructions has a straightforward characterization in terms of the ECC: it designates the field, identifiable as the conceptualizer's scope of awareness. Being abstract and diffuse, the field is inherently non-salient. As a kind of global setting, however, it is a natural point of entry for mentally accessing a proposition that emerges within it. And that is just what a subject is claimed to be: the **starting point** for purposes of conceptualizing the profiled clausal process.[14] Thus a sentence like (25)a, with *it* as subject, exemplifies the common strategy of starting with something large and "zooming in" to examine what is found inside.

The expressions in (25) involve three variants of the predicate *likely*, shown respectively in Figure 10.15. All of them situate a proposition or event toward the higher end of a scale (single arrow) representing the probability that the profiled event will occur. The double arrow indicates the conceptualizer's mental effort in making this judgment – this is a state of tension, *likely* being an inclination predicate. It is also impersonal, in that the conceptualizer is left

13 Using the terminology of Chapter 2 (§ 2), the event functions as **active zone** for locating the person with respect to the scale (Langacker 1984). This type of discrepancy between subject and active zone is normal, not exceptional, and exemplifies the ubiquitous phenomenon of metonymy.

14 More precisely, a subject specifies the trajector, characterized as the initial reference point invoked for building up to the full conception of a profiled relationship.

implicit. In fact, C can be thought of as a virtual or generalized conceptualizer, as in the case of grounding elements. This leaves three possible candidates for the entity to be focused as trajector: the field (F), the proposition, or the central participant of the profiled event. Because trajector status is simply a matter of prominence, the choice of trajector does not affect the "logical" properties of the predicate, which are the same in all three variants.

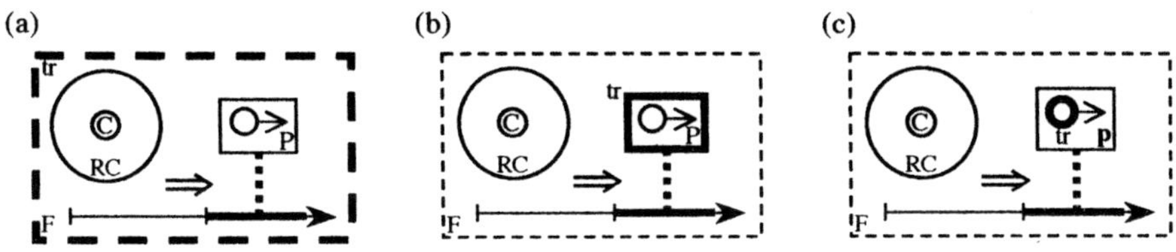

Figure 10.15

Our concern is with predicates allowing *it* as subject, as in diagram (a).[15] As with personal subjects, some predicates invoke the ECC only secondarily, i.e. P's epistemic status is presupposed but does not constitute the profiled relationship. In particular, the predicates in (27) all invoke the result phase, since they presuppose the validity of P (which makes them factive). What they designate is some kind of reaction or judgment in regard to this state of affairs.

(27) a. **Experiential:** *surprising, shocking, astounding, amazing, annoying, disturbing, frightening, scary, encouraging, discouraging, puzzling, mystifying, instructive, understandable, acceptable, unacceptable, inexcusable*

b. **Evaluative:** *good, bad, great, fine, okay, nice, sad, tragic, wonderful, marvelous, terrible, horrible, terrific*

c. **Consequential:** *important, significant, crucial, essential, relevant, irrelevant, helpful*

d. **Normative:** *unusual, odd, strange, bizarre, funny, normal, typical, appropriate, inappropriate, fitting, proper, right, justifiable*

On purely semantic grounds, the categories in (27) can be argued for but are less than fully obvious. They are overlapping rather than sharply distinct, and these predicates might well be grouped in other ways. In making these distinctions, I have been guided in part by the possibility of adding an indirect object,

15 Virtually all such predicates also allow the complement to function as subject, as in Figure 10.15(b). The obvious exceptions are *seem* and *appear*. Complement subjects are uncommon in casual speech.

marked with *to*, in order to specify the conceptualizer; I suspect that in actual speech this is almost always the speaker. My own judgments (which ought to be checked using corpus data) are that the predicates I have labeled **experiential** and **consequential** allow the phrase *to me*, while those labeled **evaluative** and **normative** resist it, as exemplified in (28). The question, then, is whether the groupings suggested by this property prove to be semantically coherent, or whether the possibility of an indirect object is purely a matter of convention, with no real semantic basis.[16]

(28) a. *It is {surprising / shocking / puzzling / unacceptable} to me that they are so poor.*
  b. *It is {good / sad / wonderful / terrible} (*to me) that the polar ice is melting.*
  c. *It is {important / crucial / irrelevant / helpful} to me that she knows Chinese.*
  d. *It is {unusual / typical / appropriate / right} (*to me) that he accepted the offer.*

The experiential predicates are all derived from verbs. Moreover, the verbs in question all involve a conceptualizer who has a particular kind of mental experience. Most of these verbs describe the process of causing the landmark (expressed by the object nominal) to have this experience: *surprise*, *shock*, *annoy*, *frighten*, *encourage*, *puzzle*, etc. Others describe the process of the trajector (expressed by the subject) engaging in a certain mental activity: *understand*, *accept*, *excuse*. So it is not at all surprising that the adjectives based on these verbs allow the conceptualizer to be expressed.

By contrast, the evaluative predicates do not derive from verbs.[17] While they do of course imply a conceptualizer who makes the evaluation, they do not refer to any specific kind of experience – their characterization of C's experience is primarily limited to whether it is positive (*good*, *nice*, *wonderful*) or negative (*bad*, *tragic*, *terrible*) and how intense it is (e.g. *good* vs. *great* vs. *wonderful*). Indeed, these predicates are less concerned with experience or mental activity per se than with locating P along an evaluative scale. This property is ascribed to P itself (or more precisely, to the circumstance of P being valid). The implication, in other words, is that P itself merits the positive or negative evaluation, so that any conceptualizer would have this attitude.

16 CG does not prejudge this issue. Classes defined by grammatical behavior may have any degree of semantic coherence.

17 Even though *wonder* and *marvel* are verbs, the adjectives *wonderful* and *marvelous* are based on the corresponding nouns.

The other two classes in (27) have even less to do with mental experience. As the label suggests, consequential predicates pertain to the consequences of the proposition being valid. They serve mainly to convey the extent to which this matters. Because some things matter for people in general, and others only for certain individuals, we have the option of either invoking a generalized conceptualizer or adding an indirect object to specify a particular experiencer. By contrast, normative predicates are mostly concerned with how P relates to social norms, in terms of either frequency or correctness. Their normative nature makes them less amenable to specifying a particular conceptualizer.

It is noteworthy that all the predicates in (27) are adjectives. This is not unexpected given that adjectives describe stable situations (states) and that the abstract entity designated by *it* is hardly capable of action (except metaphorically). If *it* refers to the scope of awareness, it is however capable of passively stimulating some mental reaction on the part of the conceptualizer. Thus among the impersonal predicates are verbs describing the causation of mental experience, as in (29)a. These are the same verbs from which the *V+ing* adjectives in (27)a derive. They do not of course imply (even metaphorically) that the field engages in any conscious act of inducing an experience, but merely that it provides the context in which awareness of P prompts C's mental reaction. So although they do not describe actions, the sentences in (29)a do describe events – events of mental stimulation. But even these verbs are more likely to be used as imperfectives, designating stable situations, as in (29)b. In this use they do not describe events, but rather a steady mental attitude toward P, one which might be manifested whenever C happens to think about the matter.

(29) a. *It {surprised / shocked / scared / puzzled} me that he couldn't remember his name.*
b. *It {surprises / shocks / scares / puzzles} me that he can't remember his name.*

In either use, the verbs in (29) correspond to the result phase of the ECC. The matrix clause in (29) does not profile the event of P being incorporated in RC, but rather the event of C reacting to the fact of its being there. Hence these verbs do not represent the ECC in the sense of designating one of its phases – they simply invoke the result phase as a background condition. When we turn to predicates which do represent the ECC, we find once more that most of them are adjectives. Moreover, almost all these predicates profile stable situations as opposed to actions or events. In terms of the stages indicated in (18) and Figure 10.13, for personal predicates, there are no examples for the assessment phase and very few for the action phase. This skewing, whereby personal and impersonal expressions correspond to different aspects of the ECC, is evidence that the various grammatical patterns we are dealing with are meaningful, not just arbitrary formal structures.

Leaving aside periphrastic expressions (e.g. *become apparent*), predicates representing the action phase may be limited to the ones in (30). They all require that the conceptualizer (usually the speaker) be specified by means of either a direct or an indirect object. Except for *occur*, they are all clearly perceived as being metaphorical. And they all portray the conceptualizer as having a passive role. The metaphorical image is that of P appearing in the field and reaching or impacting C, with the result that C attends to P and accepts it as being valid.[18] In this way the field provides the stimulus for C's incorporation of P in RC.

(30) a. *It {dawned on / struck / ?hit} me that she might be angry.*
b. *It {occurred / ?came} to me that she might be angry.*

Hence these locutions reflect the action phase of the ECC less directly than do personal predicates such as *learn*, *figure out*, *decide*, etc. Instead of describing a particular phase in the striving for epistemic control, they actually represent an alternate path to such control, where P simply "comes to" C, without C having to assess it and make a decision. And since there are no impersonal assessment predicates (impersonal counterparts of verbs like *consider*, *ponder*, and *wonder*), impersonals directly based on the ECC are all imperfective, describing stable situations rather than events. These phases are shown in Figure 10.16.[19]

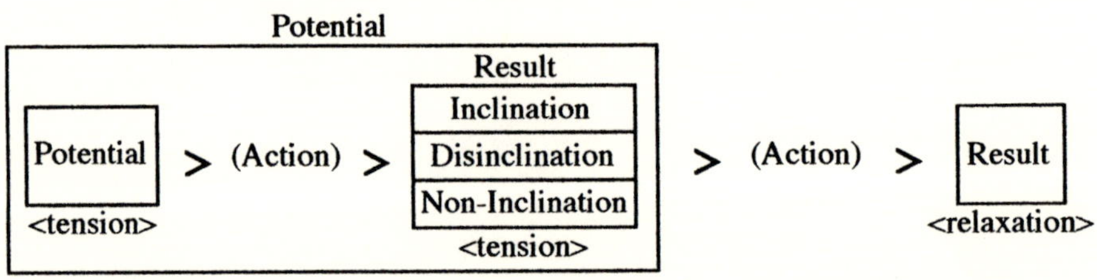

Figure 10.16

As for personal predicates (Figure 10.13), the potential phase of the impersonal ECC consists of a mini-cycle. But instead of **action** and **result**, the phases of this mini-cycle are **potential** and **result**. Functioning as potential phase predicates are *conceivable*, *plausible*, and *possible*. What they indicate

18 Note the periphrastic locution *It has come to my attention that P.*
19 Compare this to the last line in Figure 10.10.

is simply that C is in the conceptualizer's field, thus it has to be dealt with in some fashion. This is prior to any actual assessment on the part of C, hence these predicates are impersonal (whereas assessment predicates like *consider* take personal subjects and represent the action phase of the mini-cycle). What these predicates do, so to speak, is set the stage for action by announcing the existence in F of a proposition which has the potential for being valid, so that it cannot just be ignored. In this way they **initiate** the ECC.

(31) a. **Potential:** (i) *conceivable, plausible*; (ii) *possible*
b. **Inclination:** (i) *seem, appear*; (ii) *likely, probable*
c. **Disinclination:** (i) *doubtful, dubious*; (ii) *unlikely, improbable*
d. **Non-inclination:** (i) *unclear, uncertain, mysterious*; (ii) *debatable, arguable, questionable, indefinite*
e. **Result:** (i) *obvious, clear, evident, apparent, plain*; (ii) *true, false, right, correct, incorrect, valid, certain, definite, provable, demonstrable, undeniable*

As noted, with impersonals there are no true action predicates, in either the mini-cycle or the main cycle. All the predicates are imperfective, describing stable situations. Within the mini-cycle, the result phase predicates indicate different kinds of inclination: (positive) inclination, disinclination, or non-inclination. These are states of tension, since the overall issue has not yet been resolved. At the global level, the result phase is one of relaxation, since P has either been incorporated in RC or excluded from it.

I am claiming, of course, that despite being impersonal all these predicates invoke a conceptualizer who apprehends the complement proposition. With each predicate C can be left implicit, in which case it may simply be construed as a virtual or generalized conceptualizer (anyone in the role of C would arrive at the judgment indicated). In context C will naturally tend to be identified with the speaker or some other individual. The predicates differ, however, as to whether they allow this individual to be expressed by means of an indirect object. In fact, predicates in each category differ in this manner, thereby giving an indication whether C has a fairly salient role (even when left implicit) or remains in the background.

According to my own judgments, within each class the predicates in group (i) allow an indirect object, usually *to me*, while those in group (ii) do not:

(32) a. *It is {conceivable / plausible / *possible} to me that the president will resign.*
b. *It {seems / appears / *is likely / *is probable} to me that he has lied to us again.*

c. *It is {doubtful / ?dubious / *unlikely / *improbable} to me that he is innocent.*
d. *It is {unclear / uncertain / *debatable / *questionable} to me whether he ever tells anyone the truth.*
e. *It is {obvious / clear / *true / *incorrect / *definite / *undeniable} to me that he is completely dishonest.*

Accordingly, the former are more subjective in the sense of describing how the situation appears to a given conceptualizer. Most group (i) predicates invoke a specifically mental process (*conceive*, *doubt*), focus on appearance (*seem*, *appear*), or pertain to ease of observation (*(un)clear*, *obvious*, *evident*, *apparent*). Conversely, group (ii) predicates take a more objective stance. Some merely locate P on a scale of likelihood (*possible*, *(un)likely*, *(im)probable*). Others suggest the possibility of public debate (*debatable*, *arguable*, *questionable*) whereby any conceptualizer who might be involved would be able to objectively demonstrate (*provable*, *demonstrable*, *undeniable*) P's validity or incorrectness (*true*, *false*, *right*, *correct*, *incorrect*, *valid*).

Chapter 11
Subordination in Cognitive Grammar

My basic position on subordination was written many years ago (Langacker 1991: 419):

> Despite their familiarity, … such standard terms as *coordination*, *subordination*, *relative clause*, etc. do not necessarily refer to notions that are clearly defined or thoroughly understood, nor can they be accepted as representing an optimal, revelatory, or even adequate classificatory system. Indeed, it is doubtful that any single classification could accommodate the actual diversity of multiclausal constructions together with the many kinds and degrees of similarity displayed by overlapping subgroups. A better strategy is to examine individually the various factors that figure in a full characterization of such constructions; a particular construction is then defined by a constellation of properties, each of which is shared by certain others.

I still subscribe to this view, recognizing the inadequacy and non-unitary nature of the traditional categories.

In the same chapter, I nonetheless suggested that a single, unified characterization might be possible for the full range of clauses traditionally regarded as subordinate, including complement, relative, and adverbial clauses: "A **subordinate clause** is … describable as one whose profile is overridden by that of a main clause" (Langacker 1991: 436). Strictly speaking, I do not believe this passage contradicts the preceding one. It is rather an attempt to explicate the traditional notion of subordination – to offer a reasonably precise definition based on an independently justified construct (profiling) – to the extent that this notion is descriptively useful. Still, it does run counter to the spirit of the earlier passage. More importantly, certain questions arise concerning the adequacy of the proposed characterization. It is thus worth taking a closer look. Though it will not lead to a simple, definitive analysis, it may at least expose some fundamental issues.

1. Sources of asymmetry

My original definition of subordination was based on certain assumptions about profiling in complex sentences. These are exemplified in (1), where boldface indicates a clause whose profile is said to be inherited by the sentence as a whole. Coordination represents the special case of multiple, co-equal profiles.

Taken as a whole, sentence (1)a does not profile either clausal process – that of lending or that of wasting – to the exclusion of the other. Thus neither clause is subordinate to the other. In (1)b, the sentence as whole is said to designate the act of deciding, not the conjectural status of evolution; whatever one believes concerning evolution, the truth or falsity of the sentence as a whole is solely based on what the president decided. In (1)c, the profile of the relative clause *they brought him* is overridden even at the level of the subject nominal: *the crown they brought him* designates the crown, not the act of bringing. And in (1)d, the event of going to bed (rather than getting home) is profiled at the composite structure level.

(1) a. ***I lent him some money*** *and* ***he simply wasted it****.* [conjoined clauses]

b. ***The president has decided*** *that evolution is only conjecture.* [complement clause]

c. ***The crown*** *they brought him* ***was too small for his head****.* [relative clause]

d. ***I went straight to bed*** *when I got home.* [adverbial clause]

A number of questions can be raised about this analysis. There is first the question of whether adverbial clauses are really subordinate. The traditional label "subordinating conjunction", applied to elements like *because*, *since*, *when*, and *if*, suggests ambivalence in this regard, as well as the absence of any clear boundary between subordination and coordination. In recent years, substantive arguments have been put forth by Diessel and Tomasello (2001), Thompson (2002), and Verhagen (2005) against the subordinate status of complement clauses, especially from the standpoint of acquisition and use in spoken discourse. There is also room for doubt concerning profiling. While the need for this descriptive construct and the details of its application seem fairly clear at lower levels of structural organization, they are far less evident at higher levels. And finally, appeal to this construct may not be necessary. There may be other ways to account for the perceived asymmetries which motivate the term "subordination".

While the term subordination is not self-explanatory, neither is it arbitrary. It reflects a perceived asymmetry in the status of clauses in a complex sentence. My characterization in terms of profiling was an attempt to capture this asymmetry in a unified manner. But perhaps the asymmetries in question are not in fact all comparable (or are comparable only at a higher level of abstraction). Profiling is not the only possible source of a difference in status reasonably described impressionistically with labels like "main" vs. "subordinate".

Another possibility is trajector/landmark alignment, i.e. the difference between the primary and secondary focal participants in a profiled relationship.

Trajector/landmark alignment is inherent in elements like *when*, *while*, *before*, *after*, *if*, *unless*, *because*, *although*, and *since*, which introduce adverbial clauses. If not due to profiling, the perceived asymmetry between an adverbial clause and the clause it modifies may thus be ascribable to the latter being the primary focal participant in the relationship serving to connect them. Suppose it is argued that the clauses in (1)d are equally prominent in terms of profiling; in that respect, (1)d would be analogous to the coordinate structure in (1)a. It would still be the case that *I went straight to bed* is primary, and *I got home* secondary, with respect to the connecting relationship expressed by *when*: they respectively elaborate its trajector and its landmark. While the profiled events are equally focused at the composite structure level, getting home is nonetheless invoked as a temporal landmark for going to bed.

The alternative analyses are presented in Figure 11.1, where X and Y are the component clauses, and CONN a connecting element. Diagram (a) represents the analysis I previously assumed as the basis for defining subordination. It implies that Y is a complement of CONN, which functions as the head (i.e. the profile determinant) at the lower level of organization, while at the higher level the sequence CONN +Y serves to modify X, which is the head at that level and for the sentence as a whole. With respect to (1)d, it implies that *when I got home* profiles the *when* relationship, and that the entire sentence profiles the act of going to bed.

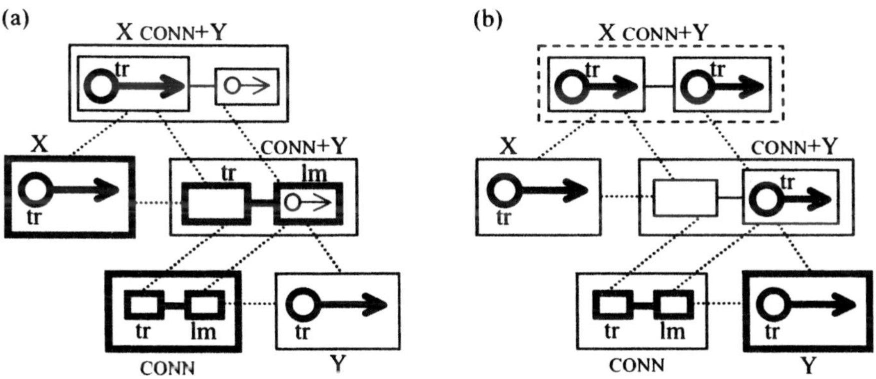

Figure 11.1

The alternative is to claim that both events are profiled at the composite structure level. This implies the analysis sketched in diagram (b). The correspondences are the same as in diagram (a): in both structures, Y elaborates the landmark of CONN, and X its trajector. However, the sequence CONN +Y is presumed to profile the clausal process (not the connecting relationship). And at the higher level of composition, both components contribute their processual profiles to the composite structure – if, indeed, there is such a structure (a matter we will return to).

Turning now to complement clauses, we can also find an alternative to profiling as the basis for perceived asymmetry. My characterization of subordination presupposed the analysis sketched in Figure 11.2(a) for a complement clause construction. The complement clause elaborates the trajector or the landmark of the process profiled by the matrix clause, which functions as profile determinant. In diagram (a), *Doris left* specifies the landmark of *Chris knows*, whose profile prevails at the composite structure level. *Chris knows Doris left* is said to designate the process of knowing, not the act of leaving.

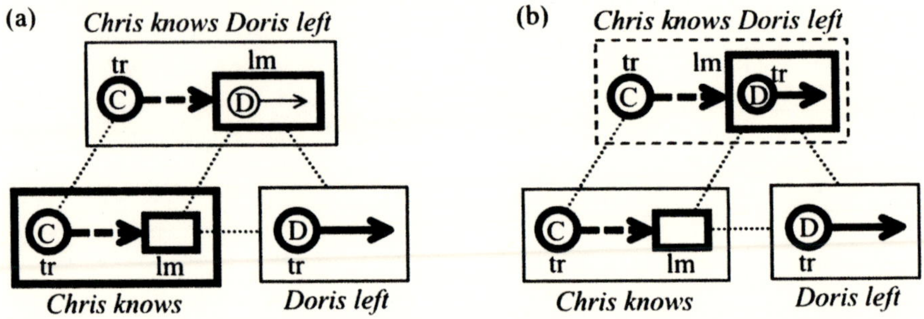

Figure 11.2

However, the component clauses display an evident asymmetry independently of any claims about profiling. The clause *Doris left* specifies a central participant in the relationship coded by *Chris knows*, but not conversely. At the conceptual level, this translates into the layering of mental spaces: *know* is a space-builder (Fauconnier 1985), and the event of Doris leaving occupies the space it evokes. Perhaps, then, a complement clause is subordinate to the matrix clause in the sense that the relationship it designates is embedded in a mental space which the matrix clause introduces. As shown in diagram (b), this layering constitutes a conceptual asymmetry even if one assumes that both clausal processes are profiled at the composite structure level.

As in Figure 11.1(b), I have enclosed the composite structure in a dashed-line box because I have some doubt that we need to posit it as part of the grammatical structure of such expressions. Perhaps in terms of grammar (though not in terms of meaning) we can simply omit the topmost structure both in Figure 11.1(b) and in 11.2(b). The matter hinges on issues that have barely begun to be explored, let alone resolved. At this stage I can only try to indicate the issues I consider to be most fundamental.

2. Constituency and profiling

Grammar, I claim, consists in assemblies of symbolic structures (form-meaning pairings). It is certainly not the case that these assemblies are always strictly hierarchical, in the manner of Figure 11.1(a). It is neither required nor assumed that the symbolic structures in an assembly form a single, consistent constituency hierarchy analogous to the classic tree structures of generative syntax. In particular, it is not assumed that a symbolic assembly is always graced by a single composite structure (at the "top") subsuming all the other symbolic structures (directly or indirectly) as components. Constituency of the "classical" sort is non-essential and therefore often variable (Langacker 1995a, 1997a). A classical constituent emerges when a particular kind of conceptual grouping (based on a correspondence between focused elements) happens to be symbolized by a particular kind of phonological grouping (based on linear contiguity). A classical constituency hierarchy emerges when this occurs at multiple levels of organization, the grouped (or composite) structure at one level functioning as a component structure at the next. However, such hierarchies are not exhaustive of the structures and relationships inherent in complex expressions.

One argument for this flexible view of constituency is that it straightforwardly accommodates the intonational groupings commonly observed in complex sentences, e.g. in (2). Almost to a person, syntacticians posit the constituency shown in (2)a, a strictly nested structure where each "embedded" clause is literally "contained" in the clause whose landmark it specifies. Phonologically, however, each clause is most naturally produced as a separate intonational unit, as shown in (2)b. To handle this discrepancy between the presumed syntactic organization and the observed phonological organization, Chomsky and Halle (1968: § 6.5) were forced to posit ad hoc "phonological adjustment rules". But there is no need for such devices if grammatical structure resides in symbolic assemblies rather than rigid constituency hierarchies. One can simply say, instead, that the hierachical organization in (2)a is a matter of conceptual structure – the successive embedding of mental spaces – but is not reflected in the expression's phonological or grammatical organization.

(2) a. *[Amy says [Bob thinks [Chris knows [Doris left]]]]*
b. *Amy says / Bob thinks / Chris knows / Doris left*

It would be both gratuitous and descriptively problematic to assume that, in assembling symbolic structures to form a complex expression, we are limited to building a strictly hierarchical structure where an integrated composite conception predominates at each successive level. Another form a symbolic assembly can take is a chain-like structure, based on local connections between successive windows of attention. This kind of serial organization is characteristic of the "intonation units" discussed by Chafe (1994). While flexible in their application, these units tend to coincide with clauses. I have suggested that such a unit can be characterized schematically as the symbolic pairing between a conceptual window of attention and a phonological intonation group (Langacker 2001b). The expression in (2)b can then be described as a chain-like symbolic assembly where each successive clause is identified with an attentional frame of this sort. This is sketched in Figure 11.3, where a box with rounded corners represents an attentional frame, and the arrow labeled T stands for processing time.

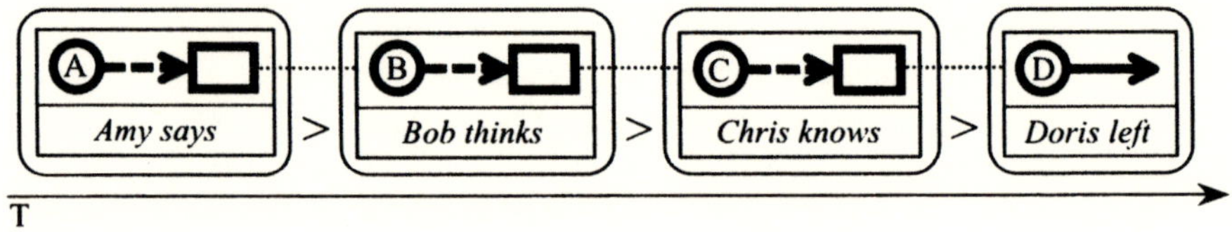

Figure 11.3

I am not suggesting that this sequence of attentional frames represents everything that is going on, either linguistically or in processing terms. Language processing occurs simultaneously at multiple levels of organization, on different time scales, and with varying degrees of conscious awareness (Langacker 2001c). In proceeding through a sentence like (2)b, focusing in turn on each successive clause, we also apprehend each in relation to its predecessor, as shown in Figure 11.4(a). At least implicitly, moreover, we are building up a global conception of the full mental space configuration, as shown in 11.4(b). But there is no particular reason to assume that, at every step along the way, an overarching composite structure emerges which subsumes the content of all the preceding stages and imposes a single profile on the entire conception. And in general, I do not believe that any such structure is descriptively necessary.

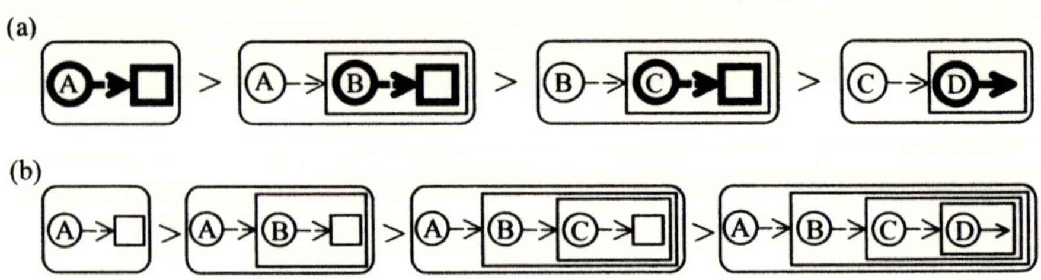

Figure 11.4

Should an account along these lines prove viable, it would still capture the asymmetry which motivates the traditional notion that a complement clause is "subordinate" to the matrix clause. Even if there is no constituency hierarchy with a single "highest" clause and a single overall profile, a complement clause is still subordinate in the sense that it specifies a central participant in the matrix clause. Moreover, the matrix clause is the "main" clause in the sense that it represents the most accessible mental space, i.e. the one most directly connected to the speaker's conception of reality.

I should emphasize that this alternative does not constitute an abandonment of the notion profiling. The only thing at stake is the proper range of application for this notion – a single construct cannot and should not do everything. At lower levels of grammatical structure, it is generally fairly clear which element is profiled, according to the definition that an expression's profile is what it designates (its conceptual referent). In English compounds, for example, the second element imposes its profile on the whole. Thus *hairspray* designates a kind of spray (not hair); *hairspray can* refers to the can; and within the conceptual complex it evokes, *hairspray can label* profiles the label. Similarly, *Sally's desk* refers to the desk (not to Sally); *on Sally's desk* profiles the locative relationship; while *the lamp on Sally's desk* designates the lamp. And the process of liking is profiled by *really like*, *really like it*, and the entire finite clause *most people really like it*.

By contrast, it is not at all self-evident (as assumed in Langacker 2001b) that a sentence like (2)b designates just the act of saying, or that conditionals of the form *if X then Y* profile just situation Y. Nor is it clear, even in principle, precisely what it means to say that complex sentences like these have a single overall referent. There has to be some upper limit on the size of the structures to which this notion is applicable.[1] Of course, the definition of profiling might prove to be a special case of a more abstract notion that would be applicable to higher-level structures. But that would require a specific proposal tangible enough to investigate.

In short, while lower-level structures strongly support the adoption of profiling as a descriptive construct, the extent of its proper use is not apparent apriori, but has to be determined by careful investigation taking a wide range of considerations into account. Its use in defining subordination may very well prove to be erroneous. A natural limit for profiling – the domain in which its application is unproblematic – would be a single grounded structure, i.e. a full nominal or a finite clause. Grounding is itself a matter of reference: singling out a particular instance of a thing or process type in relation to the interlocutors and the speech event. If profiling represents a general notion of conceptual reference, grounding represents the special case of deictic reference. Admittedly,

1 For example, it cannot be applied to an entire discourse or a novel.

though, the definition of profiling is more impressionistic than it is a precise psychological characterization. That will require a much better understanding of the varied phenomena which go by such labels as "attention", "prominence", and "focusing", and how they relate to one another.

A nominal or a finite clause is a natural domain for profiling because it contains its own internal vantage point (the ground). As such, a grounded structure has the potential to be apprehended independently, in the manner of Figure 11.3, as opposed to being viewed solely in relation to another. It would however be too strong to claim that no grounded structure is ever incorporated as part of another, i.e. that its content is never subsumed by a higher-level composite structure which imposes a different profile. That seems problematic for many structures, including the following. In possessives, such as *Jack's wife*, the possessor is a full, grounded nominal, but so is the higher-level structure containing the noun it modifies, which imposes its profile on the whole. Since *Jack* is part of the nominal *Jack's wife*, and the composite expression designates the wife, the profile of *Jack* is overridden at the higher level. Likewise, a relative clause can form a constituent with the noun it modifies, with the latter functioning as head (or profile determinant): the referent of *the proposal I made* is the proposal rather than the process of making it. And a finite clause profiles a process rather than a thing, even though it incorporates nominal arguments, e.g. the process *admire* in *I admire her.*

A more defensible position is that a grounded structure is a natural candidate to be apprehended independently, in its own attentional frame, and that grounding diminishes the likelihood of a structure being incorporated as part of another with its profile overridden. This is a matter of degree, and certainly it interacts with other factors. In particular, clauses tend more strongly than nominals to retain their independence. This no doubt reflects their greater internal complexity, as well as their status as the basic units of discourse. Although nominals are conceptually autonomous, in and of themselves they do little by way of moving the discourse along – their typical role is rather to support the conception of relationships, which primarily fulfill this function.

3. An alternative account

I am suggesting, then, that at higher levels of organization both constituency and profile determinance are variable. Consider the relative clauses in (3). Proceeding from (3)a to (3)e, the conceptual and structural integration of the relative clause and the noun it modifies becomes progressively looser. In (3)a, *that book I read* represents a canonical example of the standard syntactic account of relative clauses: it is a single constituent referring to a book which the relative serves to identify.[2] The relative construction in (3)b is also canonical, but here the relative clause is less in the shadow of the noun it modifies. It is more complex, it makes a greater, less predictable semantic contribution, and prosodically it is unreduced (in contrast to the relative in (3)a, which is unstressed and rhythmically compressed). The relative clause in (3)c has a greater measure of independence, in that its content is really not used to identify the book, but only to further characterize it. Indeed, its content is the main point of the sentence. In (3)d, the relative is still more independent, as it is not even adjacent to the noun it modifies. Hence they do not form a classical grammatical constituent. Finally, the second clause in (3)e is a canonical non-restrictive relative, which is generally accepted as being external to the nominal it characterizes. This is often likened to a coordinate construction, implying separate and equal profiles.

(3) a. *There were some really outrageous claims in that book I read.*
 b. *A book which makes outrageous claims is often a best-seller.*
 c. *I just read a book which makes some outrageous claims.*
 d. *I read a book last night which makes some outrageous claims.*
 e. *I just read a book, which makes some outrageous claims.*

The extreme cases, the relative constructions in (3)a and (3)e, are roughly sketched in Figure 11.5. In the first case, the relative clause is subordinate as originally defined: it combines with the head to form a composite symbolic structure which profiles the book rather than the clausal process. In the second case, the components are clauses which retain their independence, as in Figure 11.3. Each constitutes a separate attentional frame, so there is no single window of attention which subsumes their content but selects just one component process for its profile. While I am not ready to venture a detailed characterization of all the intermediate cases, it may at least be apparent that relative clauses have variable implementation in terms of symbolic assemblies, constituency, and profiling.

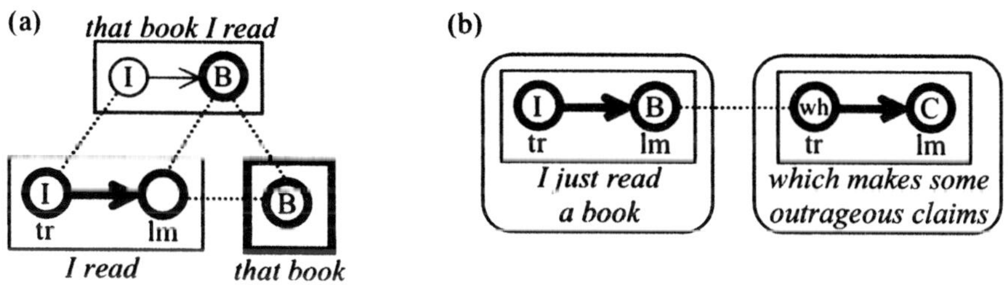

Figure 11.5

2 Hence it is quite analogous to *that book on the floor.*

Comparable remarks can be made for adverbial and complement clauses. In (4)a–e, for example, the adverbial introduced by *after* becomes progressively more elaborate and more plausibly describable as occupying a separate attentional frame with its own independent profile. Sentence (4)c might be considered transitional, since the *after*-clause is finite but not set off as a separate intonational group by the slight pause usually written as a comma. Observe that both pronunciations in (5) are quite natural, depending on whether the second clause constitutes old or new information. Compared to (5)b, the *after*-clause in (5)a is prosodically compressed in several respects: it has no word with unreduced stress (small caps); it is lower in pitch; and it is pronounced more rapidly. We might speculate that this phonological compression correlates with, or even symbolizes, a conceptual subordination of the adverbial clause whereby its profile is overridden. The pronunciation in (5)b would then correlate with both clauses retaining their processual profiles at the composite structure level.

(4) a. *He took a nap after lunch.*
b. *He took a nap after eating.*
c. *He took a nap after he ate.*
d. *He took a nap, after he ate lunch.*
e. *After he ate an enormous lunch, he took a nap.*

(5) a. *He took a* NAP *after he ate.*
b. *He took a* NAP *after he* ATE.

As for complement clauses, I fully agree with Thompson (2002) and Verhagen (2005) that complements tend to be primary in the sense of providing the most important content. I further agree with Diessel and Tomasello (2001) that, in acquisition and to some extent in adult language use, the matrix clause tends to be apprehended holistically and only as an appendage to the complement, so that only the complement expresses a proposition. They recognize, however, that these are matters of degree and subject to variation.[3] Whatever the proportion, it would be as wrong to claim that a matrix clause never expresses the proposition of primary interest as it is to claim that it always does. The problem is to come up with a unified description that accounts in a natural and revealing way for the full range of options.

The examples in (6) afford some idea of the range. In (6)a, it is certainly the matrix clause that expresses the proposition of primary interest. One can plausibly maintain that the complement's profile is overridden by that of the ma-

3 This point that is argued quite forcefully by Boye and Harder (2007).

trix clause in a composite conception viewed in a single window of attention. In (6)b, the clauses would seem to be of roughly equal status as informative propositions. In (6)c the balance tips in favor of the complement, and in (6)d *I think* is clearly an appendage to it, an epistemic afterthought. It is phonologically reduced to the point that it can hardly be taken as representing a separate window of attention. For (6)d I would posit an overall composite structure in which the profile of *think* is overridden.

(6) a. *Is evolution only conjecture? Well, the president has definitely decided that it is.*
  b. *Bush has conclusively demonstrated that evolution is only conjecture.*
  c. *I suspect that evolution is only conjecture.*
  d. *Evolution is only conjecture, I think.*

Here cases like (6)c may be transitional. Note the alternate pronunciations in (7): the matrix clause can either be fully realized phonologically, with normal focus stress, or else compressed in the same manner as the adverbial clause in (5)a and the appendage in (6)d. Possibly this marks the transition between a composite conception where both clauses retain their profile and one where the matrix clause profile is overridden.

(7) a. *I SUSPECT that EVOLUTION IS ONLY CONJECTURE.*
  b. *I suspect that EVOLUTION IS ONLY CONJECTURE.*

Wherever the transition occurs, and whether it is abrupt or gradual, at some point along the spectrum the matrix clause loses any vestige of prominence and becomes decidedly secondary to the complement. Thompson describes the matrix as having an "epistemic/evidential/evaluative" function. Diessel and Tomasello describe it (for young children) as an "epistemic marker", an "attention getter", or a "marker of illocutionary force". Accepting that something along these lines properly characterizes one end of the spectrum, the ultimate descriptive challenge is to provide an explicit account of all the varied structures that constitute it, and how they relate to one another synchronically, diachronically, and developmentally. Part of the challenge is to determine precisely what descriptive constructs are necessary and how to optimally apply them. In particular, we need to ascertain – for those cases where the matrix is clearly secondary to the complement – just what kind of prominence the latter has by virtue of which the matrix is secondary to it.

4. Broader issues

I would hypothesize that the prominence responsible for secondary status is indeed to be identified as profiling. Depending on the factors I have mentioned, and no doubt others, a matrix clause and its complement can be integrated in various ways, as shown in Figure 11.6. Either clause can impose its profile on the composite conception, or alternatively, each can maintain its status as a momentary focus of attention. It is ultimately a matter of timing and how much content is subsumed in a single window of attention. Since it is hard to deal with simultaneous foci of attention, it is easiest for both clauses to be profiled when each occupies its own attentional frame, as in diagram (b). In that case an integrated conception may well emerge, but the primary focus is at the component structure level. If two processual profiles are squeezed into a single attentional frame, e.g. for expressions like (7)a, I presume they are nonetheless accessed in sequence. Diagrams (a) and (c) show the primary focus at the composite structure level. It is easier for the full, integrated conception to fit in a single window of attention if only one component process retains its profile at this level.

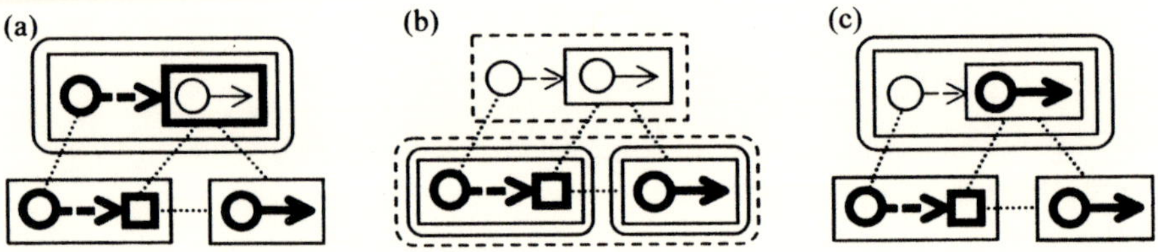

Figure 11.6

If a finite clause is a natural candidate to be apprehended independently, in its own attentional frame, the configurations in Figures 11.6(a) and (c) are less than fully optimal in this respect. I suggest, however, that both are quite natural in another respect: each is the analog, at a higher level of organization, of a basic aspect of the structure which finite clauses canonically exhibit internally (cf. Achard 1998; Chapter 9). In the case of 11.6(a), the multiclause configuration approximates the single-clause structure of a verb and its nominal arguments. To varying degrees, the complement is reduced in size and becomes less clause-like, to the point that it is almost like a pronoun, as seen in (8).

(8) a. *BUSH most CERTAINLY BELIEVES it's only conjecture.*
b. *BUSH most CERTAINLY BELIEVES it is.*
c. *BUSH most CERTAINLY BELIEVES it.*

As for Figure 11.6(c), I perceive a similarity to clausal grounding. Internally, a finite clause profiles the grounded process, not the grounding relationship. I have argued (Langacker 2002a) that this is also true of the grammaticized grounding elements (for English, tense and the modals). In diagram (c), where each component is itself a grounded clause, the composite conception shows the analogous organization in which an unprofiled relationship serves to epistemically qualify a profiled process. For instance, the relation which *may* bears to *like* in (9)a is analogous to that which *I think* bears to *he likes her* in (9)b.

(9) a. *He may* ***like*** *her.*
   b. *I think* ***he likes her.***

If the analogy is valid, it provides an argument for the hypothesis that profiling is the pivotal construct for describing different positions along the spectrum, in the manner of Figure 11.6. We could then go on to define the notions "main" and "subordinate clause" in discourse terms: a main clause is one whose profile is maintained as such, and a subordinate clause one whose profile is overridden, in a window of attention. Perhaps ironically, these are essentially the same definitions we started with, the only difference being that profiling is considered in relation to a variable window of attention instead of a composite structure presumed to be invariant. But if the definitions are the same, the extensions are not. The clauses identified as "main" and "subordinate" – in discourse terms – coincide with those traditionally labeled as such only toward one end of the spectrum.

The discourse definitions accord quite well with the characterization offered by Thompson and by Diessel and Tomasello for expressions at the opposite end. Nor do I seriously disagree with their characterization of the matrix as being formulaic and unanalyzable. I have been assuming, for sake of discussion, that the matrix clause retains its analyzability. But this is undoubtedly a matter of degree. In the case of acquisition, originally holistic elements become analyzable to various extents as the child gradually masters the grammar of complex sentences. Diachronically, we might posit the opposite development, where independent clauses gradually lose their independence and their analyzability. In the acquisition process they would then be analyzed by successive generations to a lesser and lesser degree, eventually losing their clausal status altogether. Whatever the details, acquisition and grammaticization are essential components of an overall account (cf. Boye and Harder 2007).

The proposals I have made are at best exploratory. They might well be criticized for an inappropriate mixing of considerations that properly belong to the separate domains of grammar, processing, and discourse. I am certainly mixing these considerations, but I doubt very much that this is inappropriate. I do not believe that grammar, in all its actual complexity, is coherently describable independently from processing and discourse, or that those are neatly distinct from one another. I believe we need an integrated account of all three domains for any of them to be properly understood.

Chapter 12
The conceptual basis of coordination

Despite their apparent simplicity, the notions AND and OR are not at all straightforward from the linguistic standpoint. Semantically, elements with these glosses are not necessarily equivalent to the corresponding logical connectives defined in terms of truth tables. Nor do such definitions constitute the kind of conceptual characterizations sought in cognitive linguistics. Grammatically, coordinate constructions are notoriously complex and resistant to analysis. My goal here is to improve on the preliminary account offered in Langacker 1991 (§ 11.2). I will show that basic notions of cognitive linguistics, proposed and justified quite independently of coordination, provide the essential tools for describing it.

1. Prerequisites

Despite being non-canonical in various respects, coordinate structures are amenable to analysis in terms of symbolic assemblies based on a conceptualist semantics. They do not require any new descriptive constructs or theoretical innovations. To see this, let us start with a brief survey of relevant semantic and grammatical phenomena, all evident in non-coordinate expressions.

1.1. Conceptual semantics

Certain properties of linguistic meaning follow directly from its conceptual nature. Most broadly, meaning includes not only conceptual **content**, but also **construal**: our ability to conceive and portray the same situation in alternate ways. One dimension of construal is the **prominence** conferred on conceptual elements, and one kind of prominence – profiling – is of central importance in coordination.

Another basic feature of linguistic meaning is **dynamicity** (Langacker 2001c). Conceptualization requires time. It takes place through processing time. And how it develops through processing time is often crucial to an expression's meaning. The sentences in (1), for example, are semantically non-equivalent even though they contain the same locative expressions and describe the same objective situation. They differ in how the scene is mentally accessed: whether we "zoom in" from a global location to successively more local ones, or whether we do the opposite by "zooming out".

(1) a. *The brushes are in the garage, in the cabinet, on the top shelf, behind the paint cans.*

b. *The brushes are behind the paint cans, on the top shelf, in the cabinet, in the garage.*

When we conceptualize multiple entities, there are several basic ways to access them, sketched in Figure 12.1. They may all be accessed as a single gestalt, simultaneously available at a single point in processing time. This happens, for instance, when we determine the size of a small group by subitization. Another option is sequential access (represented by a dashed arrow), as in counting the members of a larger group, or mentally reciting the alphabet. A special case of sequentiality is alternation (represented by a double-headed dashed arrow). An example is the perception of an ambiguous figure, where we flip back and forth between alternate interpretations (rather than entertaining them simultaneously). These are not mutually exclusive. Although the sentences in (1) provide contrasting sequential access to a complex situation, through either path of access we are able to build up a holistic conception of the scene, which may then be available as a single gestalt.

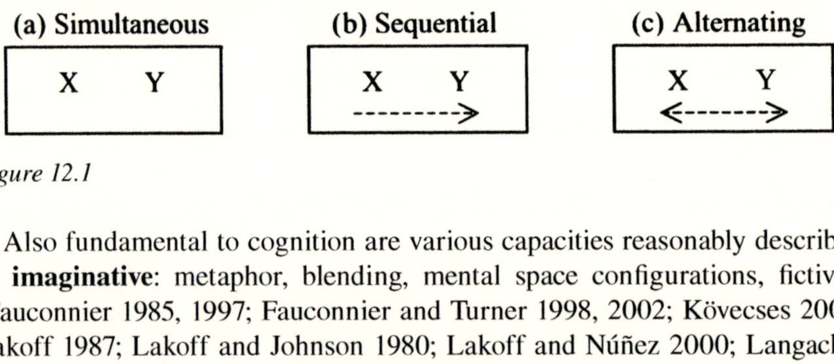

Figure 12.1

Also fundamental to cognition are various capacities reasonably described as **imaginative**: metaphor, blending, mental space configurations, fictivity (Fauconnier 1985, 1997; Fauconnier and Turner 1998, 2002; Kövecses 2000; Lakoff 1987; Lakoff and Johnson 1980; Lakoff and Núñez 2000; Langacker 1999d, 2005b; Matsumoto 1996; Talmy 1996). In metaphor, we invoke one domain of experience, a source domain, to apprehend another, the target domain. What is important here is that metaphor is partially based on structural analogy (Gentner 1983). This involves establishing correspondences (mappings) between elements of the source and target, and observing that parallel relationships hold between corresponding elements in the two domains (Lakoff 1990). Metaphor is a special case of blending, where elements of two input spaces are projected to form a third space, the blend, with its own distinct properties. Blending in turn is a special case of mental space configurations: the organization of conceptual content into separate "working areas" connected by correspondences between their elements. We invoke mental spaces for many purposes, only one of which is the representation of actual situations. And even for actual situations, the entities directly described linguistically are often fictive (or virtual) in nature, being "conjured up" (imagined) for a special purpose, with no status outside the mental space constructed for that purpose (Chapter 4: § 4).

A final point is that conceptual structures involve multiple **levels of organization**. Consider the notion *stack*. A stack is internally complex, consisting of a number of distinct entities, e.g. plates. But it is also conceived, at a higher level of conceptual organization, as a single, unitary entity. For this reason *stack* functions grammatically as a singular noun, even though *plates* is a plural noun. A number of *stacks* can form a *row* at a higher level of organization. If a number of *rows* are close together, they constitute a *cluster*, at a still higher level. At a higher level yet, a set of such clusters might form a *line*, and so on. With effort, we can fully apprehend an expression like (2)a, and even though, objectively, the scene described consists of nothing other than plates, conceptually and linguistically it is populated with higher-level things – stacks, rows, clusters, and a line.

(2) a. *a line of clusters of rows of stacks of plates*
  b. *I washed the whole stack (of plates).*
  c. *A flock of geese is flying overhead.*

We not only conceptualize things at multiple levels of organization, but also relationships (Chapter 2: § 4). For example, (2)b–c profile complex relationships decomposable into simpler ones. Though I probably washed the plates individually, (2)b portrays the washing as being directed at the stack. And while the geese fly individually (unless they happen to be riding in a plane), (2)c ascribes the flying to the flock (note the singular verb). These conceptions are sketched in Figure 12.2.

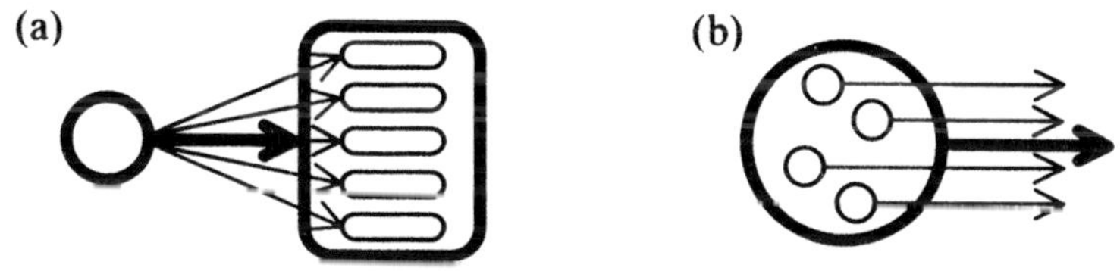

Figure 12.2

1.2. Symbolic grammar

As viewed in CG, grammar consists in symbolic structures (each the pairing of a semantic and a phonological structure) linked by correspondences to form assemblies. To some extent these assemblies are organized hierarchically, with component symbolic structures being integrated to form composite structures that subsume their content and impose a single profile on the overall conception that emerges (Chapter 1: § 3). When this happens at multiple levels of organization – the composite structure at each successive level functioning in turn as one component at the next – it results in tree-like configurations that linguists recognize as grammatical constituency.

It is commonly assumed that constituency is fundamental to grammar and that the syntactic structure of a sentence comprises a single, well-behaved constituency hierarchy. The grammar of a particular expression, e.g. *Alice threw the ball*, is therefore represented by means of a single tree-like diagram or – equivalently – a nesting diagram like Figure 12.3(a). In a well-behaved hierarchy, the branching or nesting is complete (with no crossing lines) and exhaustive of the expression. From the CG perspective, however, symbolic assemblies are flexible and assume varied forms, even for a single expression. It is not the case that constituency always emerges or exhausts the structure of expressions. When it does emerge, it represents a special case of more general phenomena: conceptual grouping, phonological grouping, and symbolic links between the two (Langacker 1995a, 1997a). In CG, therefore, it is merely claimed that semantic, phonological, and symbolic structures form an assembly linked by correspondences.

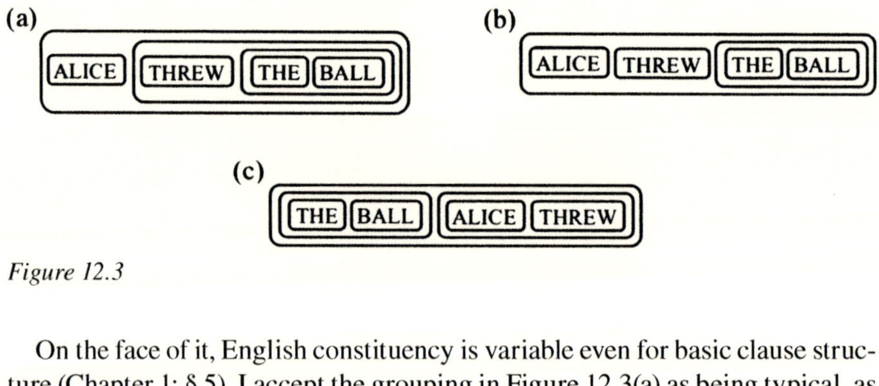

Figure 12.3

On the face of it, English constituency is variable even for basic clause structure (Chapter 1: § 5). I accept the grouping in Figure 12.3(a) as being typical, as indicated by the possibility of a slight hesitation between the subject and predicate, as shown in (3)a. But it is not the only possible constituency. The careful, deliberate pronunciation represented in (3)b suggests a tripartite constituency, as in diagram (b). Moreover, the grouping in diagram (c) occurs in both relative clauses and in expressions with preposed objects, exemplified in (3)d–e.

(3) a. *Alice / threw the ball.*
b. *Alice / threw / the ball.*
c. *the ball / Alice threw*
d. *The ball Alice threw hit a cat.*
e. *The ball Alice threw. The rock she didn't.*

Furthermore, the elements of symbolic assemblies show varying degrees of conceptual and phonological integration. It is not invariably the case that component elements give rise to a distinct composite structure subsuming their content in a single window of attention with a single overall profile (Chapter 11). As an extreme example, consider a graduation ceremony, where the names of students are read – essentially as an unstructured list – as they file across the stage one by one. Each name occupies its own window of attention, and there is no intrinsic connection between one name and the next. They form an assembly only by virtue of representing successive steps in an overall script, as part of the graduation scenario. In Figure 12.4(a), the arrow represents speech time. Through time, each successive name occupies its own brief window of attention. Instead of there being a single overall profile, there is thus a succession of profiles.

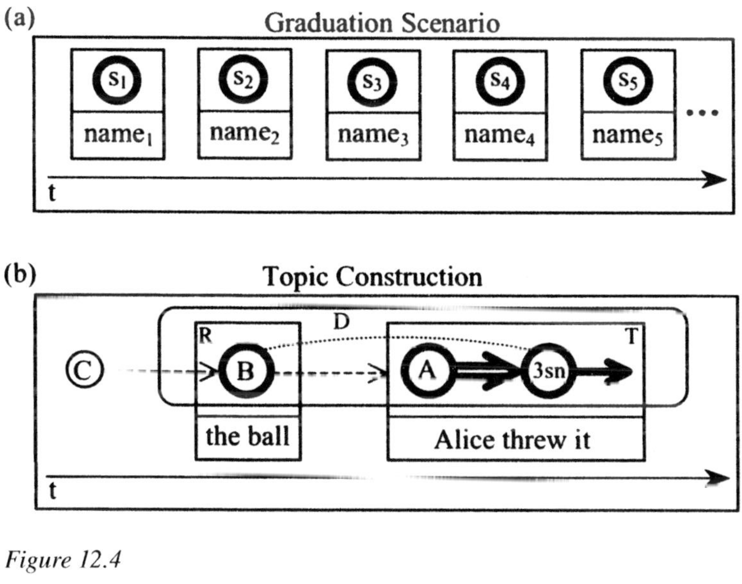

Figure 12.4

Representing an intermediate case is a topic construction, as shown in Figure 12.4(b): *The ball, Alice threw it.* Here the topic nominal and the comment clause are loosely integrated phonologically under a single intonation contour, not separated by the falling intonation that closes an utterance. Semantically their integration is also a loose one, but they are indeed directly connected. For one thing, the topic corresponds to an element of the comment clause, in this example expressed by the object pronoun *it*. Also, the topic functions as a conceptual reference point, which evokes a dominion (domain of knowledge) in which the target (the comment clause) is to be interpreted and incorporated (Chapter 2: § 3). The question then arises as to what the overall expression profiles. I believe it has no overall profile. That is, I see no reason to posit the emergence of a composite structure, all accessible in a single window of attention, which profiles one entity (presumably the clausal process) rather than the other (the nominal referent). Instead I suggest that this construction is by nature dynamic, involving a succession of profiles. While the overall expression forms a constituent, it is not a classical constituent.[1]

Both cases represent looser integration than classical constituency. But there can also be closer integration, most obviously at the phonological pole. Phonological integration is not in general limited to simply juxtaposing the components, in linear sequence and without modification. While simple juxtaposition may be a default, in general it is merely required that the composite phonological structure be some function of the components, which need not be manifested in just the same way that they would in isolation. This is quite familiar in morphological constructions. For instance, the integration of the verb *keep* and the past-tense marker *-t* does not yield *keeped*, but rather *kept*. It is also possible for one component structure to be incorporated in the other, rather than being juxtaposed to it. When a clause is nominalized, for example, the nominalizing marker sometimes appears inside the clause, often attached to the verb, even though it and the clause should probably be analyzed as co-constituents for semantic and grammatical purposes. This may be the case with English gerundive *-ing*, as in ***Alice quitting her job*** *put them in a difficult financial situation.*

A special case of integration by incorporation are the various kinds of constructions loosely described as "parenthetical insertion", so called because the incorporated element is sometimes marked orthographically with parentheses. One type of example involves an incorporated clause expressing an epistemic judgment, e.g. *He is, I think, quite untrustworthy* (cf. Diessel and Tomasello

1 The topic construction in (3)e, e.g. *The ball Alice threw*, is also dynamic, but the reference point relation holds within a single clause, presented without a pause between the topic and the remainder. Thus it is all compressed into a single window of attention. I analyze the clause as a classical constituent, with a composite structure that profiles the process *throw*.

2001; Thompson 2002; Langacker 1995a, 1997a; Chapter 11), diagrammed in Figure 12.5. If we consider only linear order, one clause is interrupted by the other, as in diagram (a), hence it is not a contiguous phonological grouping. But this represents a very limited view of phonological structure – there are parameters to consider other than temporal order. In this case the incorporated clause tends to be set off from the remainder by several factors: lower pitch, lesser amplitude, more rapid production (all symptoms of a general phonological compression). If we consider both temporal order and (say) pitch, the two clauses are segregated phonologically on the basis of the latter, thus each is apprehended as a group despite the temporal intercalation, as shown in diagram (b).

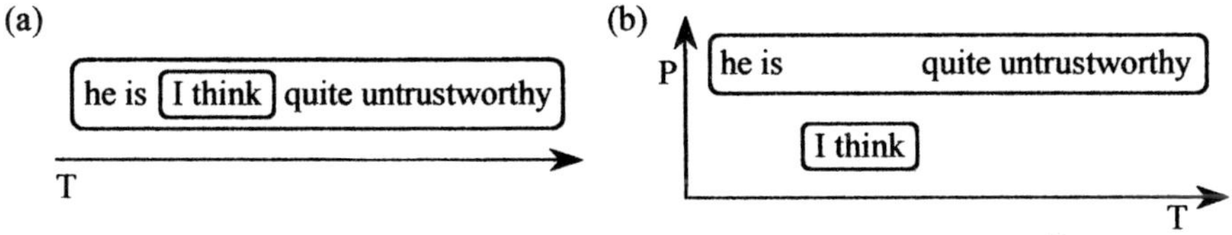

Figure 12.5

Constituency reflects the general human propensity for grouping and hierarchy, so while often variable, it does tend strongly to emerge at lower levels of organization. When it does, though, we sometimes find not a single, well-behaved hierarchy, but intersecting hierarchies, where some constituent simultaneously plays a role in both. Some cases are roughly sketched in Figure 12.6. Sentence (a) is possible in some varieties of colloquial English. It represents a blend of two presentative expressions, either of which might serve to introduce a discourse: *There was a farmer* and *A farmer had a dog*. The nominal *a farmer* is simultaneously the predicate nominative in one clause and the subject in the

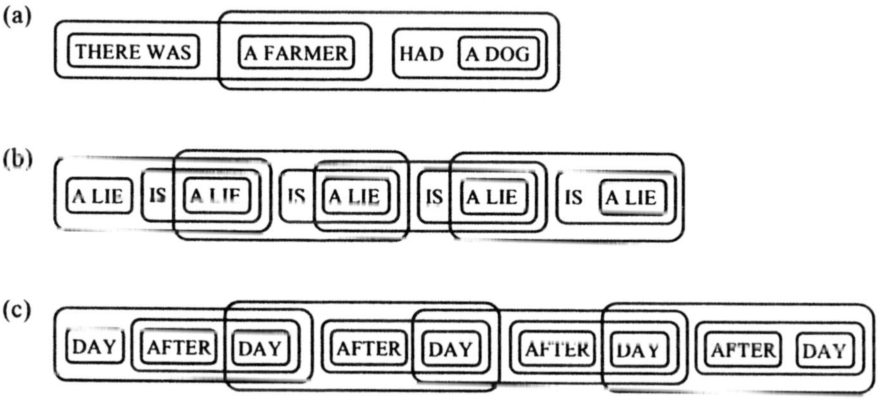

Figure 12.6

other (Lambrecht 1988). Likewise in 12.6(b), the predicate nominative of each component clause is also the subject of the next. What this amounts to is four iterations of the clause *A lie is a lie*, but they are overlapping, not disjoint. This is not limited to predicate nominative constructions. For instance, it also happens with prepositional phrases, as in 12.6(c): *day after day after day after day after day.*

Finally, I note that some symbolic structures are based on a **global comparison** of others. This can result in another level of symbolic organization which cross-cuts constituency groupings. An example is **focus**, roughly describable as that portion of an expression which, in the immediate discourse context, provides the information considered new or noteworthy. In English, focus is marked by unreduced stress; elements which repeat what has just been said have reduced stress. The focus is often a constituent, as in (4)a. But it can also cross-cut basic grammatical constituency, as in (4)b. It can even be discontinuous, as in (4)c (cf. Jackendoff 1972).

(4) a. *Jack drinks beer. He also drinks* ***red wine.***
b. *Jack drinks whisky with ice. He drinks* ***gin without*** *it.*
c. *Jack likes whisky.* ***Jill*** *prefers* ***gin.***

The nature of a focus construction is sketched in Figure 12.7, where capital letters represent the semantic pole of symbolic structures, and small letters the phonological pole. One stretch of discourse is used as **standard of comparison** to assess the following stretch of discourse, the **target of comparison**. The **differential** – that segment of the target which contrasts with the standard – constitutes the focus, symbolized by unreduced stress. This symbolic structure need not coincide with semantic or phonological groupings formed on any other basis. Being what the act of comparison is meant to detect, the differential stands in the **foreground** of awareness, the standard and shared elements of the target constituting the **background**. This conceptual salience is symbolized by a kind of phonological salience.

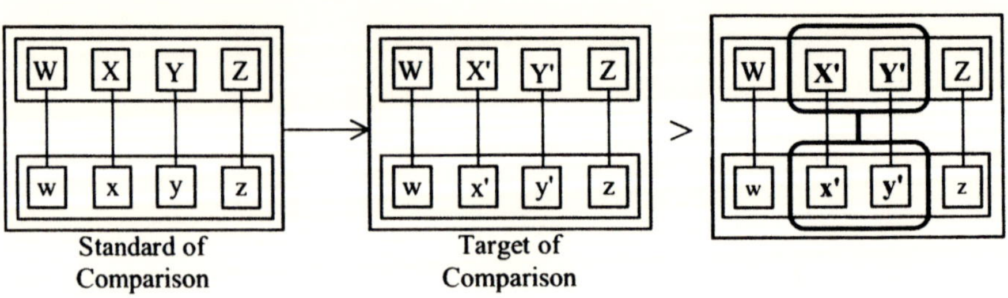

Figure 12.7

2. Conjunction and/or disjunction

2.1. AND

We turn now to the conceptual import of coordination, starting with AND. As a first approximation we can say that in a coordinate structure the conjuncts are **parallel** and **co-equal**. But what exactly does that mean? This is a classic problem which I have not investigated in depth. At best I can offer some comments by way of a rough, second approximation.

One aspect of parallelism is that the conjuncts belong to the same grammatical category. Thus two nominals are conjoined in (5)a, and two verbs in (5)b. There are some apparent exceptions, like (5)c, where the two conjuncts are an adjectival phrase and a prepositional phrase. Possibly the problem lies with traditional schemes of grammatical categorization. In CG, adjectives and prepositions share an abstract semantic characterization (both profile non-processual relationships), and since grammatical category depends on profiling, there is indeed a general category they both belong to. Whether or not all apparent exceptions can be handled in this manner is not essential. In the CG perspective, common category membership is just one kind of semantic parallelism, and not the only kind that matters. This is well known from cases of zeugma, e.g. (5)d, where coordination is infelicitous even between two prepositional phrases or two nominals. Even the coordination of clauses with comparable syntactic structure is sometimes problematic, as in (5)e. Thus it is not sufficient that the conjuncts be abstractly similar (i.e. that there be a schema which they both instantiate).

(5) a. *I bought a newspaper and a loaf of bread.*
  b. *She likes and admires her teacher.*
  c. *His mother is very old and in a hospital.*
  d. **She cut the meat with enthusiasm and (with) a sharp knife.*
  e. *??Jill likes her cat and the moon orbits the earth.*

I am not able to give a precise and definitive characterization of the requisite conceptual parallelism. However, besides the conjuncts themselves being abstractly similar, it is evidently necessary that they be connected in parallel fashion to other structures. The most obvious connections are basic grammatical correspondences between focused elements. In (5)a, for instance, the landmark of *buy* corresponds in parallel fashion to the profiles of both object nominals, *a newspaper* and *a loaf of bread*. In (5)c, the adjectival and prepositional phrases both function as complements of *be*, and in each case the trajector corresponds to the profile of the subject nominal, *his mother*.

But the relevant connections go beyond these basic correspondences. In (5)d, *with enthusiasm* and *with a sharp knife* both function as adverbial modifiers of the clausal process. The non-parallelism of their connections shows up in a finer-grained description. *With a sharp knife* specifies the instrument of cutting, hence it relates to *cut* in terms of the action itself, i.e. the chain of causation (or transmission of force) leading from the agent to the patient. On the other hand, *with enthusiasm* pertains to the agent's mental attitude in carrying out the action. With conjoined clauses, as in (5)e, it is not so easy to identify the "other structures" the conjuncts are connected to. It might be that they are conceived as being aspects of the same domain of knowledge. Alternatively, there is conceived to be a common purpose for putting them forth at the current stage of the discourse.

What we have so far is sketched in Figure 12.8. Conceptually, the conjuncts both instantiate a schematic characterization, and exhibit parallel connections with other structures. The heavy-line boxes represent the profiles of the respective conjuncts. This notation is meant to be neutral as to whether the profiles are things or relationships. At least in typical cases, their profiles establish the conjuncts as members of the same grammatical category. Of course, there can be any number of conjuncts, so the description has to be generalized. For the most part I will limit myself to coordinate structures with just two conjuncts, just to keep the diagrams simple.

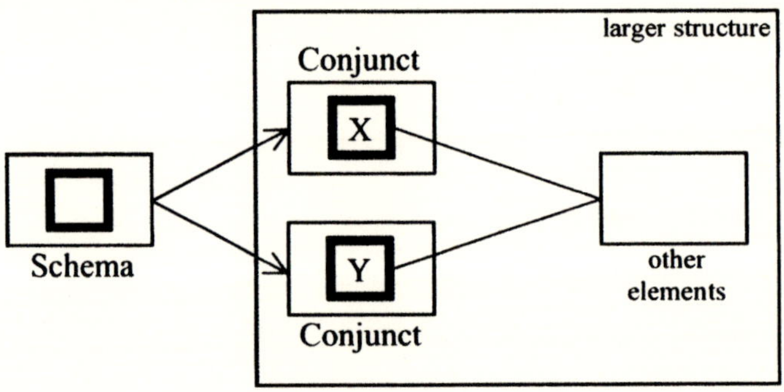

Figure 12.8

Profiling is indicated in Figure 12.8 not only because it is an aspect of conceptual parallelism, but also because it constitutes co-equality. An expression's profile is prominent in the sense of being the entity it designates, or refers to, and as such is a kind of focus of attention. In a coordinate structure, the conjuncts are equal in the sense that neither of their profiles overrides that of the other, as is usual in grammatical constructions. For example, in a verb + object combination like *buy a newspaper*, the verb's profile overrides that of its nominal complement in forming the composite structure. But this is not so within a coordinate structure. Thus in (6)a the profiles of the two object nominals, *a house* and *a garden*, have equal status. But in (6)b, *a house with a garden* has a single overall profile, namely the house. At the composite structure level, the profile of *house* overrides that of *garden*. Even though the sentence implies that she wants a garden as well as a house, it is only the house that corresponds to the landmark of *want*. The house and the garden are not co-equal in this expression, which exemplifies modification rather than coordination.

(6) a. *She wants [a* ***house****] and [a* ***garden****].*
b. *She wants [a* ***house*** *[with a garden]].*

When the elements involved are full clauses instead of nominals, the matter is not so clear. Certainly I would analyze (7)a as having two processual profiles, each occupying its own window of attention. It is not however a necessary condition for coordination that the conjuncts occupy separate windows of attention. Arguably the clauses in (7)b are compressed into a single window, especially in rapid speech where the entire expression has a single intonation contour, with no pauses. And for coordination at lower levels of organization, as in (6)a, positing separate windows of attention would seem implausible (barring special intonation).

(7) a. *Joe really likes good whisky, and for that reason he drinks it often.*
b. *Joe likes whisky and he drinks it often.*
c. *Joe drinks whisky because he really likes it.*

At the same time, having two profiles is not a sufficient condition for coordination. Consider (7)c. Here grammatical tradition is ambivalent. On the one hand, *Joe drinks whisky* is sometimes regarded as a main clause, and *(because) he really likes it* as a subordinate clause. On the other hand, *because* is sometimes called a "conjunction", implying coordination. The common term "subordinating conjunction" reflects this ambivalence. As discussed in Chapter 11, there is no real reason to posit a single, all-subsuming composite structure with a single overall profile. Instead, expressions like (7)c may exhibit a lesser degree of conceptual and phonological integration, with each clause appearing in its own window of attention and retaining its own profile.[2] If so, it has two successive profiles, like (7)a. But it is not a coordinate structure in the narrow sense of the term.

2 This depends in part on the complexity of the clauses. If they are very brief, they can be compressed into a single window: *He drinks it because he likes it.*

The analysis I adopt for (7)c is sketched in Figure 12.9. At the lower level of composition, the clause *he really likes it* specifies one participant in the relation profiled by *because* (the causing circumstance). At the higher level, *Joe drinks whisky* specifies the other participant (the caused circumstance). Each clause retains its profile at higher levels. The overall expression is a constituent, but not a classical constituent. The integration of the component structures is only partial, as no single overall profile emerges.

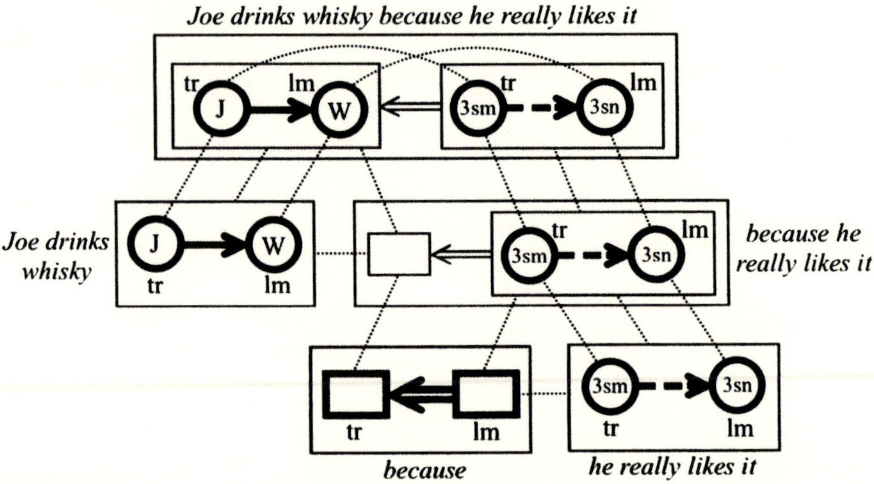

Figure 12.9

Why is (7)c not, strictly speaking, a coordinate expression? It departs from "pure" coordination in the nature of the connection between the two clauses. For one thing, *because* has more elaborate conceptual content than the basic conjunctions (AND and OR). Also, *because* designates an asymmetrical relationship between the two clauses, which runs counter to the notion that conjuncts are parallel and co-equal.[3] Since *because* is internally asymmetrical, the clauses it joins are not portrayed as equal in status. This I take to be the basis for the characterization of one as the "main" clause and the other as "subordinate".

We obtain a coordinate structure, in the narrow sense of the term, just by changing *because* to *and* in (7)c. What is the difference in their meanings? First, *and* exhibits no internal asymmetry, hence the clauses it joins are co-equal in status. Second, it has little if any intrinsic content. *Because* contrasts

3 The same can be said for other subordinating conjunctions, such as *if, although, since, while, when, before, after*, etc.

in meaning with a whole series of other subordinating conjunctions – it is semantically distinct from *although*, *while*, *if*, *before*, etc. On the other hand, *and* contrasts with only *or* and *but*. Moreover, the AND conjunction would seem to be unmarked, the most neutral semantically. Others can be analyzed as elaborating its basic conceptual import by introducing other factors.

If we take the requirements of minimal content and minimal asymmetry to the extreme, we wind up with the configuration in Figure 12.8. Apart from the notion of parallelism (in terms of a common schema and analogous connections to other structures), there is no relation at all between the conjuncts. They are simply co-conceived, or mentally juxtaposed. In its pure form, in other words, AND amounts to a schematized representation of coordination. Or to put it another way, coordination is just the grammatical manifestion of the mental juxtaposition of co-equal structures.

Of course, the ideal is seldom fully realized in actual practice. I am not claiming that an AND-type conjunction is necessarily limited to this abstracted value. A particular conjunction in a given language may well incorporate additional content (English *but* being one example). I would speculate, however, that this maximally general conceptual import is what particular conjunctions share, and serves as the endpoint for paths of grammaticization which elements follow as they develop into conjunctions.

At the same time, the ideal is probably **too** ideal to occur very often without embellishment. When events or situations are co-conceived and mentally juxtaposed, it is natural to see some further relation between them. We tend to interpret them as occurring in the order described, or as being causally related. We often mark this explicitly with a complex conjunction, like *and then* or *and so*. But additional marking is not required. For instance, it is hard not to interpret the first conjunct in (7)b as providing the reason for the situation described in the second conjunct. Similarly, we are likely to interpret *She quit her job and got married* as indicating that she quit her job first. *She got married and quit her job* suggests the opposite order, and also that getting married made it possible to quit her job.

2.2. OR

Let us now extend the analysis from AND to OR, i.e. from **con**junction to **dis**junction. Most of what I have said about AND carries over to OR. Grammatically, AND-constructions and OR-constructions are both instances of coordination. For the most part, the analysis I have presented for AND applies to OR as well.

There is however an apparent problem with the semantic description of AND in terms of mental juxtaposition. I pointed out that this could be considered the conceptual characterization of coordination itself. Now, since OR-constructions are also instances of coordination, they too should be describable in terms of mental juxtaposition. But that seems quite problematic in the case of OR. Whereas AND involves a kind of simultaneous applicability – both conjuncts being valid for some purpose – with OR the key notion is alternation, where only one is valid. How can this be reconciled with the simultaneity implied by mental juxtaposition?

The key to the matter is that OR is semantically more complex than AND. It incorporates the value of AND, which is responsible for OR-constructions being coordinate in nature. In the case of OR, however, this mental juxtaposition is embedded in a more elaborate conceptual structure, which is responsible for the notion of alternation (Langacker 1991, 2005d). Important factors in describing this conceptual structure are very general phenomena independently established in cognitive semantics, notably dynamicity, fictivity, and mental spaces.

As indicated in Figure 12.8, the basic import of AND consists in the mental juxtaposition of conjuncts and parallelism in their connection to other structures. For present purposes, it will be more useful to talk instead – but equivalently – about the position of conjuncts in a larger structural configuration. In Figure 12.10(a), the outer box labeled Z stands for the larger structural configuration, while the inner box represents some position, or "role", within it. In diagrams (b) and (c), X and Y represent two conjuncts, both of which fill the role. This can happen in two different ways. On the one hand, they can fill the role individually, so that actually there is a dual filling of it (e.g. *X and Y are tall*). On the other hand, they can fill it jointly (e.g. *X and Y are alike*). But in either case, X and Y are co-conceived in relation to the role. They are mentally juxtaposed, both present in a single, consistent conception possibly all activated simultaneously, at a single moment in processing time.

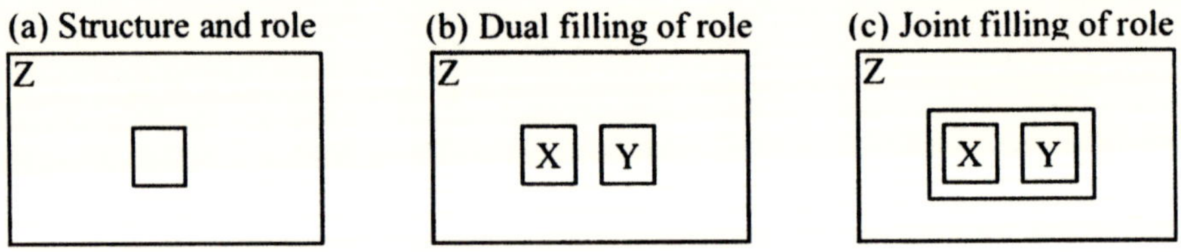

Figure 12.10

The conceptual import of OR is more elaborate and harder to describe. As shown in Figure 12.11, its characterization involves two levels, or mental spaces. There is first a **target situation**, where a single entity fills a given role in structure Z. Also included are alternative conceptions of what that entity might be. The conjuncts, given as X and Y, are **candidates** to fill this role in the target situation. Conceiving of them as candidates amounts to conceptualizing each of them in the role. However, relative to the target situation, these conceptions – of X filling the role, and of Y filling the role – are only virtual, or fictive in nature. They represent potential forms that the target situation might assume, without either one being conceived as its actual form. What does it mean for the candidates to be conceived as "alternatives"? This notion is partially captured by the correspondence lines: X and Y both correspond to a single position in the target situation. But there is also a temporal aspect to this notion. I suggest that their status as alternatives consists in part, at some level of cognitive processing, in their not being activated simultaneously, but one at a time, in alternating fashion (Figure 12.1(c)). Once again I draw the analogy to the perception of an ambiguous figure, where we flip back and forth between the alternate interpretations rather than entertaining them simultaneously. In addition to mental spaces and fictivity, dynamicity is thus a crucial factor distinguishing AND from OR.[4]

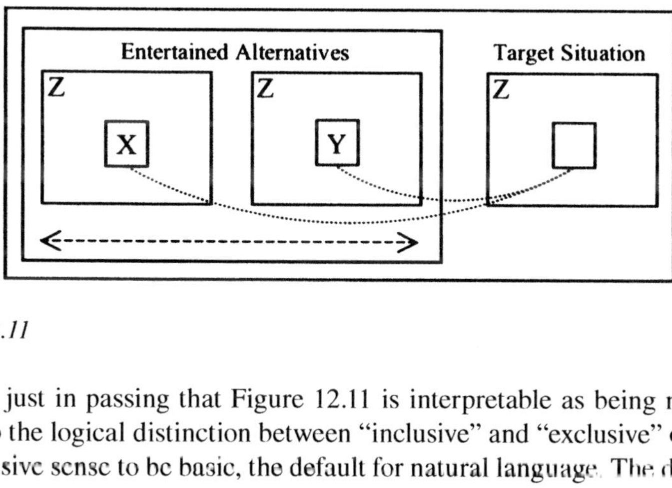

Figure 12.11

I note just in passing that Figure 12.11 is interpretable as being neutral in regard to the logical distinction between "inclusive" and "exclusive" OR. I take the exclusive sense to be basic, the default for natural language. The difference

4 OR is also dynamic in the sense implied by the notion of "candidates". Conceptually, both candidates are competing for the privilege of being realized in the target situation. There is thus a kind of mental progression from the alternatives to the target. In contrast to AND, the configuration invoked by OR is abstractly force-dynamic (Talmy 1988). There is a state of conceptual tension which has to be resolved in some fashion, whereas AND represents a state of relaxation (Chapter 9).

is then a matter of whether the configuration shown for Z, with just a single slot representing the role, is taken as being a **minimal** characterization of the target situation or the **full** characterization.

If the alternatives are apprehended in alternating fashion rather than simultaneously, how then can we say that OR involves mental juxtaposition of the conjuncts? There are different ways to think about this (not mutually exclusive). One option is to interpret the notion of "juxtaposition" loosely enough that it encompasses adjacency in processing time, as well as adjacency within the configuration evoked at a given instant. Another option involves our mental ability to summarize over temporally distributed occurrences and view them holistically, as part of a single conceptual gestalt. This is common and very basic. It happens, for instance, when a sentence like *Alice and Bill resigned* is used to describe a sequence of events, e.g. Alice resigned one day and Bill the next. We simply abstract away from time and present the summation of temporally distinct occurrences. In the case of Figure 12.11, it is a matter of abstracting away from the inherent dynamicity of the configuration and taking a summary view of the alternatives – at this slightly higher level of abstraction, they are seen as simultaneously having the status of candidates for the target situation. To put it another way, it is a matter of imposing a simultaneous, summary view on an inherently dynamic configuration at a higher level of conceptual organization. As the diagram suggests, at this higher level of organization the candidate situations are simultaneously apprehended in their shared role as alternatives (the entire configuration functioning as structure Z at this level, for this purpose).

Importantly, the notions "virtual" and "actual" are relative, not absolute. The candidates in Figure 12.11 are necessarily virtual in the sense of representing potential forms that the target situation might actually assume. It need not however be the case that the target situation is real or actual except in relation to this potentiality. For example, (8)a does not imply that Joe's meeting an actress or movie star is an actual event; even the target situation is limited to the mental space representing Joe's desire. The target situation is also virtual in the sense that neither candidate is identified as the one filling the role in question. That is, the target situation represents the idea of a single entity filling that role, but does not specify which one this might be; there is only a partial characterization of the entity filling the role, one that is not sufficient to distinguish between the candidates. Within the target situation, therefore, the role is a virtual entity rather than an actual individual. So in Figure 12.11 both the entertained alternatives and the target situation are virtual in nature (though in slightly different ways). By contrast, everything in Figure 12.10 has the possibililty of being real and actual, e.g. in (8)b. Of course, it does not have to be, as we observe in (8)c.

(8) a. *Joe wants to meet an actress or a movie star.*
b. *Joe met an actress and a movie star.*
c. *Joe wants to meet an actress and a movie star.*

A final point concerning conjunctions is that sometimes *and* and *or* seem interchangeable (cf. LeGrand 1974):

(9) a. *If our team wins we'll have a party, {and / or} if it loses we'll have a party.*
b. *Alice is more intelligent than Bill {and / or} Sam.*
c. *Knowing Latin is helpful in linguistics {and / or} in medicine.*
d. *Dogs {and / or} cats make good pets.*
e. *We have gin {and / or} vodka.*

In each example in (9), replacing *and* with *or* results in an expression interpretable as being logically equivalent. I take this **conjunctive** use of *or* as representing a conceptual blend whose input structures are the basic meanings of *and* and *or* (Figures 12.10 and 12.11). As shown in Figure 12.12, the blend is obtained by superimposing the dynamicity of *or* – its alternating character – on the basic, simpler value of *and*, which is otherwise preserved. The virtuality of *or* is not projected into the blend: the conjuncts are still conceived as being simultaneously valid, i.e. part of a single, consistent configuration (the target situation). All that changes is the way of mentally accessing the conjuncts, considering (or entertaining) them in turn as one facet of the overall cognitive processing involved.[5]

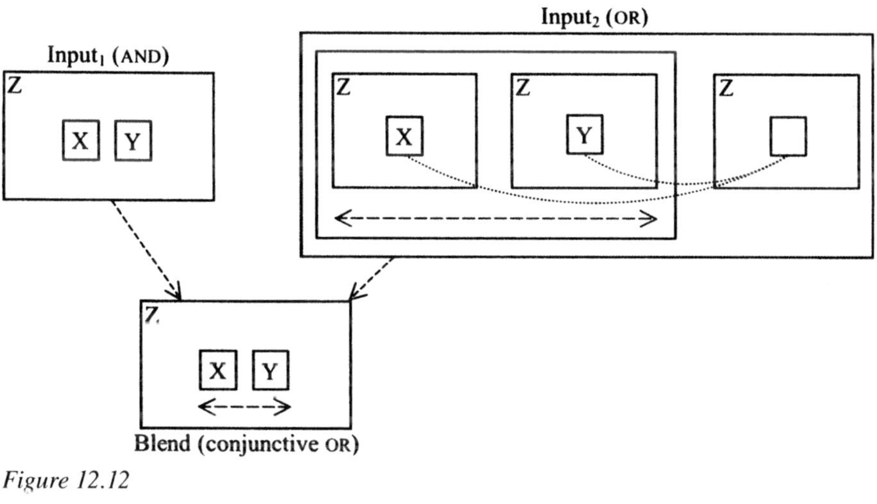

Figure 12.12

5 I will not consider in any detail the question of when *or* can have this interpretation. Some preliminary observations are made in Langacker 2009.

As might be expected, conjunctive *or* tends to be used when some vestige remains of the notion of choosing between alternatives – first considering one option, then another, when the options are simultaneously available. Very roughly, using *or* in (9)e is comparable to saying both *we have gin and vodka* and *you can choose either gin or vodka*. The notion of alternatives is still very much part of the contextual understanding of the expression, though implicit apart from *or*.

3. Basic coordination

Coordination is known for its complexity and analytical difficulty. Coordinate structures in English are quite varied and raise many descriptive and theoretical problems. Obviously, the best I can do here is sketch a possible path through this linguistic jungle. I believe the general framework of CG and the various points I have made and tried to establish independently give some hope that the problem can in principle be successfully dealt with in this perspective.

Let us start with the simplest case, a coordinate structure of the form *X and Y*, where X and Y are clearly constituents, for instance nominals. The internal structure of *and* is sketched in Figure 12.13(a). The ellipses indicate that there can be any number of conjuncts, as long as there are a minimum of two. Each conjunct is a schematic symbolic structure. At the semantic pole, their profiles (shown as boxes) can be of any sort (i.e. the conjuncts can be of any category). At the phonological pole, x and y are used as schematic representations of their form. The specific phonological content of English *and* is, of course, *and* (given here orthographically), specified as occurring just prior to the final conjunct in the stream of speech (the arrow labeled t is for speech time, the temporal dimension of phonological space). As in Figure 12.8, indications are given that semantically the conjuncts are abstractly similar (they instantiate a schema) and exhibit parallel connections to other structures.

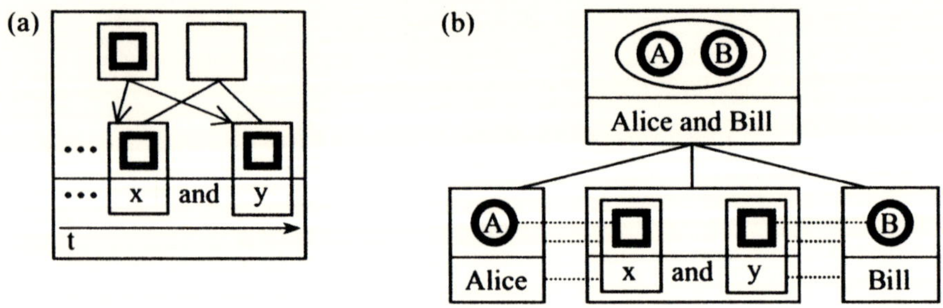

Figure 12.13

Diagram (b) shows the formation of the specific coordinate expression *Alice and Bill*. For diagrammatic ease, I have simplified the representation of *and* by omitting several elements: the arrow for speech time, the schematic commonality, parallel connections, and the possibility of more than two conjuncts. The conjuncts schematically evoked by *and* are specified by the nominals *Alice* and *Bill*. Correspondence lines indicate identity of their semantic poles (implying that their profiles also correspond) as well as their phonological poles. When corresponding entities are superimposed, the result is the composite symbolic structure shown at the top. Phonologically, the sequence is *Alice and Bill*. Semantically, there are two co-equal profiles.

I have also enclosed these elements in an ellipse, which represents the group comprising Alice and Bill. The very fact of mentally juxtaposing two comparable elements effects their conceptual grouping. At least implicitly it establishes them as a higher-order thing, analogous to a stack of plates or a flock of geese, except that the grouping is ad hoc rather than a familiar category. And as in the case of expressions like *flock of geese*, it would be a very easy matter for the profile to shift to the higher-order thing. There is a kind of inherent ambivalence between the co-profiling of constitutive elements and the profiling of the collective entity they constitute. Various factors can encourage this alternate profiling.

Descriptive challenges start to emerge as soon as we consider how a conjoined nominal combines with other structures. Take the sentence *Alice and Bill resigned*, where *Alice and Bill* specifies the verb's trajector, making it the clausal subject. In this case the verb *resign(ed)* functions as the "other structures" with which the conjuncts are connected in parallel fashion. Thus each nominal referent corresponds to the verb's trajector, as shown in Figure 12.14(a). The descriptive challenge that arises at this juncture is to be clear about the import of this notation and what the composite semantic structure should look like. Since resigning is usually an individual action, let us assume the default interpretation where Alice and Bill resigned individually. Thus there were two instances of resigning, but in diagram (a) only one is shown at the component structure level. It would be contradictory to say that Alice and Bill each, individually, function as trajector for the same instance of this event type. Rather, as shown at the composite structure level, we want to say that there are two instances of resigning, in each of which one person participates.

I call this a "challenge" because it is not a real "problem" for the analysis. It is rather a matter of being clear about what notations are meant to indicate, and about further, finer-grained details of grammatical description that have to be dealt with independently. A key point is that English verbs (also adjectives) do not lexicalize the distinction between **simplex** and **complex** relationships.

If I say *Alice kicked her dog*, it makes perfect sense to reply by asking *How many times?*. Though one instance is the default, a simple verb stem is routinely and conventionally used for complex occurrences involving any number of instances. In contrast with nouns, where a singular/plural distinction is generally indicated morphologically, there is no such morphological distinction marked on verbs in English.[6]

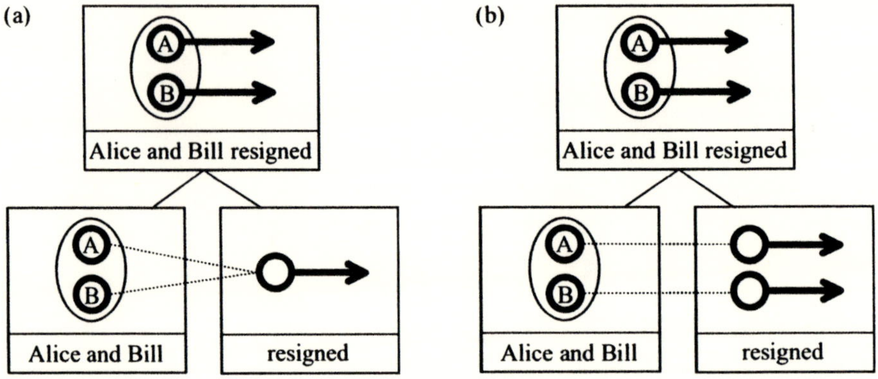

Figure 12.14

We could then say that the depiction of *resign* at the component structure level is a fictive instance, invoked as being representative of any number of actual instances. The complex subject then implies that there are multiple actual instances, as seen at the composite structure level. Alternatively, as shown in Figure 12.14(b), we could say that *resign* (as one of its possible values – the one relevant in the context of the overall expression) profiles a complex event comprising two **atomic** events, whose trajectors correspond to the nominal profiles. Ultimately, I believe these options are equivalent.

Just as a set of things constitutes a complex or higher-order thing, so we can consider a set of relationships to constitute a complex or higher-order relationship. This was shown in Figure 12.2(b), corresponding to a sentence like (2)c, *A flock of geese is flying overhead*. In Figure 12.15(a), I have taken the composite structure from Figure 12.14 and added an arrow representing the com-

6 I leave aside verb "agreement", which is part of the inflectional system for grounding, thus analogous to nominal determiners rather than pluralization. In any case, the indication of number it gives pertains to the trajector, not specifically to the complexity of the profiled relationship. For instance, *The boxes are heavy* uses a plural verb whether the boxes are heavy individually or only collectively.

plex relationship, whose constitutive elements are the profiled atomic events. As indicated, this structure corresponds to the default interpretion of *Alice and Bill resigned*, where they resigned individually, the clause merely serving to summarize two separate events. There are however other interpretations. It could be, for instance, that either or both people resigned on multiple occasions. We will not consider this option. Instead of Figure 12.15(a), I believe we can also impose the profiling of diagram (b). This would correspond to the situation where Alice and Bill are resigning in concert with one another, as a joint action, even though technically each resigns independently. It is simply a matter of shifting the emphasis, conceptually, from the individual to the collective aspect of a complex situation which has both facets. Certainly it will not always be evident which interpretation is intended, perhaps even in the mind of the speaker. Conceivably it is just a matter of degree. In any case, we need to recognize still another option, shown in diagram (c), where there is only one atomic event of resigning, on the part of a group. This corresponds to the situation where Alice and Bill are a team of some sort, and hired as a team for a single function, so that there is only one job and one act of resignation. These can all arise from two component structures, *Alice and Bill* and *resigned*, depending on precisely what correspondences are established between their elements.

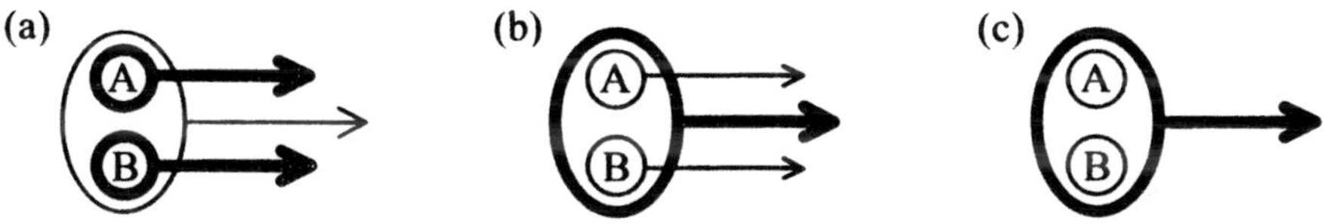

Figure 12.15

I should point out that these different interpretations are independent of the phenomenon of coordination. They can also be observed with plurals, as in Figure 12.16, for the sentence *The women are smart*. In this case the profiled relationship, *(be) smart*, ascribes a property to the trajector. This property is indicated with a box labeled 's'. The property *smart* is usually associated just with individuals, as in diagram (a). I believe, however, that the interpretion in (b) is possible (albeit only subtly different). Even though the women are smart individually, the emphasis is on the overall aura of intelligence they project collectively. The situation in (c) is more clearly distinct conceptually (however rare it might be in practice): individually the women may be of just ordinary intelligence – it is only when acting as a unit that they are (collectively) smart.

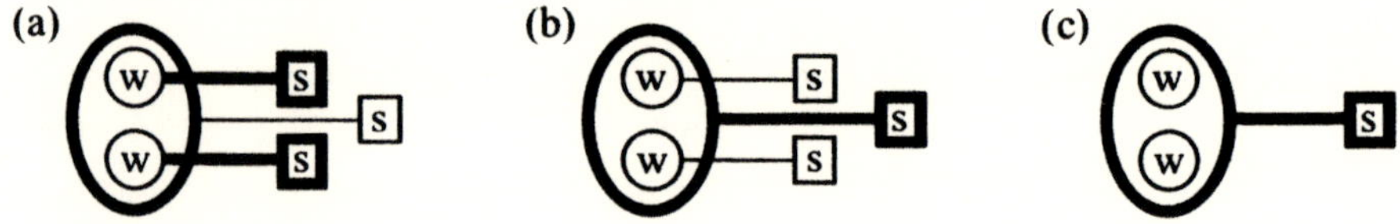

Figure 12.16

The phenomena in Figures 12.15 and 12.16 have to be distinguished from another sort of case: that where the profiled relationship intrinsically requires a complex trajector. An example is the verb *meet*, as in Figure 12.17. The profiled relationship is basically symmetrical, and its two participants are specifically construed as a group, a higher-order thing. It is this higher-order entity that is put in focus as trajector, hence it combines with a subject nominal which profiles such an entity. This can either be a plural, as in *The women met*, or a coordinate structure.

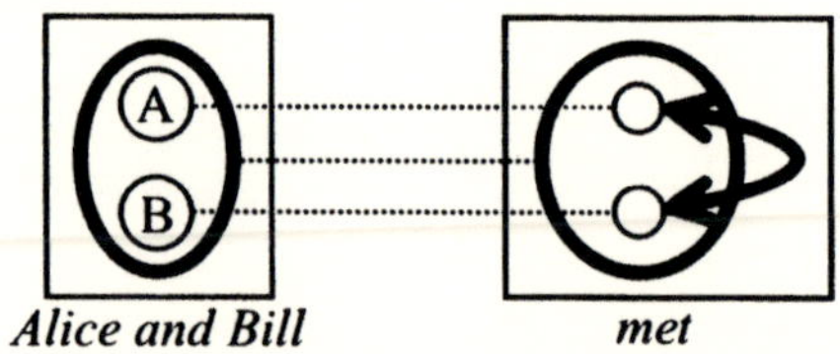

Figure 12.17

There is more to say about higher-order entities. Usually such an entity is more than just the sum of its parts. Even in Figure 12.15(b), where Alice and Bill resign together, the very fact that they are acting in concert makes them and their resignation something more than just individual people and individual acts. Their collective nature has conceptual and even causal import (perhaps only a joint resignation will have an impact on the organization). If Alice and Bill are a team, that is clearly something above and beyond individuals (just as a *stack* is more than just plates). With varying degrees of clarity and salience, higher-order entities are viewed as representing distinct and separate **types**, with emergent properties not reducible to those of their components.

Let us once more consider (2)c, *A flock of geese is flying overhead*, diagrammed in Figure 12.2(b).[7] There is a qualitative difference between the way a flock flies and the way individual geese do. Individual geese flap their wings

7 What about *A flock of geese are flying overhead*? I would say that it focuses the plural mass, *geese*, as opposed to the *flock*, and that the processual profile is complex, as in Figure 12.15(a) or 12.16(a). The contrast was shown in Figure 2.10.

to propel themselves through the air. In a sense, of course, the flying of a flock of geese is the sum of all these individual activities. But in addition, we have the visual impression, in seeing or imagining this, of a bounded entity moving as a unit across the sky. This higher-order entity does not per se have wings or flap them; it simply moves, and we can describe it in this way even if we cannot make out the individual birds or their wings. This emergent property shows up in the infelicity of (10)b, as opposed to (10)a.

(10) a. *A flock of geese are flying overhead by flapping their wings.*
b. **A flock of geese is flying overhead by flapping {its / their} wings.*

The distinct, emergent nature of the higher-order entity is generally more apparent when the constitutive elements are themselves distinct in nature, rather than multiple instances of the same type. Many fixed expressions have coalesced as standard labels for these higher-order types. The conjoined elements can be nouns, as in *gin and tonic*, *whisky and soda*, *rum and coke*, etc. Drinking a *gin and tonic* is not at all just the sum of drinking gin and drinking tonic – their combination is a qualitatively different substance with its own distinct properties. In this case the coordinate expression necessarily profiles the higher-order thing, as shown in Figure 12.18(a), where X stands for emergent properties not inherited from the component ingredients. There are fixed expressions of this sort for verbs, e.g. *toss and turn*, which means 'sleep restlessly'. Also for adjectives, e.g. *tried and true*. But the phenomenon is not limited to fixed expressions (lexical items). New examples are productively created. For instance, I can speak of a *red and yellow shirt*, a novel expression, which is readily understood in the manner shown in 12.18(c). The shirt as a whole is not red, nor is it yellow. The coordinate expression *red and yellow* is construed as describing a complex color property, where certain portions of its trajector project to the red region of color space, and certain portions to the yellow region.[8] Of course, once the higher-order entity is created and put in profile, the expression combines with other structures in the usual way, analogous to the behavior of simplex entities.

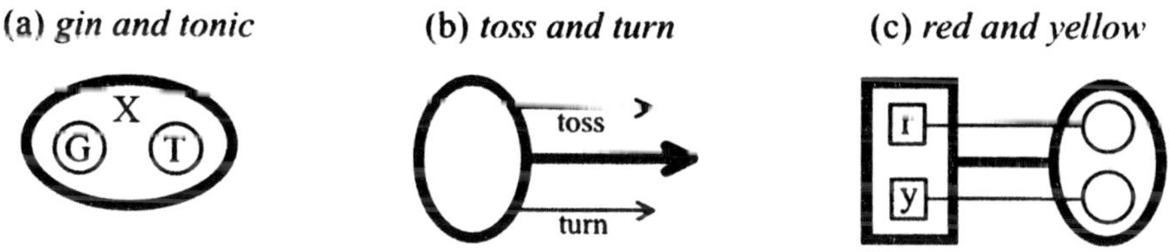

Figure 12.18

8 Cf. *plaid shirt*, where the complexity of a visual property is lexicalized.

4. Complex constructions

So far we have only looked at examples where the conjuncts are single-word expressions. But naturally, coordination happens at different levels of structural organization, and the conjuncts can be of any size. In Figure 12.19 the conjuncts are complex predicates consisting of a verb and its object. Although I have not shown it, the two component structures – *fed the dog* and *washed the cat* – are to be understood as composite structures arising from lower levels of grammatical composition. At the higher level of organization, the nominal *Alice* simultaneously specifies the trajectors of both profiled relationships, and is thus the subject with respect to each conjunct. This is their parallelism in grammatical connections with other structures.

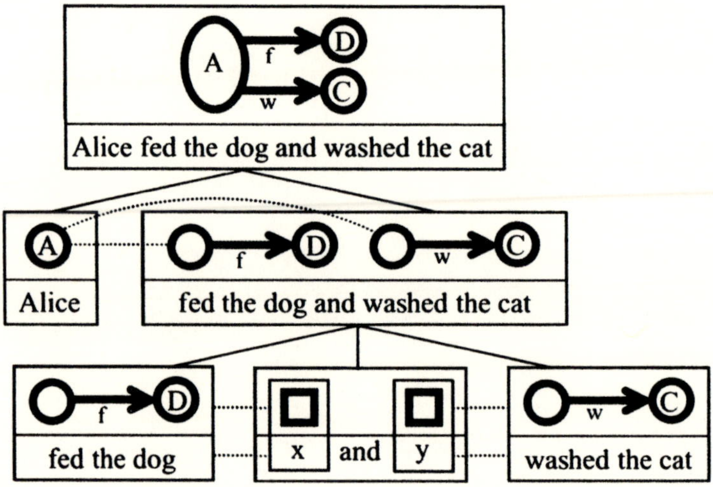

Figure 12.19

4.1. Non-constituent coordination

Now things start to get difficult. How does one analyze a sentence like (11)? The conjuncts consist of a subject-verb combination that excludes the object. While this is not a usual constituency in English, there are cases where it definitely occurs, e.g. relative clauses and clause-internal topic constructions, as noted in (3)d–e. One option, then, is to simply posit this alternate constituency for expressions like (11). The structure would be precisely analogous to Figure 12.19, except that the conjuncts are subject-verb combinations instead of verb-object combinations. At the higher level of composition, *the cat* simultaneously corresponds to and specifies the landmarks of both conjuncts.

(11) *Alice washed, and Bill dried, the cat.*

I do not think this is wrong, but I also think it is only part of the story. In contrast to the sentence in Figure 12.19, which is easily pronounced without any noticeable pause, the natural pronunciation of (11) places very clear pauses around the second conjunct. That suggests to me that in some sense it is intrusive, actually interrupting the clause *Alice washed the cat*. This implies a more complex analysis, which relates the expression to phenomena like ellipsis and parenthetical insertion. That does not necessarily mean the structure is non-coordinate; it is, after all, marked with *and*, and semantically it involves parallel events. Now I can pronounce (11) with no hesitation anywhere, just as for Figure 12.19; it might then be written without commas. This is secondary, but so is subject-verb constituency the secondary pattern in English. What I suspect, then, is that a sentence like (11) has two alternate grammatical structures. On one analysis, it is indeed parallel to Figure 12.19, with subject-verb constituents as conjuncts. On the other analysis, which would tend to correlate with the occurrence of pauses, it is actually a special manifestation of conjoined clauses. What that analysis looks like from a CG perspective is our next topic.

In one way this is not a new proposal. In the generative tradition, transformations were sometimes posited that reduced conjoined clauses to single clauses with conjoined constituents.[9] It was further noted that not all cases of conjoined constituents could be derived in this manner, and that some expressions were ambiguous in a way best explained by allowing both the direct combination of constituents and a derivation from conjoined clauses (Smith 1969).

Let me rephrase this in my own terms. Some cases of non-clausal coordination clearly **cannot** be derived from or related to clausal coordination. For instance, *I drank gin and tonic* is not equivalent to *I drank gin and I drank tonic*. *Alice and Bill met* is not equivalent to **Alice met and Bill met*. Some cases of non-clausal coordination **may** be related to clausal coordination. An example is (11), which may in fact have alternate analyses. I would not rule out the possibility that most cases of coordination with non clausal conjuncts have alternate analyses. If so, *Alice and Bill resigned* would have the structure shown in Figure 12.14 and another structure along the lines of what follows. Similarly, *Alice fed the dog and washed the cat* would have both the structure in Figure 12.19

9 "Conjunction reduction" was a common term. For sentences like (11), where the conjuncts were not seen as constituents, a special rule called "right node raising" was suggested.

and a structure relating to clausal coordination. And lastly, some evident cases of non-clausal coordination **must** be related to clausal coordination. The basic reason is that the apparent conjuncts are implausible as independent groupings – conceptually they make no sense alone, nor do they instantiate independently attested patterns. Another reason is that in some cases the seeming conjuncts are disparate in nature. One example: *Jack went to the party with, and Jill without, a date.* These problems disappear if the expressions are seen as alternate manifestations of configurations which would normally be manifested by conjoined clauses.

Since CG does not allow transformations or derivations from underlying structures, I cannot say that such expressions derive from conjoined clauses. Nor do I take them as evidence for the need to posit deep structures and derivations. It is possible to accommodate both the clausal and non-clausal aspects of the expressions in a framework that only posits assemblies of symbolic structures, all simultaneously available. The key is to recognize that symbolic assemblies have many possible configurations, with organization into a well-behaved constituency hierarchy being only one.

Although I could in principle supply diagrams in the format of Figure 12.19, showing the details of semantic structure, correspondences, and composition at multiple levels, in practical terms we will be better served by nesting diagrams like those in Figure 12.3, where small caps abbreviate symbolic structures. For sake of discussion I will assume the standard constituency of Figure 12.3(a). If we analyze (11) as being based on clausal coordination, two constituency hierarchies analogous to Figure 12.3(a) will be among its component structures. These are given in Figure 12.20(a). Of course, the central fact we have to deal with is that the two clausal structures are not fully realized, at least not individually. Though each structure takes *the cat* as its object, in (11) that nominal appears only once. Accordingly – and unproblematically from the standpoint of CG – I take the two clausal constituency hierarchies as being overlapping rather than disjoint. They share an object nominal, as shown in diagram (b). This is just a special case of an independently established phenomenon, illustrated previously in Figure 12.6.[10]

10 A complex matter I cannot investigate here concerns the conditions under which clausal elements can be conflated in this manner. Semantically, for instance, strict referential identity is not always required. In the following example, *a cat* does not necessarily have the same reference in the component clauses: *Alice washed, and Bill dried, a cat.* Nor is strict phonological or morphological identity always required: *I am very tall, and Bill rather short.* These problems are not unique to coordination, however.

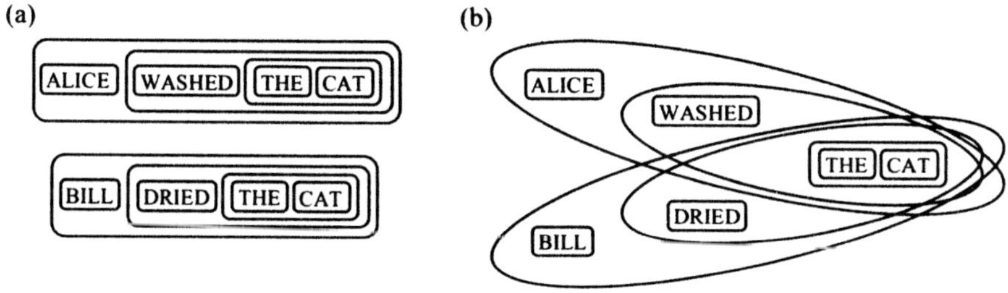

Figure 12.20

We must next consider the conjunction and what it conjoins. The presumed difference from previous examples is that the conjuncts are not established independently as constituents. Rather, they consist of portions of clausal structures which generally cross-cut regular constituency groupings. I would say that the very fact of being coordinated (used as conjuncts) imposes a grouping, so that they become constituents through participation in this construction. They are not however classical constituents, since it is not necessarily the case that a single, self-contained composite structure emerges with a single overall profile.

What is involved here is global comparison, of the sort described for focus in Figure 12.7. In the focus construction, two structures are globally compared to determine which elements of the target stand out as being different from corresponding elements of the standard. The differential between the standard and target has a certain kind of salience, standing in the foreground of awareness. In cases like (11), we are not dealing with focus in the discourse sense, where the standard and target are successive expressions, often separate sentences. Instead, the global comparison is put to work in the formation of a single sentence, applying to partially overlapping component structures within the same symbolic assembly. This is shown in Figure 12.21(a). Within the target, *Bill dried* stands out as the differential, its salience indicated by the thicker line of the box enclosing it in diagram (b). The very act of comparison and detection of contrast effects the grouping of *Bill dried*, which thus emerges as a kind of constituent, and implicitly also effects the grouping of *Alice washed*, as the segment of the standard it contrasts with.

These emergent constituents are the conjuncts joined by *and*, as shown in diagram (b). This implies a slightly generalized version of *and*, one which does not require that the conjuncts have a single overall profile. Apart from that, it joins the conjuncts in the manner shown in Figure 12.19, producing a composite structure which – were it pronounced in isolation – would have the form *Alice washed and Bill dried*. The configuration in 12.21(b) is simply an assembly of symbolic structures, but it does have some special properties. First, it involves both parallelism and asymmetry. The clausal structures are parallel from the standpoint of their semantic and grammatical organization. The asymmetry resides in the status of the conjuncts, as determined by the global comparison giving rise to these conjuncts. There is nothing contradictory about both factors being present. Second, we can describe this assembly as comprising three complex structures derived by composition from constitutive elements. These are the two clausal structures, *Alice washed the cat* and *Bill dried the cat*, as well as the coordinate structure *Alice washed and Bill dried.* These function as component structures for purposes of deriving the composite structure representing the form and meaning of the full expression. It happens to be the case, however, that these component structures are overlapping in the ways shown, rather than disjoint.

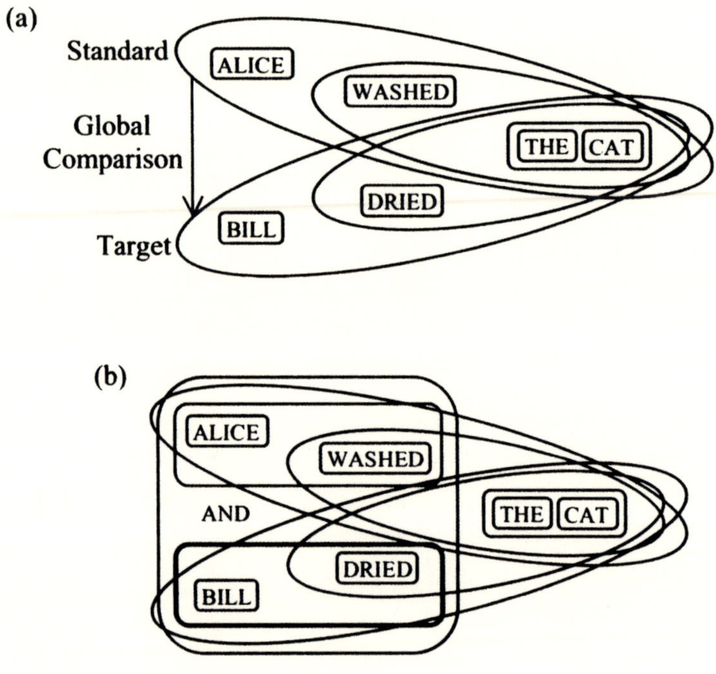

Figure 12.21

What, then, does the composite structure look like? Here we need to consider the semantic and phonological poles individually. A first approximation to its semantic pole is given in Figure 12.22. Diagram (a) shows the three component semantic structures: the two clausal components, and the one defined by the differential. Correspondence lines indicate their conceptual overlap, which is reflected more directly in 12.21(b). Showing the component structures as discrete elements, in separate boxes, is done for analytical purposes, to represent them in the format used for constructions in general. But this should not obscure the construction's special nature, in which the composite conception's dissociation into separate clausal structures for purposes of linguistic expression is only partial (as opposed to non-overlapping clauses, as in *Alice washed the cat and Bill dried it*).

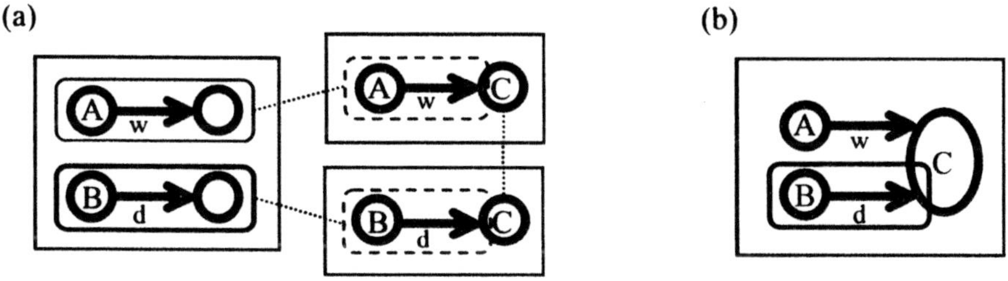

Figure 12.22

Since the clauses are conjoined by AND, the composite semantic structure profiles both the washing and the drying, both directed at the cat, as shown in 12.22(b). Beyond this, the composite conception includes the foregrounding of Bill and his drying, reflecting their status as the differential.

As for the phonological pole, the key factor is the apparent incorporation of the differential, *and Bill dried*, in the clause functioning as standard. I have pointed out that this phenomenon is independently attested and readily accommodated in the general CG account of phonological integration (Figure 12.5).

The phonological composition is sketched in Figure 12.23. The three component structures are *Alice washed the cat*, *Bill dried the cat*, and *Alice washed and Bill dried*. At the component structure level, each represents a linearly contiguous phonological grouping. Once more, however, they are not disjoint but overlapping, as shown more directly in Figure 12.21. The overlap is indicated with underscores and correspondence lines. I have further identified *and Bill dried* as the phonological pole of the differential. As the diagram shows, the composite phonological structure consists of the standard of comparison, *Alice washed the cat*, with the differential incorporated in it with respect to the temporal sequence. The target clause, *Bill dried the cat*, is not separately manifested at the composite structure level, as it overlaps fully with the other components.[11]

11 In Figure 12.23 I show the conjunction *and* as being part of the differential. It does form a phonological grouping with the final conjunct, and it is part of the differen-

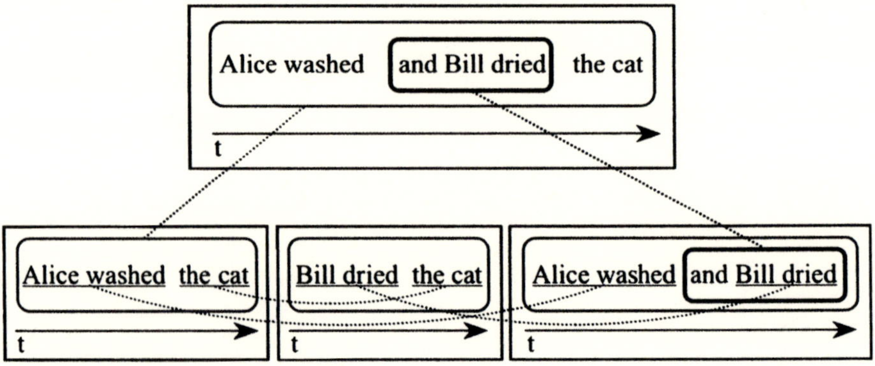

Figure 12.23

I am not claiming that the differential is necessarily set off from the remainder by pitch, as in Figure 12.5(b), or by other phonetic parameters like amplitude or rate of production. Indeed, I find it most natural to keep these basically constant for the entire expression. It is however bracketed by pauses, represented orthographically as commas. I take this to be a way of signalling its intrusive status, and an indication that the speaker apprehends the remainder as a coherent phonological grouping despite the temporal interruption. I am also not claiming that the differential is inherently more prominent phonetically, or semantically prominent in any way similar to profiling. At either pole it is simply more salient in the sense of being recognized as different from the standard of comparison.

4.2. Discontinuity

As with the focus construction, the analysis has to be generalized to accommodate examples where the differential is discontinuous. This is perfectly straightforward in principle, but difficult from the standpoint of producing readable diagrams in two dimensions, while using one dimension for temporal order. I will thus adopt the notation in Figure 12.24, purely as a device for simplifying diagrams. Despite apparent discontinuity, X and Y constitute a group.

Figure 12.24

tial in the sense of going beyond what is provided by the standard of comparison. In more elaborate diagrams, I would show an intermediate-level grouping that includes both the conjunction and the second conjunct: [[X] [*and* [Y]]].

Consider the expression in (12), which displays the grouping in Figure 12.25. The differential is the phonologically and conceptually discontinuous combination of BILL and WITHOUT.

(12) *Alice came with, and Bill without, a date.*

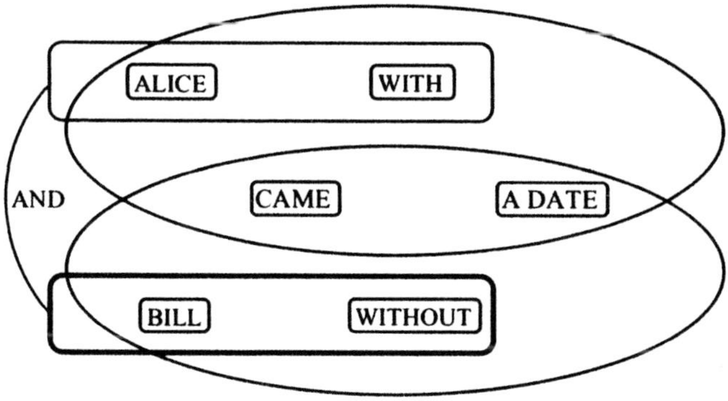

Figure 12.25

The semantic integration of (12) is shown in Figure 12.26. The component structures, represented separately in diagram (a), are the clauses, *Alice came with a date* and *Bill came without a date*, as well as the coordinate structure *Alice with and Bill without*. This being a type of clausal coordination, the composite structure profiles both instances of *come*, as shown in diagram (b). Once more, the differential (*Bill without*) is foregrounded by virtue of the clausal comparison.[12]

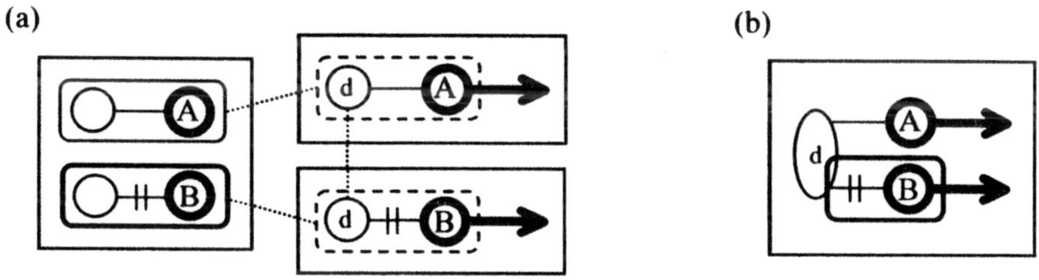

Figure 12.26

12 Note that the two instances of *a date* are identified, even though – in terms of real-world reference – the date Alice came with is not the same as the imagined date Bill came without. Their identity holds instead at the **role** level (Fauconnier 1985): both clauses allude to the fictive instance of *date* defined by its role in the come-to-a-party-with-a-date scenario. It is the role, rather than a **value** of that role, which is coded in (12).

The phonological pole of (12) is given in Figure 12.27. The formation of the composite structure comes about in just the same way as in Figure 12.23: the composite expression consists of the standard clause plus the differential, the latter incorporated in the former. In this case there is an alternate word order, where the standard and differential are juxtaposed, occurring in sequence. This is shown in Figure 12.28.

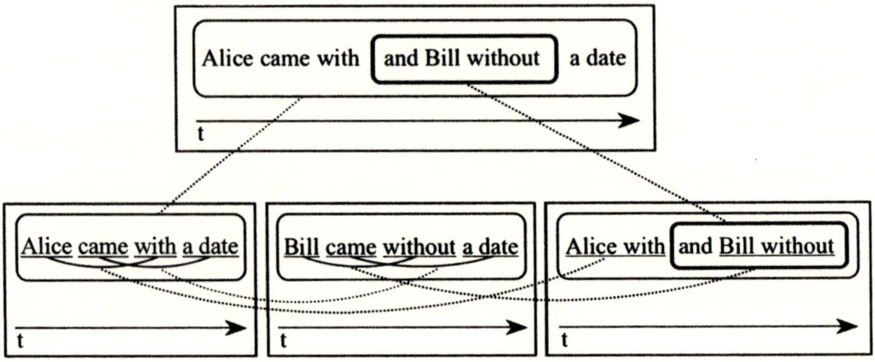

Figure 12.27

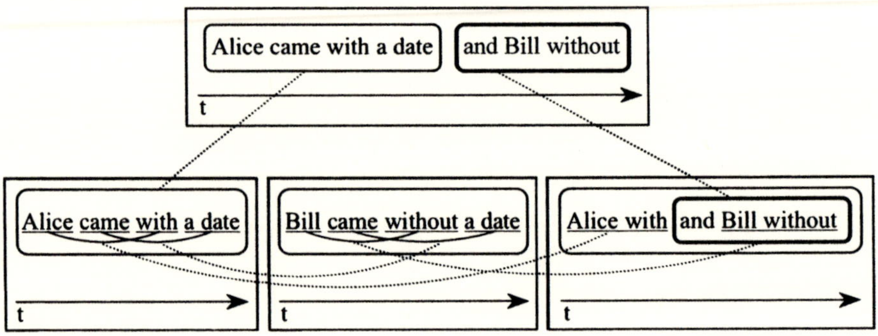

Figure 12.28

This second variant illustrates the phenomenon known as **gapping** (Ross 1970), so called because the second conjunct – what I have identified as the differential – contains a gap. Gapping is thus related to a more general phenomenon. A somewhat simpler example is (13), with the grouping shown in Figure 12.29.[13] The semantic pole of (13) is shown in Figure 12.30, and its phonological pole in 12.31.

13 I have not investigated the full range of these variants. They are not always freely interchangeable. Corresponding to (11), for instance, we do not have the following:

(13) *Alice washed the dog, and Bill the cat.*

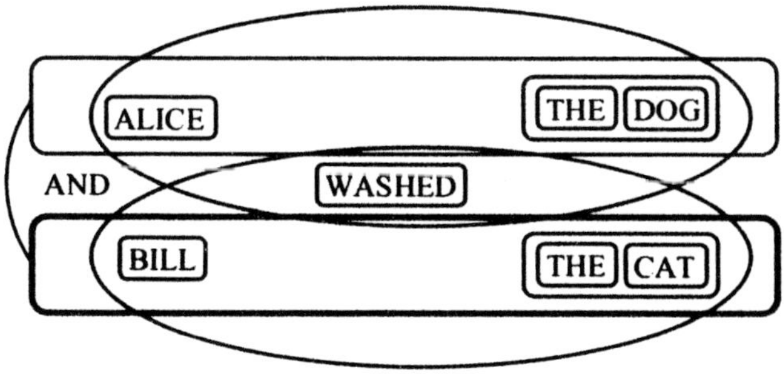

Figure 12.29

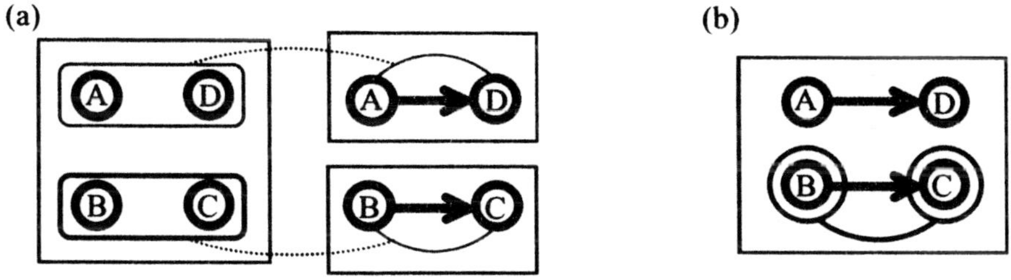

Figure 12.30

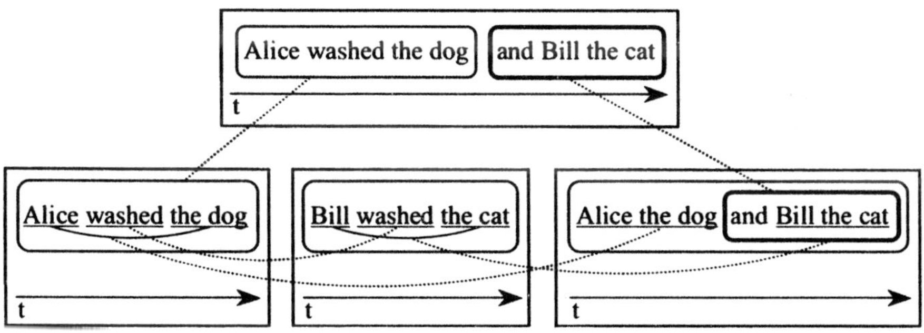

Figure 12.31

**Alice washed the cat, and Bill dried.* It is not that there always has to be a gap in the differential, e g we have both *Alice walked, and Bill ran, to the store* and *Alice walked to the store, and Bill ran*. Nor is the intercalated variety always possible: *Alice washed the dog, and Bill the cat*, but not **Alice washed, and Bill the cat, the dog* or **Alice, and Bill the cat, washed the dog.*

Of course, we always have the option of full clause coordination, as in (14)a. And instead of discontinuous conjuncts we sometimes have the option of multiple conjuncts, as in (14)b. Because (14)b has multiple interpretations, the adverb *respectively* can be used to indicate that the specific interpretation in (14)a is the one intended. The options represent alternate ways of dissociating the same composite conception into component conceptions for purposes of linguistic expression.

(14) a. *Alice washed the dog, and Bill washed the cat.*
b. *Alice and Bill washed the dog and the cat (respectively).*

A final point is that the mechanism of global comparison is available even when the conjuncts are constituents, so that regular constituent coordination would be possible. The contrast shows up intonationally:

(15) a. *Alice and Bill washed the cat.*
b. *Alice, and Bill, washed the cat.*
c. *Alice washed the cat, and Bill.*

The moral, I guess, is that just as there is more than one way to skin a cat, there is more than one way to coordinate its washing.

5. Final word

I hardly need mention how preliminary these proposals are and how much remains to investigate and analyze. I have however dealt with a considerable variety of central problems in a way that has some chance of proving plausible from the cognitive standpoint and viable from the linguistic standpoint. There are two points I should emphasize in conclusion. First, an attempt has been made to characterize coordination and conjunctions in conceptual terms. If successful, such a characterization should ultimately serve to explicate their "logical" properties without however being limited to them. Second, the analysis has not required that anything really new be added to the descriptive apparatus already available or independently needed in cognitive linguistics and Cognitive Grammar. Coordination is very complex, and often puzzling due to the multiplicity of factors involved, but from the CG perspective it is neither mysterious nor fundamentally different. I regard that as some validation for the approach.

References

Achard, Michel

1998 *Representation of Cognitive Structures: Syntax and Semantics of French Sentential Complements*. Berlin/New York: Mouton de Gruyter.

Anderson, John M.

1971 *The Grammar of Case: Towards a Localistic Theory*. Cambridge: Cambridge University Press.

Ariel, Mira

1988 Referring and accessibility. *Journal of Linguistics* 24: 65–87.

Austin, J. L.

1962 *How to Do Things with Words*. Cambridge, MA: Harvard University Press.

Barlow, Michael

1992 *A Situated Theory of Agreement*. New York: Garland.

Barlow, Michael, and Suzanne Kemmer (eds.)

2000 *Usage-Based Models of Language*. Stanford: CSLI Publications.

Barsalou, Lawrence W.

1999 Perceptual symbol systems. *Behavioral and Brain Sciences* 22: 577–660.

Bendix, Edward Herman

1966 *Componential Analysis of General Vocabulary: The Semantic Structure of a Set of Verbs in English, Hindi, and Japanese*. Bloomington: Indiana University Research Center in Anthropology, Folklore, and Linguistics.

Bergen, Benjamin

2005 Mental simulation in literal and figurative language understanding. In *The Literal and Nonliteral in Language and Thought*, Seana Coulson and Barbara Lewandowska-Tomaszczyk (eds.), 255–278. Frankfurt am Main: Peter Lang.

Bolinger, Dwight

1973 Ambient *it* is meaningful too. *Journal of Linguistics* 9: 261–270.

Bolinger, Dwight

1977 *Meaning and Form*. London/New York: Longman.

Boye, Kasper, and Peter Harder

2007 Complement-taking predicates: Usage and linguistic structure. *Studies in Language* 31: 569–606.

Brisard, Frank

1999 *A Critique of Localism in and about Tense Theory*. Antwerp: University of Antwerp doctoral dissertation.

Brisard, Frank

2001 *Be going to*: An exercise in grounding. *Journal of Linguistics* 37: 251–285.

Brisard, Frank
2002 The English present. In *Grounding: The Epistemic Footing of Deixis and Reference*, Frank Brisard (ed.), 251–297. Berlin/New York: Mouton de Gruyter.

Brisard, Frank (ed.)
2002 *Grounding: The Epistemic Footing of Deixis and Reference*. Berlin/New York: Mouton de Gruyter.

Casad, Eugene H., and Ronald W. Langacker
1985 "Inside" and "outside" in Cora grammar. *International Journal of American Linguistics* 51: 247–281.

Chafe, Wallace L.
1970 *Meaning and the Structure of Language*. Chicago: University of Chicago Press.

Chafe, Wallace L.
1994 *Discourse, Consciousness, and Time: The Flow and Displacement of Conscious Experience in Speaking and Writing*. Chicago/London: University of Chicago Press.

Chomsky, Noam
1957 *Syntactic Structures*. The Hague: Mouton.

Chomsky, Noam, and Morris Halle
1968 *The Sound Pattern of English*. New York: Harper & Row.

Croft, William
2001 *Radical Construction Grammar: Syntactic Theory in Typological Perspective*. Oxford: Oxford University Press.

Croft, William
2007 The origins of grammar in the verbalization of experience. *Cognitive Linguistics* 18: 339–382.

Dapremont, Elena M.
2001 Assembled data, mounting evidence: Conceptual contrasts between past and present participle based change. Paper presented at the Seventh International Cognitive Linguistics Conference. Santa Barbara.

Diessel, Holger, and Michael Tomasello
2001 The acquisition of finite complement clauses in English: A corpus-based analysis. *Cognitive Linguistics* 12: 97–141.

Diver, William
1995 Theory. In *Meaning as Explanation: Advances in Linguistic Sign Theory*, Ellen Contini-Morava and Barbara Sussman Goldberg (eds.), 43–114. Berlin/New York: Mouton de Gruyter.

Dowty, David
2000 "The garden swarms with bees" and the fallacy of "argument alternation". In *Polysemy: Theoretical and Computational Approaches*, Yael Ravin and Claudia Leacock (eds.), 111–128. Oxford: Oxford University Press.

Du Bois, John W.
1987 The discourse basis of ergativity. *Language* 63: 805–855.

Epstein, Richard
2001 The definite article, accessibility, and the construction of discourse referents. *Cognitive Linguistics* 12: 333–378.

Epstein, Richard
2002 Grounding, subjectivity and definite descriptions. In *Grounding: The Epistemic Footing of Deixis and Reference*, Frank Brisard (ed.), 41–82. Berlin/New York: Mouton de Gruyter.

Evans, Vyvyan
2004 *The Structure of Time: Language, Meaning and Temporal Cognition.* Amsterdam/Philadelphia: John Benjamins.

Fauconnier, Gilles
1985 *Mental Spaces: Aspects of Meaning Construction in Natural Language.* Cambridge, MA/London: MIT Press/Bradford.

Fauconnier, Gilles
1997 *Mappings in Thought and Language.* Cambridge: Cambridge University Press.

Fauconnier, Gilles, and Mark Turner
1998 Conceptual integration networks. *Cognitive Science* 22: 133–187.

Fauconnier, Gilles, and Mark Turner
2002 *The Way We Think: Conceptual Blending and the Mind's Hidden Complexities.* New York: Basic Books.

Fillmore, Charles J.
1988 The mechanisms of "construction grammar". *Proceedings of the Annual Meeting of the Berkeley Linguistics Society* 14: 35–55.

Fillmore, Charles J., Paul Kay, and Mary Catherine O'Connor
1988 Regularity and idiomaticity in grammatical constructions: The case of *let alone. Language* 64: 501–538.

Fodor, Jerry A.
1970 Three reasons for not deriving "kill" from "cause to die". *Linguistic Inquiry* 1: 429–438.

Freeze, Ray
1992 Existentials and other locatives. *Language* 68: 553–595.

Gensler, Orin D.
1977 Non-syntactic antecedents and frame semantics. *Proceedings of the Annual Meeting of the Berkeley Linguistics Society* 3: 321–334.

Gentner, Dedre
1983 Structure mapping: A theoretical framework for analogy. *Cognitive Science* 7: 155–170.

Goldberg, Adele E.
1995 *Constructions: A Construction Grammar Approach to Argument Structure.* Chicago/London: University of Chicago Press.

Goldberg, Adele E.
2006 *Constructions at Work: The Nature of Generalizations in Language.* Oxford: Oxford University Press.

Goldsmith, John, and Erich Woisetschlaeger
1982 The logic of the English progressive. *Linguistic Inquiry* 13: 79–89.

Gundel, Jeanette K., Nancy Hedberg, and Ron Zacharski
1993 Cognitive status and the form of referring expressions in discourse. *Language* 69: 274–307.
Hankamer, Jorge, and Ivan Sag
1976 Deep and surface anaphora. *Linguistic Inquiry* 7: 391–428.
Harder, Peter
1996 *Functional Semantics: A Theory of Meaning, Structure and Tense in English*. Berlin/New York: Mouton de Gruyter.
Hawkins, Bruce W.
1984 *The Semantics of English Spatial Prepositions*. San Diego: University of California doctoral dissertation.
Hawkins, John
1978 *Definiteness and Indefiniteness: A Study in Reference and Grammaticality Prediction*. London: Croom Helm.
Heine, Bernd
1992 Grammaticalization chains. *Studies in Language* 16: 335–368.
Heine, Bernd
1997 *Cognitive Foundations of Grammar*. New York/Oxford: Oxford University Press.
Heyvaert, Liesbet
2003 *A Cognitive-Functional Approach to Nominalization in English*. Berlin/New York: Mouton de Gruyter .
Higuchi Goto, Mariko
2008 *The Semantic Function of the English Present Tense Morpheme*. Kyushu (Japan): Kyushu University doctoral dissertation.
Hudson, Richard A.
1987 Zwicky on heads. *Journal of Linguistics* 23: 109–132.
Ikegami, Yoshihiko
1985 "Activity"-"accomplishment"-"achievement"—A language that can't say "I burned it, but it didn't burn" and one that can. In *Linguistics and Philosophy: Essays in Honor of Rulon S. Wells*, Adam Makkai and Alan K. Melby (eds.), 265–304. Amsterdam/Philadelphia: John Benjamins.
Jackendoff, Ray S.
1972 *Semantic Interpretation in Generative Grammar*. Cambridge, MA/London: MIT Press.
Janssen, Theo A. J. M.
1995 Deixis from a cognitive point of view. In *Meaning as Explanation: Advances in Linguistic Sign Theory*, Ellen Contini-Morava and Barbara Sussman Goldberg (eds.), 245–270. Berlin/New York: Mouton de Gruyter.
Johnson, Mark
1987 *The Body in the Mind: The Bodily Basis of Meaning, Imagination, and Reason*. Chicago/London: University of Chicago Press.
Kiparsky, Paul, and Carol Kiparsky
1970 Fact. In *Progress in Linguistics*, Manfred Bierwisch and Karl Erich Heidolph (eds.), 143–173. The Hague: Mouton.

Kirsner, Robert S.
1979 *The Problem of Presentative Sentences in Modern Dutch*. Amsterdam: North-Holland.

Kirsner, Robert S.
1993 From meaning to message in two theories: Cognitive and Saussurean views of the Modern Dutch demonstratives. In *Conceptualizations and Mental Processing in Language*, Richard A. Geiger and Brygida Rudzka-Ostyn (eds.), 81–114. Berlin/New York: Mouton de Gruyter.

Kirsner, Robert S., and Sandra A. Thompson
1976 The role of pragmatic inference in semantics: A study of sensory verb complements in English. *Glossa* 10: 200–240.

Kövecses, Zoltán
2000 *Metaphor and Emotion: Language, Culture, and Body in Human Feeling*. Cambridge: Cambridge University Press.

Kumashiro, Toshiyuki
2000 *The Conceptual Basis of Grammar: A Cognitive Approach to Japanese Clausal Structure*. San Diego: University of California doctoral dissertation.

Kumashiro, Toshiyuki, and Ronald W. Langacker
2003 Double-subject and complex-predicate constructions. *Cognitive Linguistics* 14: 1–45.

Lakoff, George
1987 *Women, Fire, and Dangerous Things: What Categories Reveal About the Mind*. Chicago/London: University of Chicago Press.

Lakoff, George
1990 The invariance hypothesis: Is abstract reason based on image-schemas? *Cognitive Linguistics* 1: 39–74.

Lakoff, George, and Mark Johnson
1980 *Metaphors We Live By*. Chicago/London: University of Chicago Press.

Lakoff, George, and Rafael E. Núñez
2000 *Where Mathematics Comes From: How the Embodied Mind Brings Mathematics into Being*. New York: Basic Books.

Lambrecht, Knud
1988 There was a farmer had a dog: Syntactic amalgams revisited. *Proceedings of the Annual Meeting of the Berkeley Linguistics Society* 14: 319–339.

Langacker, Ronald W.
1969 On pronominalization and the chain of command. In *Modern Studies in English*, David A. Reibel and Sanford A. Schane (eds.), 160–186. Englewood Cliffs, NJ: Prentice-Hall.

Langacker, Ronald W.
1973 Predicate raising: Some Uto-Aztecan evidence. In *Issues in Linguistics: Papers in Honor of Henry and Renée Kahane*, Braj B. Kachru, *et al.* (eds.), 468–491. Urbana: University of Illinois Press.

Langacker, Ronald W.
1976 *Non-Distinct Arguments in Uto-Aztecan*. Berkeley/Los Angeles: University of California Press.

Langacker, Ronald W.
1982 Space grammar, analysability, and the English passive. *Language* 58: 22–80.

Langacker, Ronald W.
1984 Active zones. *Proceedings of the Annual Meeting of the Berkeley Linguistics Society* 10: 172–188.

Langacker, Ronald W.
1985 Observations and speculations on subjectivity. In *Iconicity in Syntax*, John Haiman (ed.), 109–150. Amsterdam/Philadelphia: John Benjamins.

Langacker, Ronald W.
1987a *Foundations of Cognitive Grammar*, vol. 1, *Theoretical Prerequisites*. Stanford: Stanford University Press.

Langacker, Ronald W.
1987b Nouns and verbs. *Language* 63: 53–94.

Langacker, Ronald W.
1987c Grammatical ramifications of the setting/participant distinction. *Proceedings of the Annual Meeting of the Berkeley Linguistics Society* 13: 383–394.

Langacker, Ronald W.
1988a A usage-based model. In *Topics in Cognitive Linguistics*, Brygida Rudzka-Ostyn (ed.), 127–161. Amsterdam/Philadelphia: John Benjamins.

Langacker, Ronald W.
1988b The nature of grammatical valence. In *Topics in Cognitive Linguistics*, Brygida Rudzka-Ostyn (ed.), 91–125. Amsterdam/Philadelphia: John Benjamins.

Langacker, Ronald W.
1990a *Concept, Image, and Symbol: The Cognitive Basis of Grammar*. Berlin/New York: Mouton de Gruyter.

Langacker, Ronald W.
1990b Subjectification. *Cognitive Linguistics* 1: 5–38.

Langacker, Ronald W.
1991 *Foundations of Cognitive Grammar*, vol. 2, *Descriptive Application*. Stanford: Stanford University Press.

Langacker, Ronald W.
1992a The symbolic nature of cognitive grammar: The meaning of *of* and of *of*-periphrasis. In *Thirty Years of Linguistic Evolution: Studies in Honour of René Dirven on the Occasion of his Sixtieth Birthday*, Martin Pütz (ed.), 483–502. Philadelphia/Amsterdam: John Benjamins.

Langacker, Ronald W.
1992b Prepositions as grammatical(izing) elements. *Leuvense Bijdragen* 81: 287–309.

Langacker, Ronald W.
1993a Universals of construal. *Proceedings of the Annual Meeting of the Berkeley Linguistics Society* 19: 447–463.

Langacker, Ronald W.
1993b Grammatical traces of some "invisible" semantic constructs. *Language Sciences* 15: 323–355.

Langacker, Ronald W.
1993c Reference-point constructions. *Cognitive Linguistics* 4: 1–38.

Langacker, Ronald W.
1993d Clause structure in cognitive grammar. *Studi Italiani di Linguistica Teorica e Applicata* 22: 465–508.

Langacker, Ronald W.
1995a Conceptual grouping and constituency in cognitive grammar. In *Linguistics in the Morning Calm 3*, Ik-Hwan Lee (ed.), 149–172. Seoul: Hanshin.

Langacker, Ronald W.
1995b Possession and possessive constructions. In *Language and the Cognitive Construal of the World*, John R. Taylor and Robert E. MacLaury (eds.), 51–79. Berlin/New York: Mouton de Gruyter.

Langacker, Ronald W.
1995c Raising and transparency. *Language* 71: 1–62.

Langacker, Ronald W.
1995d Viewing in cognition and grammar. In *Alternative Linguistics: Descriptive and Theoretical Modes*, Philip W. Davis (ed.), 153–212. Amsterdam/Philadelphia: John Benjamins.

Langacker, Ronald W.
1996 Conceptual grouping and pronominal anaphora. In *Studies in Anaphora*, Barbara Fox (ed.), 333–378. Amsterdam/Philadelphia: John Benjamins.

Langacker, Ronald W.
1997a Constituency, dependency, and conceptual grouping. *Cognitive Linguistics* 8: 1–32.

Langacker, Ronald W.
1997b Generics and habituals. In *On Conditionals Again*, Angeliki Athanasiadou and René Dirven (eds.), 191–222. Amsterdam/Philadelphia: John Benjamins.

Langacker, Ronald W.
1998a Indeterminacy in semantics and grammar. In *Estudios de Lingüística Cognitiva II*, José Luis Cifuentes Honrubia (ed.), 649–672. Alicante: Universidad de Alicante.

Langacker, Ronald W.
1998b On subjectification and grammaticization. In *Discourse and Cognition: Bridging the Gap*, Jean-Pierre Koenig (ed.), 71–89. Stanford: CSLI Publications.

Langacker, Ronald W.
1999a *Grammar and Conceptualization*. Berlin/New York: Mouton de Gruyter.

Langacker, Ronald W.
1999b Correspondences, compositionality, and grammar. In *Actas del XXI Congreso Internacional de AEDEAN*, Fernando Toda Iglesia, *et al* (eds.), 55–74. Seville: Universidad de Sevilla.

Langacker, Ronald W.
1999c Assessing the cognitive linguistic enterprise. In *Cognitive Linguistics: Foundations, Scope, and Methodology*, Theo Janssen and Gisela Redeker (eds.), 13–59. Berlin/New York: Mouton de Gruyter.

Langacker, Ronald W.
1999d Virtual reality. *Studies in the Linguistic Sciences* 29 (2): 77–103.

Langacker, Ronald W.
1999e Losing control: Grammaticization, subjectification, and transparency. In *Historical Semantics and Cognition*, Andreas Blank and Peter Koch (eds.), 147–175. Berlin/New York: Mouton de Gruyter.

Langacker, Ronald W.
2000 A dynamic usage-based model. In *Usage-Based Models of Language*, Michael Barlow and Suzanne Kemmer (eds.), 1–63. Stanford: CSLI Publications.

Langacker, Ronald W.
2001a Topic, subject, and possessor. In *A Cognitive Approach to the Verb: Morphological and Constructional Perspectives*, Hanne Gram Simonsen and Rolf Theil Endresen (eds.), 11–48. Berlin/New York: Mouton de Gruyter.

Langacker, Ronald W.
2001b Discourse in cognitive grammar. *Cognitive Linguistics* 12: 143–188.

Langacker, Ronald W.
2001c Dynamicity in grammar. *Axiomathes* 12: 7–33.

Langacker, Ronald W.
2001d What WH means. In *Conceptual and Discourse Factors in Linguistic Structure*, Alan Cienki, Barbara J. Luka, and Michael B. Smith (eds.), 137–152. Stanford: CSLI Publications.

Langacker, Ronald W.
2001e Viewing and experiential reporting in cognitive grammar. In *Linguagem e Cognição: A Perspectiva da Linguística Cognitiva*, Augusto Soares da Silva (ed.), 19–49. Braga: Associação Portuguesa de Linguística and Universidade Católica Portuguesa.

Langacker, Ronald W.
2001f The English present tense. *English Language and Linguistics* 5: 251–271.

Langacker, Ronald W.
2002a Deixis and subjectivity. In *Grounding: The Epistemic Footing of Deixis and Reference*, Frank Brisard (ed.), 1–28. Berlin/New York: Mouton de Gruyter.

Langacker, Ronald W.
2002b A study in unified diversity: English and Mixtec locatives. In *Ethnosyntax: Explorations in Grammar and Culture*, N. J. Enfield (ed.), 138–161. Oxford/London: Oxford University Press.

Langacker, Ronald W.
2002c The control cycle: Why grammar is a matter of life and death. *Proceedings of the Annual Meeting of the Japanese Cognitive Linguistics Association* 2: 193–220.

Langacker, Ronald W.
2002d Remarks on the English grounding systems. In *Grounding: The Epistemic Footing of Deixis and Reference*, Frank Brisard (ed.), 29–38. Berlin/New York: Mouton de Gruyter.

Langacker, Ronald W.
2003a Constructions in cognitive grammar. *English Linguistics* 20: 41–83.

Langacker, Ronald W.
2003b Context, cognition, and semantics: A unified dynamic approach. In *Job 28: Cognition in Context*, Ellen van Wolde (ed.), 179–230. Leiden/Boston: Brill.

Langacker, Ronald W.
2003c Constructional integration, grammaticization, and serial verb constructions. *Language and Linguistics* 4: 251–278.

Langacker, Ronald W.
2004a Metonymy in grammar. *Journal of Foreign Languages* 27: 2–24.

Langacker, Ronald W.
2004b Possession, location, and existence. In *Linguagem, Cultura e Cognição: Estudios de Linguística Cognitiva*, vol. I, Augusto Soares da Silva, Amadeu Torres, and Miguel Gonçalves (eds.), 85–120. Coimbra: Almedina.

Langacker, Ronald W.
2004c Remarks on nominal grounding. *Functions of Language* 11: 77–113.

Langacker, Ronald W.
2004d Aspects of the grammar of finite clauses. In *Language, Culture and Mind*, Michel Achard and Suzanne Kemmer (eds.), 535–577. Stanford: CSLI Publications.

Langacker, Ronald W.
2004e Grammar as image: The case of voice. In *Imagery in Language: Festschrift in Honour of Professor Ronald W. Langacker*, Barbara Lewandowska-Tomaszczyk and Alina Kwiatkowska (eds.), 63–114. Frankfurt am Main: Peter Lang.

Langacker, Ronald W.
2005a Integration, grammaticization, and constructional meaning. In *Grammatical Constructions: Back to the Roots*, Mirjam Fried and Hans C. Boas (eds.), 157–189. Amsterdam/Philadelphia: John Benjamins.

Langacker, Ronald W.
2005b Dynamicity, fictivity, and scanning: The imaginative basis of logic and linguistic meaning. In *Grounding Cognition: The Role of Perception and Action in Memory, Language and Thinking*, Diane Pecher and Rolf A. Zwaan (eds.), 164–197. Cambridge: Cambridge University Press.

Langacker, Ronald W.
2005c Construction grammars: Cognitive, radical, and less so. In *Cognitive Linguistics: Internal Dynamics and Interdisciplinary Interaction*, Francisco J. Ruiz de Mendoza Ibáñez and M. Sandra Peña Cervel (eds.), 101–159. Berlin/New York: Mouton de Gruyter.

Langacker, Ronald W.
2005d Two problems virtually resolved. In *De Lingua et Litteris: Studia in Honorem Casimiri Andreae Sroka*, Danuta Stanulewicz, *et al.* (eds.), 65–70. Gdańsk: University of Gdańsk Press.

Langacker, Ronald W.
2006a Dimensions of defocusing. In *Voice and Grammatical Relations*, Tasaku Tsunoda and Taro Kageyama (eds.), 115–137. Amsterdam/Philadelphia: John Benjamins.

Langacker, Ronald W.
2006b Subjectification, grammaticization, and conceptual archetypes. In *Subjectification: Various Paths to Subjectivity*, Angeliki Athanasiadou, Costas Canakis, and Bert Cornillie (eds.), 17–40. Berlin/New York: Mouton de Gruyter.

Langacker, Ronald W.
2007 The present tense in English adverbial clauses. In *Cognition in Language: Volume in Honour of Professor Elzbieta Tabakowska*, Władysław Chłopicki, Andrzej Pawelec, and Agnieszka Pokojska (eds.), 179–209. Cracow: Tertium.

Langacker, Ronald W.
2008a *Cognitive Grammar: A Basic Introduction.* New York: Oxford University Press.

Langacker, Ronald W.
2008b Enunciating the parallelism of nominal and clausal grounding. In *Du Fait Grammatical au Fait Cognitif [From Gram to Mind: Grammar as Cognition]*, vol. 1, Jean-Rémi Lapaire, Guillaume Desagulier, and Jean-Baptiste Guignard (eds.), 17–65. Pessac: Presses Universitaires de Bordeaux.

Langacker, Ronald W.
2008c Finite complements in English. *Journal of Foreign Languages* 31: 2–35.

Langacker, Ronald W.
2009 On AND and OR and OR as AND. In *Cognitive Approaches to Language and Linguistic Data: Studies in Honor of Barbara Lewandowska-Tomaszczyk*, Wiesław Oleksy and Piotr Stalmaszczyk (eds.), 151–169. Frankfurt am Main: Peter Lang.

Langacker, Ronald W.
To app. a On the subject of impersonals.
To app. b A lot of quantifiers.
To app. c A constructional approach to grammaticization.
To app. d The English present: Temporal coincidence vs. epistemic immediacy.
To app. e The conceptual basis of coordination.
To app. f Control and the mind/body duality: Knowing vs. effecting.

LeGrand, Jean E.
1974 AND and OR: Some SOMEs and all ANYs. *Papers from the Regional Meeting of the Chicago Linguistic Society* 10: 390–401.

Li, Charles N., and Sandra A. Thompson
1976 Subject and topic: A new typology of language. In *Subject and Topic*, Charles N. Li (ed.), 457–489. New York: Academic Press.

Lindholm, James M.
1969 Negative-raising and sentence pronominalization. *Papers from the Regional Meeting of the Chicago Linguistic Society* 5: 148–158.

Lyons, John
1967 A note on possessive, existential and locative sentences. *Foundations of Language* 3: 390–396.

Matlock, Teenie
2004 Fictive motion as cognitive simulation. *Memory and Cognition* 32: 1389–1400.

Matsumoto, Yo
1996 Subjective-change expressions in Japanese and their cognitive and linguistic bases. In *Spaces, Worlds, and Grammar*, Gilles Fauconnier and Eve Sweetser (eds.), 124–156. Chicago/London: University of Chicago Press.

Matsumoto, Yo
1997 Linguistic evidence for subjective (fictive) motion. In *The Locus of Meaning: Papers in Honor of Yoshihiko Ikegami*, Kei Yamanaka and Toshio Ohori (eds.), 209–220. Tokyo: Kuroshio.

Postal, Paul M.
1974 *On Raising: One Rule of English Grammar and its Theoretical Implications.* Cambridge, MA/London: MIT Press.

Reid, Wallis
1991 *Verb and Noun Number in English: A Functional Explanation.* London/ New York: Longman.

Reinhart, Tanya
1983 *Anaphora and Semantic Interpretation.* Chicago: University of Chicago Press.

Rice, Sally
1987a *Towards a Cognitive Model of Transitivity.* San Diego: University of California doctoral dissertation.

Rice, Sally
1987b Towards a transitive prototype: Evidence from some atypical English passives. *Proceedings of the Annual Meeting of the Berkeley Linguistics Society* 13: 422–434.

Rosenbaum, Peter S.
1967 *The Grammar of English Predicate Complement Constructions.* Cambridge, MA: MIT Press.

Ross, John Robert
1970 Gapping and the order of constituents. In *Progress in Linguistics*, Manfred Bierwisch and Karl Erich Heidolph (eds.), 249–259. The Hague: Mouton.

Shen, Ya-Ming
1996 The semantics of the Chinese verb "come". In *Cognitive Linguistics in the Redwoods: The Expansion of a New Paradigm in Linguistics*, Eugene H. Casad (ed.), 507–540. Berlin/New York: Mouton de Gruyter.

Shibatani, Masayoshi

1985 Passives and related constructions: A prototype analysis. *Language* 61: 821–848.

Smith, Carlota S.

1969 Ambiguous sentences with *and*. In *Modern Studies in English*, David A. Reibel and Sanford A. Schane (eds.), 75–79. Englewood Cliffs, NJ: Prentice-Hall.

Smith, Michael B.

1994 Agreement and iconicity in Russian impersonal constructions. *Cognitive Linguistics* 5: 5–56.

Smith, Michael B.

2000 Cataphors, spaces, propositions: Cataphoric pronouns and their function. *Proceedings from the Meeting of the Chicago Linguistic Society* 36 (1): 483–500.

Sumnicht, Anne

2001 A cognitive approach to negative raising. Paper presented at the Seventh International Cognitive Linguistics Conference. Santa Barbara.

Sumnicht, Anne

2004 A new look at negative raising. In *Linguagem, Cultura e Cognição: Estudios de Linguística Cognitiva*, vol. I, Augusto Soares da Silva, Amadeu Torres, and Miguel Gonçalves (eds.), 607–626. Coimbra: Almedina.

Sweetser, Eve E.

1982 Root and epistemic modals: Causality in two worlds. *Proceedings of the Annual Meeting of the Berkeley Linguistics Society* 8: 484–507.

Sweetser, Eve E.

1990 *From Etymology to Pragmatics: Metaphorical and Cultural Aspects of Semantic Structure*. Cambridge: Cambridge University Press.

Sweetser, Eve E.

1997 Role and individual interpretations of change predicates. In *Language and Conceptualization*, Jan Nuyts and Eric Pederson (eds.), 116–136. Cambridge: Cambridge University Press.

Sweetser, Eve E.

1999 Compositionality and blending: Semantic composition in a cognitively realistic framework. In *Cognitive Linguistics: Foundations, Scope, and Methodology*, Theo Janssen and Gisela Redeker (eds.), 129–162. Berlin/New York: Mouton de Gruyter.

Talmy, Leonard

1988 Force dynamics in language and cognition. *Cognitive Science* 12: 49–100.

Talmy, Leonard

1996 Fictive motion in language and "ception". In *Language and Space*, Paul Bloom, *et al.* (eds.), 211–276. Cambridge, MA/London: MIT Press/Bradford.

Taylor, John R.
1996 *Possessives in English: An Exploration in Cognitive Grammar.* Oxford: Oxford University Press/Clarendon.

Thompson, Sandra A.
2002 "Object complements" and conversation: Towards a realistic account. *Studies in Language* 26: 125–164.

Traugott, Elizabeth
1988 Pragmatic strengthening and grammaticalization. *Proceedings of the Annual Meeting of the Berkeley Linguistics Society* 14: 406–416.

Traugott, Elizabeth
1989 On the rise of epistemic meanings in English: An example of subjectification in semantic change. *Language* 65: 31–55.

Tuggy, David
2003 *Abrelatas* and *scarecrow* nouns: Exocentric verb-noun compounds as illustrations of basic principles of cognitive grammar. *International Journal of English Studies* 3 (2): 25–61.

van Hoek, Karen
1995 Conceptual reference points: A cognitive grammar account of pronominal anaphora constraints. *Language* 71: 310–340.

van Hoek, Karen
1997 *Anaphora and Conceptual Structure.* Chicago/London: University of Chicago Press.

van Oosten, Jeanne
1977 Subjects and agenthood in English. *Papers from the Regional Meeting of the Chicago Linguistic Society* 13: 459–471.

van Oosten, Jeanne
1986 *The Nature of Subjects, Topics and Agents: A Cognitive Explanation.* Bloomington: Indiana University Linguistics Club.

Vandeloise, Claude
1991 *Spatial Prepositions: A Case Study from French.* Chicago/London: University of Chicago Press.

Vendler, Zeno
1967 *Linguistics in Philosophy.* Ithaca: Cornell University Press.

Verhagen, Arie
1986 *Linguistic Theory and the Function of Word Order in Dutch: A Study on Interpretive Aspects of the Order of Adverbials and Noun Phrases.* Dordrecht: Foris.

Verhagen, Arie
2005 *Constructions of Intersubjectivity: Discourse, Syntax, and Cognition.* Oxford: Oxford University Press.

Verstraete, Jean-Christophe
2002 *Interpersonal Grammar and Clause Combining in English.* Leuven: University of Leuven doctoral dissertation.

Wierzbicka, Anna
1975 Why "kill" does not mean "cause to die": The semantics of action sentences. *Foundations of Language* 13: 491–528.

Wierzbicka, Anna
1988 *The Semantics of Grammar.* Amsterdam/Philadelphia: John Benjamins.

Yamanashi, Masa-aki
2003 Anaphora and reference-point ability. In *Empirical and Theoretical Investigations into Language: A Festschrift for Masaru Kajita*, Shuji Chiba, *et al.* (eds.), 846–857. Tokyo: Kaitakusha.

Zwicky, Arnold M.
1985 Heads. *Journal of Linguistics* 21: 1–29.

Author index

Subject index